"This is a very unusual and important book. In this volume, William Lane Craig brings together a superb combination of the three essential dimensions of the Doctrine of the Atonement: the biblical, the theological, and the philosophical. Most significantly, he starts with the foundation in biblical exegesis and theology, both Old and New Testament, and uses it as an anchor for his handling of the systematic theological and analytical philosophical discussions that follow. In this way, he is able to set the whole discussion in perspective, recognize the central importance as well as the theological and philosophical coherence of penal substitution, and show how some of the other views of the Atonement also have something to contribute. This is a magnificent accomplishment, for which we should all be truly grateful. With enthusiasm, I heartily recommend it to all who pursue the serious study of this all-important biblical doctrine."

—RICHARD E. AVERBECK, *Professor of Old Testament and Semitic Languages, Trinity Evangelical Divinity School*

"Atonement and the Death of Christ is the definitive work on penal substitution. Those who want to argue against penal substitution must first get familiar with this volume. It is a welcome addition to the now growing philosophical literature on the atonement."

—TYLER MCNABB, *Post-doctoral Fellow, University of Macau*

"In *Atonement and the Death of Christ* William Lane Craig defends a classical Reformed understanding of the atonement. However, unlike other works on this subject, this book addresses issues in patristics, Anglo-American law, and philosophy, making the case that insights from these areas of study may illuminate our understanding of the atonement. Craig shows us that the doctrine of the atonement—though an essential belief of Christian theology—is no different than fundamental beliefs within other disciplines insofar as it may be analyzed with intellectual tools outside the domains from which it originally arose. Craig should be commended for reminding us that the proper development of Christian theology is enhanced when it is in conversation with other academic fields."

—FRANCIS J. BECKWITH, *Professor of Philosophy & Church State Studies, Baylor University*

ATONEMENT AND THE DEATH OF CHRIST

An Exegetical, Historical, and Philosophical Exploration

William Lane Craig

BAYLOR UNIVERSITY PRESS

Cover Design: Kasey McBeath
Cover image: detail from Dalí, Salvador (1904-89) / Spanish, *Christ of St. John of the Cross*, 1951 (oil on canvas), © CSG CIC Glasgow Museums Collection / Bridgeman Images

Hardcover ISBN: 978-1-4813-1204-2
Library of Congress Control Number: 2020008694

Printed in the United States of America on acid-free paper with a minimum of thirty percent recycled content.

CONTENTS

Preface   vii

1   Introduction   1

I
Biblical Data Concerning the Atonement

2   Sacrifice   13

3   Isaiah's Servant of the LORD   37

4   Divine Justice   51

5   Representation and Redemption   79

II
Dogmatic History of the Doctrine of the Atonement

6   Patristic Theories   91

7   Medieval Theories   113

8   Reformation and Post-Reformation Theories   125

III
Philosophical Reflections on
the Doctrine of the Atonement

9   Penal Substitution: Its Coherence   147

10   Penal Substitution: Its Justification   173

11   Satisfaction of Divine Justice   195

12   Redemption: Divine Pardon and Its Effects   215

13   Redemption: Justification and
     Appropriation of a Divine Pardon   237

14   The Moral Influence of Christ's Passion   259

15   Conclusion   265

Bibliography   273
Index of Authors and Subjects   293
Index of Ancient Sources   307
Index of Scripture   311
Index of Court Opinions   317

PREFACE

O ne of the most noteworthy developments in contemporary philosophy of religion has been the ingress of Anglo-American Christian
philosophers into areas normally considered the province of systematic
theologians. In particular, many Christian philosophers have taken
up the task of helping to formulate and defend coherent statements
of Christian doctrine. So Christian philosophers have been actively
engaged, for example, in discussion of the doctrines of the Trinity,
incarnation, and atonement, which might be called "the big three" of
peculiarly Christian doctrines.[1] The work of Christian philosophers in
systematic theology has even served to spawn a new subdiscipline of
theology: analytic theology, which is committed to using the tools
of analytic philosophy in exploring Christian doctrine.

The activity of Anglo-American Christian philosophers in the
field of systematic theology has even come to the attention of German
theologians. In the standard German reference work in theology, the

---

[1] See, for example, the entry in the *Stanford Encyclopedia of Philosophy*, s.v. "Philosophy and Christian Theology," by Michael J. Murray and Michael Rae, August 9,
2012, https://plato.stanford.edu/entries/christiantheology-philosophy/, which
singles out for discussion the doctrines of the Trinity, incarnation, and atonement. It is surprising that this article includes no discussion of penal substitutionary theories apart from satisfaction theories.

Theologische Realenzyklopädie (*TRE*), Christoph Gestrich draws attention to the contribution of Anglo-American analytic philosophy to the
subject of the incarnation and its possible relevance for the subject of the
atonement:

> In Great Britain there was already during the 19th century a widespread
> and growing *atonement-literature* spanning theological lines and confes-
> sions and a nearly general consensus concerning Christ's substitutionary
> atonement. It was extensively debated, for example, whether one should
> speak of the "objective" validity of this atonement or the necessity of a "sub-
> jective" realization in faith and morals. By the 20th century this topic had
> for the most part been exhausted in the English-speaking realm—until
> during the '70s a lively discussion about the historicity of the incarna-
> tion of the Son of God, stimulated by analytic philosophy, was kindled.
> Is the atoning descent of the heavenly Son of God to earthly flesh "only"
> a metaphor—and thus by no means a part of objective history? Chiefly
> related to this question there was once more in the '80s and '90s of the
> 20th century a whole series of English-language theological investigations
> concerning the "problem" of the *atonement*. The predominant result: the
> admittedly metaphorical talk of the incarnation of the Son of God in
> the Christian confession remains now as always indispensable and refers
> to an actual event. Nevertheless, one must consider anew *in what way* it
> leads to the divine *atonement*.[2]

The present book is intended to be a contribution to this ongoing
debate, exploring the relation between atonement and the death of
Christ. I shall explore this question exegetically, historically, and finally
philosophically. My aim is articulate the core of an atonement theory
which is both biblical and philosophically coherent.

I am especially indebted to Dr. Daniel P. Bailey for extensive
conversation and correspondence as well as literature concerning the

---

2   *Theologische Realenzyklopädie*, ed. Gerhard Müller, vol. 32, *Spurgeon-Taylor* (Ber-
    lin: Walter de Gruyter, 2001), s.v. "Sühne V: Kirchengeschichtlich und dogma-
    tisch," by Christoph Gestrich. A list of references to English-language resources
    by Christian philosophers and theologians then follows. The nineteenth-century
    British literature alluded to by Gestrich is still worth reading and is, sadly,
    largely overlooked by Christian philosophers today. Standouts include George
    Smeaton, *The Doctrine of the Atonement, as Taught by the Apostles* (Edinburgh:
    T&T Clark, 1870); R. W. Dale, *The Atonement*, 9th ed. (London: Hodder &
    Stoughton, 1884); and a bit later James Denney, *The Death of Christ: Its Place and
    Interpretation in the New Testament* (London: Hodder & Stoughton, 1907).

meaning of Paul's term *hilastērion* in Romans 3:25. I am also grateful to Dr. E. Descheemaeker of the Edinburgh Law School for stimulating correspondence concerning the relevance of the philosophy of law to the subject of the atonement and for guidance into the legal literature. I am grateful, too, to Shaun McNaughton at Brown & Streza, LLP, for help in obtaining court opinions. I am also thankful to my research assistant Timothy Bayless for procuring for me research materials, as well as proofreading and preparing the bibliography and indices. As always, I am thankful for my wife Jan's faithful support and interest in this subject.

My short book *The Atonement* (Cambridge University Press, 2018) in the Cambridge Elements of Philosophy series is an extract of this book and serves as a sort of précis of it. Material from this book has also been published in various journals: "Is Penal Substitution Incoherent? An Examination of Mark Murphy's Criticisms," *Religious Studies* 54, no. 4 (2018): 509–26; "Is Penal Substitution Unjust?" *International Journal for Philosophy of Religion* 83 (2018): 231–44; "Is Penal Substitution Unsatisfactory?" *Philosophia Christi* 21, no. 1 (2019): 155–68; and "Divine Forgiveness and Legal Pardon," in *The Philosophy of Forgiveness*, vol. 4, *Christian Perspectives on Forgiveness*, ed. G. L. Bock (Wilmington, Del.: Vernon Press, 2018), 1–22.

William Lane Craig
Atlanta, Georgia

Chapter 1

INTRODUCTION

This is a book about the relationship between the death of Christ and atonement for sin. Its controlling question is, How is it that Christ's death atones for our sins? In attempting to address this question, we are immediately confronted with the problem that the word "atonement" and its cognates are ambiguous, having two very different meanings.

THE MEANING OF "ATONEMENT"

The word "atonement" derives not from Greek or Latin, as is the case with most theological terms in English, but rather from Middle English; namely, the phrase "at onement," designating a state of harmony. The closest New Testament (NT) word for atonement in this etymological sense is *katallagē* or reconciliation, specifically reconciliation between God and man. Paul characterizes the apostolic vocation in just such terms:

> So if anyone is in Christ, there is a new creation: everything old has passed away; see, everything has become new! All this is from God, who reconciled us to himself through Christ, and has given us the ministry of reconciliation; that is, in Christ God was reconciling the world to himself, not counting their trespasses against them, and entrusting the message of reconciliation to us. So we are ambassadors for Christ, since God

1

is making his appeal through us; we entreat you on behalf of Christ, be reconciled to God. (2 Cor 5:17-20)

When William Tyndale produced the first English translation of the NT from the Greek in 1526, the etymological meaning of "atonement" as "at-onement" was clear in his rendering of 2 Corinthians 5:18-20. "The ministry of *reconciliation*" was "the office to preach *the atonement*" (5:18), and the call "to be *reconciled* to God" was to "be *at-one* with God" (5:20).

The concept of being in harmony with God is not uniquely expressed in the NT by *katallagē*, however. As I. H. Marshall explains, words like "reconciliation," "justification," "redemption," and "salvation" all refer to the state of believers that results from God's salvific action through Christ.[1]

How is reconciliation with God achieved? Paul believed that it was through Christ's death on the cross that we obtained reconciliation with God: "We were reconciled to God through the death of his Son" (Rom 5:10; cf. Col 1:19-22). But how does the death of Christ achieve the reconciliation of condemned sinners with God? Here we confront a quite different sense of the word "atonement," which is expressed by the Hebrew and Greek words typically translated by the English words "atonement" or "to make atonement." In the Old Testament (OT) "atonement" and its cognates translate words having the Hebrew root *kpr*.[2] The Greek equivalent in the Septuagint (LXX) and NT is *hilaskesthai*. To "atone" in

---

1 I. Howard Marshall, *Aspects of the Atonement: Cross and Resurrection in the Reconciling of God and Humanity* (London: Paternoster, 2007), 124.

2 See Richard E. Averbeck, "kpr [4105/4106]," *New International Dictionary of Old Testament Theology and Exegesis*, ed. Willem A. VanGemeren (Grand Rapids: Zondervan, 1997), 689–710. Three of the four OT words related to the root *kpr* appear in Exod 30:11-16, where each person is commanded to give "a ransom (*kōper*) for his life" (v. 12) in order to "make atonement (*kpr*) for your lives" (vv. 15b and 16b) by giving an offering of "the atonement (*kippurim*) money" (v. 16). The fourth word, *kappōret*, designates the "mercy seat" or cover of the ark of the covenant secreted away in the innermost sanctum of the Tabernacle or, later, of the Temple (Lev 16:2). In the NT the Greek equivalents of Hebrew atonement words occur in Rom 3:25 (*hilastērion* = *kappōret*); in Luke 18:13; Heb 2:17 (*hilaskomai* = *kpr*); and in 1 John 2:2; 4:10 (*hilasmos* = *kippurim*). Daniel Bailey complains that biblical translators have traditionally obscured the connection between the two testaments by using English atonement words for the OT Hebrew terms but not for the NT Greek terms. The two most popular English Bibles, the NIV and NRSV, now use English atonement words consistently across the two

this sense takes as its object impurity or sin and has primarily the sense "to purify, to cleanse." As we shall see, in Paul's thinking, Christ's death was a sacrificial offering to God, akin to the Levitical animal sacrifices described in the OT, which cleansed us from sin, thereby reconciling us with God. While the result of atonement in this narrow sense (cleansing of sin) may be said to be atonement in the broad sense (reconciliation with God), nevertheless the biblical words translated "atonement" or "to atone" need to be interpreted in the narrower sense if we are to understand correctly the meaning of the *kpr-* and *hilas-*texts.

We may say, then, somewhat paradoxically, that atonement (in the broad sense) is achieved through atonement (in the narrow sense).[3] Theological treatments of atonement in German enjoy a decided advantage in this regard over treatments in English. In German theological vocabulary, *Versöhnung* (reconciliation) is distinguished from *Sühne* (expiation of sin). Hence, one may say without confusion that *Versöhnung* is achieved through *die Sühne*.[4] But the English word "atonement" is ambiguous, having, as we have seen, two very different meanings.

Avoiding Confusion

This ambiguity may occasion confusion. For example, in her recent book *Atonement*, Eleonore Stump objects to penal substitutionary theories because they fail to provide a complete solution to achieving union with God, lacking a role, for example, for the Holy Spirit, for the life of Christ, and for a connection between Christ's passion and the concerns

---

testaments (Daniel P. Bailey, "Atonement in the Hebrew Bible, Early Judaism, and the New Testament: An Overview," *Biblical Research* 60 [2015]: 5–6).

3 As P. T. Forsyth puts it, reconciliation rests upon atonement as its ground; reconciliation is the end and atonement is the means (Peter Taylor Forsyth, *The Work of Christ*, 2nd ed. [London: Independent Press, 1938], 56, 59). This insight is unaffected by Forsyth's outmoded understanding of "atonement" as a covering of sin from God's sight. He rightly complains that liberal theologians like Albrecht Ritschl had emptied reconciliation of atonement (66).

4 See, e.g., Otfried Hofius, "Sühne und Versöhnung: Zum paulinischen Verständnis des Kreuzestodes Jesu," in *Versuche, das Leiden und Sterben Jesu zu verstehen*, ed. W. Maas, Schriftenreihe der Katholischen Akademie der Erzdiözese Freiburg (Munich: Verlag Schnell & Steiner, 1983), 25–46; Otfried Hofius, "Erwägungen zur Gestalt und Herkunft des paulinischen Versöhnungsgedankens," *Zeitschrift für Theologie und Kirche* 77, no. 2 (1980): 189–90.

of theodicy.[5] These objections are, however, misplaced, I think, for two reasons.

First, penal substitution is not usually intended by its proponents to be one's entire atonement theory but just a central facet thereof. Theologians have often noted the multiplicity of metaphors and motifs characterizing the atonement found in the NT. The doctrine has been aptly compared to a multifaceted jewel. Sacrifice, ransom, governmental and judicial motifs, moral influence, and so on are all facets of a full atonement theory. Hence, it is not so important if certain motifs, like Christ's life or the Holy Spirit's role, feature more prominently in some facets of the atonement than in others. Together they build a full-orbed atonement theory.

But second, and more fundamentally, Stump's indictment of penal substitutionary theories fails to take sufficient cognizance of the crucial ambiguity concerning the meaning of the word "atonement." Theologically, the traditional doctrine of the atonement is focused on atonement in the narrow sense. In Protestant Scholasticism Christ was thought to discharge the three offices of prophet, priest, and king, and his atoning death was a function of his priestly office. But Stump defends a theory of reconciliation (*Versöhnung*) that does not feature atonement (*Sühne*) at its core. She wants to investigate how it is that sinners may come to enjoy union with God. Stump signals her broader etymological use of "atonement" by employing in her opening chapter the expression "at onement." Her book turns out to be primarily not about Christology but about soteriology and, especially, pneumatology. The Holy Spirit displaces Christ as the central figure in her account of achieving union with God. The death of Christ plays a relatively minor role in her theory of *at onement*, and atonement in the narrow sense no role at all.

According to Stump, the problem that the atonement of Christ is intended to solve in order to enable everlasting union between God and fallen human persons includes three elements:

(1) occurrent dispositions to moral wrongdoing, with their liability to future morally wrong acts, and past morally wrong acts; with their consequent
(2) guilt, both in (a) its impairments in the psyche of the wrongdoer and (b) the ill effects of the wrongdoing in the world; and
(3) shame.[6]

5 Eleonore Stump, *Atonement* (Oxford: Oxford University Press, 2018), 31–35.
6 Stump, *Atonement*, 19; cf. 340.

An acceptable interpretation of the atonement, Stump asserts, needs to show that these elements of the problem are solved by one's theory of the atonement.

It is striking that the theory of the atonement articulated by the Protestant divines is intended to address none of these problems! The closest would be (2), except that Stump speaks here not of the removal of guilt, which is, indeed, the object of Christ's atonement, but rather of the effects of guilt on the psyche of the wrongdoer and the effects of sin in the world. Seen in this light, Stump's book is not a book about the atonement (*Sühne*) at all. She and the Reformers are simply addressing different problems. This is not to say that the Reformers did not have much to say about regeneration, the indwelling of the Holy Spirit, infused grace, and so on, but just that these topics did not belong to the doctrine of the atonement but to soteriology and especially pneumatology. It is no indictment of theories of the atonement in the narrow sense that they do not address problems about achieving *at onement* in the broad sense of union with God, problems that are addressed in other loci of the theological curriculum.

OUR FOCUS

In our investigation of the atonement, we are primarily interested in how Christ's death served to atone for sin (and so with atonement in the narrow sense), thereby facilitating our reconciliation with God. The role of Christ's death in achieving atonement for sin and, hence, reconciliation with God is central to the NT. The message of the NT is that God, out of His great love, has provided the means of atonement for sin through Christ's death on the cross. By his death on the cross, Christ has thus made possible the reconciliation of alienated and condemned sinners to God. "For God so loved the world that he gave his only Son, that whoever believes in him should not perish but have eternal life" (John 3:16). Thus, "the cross" came to be a metaphor epitomizing the Gospel message, such that Paul could call the Gospel "the word of the cross" (1 Cor 1:18), reminding his Corinthian converts that "I decided to know nothing among you except Jesus Christ and him crucified" (1 Cor 2:2). Hence, Paul would glory in nothing "except the cross of our Lord Jesus Christ" (Gal 6:14).

The importance of the death of Christ for the NT church may be seen in the disproportionate space that the four Gospels devote to Jesus' so-called passion, the final week of his suffering and crucifixion, thereby emphasizing his death. Of course, Jesus' death is not the end of the passion story: the Gospels all conclude with the proclamation of Jesus' victorious resurrection, vindicating him as God's chosen one. The death and resurrection of Jesus are two sides of the same coin: he "was put to death for our trespasses and raised for our justification" (Rom 4:25).

Paul quotes the earliest summary of the Gospel message, a four-line formula dating to within five years of Jesus' crucifixion, reminding the Corinthian believers:

> I delivered to you as of first importance what I also received:
>> that Christ died for our sins in accordance with the Scriptures,
>> and that he was buried,
>> and that he was raised on the third day in accordance with the
>>> Scriptures,
>> and that he appeared to Cephas, then to the Twelve. (1 Cor 15:3-5)

This is the message, Paul says, that was proclaimed by all the apostles (1 Cor 15:11), and it is the message that dominates the NT.

The first line of the pre-Pauline formula encapsulates in a pithy way the NT doctrine of the atonement. Christ is said to have "died for our sins" (1 Cor 15:3), just he is said to have been "put to death (or delivered up) for our trespasses" (Rom 4:25). How is it that Jesus' death dealt with our sins? How did his death on the cross overcome the estrangement and condemnation of sinners before a holy God, so as to reconcile them to Him? This is the central question concerning the NT doctrine of the atonement.

DOCTRINE AND THEORY OF THE ATONEMENT

In handling this question we should distinguish between the *doctrine* of the atonement and a *theory* of the atonement. The NT teaches explicitly that Christ died for our sins, thereby achieving our reconciliation with God. But a bewildering variety of theories of the atonement have been offered to make sense of the fact that Christ by his death has provided the means of reconciliation with God. A theory of the atonement will seek to explicate how Jesus' death served to remove the obstacle of sin separating us from God.

As we shall see, in contrast to the church's handling of the doctrines of the Trinity and incarnation, no ecumenical council ever pronounced on the doctrine of the atonement, leaving the church without conciliar guidance as to acceptable theories of the atonement. Competing

atonement theories will therefore need to be assessed by (1) their accord
with biblical teaching and (2) their philosophical coherence.[7]

With respect to (1), the NT has a great deal to say about Christ's
atoning death on our behalf, and any theory of the atonement aspiring
to be Christian must make peace with these biblical data. Many theories
of the atonement offered by post-Enlightenment theologians—such as
Schleiermacher, Ritschl, Bushnell, Campbell, and so on—do not fare
well when judged by this criterion.[8] One might hope that a better result
might be fostered through the renaissance of Christian philosophy
among Anglo-American philosophers in our day. Unfortunately, however, the work of contemporary Christian philosophers on the doctrine

---

7 These same criteria of assessment are endorsed by Stump in *Atonement* (36).
   While applauding Stump's insistence on biblical adequacy for any acceptable
   theory of the atonement, I must say that Stump does not take this stricture with
   sufficient seriousness. For example, in discussing the biblical motif of Christ's
   death as a sacrifice, she ignores the Levitical sacrifices, which are at the heart
   of the Pentateuch and were offered for centuries in the Tabernacle and Temple
   and featured expiatory offerings for human persons, and focuses instead on the
   sacrifices of Cain and Abel, Noah, and Melchizedek, which, in contrast to
   the Levitical sacrifices, are of virtually no interest to NT writers on Christ's
   death. She also overlooks the substitutionary suffering of the Servant of the
   LORD in Isaiah 53, which features so prominently in the NT. When it comes to
   discussing Christ's "bearing our sins," Stump ignores the meaning of this common OT Hebrew idiom for bearing guilt or punishment for sin and instead proposes a psychological account of Christ's experiencing the sinful mental states
   of all fallen persons. My point is not that her reflections are not interesting
   but merely that her claim to have better biblical support than rival atonement
   theories is unjustified. Rather than building her theory on careful biblical exegesis, she first constructs her theory and then imposes it on the biblical text.
8 See Robert Franks' description of the so-called modern synthesis in Robert S.
   Franks, *A History of the Doctrine of the Work of Christ in Its Ecclesiastical Development*, 2 vols. (London: Hodder & Stoughton, [1918]), 2:364–65; and more
   recently with impressive detail Gunther Wenz, *Geschichte der Versöhnungslehre
   in der evangelischen Theologie der Neuzeit*, 2 vols. (Munich: Chr. Kaiser, 1984). Cf.
   Albrecht Ritschl, *A Critical History of the Christian Doctrine of Justification and
   Reconciliation* [1870], trans. John S. Black (Edinburgh: Edmonston and Douglas,
   1872), chap. 7: "Complete Disintegration of the Doctrines of Reconciliation and
   Justification by German Theologians," which commences his chronicle of the
   increasing departure of German theology from biblical roots; see also L. W.
   Grensted, *A Short History of the Doctrine of the Atonement*, Theological Series 4
   (Manchester: Manchester University Press, 1920), chap. 13: "The Doctrine of the
   Atonement in Modern Times."

of the atonement has been largely uninformed by biblical exegesis.[9] Theories of the atonement are usually laid out based on the way in which reconciliation is typically achieved in human relationships. If the biblical texts are discussed at all, it is only after a theory of the atonement has been formulated, which is then read back into the biblical texts. Not only does such a methodology risk distortion because of the enormous disanalogies between merely human relationships and divine-human relationships, but more fundamentally it runs the risk of developing a theory of the atonement that, however congenial, just is not a Christian theory of the atonement because it does not accord with the biblical data. Such an approach to the biblical texts is eisegesis, not exegesis. So flawed a hermeneutic will not deliver to us the meaning of the author of the text but only our own preconceived views. Because the biblical data concerning the atonement are so often neglected by Christian philosophers, it is imperative that we begin our investigation with a survey of some of the key biblical motifs.

But we must not stop there if we are to engage in serious systematic theology. With respect to criterion (2), theologians too often draw up short when it comes to reflecting philosophically on the doctrine of the atonement so as to arrive at a clear and defensible theory of the atonement. A recent volume of collected essays in defense of a biblical atonement doctrine entitled *The Glory of the Atonement* well illustrates this shortcoming.[10] The first sentence of the book informs us, "The analytic philosopher A. J. Ayer argued that a strong case could be made

---

9 This shortcoming of the work of contemporary Christian philosophers on the atonement is illustrated, howbeit unintentionally, by Brandon Warmke's survey of closely related theories of divine forgiveness in his "Divine Forgiveness I: Emotion and Punishment-Forbearance Theories," *Philosophy Compass* 12, no. 9 (2017): e12440, https://doi.org/10.1111/phc3.12440; "Divine Forgiveness II: Reconciliation and Debt-Cancellation Theories," *Philosophy Compass* 12, no. 9 (2017): e12439, https://doi.org/10.1111/phc3.12439. Even his so-called punishment-forbearance theories, which come closest to NT ideas, are not rooted in careful exegesis.

10 Charles E. Hill and Frank A. James III, eds., *The Glory of the Atonement: Biblical, Historical, and Practical Perspectives* (Downers Grove, Ill.: InterVarsity, 2004). By contrast, in part 2 of Steve Jeffery, Michael Ovey, and Andrew Sach, *Pierced for Our Transgressions: Rediscovering the Glory of Penal Substitution*, with a Foreword by John Piper (Wheaton, Ill.: Crossway Books, 2007), especially chap. 10: "Penal Substitution and Justice," a genuine effort is made to tackle philosophical problems of the atonement.

that of the world religions, Christianity was the worst" because it rests, in Ayer's words, on "the allied doctrines of original sin and vicarious atonement, which are intellectually contemptible and morally outrageous."[11] Remarkably, none of the contributors to the book attempts to respond to Ayer's challenge, nor are any of them philosophers. Rather, the book's contributors view the atonement respectively from the angles of the Bible, church history, and the Christian life, leaving us to conclude that this intellectually contemptible and morally outrageous doctrine is, indeed, taught by the Bible, espoused by the church, and worked out in practical Christian living.

"The Bible is enough for our saving faith," advises P. T. Forsyth, "but it is not enough for our scientific theology."[12] Anyone familiar with the history of the doctrine of the atonement knows that since the time of Faustus Socinus in the sixteenth century the doctrine of the atonement has been a battleground of theology. Given the widespread criticism of traditional atonement theories, it will not do simply to reassert in glowing terms the traditional doctrine or to glory in logical paradox.[13] Rather, what is needed is a defense of the coherence and morality of one's theory of the atonement using the best tools of philosophical analysis and argumentation. Only then will one's theory of the atonement commend itself to thinking men and women today.

PROSPECTUS

So in the investigation to follow, we shall study the atonement from three angles: In part 1 we shall make an effort to understand the biblical data concerning Christ's atoning death. In part 2 we shall survey some of the highlights of premodern historical theology concerning the atonement with a view toward understanding the outlines of various traditional

---

11 Frank A. James III, general introduction to Hill and James, *Glory of the Atonement*, 15; A. J. Ayer, "Christianity: Not the Only Religion nor Evidently the Best," *Guardian*, August 30, 1979, 11.

12 Forsyth, *Work of Christ*, 177. Unfortunately, Forsyth himself was all too ready to accept uncritically the revisions in the traditional doctrine of the atonement "on which the best modern authorities are substantially agreed" (180).

13 For example, Emil Brunner's modern classic *The Mediator* [*Der Mittler*]: *A Study of the Central Doctrine of the Christian Faith*, 2nd ed., trans. Olive Wyon, Lutterworth Library 3 (London: Lutterworth Press, 1934), contains no response at all to the Socinian objections that underlay nineteenth-century liberal theology's rejection of Brunner's favored penal substitutionary theory.

atonement theories. Finally, in part 3 we shall reflect philosophically on what we have learned in order to articulate options for a coherent and morally acceptable theory of Christ's atoning death. The subject is a difficult one, and therefore we may make the Psalmist's prayer our own: "Let the words of my mouth and the meditation of my heart be acceptable to you, O LORD" (Ps 19:14).

I

Biblical Data Concerning
the Atonement

Chapter 2

SACRIFICE

INTRODUCTION

Theologians have often remarked on the multiplicity of metaphors and motifs characterizing Christ's atonement found in the NT. The biblical doctrine of the atonement may be aptly compared to a multifaceted jewel, each facet contributing to the beauty of the whole gem. The various facets of a gem are transparent to and refracted in one another, thereby increasing the brilliance and beauty of the whole. On this analogy, it would be an obvious mistake to try to reduce the doctrine of the atonement to just one of its many facets, as some theorists have done. If one's theory of the atonement neglects or excludes any of the facets of the biblical doctrine, then it is not biblically adequate. If an atonement theory is merely incomplete, we might seek to enhance it further; but if it eliminates or precludes various facets of the biblical doctrine, then we may be spared pursuing such a theory further, since it fails to meet adequately our first criterion of a Christian theory of the atonement. In part I we want to survey some of the various facets that make up the biblical doctrine of the atonement.

Our interest in examining the biblical materials is not in tradition-historical analysis of the biblical text, seeking, for example, to determine the date and provenance of the priestly traditions concerning the Levitical sacrifices or to ascertain the authentic words of Jesus concerning his death. Rather, we shall adopt a canonical approach to our subject, taking the biblical text as we have it.[1] The reason for so doing is not because such historical-critical questions are uninteresting or unimportant,[2] but because the canonical text is, after all, the basis for the traditional theories of the atonement surveyed in part 2, which in turn serve as the springboard for our reflections in part 3, and because, having adopted biblical adequacy as a criterion for assessing atonement theories, we want to discover what guidelines and constraints the canonical text provides for a theory of the atonement.

In approaching the biblical teaching on the atonement, we must decide whether to approach the subject thematically or by author. This is no easy decision, for it is not without consequences. An authorial approach has the considerable advantage of giving a clearer picture of what a Paul or a John, for example, thought about the atonement, whereas a thematic approach is likely to blur these lines of distinction.[3] However, an authorial approach does not so easily enable us to identify and explore

---

1   In biblical studies, there has been a reappreciation of the value of studying the canonical text, a movement sometimes known as canonical criticism to differentiate it from source-, form-, and tradition-criticism. The OT scholar Brevard Childs draws attention to "the enormous hiatus" between the critically constructed development of the text and the actual canonical text. "The significance of the final form of the biblical text is that it alone bears witness to the full history of revelation" (Brevard S. Childs, *Introduction to the Old Testament as Scripture* [Philadelphia: Fortress Press, 1979], 40, 76). D. J. A. Clines in his pioneering study of the theme of the Pentateuch points out that biblical scholarship belongs firmly in the tradition of humanistic studies and thus has more in common with literary analysis than with the scientific search for new data. Hence, he indicts biblical scholarship for its "geneticism" and "atomism" to the neglect of the final form of the text (David J. A. Clines, *The Theme of the Pentateuch*, 2nd ed., Journal for the Study of the Old Testament Supplement Series 10 [Sheffield, England: Sheffield Academic Press, 1997], 11).

2   On the contrary, these questions are fascinating in their own right and vitally important for Christian apologetics, since it would be very serious, indeed, if, for example, historical-critical studies of the life of Jesus were to reveal that the historical Jesus, say, saw no redemptive significance at all to his death. Many of the biblical studies I cite in part I do address such historical-critical questions. My overriding concern, however, is to articulate a philosophically adequate theory of the atonement that is faithful to the canonical text.

3   For still-useful authorial approaches see George Smeaton, *The Doctrine of the Atonement, as Taught by the Apostles* (Edinburgh: T&T Clark, 1870); R. W. Dale, *The Atonement*, 9th ed. (London: Hodder & Stoughton, 1884); James

common emphases of the biblical writers as does a thematic approach. Since our aim is to identify the various facets of the biblical doctrine of the atonement, a thematic approach is better suited to our goal. We shall, therefore, take a thematic approach to the biblical materials.

A multifaceted gemstone typically has a central, larger facet that gemologists call "the table." It anchors the entire stone. On this analogy, the table of the biblical doctrine of the atonement is sacrifice. The predominant motif used in the NT to characterize the atonement is the portrayal of Christ's death as a sacrificial offering to God on our behalf. Joel Green provides a pithy summary:

> In their development of the saving significance of Jesus' death, early Christians were heavily influenced by the world of the sacrificial cult in Israel's Scriptures and by the practices of animal sacrifice in the Jerusalem temple. . . . The expression *"Christ died for all,"* widespread in this and variant forms throughout the NT (e.g., Mk 14:24; Rom 5:6, 8; 15:3; Gal 2:21; 1 Pet 3:18), is thematic in this regard, as are references to the salvific effects of *the blood of Christ* (e.g., Acts 20:28; Rom 5:9; Col 1:20). Jesus' death is presented as a *covenant sacrifice* (e.g., Mk 14:24; 1 Cor 11:25; Heb 7:22; 8:6; 9:15), a *Passover sacrifice* (e.g., Jn 19:14; 1 Cor 5:7–8), the *sin offering* (Rom 8:3; 2 Cor 5:21), the *offering of first fruits* (1 Cor 15:20, 23), the sacrifice offered on *the Day of Atonement* (Heb 9–10), and an offering reminiscent of *Abraham's presentation of Isaac* (e.g., Rom 8:32). The writer of Ephesians summarizes well: "Christ loved us and gave himself up for us, a fragrant offering and sacrifice to God" (Eph 5:2).[4]

No other atonement motif is so abundantly attested. This is convincing evidence that the motif of sacrifice anchors the doctrine of the atonement in the NT.

JESUS' ATTITUDE TOWARD HIS DEATH

The interpretation of Jesus' death as a sacrificial offering was not, according to the Gospels, an ex post facto rationalization on the part of Christians of Jesus' ignominious fate. Rather, Jesus himself had seen his

---

Denney, *The Death of Christ: Its Place and Interpretation in the New Testament* (London: Hodder & Stoughton, 1907).

4 Joel B. Green, "Kaleidoscopic View," in *The Nature of the Atonement*, ed. James Beilby and Paul R. Eddy, Spectrum Multiview Books (Downers Grove, Ill.: IVP Academic, 2006), 172 (emphases added).

impending death in this light. He predicted his death (Mark 10:33-34) and even provoked it by his messianic actions in Jerusalem (Mark 11:1-10, 13-18). As N. T. Wright has emphasized, Jesus' selection of the Passover festival as the time of the climax of his ministry was no accident. "Jesus chose Passover as the explanatory setting for what he had to do."[5] For as he celebrated with his disciples his final Passover meal, "he took a loaf of bread, and after blessing it he broke it, gave it to them, and said, 'Take; this is my body.' Then he took a cup, and after giving thanks he gave it to them, and all of them drank from it. He said to them, 'This is my blood of the covenant, which is poured out for many'" (Mark 14:22-24). Jesus saw his death symbolized in the elements of the Passover meal.[6] It was the blood of the Passover lamb, smeared on the doorposts of Jewish homes, that had saved the Jewish people from God's judgment. Jesus' blood, soon to be poured out for many, would accomplish the same purpose. The fact that the disciples then share symbolically in partaking of his body and blood shows that his death is meant to encompass them; it is a death on their behalf.

Moreover, the expression "this is my blood of the covenant"[7] recalls Moses' words at the inauguration of the old covenant, "See the blood of the covenant that the LORD has made with you" (Exod 24:8). The only other OT passage that mentions "the blood of my covenant with you" is Zechariah 9:9-12, a proclamation of the advent of a Messianic King who will restore Israel's fortunes. Jesus the Messiah is inaugurating by his death the new covenant prophesied by Jeremiah, which would bring restoration and forgiveness of sin:

> The days are surely coming, says the LORD, when I will make a new cove-
> nant with the house of Israel and the house of Judah. It will not be like the

---

5   N. T. Wright, *The Day the Revolution Began: Reconsidering the Meaning of Jesus' Crucifixion* (San Francisco: HarperOne, 2017), 277. Discerning the symbolic significance of Jesus' death as the ultimate Passover sacrifice and the inauguration of a new covenant does not imply agreeing with Wright's interpretation that Jesus thought of himself as bringing about Israel's return from exile and a new Exodus.

6   See discussion of the authenticity and meaning of Jesus' words by Joachim Jeremias, *The Eucharistic Words of Jesus*, trans. Norman Perrin (New York: Charles Scribner's Sons, 1966), chap. 5; Brant Pitre, *Jesus and the Last Supper* (Grand Rapids: Eerdmans, 2015), chap. 5.

7   Paul and Luke have explicitly "this cup is the new covenant in my blood" (1 Cor 11:25; Luke 22:20).

covenant that I made with their ancestors when I took them by the hand to bring them out of the land of Egypt—a covenant that they broke, though I was their husband, says the LORD. But this is the covenant that I will make with the house of Israel after those days, says the LORD: I will put my law within them, and I will write it on their hearts; and I will be their God, and they shall be my people. No longer shall they teach one another, or say to each other, "Know the LORD," for they shall all know me, from the least of them to the greatest, says the LORD; for I will forgive their iniquity, and remember their sin no more. (Jer 31:31-34)

Jesus saw his death as not merely averting God's judgment but as expunging Israel's sin and restoring fellowship with God.

Moreover, the words "poured out for many" hark back to Isaiah's prophecy of the Servant of the LORD, who

> poured out his soul to death,
>> and was numbered with the transgressors;
> yet he bore the sin of many,
>> and made intercession for the transgressors. (Isa 53:12)

In Luke 22:37 Jesus, on the night of his arrest, cites this very Scripture in application to himself. "For I tell you, this scripture must be fulfilled in me, 'And he was counted among the lawless'; and indeed what is written about me is being fulfilled." The "many" whose sin the Servant bears include the Gentiles, to whom the Servant would be a light of salvation (Isa 42:6; 49:6). Jesus saw himself as the suffering Servant of Isaiah 53, who "makes himself an offering for sin" (Isa 53:10). Earlier Jesus had said of himself, "The Son of man came not to be served but to serve, and to give his life a ransom for many" (Mark 10:45).[8] The Son of Man is a divine-human figure from Daniel's prophecy whom "all peoples, nations, and languages should serve" (Dan 7:14). In his paradoxical statement Jesus stands things on their head, declaring that the Son of Man has come in the role of a servant and, like the Servant of Isaiah 53, gives his life as a ransom for many. Only in Isaiah 53 do we find in the OT

---

8 For a discussion of the authenticity and interpretation of this saying, see Peter Stuhlmacher, *Reconciliation, Law, and Righteousness: Essays in Biblical Theology*, trans. Everett R. Kalin (Philadelphia: Fortress Press, 1986), chap. 2: "Vicariously Giving His Life for Many, Mark 10:45 (Matt. 20:28)," 16–29; cf. idem, "Eighteen Theses on Paul's Theology of the Cross," in *Reconciliation, Law, and Righteousness*, 165.

the complex idea of a "serving" figure who, in an eschatological context, gives his life for "the many."[9]

According to the Gospels, then, Jesus saw his death as a redemptive sacrifice, like the Passover sacrifice, and himself as a sin-bearer, like Isaiah's Servant of the LORD, inaugurating, like the Mosaic sacrifice, a fresh covenant between God and the people.

OT BACKGROUND

We can gain deeper insight into Jesus' death as a sacrificial offering by examining the function of the OT sacrifices that formed the interpretive framework for Jesus' death. In doing so, it must be said, we enter a world that is utterly foreign to modern Western readers. Most of us have never seen an animal slaughtered, much less done it ourselves, and, accustomed as we are to buying our meat and poultry in antiseptically wrapped packaging in refrigerated bins, we are apt to find the animal sacrifices described in the OT revolting. Moreover, most of us have no familiarity with a world in which ritual practices fraught with symbolic meaning play a major role in one's interactions with the spiritual realm, and so the OT cult may strike us as bizarre and opaque. If we are to understand these practices, we need to shed our Western sensibilities and try to enter sympathetically the primitive world of a bucolic society that was not squeamish about blood and guts and that had a highly developed ritual system in its approach to God.

The challenge of understanding these ancient texts is compounded by the fact that they often describe rituals without explaining their meaning, which was probably well known to their contemporary practitioners. Therefore, we must try as best we can to discern their proper interpretation based on the clues that we have. Fortunately, we have sufficient evidence to form some reliable ideas about what the sacrifices were intended to accomplish. Among their various functions the animal sacrifices filled the twin fundamental purposes of expiation of sin and propitiation of God. "To expiate" means to remove, annul, cancel; "to propitiate" means to appease, to placate, to satisfy. The object of expiation is sin; the object of propitiation is God.

---

9   Rikki E. Watts, "Jesus' Death, Isaiah 53, and Mark 10:45: A Crux Revisited," in *Jesus and the Suffering Servant: Isaiah 53 and Christian Origins*, ed. William H. Bellinger Jr. and William R. Farmer (Harrisburg, Penn.: Trinity Press International, 1998), 143.

Propitiatory Sacrifices

At least some of the sacrifices described in the OT were clearly propitiatory. A premier example is the sacrifice of the Passover lamb (Exod 12:1-27). This sacrifice was not originally instituted for the purpose of expiating sin. Rather, the blood of the lamb smeared on the doorframes of Israelite homes served to shelter them as God's judgment swept over Egypt. "When I see the blood, I will pass over you, and no plague shall destroy you when I strike the land of Egypt" (Exod 12:13). Had they not offered the sacrifices, God's deadly judgment would have fallen on the Israelites as well.

Propitiation is also in view in various Levitical sacrifices offered in the Tabernacle (and later in the Temple). The careful regulations concerning the sacrificial offerings are to be understood against the background of God's striking down Aaron's sons for their unlawful offering of sacrifices in the Tabernacle precincts (Lev 10:1-2; 16:1).[10] God was conceived to be specially present in the innermost sanctum of the Tabernacle, which therefore had to be approached with utmost care. It was a dangerous business to have a holy God dwelling in the midst of a sinful and impure people, as we see in God's refusal to accompany the people into the promised land following their apostasy with the golden calf: "Go up to a land flowing with milk and honey; but I will not go up among you, or I would consume you on the way, for you are a stiff-necked people. . . . if for a single moment I should go up among you, I would consume you" (Exod 33:3, 5). The sacrificial system functioned to facilitate the juxtaposition of the holy and the unholy. It did this, not merely by purging the Tabernacle and its paraphernalia of impurity but also by propitiating God and so averting His wrath upon the people. The roasting of the sacrificial animals, in particular, is repeatedly said to produce "a pleasing odor to the LORD" (Lev 1:9, 13, 17; 2:2; 3:5; 4:31; 8:21,

---

10 J. Oswalt observes that Lev 10:8–15:33 is a parenthesis prompted by the tragedy of 10:1-7. In Lev 1–9 God had been trying to show His people that His holiness constituted a positive danger to them and that He alone could set the terms of their relationship. Nadab and Abihu demonstrated that the lesson had not been learned. In Lev 16:1 the reader is returned to what would have been originally intended to be the climax of chapters 1–9 (*Dictionary of the Old Testament: Pentateuch*, ed. T. Desmond Alexander and David W. Baker, s.v. "Theology of the Pentateuch," by J. N. Oswalt [Downers Grove, Ill.: InterVarsity, 2003], 845–59).

etc.), which implies that the sacrifices were accepted by God and helped to cultivate His favor (cf. Gen 8:21).[11]

Expiatory Sacrifices

The Levitical sacrifices, which are the central sacrifices of the OT, came in a bewildering variety, the distinctive functions of which are not always clear.[12] In addition to regulations for offerings of grain (*minḥâ*),[13] the book of Leviticus prescribes regulations for the offering (and disposal of any remains) of four types of animal sacrifices to be brought by faithful Jews:

(1) Burnt offering (*'ōlâ*)
(2) Peace (well-being) offering (*šelāmîm*)
(3) Sin (purification) offering (*ḥaṭṭā't*)
(4) Guilt (reparation) offering (*'āšām*)

Six steps were involved in the sacrificial ritual: (1) the offerer brings the animal to be sacrificed to the sanctuary, (2) the offerer lays his hand on the animal's head, (3) the offerer kills the animal, (4) the officiating priest carries out a blood rite (such sprinkling, pouring, or applying the

---

11 Gordon Wenham says that the word "pleasing" (*niḥōaḥ*) would better be translated "soothing," "pacifying," "quietening" (Gordon J. Wenham, "The Theology of Old Testament Sacrifice," in *Sacrifice in the Bible*, ed. Roger T. Beckwith and Martin J. Selman [Grand Rapids: Baker Book House, 1995], 80).

12 For a detailed discussion see Jacob Milgrom, *Leviticus 1–16*, The Anchor Bible (New York: Doubleday, 1991), "Sacrificial Instructions Directed to the Laity 1.1–5.26." We have little knowledge of sacrifices outside the Levitical system. The so-called burnt offering seems to have existed prior to its incorporation into the Levitical sacrificial system and was offered both to propitiate God (Gen 8:21) and to expiate sin (Job 1:5; 42:8).

13 Because they lacked the crucial element of blood (Lev 17:11), the rationale for grain offerings was not to atone for sin and impurity. According to Milgrom, they served as presents made to God in order to obtain or retain His goodwill (*Leviticus 1–16*, 197). For the desperately poor, who could not afford an animal sacrifice, an offering of flour was acceptable in its place (Lev 5:7-13), but this was an accommodation by the LORD. It reflects the fact that the sacrifices did not function *ex opera operato* to atone for sin and impurity but were a gracious arrangement made by God for securing His pardon, an arrangement seen by NT authors as provisional (Heb 9:9-10). Since our interest is in atonement, we focus on the animal sacrifices.

animal's blood), (5) the priest butchers the animal and burns the various pieces on the altar, and (6) the remains are disposed of, while some cuts may be kept to be eaten. Morris provides the following helpful tableau concerning the handling of these sacrifices:[14]

The Animal Sacrifices in Leviticus
(References to chapter and verse in Leviticus)

	Burnt	Peace	Sin	Guilt
1. The worshipper "brings near"	male from flock or herd: bull, sheep or goat; dove or pigeon (1:5, 10, 14)	domestic animal, male or female (3:1, 6, 12)	for priest or people, young bull (4:3, 13-14); for leader, male goat (4:22-23); for citizen, female goat (4:27-28) or lamb (4:32)	ram plus silver (5:15)
2. The worshipper lays his hand on the head of the prescribed victim				
3. The worshipper himself kills the prescribed victim				
4. The priest puts the blood	against the altar on all sides (1:5, 11); drains blood of birds on side of altar (1:15)	against the altar on all sides (3:2, 8)	for priest or the community, seven times before the curtain, on horns of incense altar, at base of main altar (4:6-7, 17-18); for individual, on horns and at base of main altar (4:25, 30)	against the altar on all sides (7:2)
5. The priest burns on the altar	the whole animal or bird (1:9, 13, 17)	specified parts (3:3-4, 9-10, 14-15)	same as for peace offerings (4:8-10)	specified parts (7:3-4)
6. Disposal of the rest of the carcass	— (the hide to the priest, 7:8)	parts to the priest (7:31-34); the rest eaten by worshippers (7:15-21)	for priest or community, burnt outside the camp (4:11-12, 21); for individuals, eaten by priestly males (6:25-26, 29)	eaten by priestly males (7:6)

---

14 Leon Morris, *The Atonement: Its Meaning and Significance* (Downers Grove, Ill.: InterVarsity, 1983), 46.

According to Milgrom, while a comprehensive understanding of the burnt offering's rationale eludes us, the function of the remaining three can be satisfactorily explained: they were all expiatory sacrifices.[15] In the Levitical system of sacrifices, these offerings served to remove ceremonial impurity and/or moral guilt. Our interest is in the latter function. Some commentators have overemphasized the function of the sacrifices in purifying the Tabernacle and its sacred objects to the neglect of the sacrifices' role in cleansing the people themselves of guilt and impurity.[16] Reducing the function of the sacrifices to the purification of objects alone is implausible and fails to do justice to the biblical text. For purging objects of impurity while leaving the worshippers themselves guilty and unclean would fail to address the root of the problem. For human sin pollutes the sanctuary and its objects with impurity. Moreover, the text repeatedly promises, "The priest shall make atonement on your behalf for the sin that you have committed, and you shall be forgiven" (Lev 4:35; cf. 4:20, 26, 31, etc.). The word translated "make atonement" (*kippēr*) has a range of meanings—to purge, to ransom, to expiate[17]—but what is significant here is the result: *the person's sins are forgiven.*[18] Through the ritual sacrifice a person's guilt has been removed.

---

15 The burnt offering is assigned an expiatory function as well in Lev 9:7; 14:20; 16:24, and in Job 1:5; 42:8; Ezek 45:15, 17. Like the grain offering, it is offered to obtain God's favor in Judg 20:26; 1 Sam 13:12; 2 Sam 24:21-25.

16 See, e.g., *Anchor Bible Dictionary*, ed. David Noel Freedman, s.v. "Sacrifice and Sacrificial Offerings: Old Testament," by Gary A. Anderson (New York: Doubleday, 1992), 5:870–86. For a helpful review of the various interpretations of the Levitical animal sacrifices, see Jim Greenberg, "An Assessment of Jacob Milgrom's View of the *ḥaṭṭā't* Offering Using a Text-Immanent Approach to Reading the Priestly Texts" (paper presented at the annual meeting of the Society of Biblical Literature, Boston, November 18–21, 2017).

17 See Milgrom, *Leviticus 1–16*, 1079–84; Jay Sklar, "Sin and Impurity: Atoned or Purified? Yes!," in *Perspectives on Purity and Purification in the Bible*, ed. Baruch J. Schwartz, David P. Wright, Jeffrey Stackert, and Naphtali S. Meshel, Library of Hebrew Bible / Old Testament Studies 474 (London: T&T Clark, 2008), 18–31.

18 As noted by Gary A. Anderson, "Sacrifice and Sacrificial Offerings: Old Testament," in *The Anchor Bible Dictionary, O–Sh*, ed. David Noel Freedman (New York: Doubleday, 1992), 880. Greenberg observes, "Many sacrifices include preconditions the offerer must meet . . . and end with result statements expressed on behalf of the offerer, such as forgiveness, and making clean. As a result, with some confidence, scholars conclude that sacrifice fixes a problem between the offerer and *YHWH*. However, determining how and why sacrifice fixes this

So, Milgrom advises, "Although the cult concentrates heavily on the purging of sanctuary impurity, it too recognizes that the ultimate source of impurity is human sin."[19] Sin must therefore be expiated. The continual purging and reconsecration of the altar "points to the singular function of the altar: it is the medium of God's salvific expiation of the sins of Israel. Therefore, not only does it have to be purged of Israel's sins; it must be a fit instrument for effecting expiation for Israel when sacrifices are offered up on it."[20] While repentance is a necessary condition of God's forgiveness of a sin, "For the complete annulment of the sin, however, for the assurance of divine forgiveness (*sālaḥ*), sacrificial expiation (*kippēr*) is *always* required" in the Levitical system.[21] *Kippēr* in its most abstract sense thus comes to mean "atone" or "expiate." "The meaning here is that the offerer is cleansed of his impurities/sins and becomes reconciled, 'at one,' with God."[22]

In the Pentateuch three broad categories of sin are recognized: unintentional sins, intentional sins short of apostasy, and intentional sins of

---

problem is elusive" (Greenberg, "Assessment"). N.B. that for neither purgation of impurity nor expiation of sins is the blood sprinkled on the people themselves, yet the sacrifices are efficacious in rendering their offerers forgiven just as they are in rendering them clean. "Through the sin offering's blood-manipulation ritual the violator of the law could gain forgiveness before God, while the unclean person could be brought back into the condition of being ritually clean as opposed to unclean" (*Dictionary of the Old Testament: Pentateuch*, ed. T. Desmond Alexander and David W. Baker, s.v. "Sacrifices and Offerings," by R. E. Averbeck [Downers Grove, Ill.: InterVarsity, 2003], 719). Similarly, it is of no significance that grammatically *kippēr* + a preposition like *'al* or *be 'ad* is used with respect to people, whereas words for objects may be the direct object of *kippēr*. Efficacy is not determined by grammar. For a helpful summary of terms, see *Theologische Realenzyklopädie*, ed. Gerhard Müller, vol. 32, *Spurgeon-Taylor* (Berlin: Walter de Gruyter, 2001), s.v. "Sühne II: Altes Testament," by Adrian Schenker.

19 Milgrom, *Leviticus 1–16*, 1083–84.
20 Milgrom, *Leviticus 1–16*, 1038.
21 Milgrom, *Leviticus 1–16*, 377. Milgrom notes that in the OT only God is able to extend *sālaḥ*, never human persons. It involves both the pardon of sin and the restoration of relationship with God. "The offerer knows that his wrong has polluted the altar and hence has alienated him from God. By the sacrifice he hopes to repair the broken relationship. He therefore seeks more than forgiveness. If God will accept his sacrifice he will be once again restored to grace at one with his deity" (245).
22 Milgrom, *Leviticus 1–16*, 1083.

apostasy.[23] The Levitical personal sacrifices availed for expiation of sins only of the first two types; persons committing so-called high-handed sins were to be cut off from the people. The sacrifices had been given by the LORD to His covenant people to atone for their sins.[24] Someone who committed a sin amounting to apostasy was, in effect, renouncing the covenant and so no longer a beneficiary of it. Nevertheless, his situation was not entirely hopeless: through repentance and the intercession of a mediator (such as Moses), God might pardon him (Exod 32:11-14; Num 11:2; 14:13-20; 16:22; 17:6-15; 25:8). The fact that sins could be thus pardoned without sacrifice underlines the fact that the animal sacrifices served a ritual or symbolic function (cf. Heb 10:1-4).

As intimated, one of the noteworthy features of these sacrificial offerings is that they were personal offerings in which the individual bringing the sacrifice was an active participant. In particular, the offerer was required to slay the animal himself. A telling hand-laying ritual accompanied the slaughter of the animal: the offerer was to lay his hand upon the animal's head before slaying it (Lev 1:4). The Hebrew expression (*sāmak yādô*) indicates a forceful laying of the hand: one was to press his hand upon the head of the beast to be sacrificed. Although Milgrom has suggested that this "hand-leaning" ritual was meant merely to indicate ownership of the sacrificial animal,[25] such an interpretation is implausible and trivializes an apparently important feature of the ceremony.[26] Someone pulling an animal by a rope around its neck before

---

23 Jay Sklar, "Sin and Atonement: Lessons from the Pentateuch," *Bulletin for Biblical Research* 22, no. 4 (2012): 467–91.

24 As Bernd Janowski so beautifully puts it, the sacrificial system did not rest on the pagan principle *do ut des* (I [man] give so that you [God] will give) but rather on the principle *do quia dedisti* (I [man] give because you [God] have previously given) (Bernd Janowski, *Sühne als Heilsgeschehen: Studien zur Sühnetheologie der Priesterschrift und zur Wurzel KPR im Alten Orient und im Alten Testament*, WMANT 55 [Neukirchen-Vluyn, Germany: Neukirchener (Vandenhoeck & Ruprecht Verlage) 1982], 261).

25 Milgrom, *Leviticus 1–16*, 151–52. He argues as follows: the hand-laying ritual was not required for grain offerings or the offering of a bird or a monetary substitute because the person brought it in his hand, and so it was obviously his offering. But hand-laying is required for all quadrupeds because they would have to be dragged in by rope or bought from the sanctuary stock, and so in either case ownership would have to be established.

26 As Greenberg puts it, "The sacrificial remedy requires an unbroken chain of physical touch [of which the hand-laying ceremony is a part] between the offerer

the altar is just as obviously the person bringing his sacrifice as someone who carries in his hand a bird or grain for sacrifice, and if there were any doubt a verbal affirmation would suffice. Rather, this emphatic gesture of pressing one's hand on the animal's head is plausibly meant to indicate the identification of the offerer with the animal, so that the animal's fate symbolizes his own. That is why "it shall be acceptable in your behalf as atonement for you" (Lev 1:4).[27] Death is the penalty for sin,[28] and the animal dies in place of the worshipper. This is not to say that the animal was punished in the place of the worshipper; rather, the animal suffered the death that would have been the worshipper's punishment had it happened to him. This is at most a ritual punishment, a symbolic representation of what the offerer deserves. It was, in W. H. Moberly's words, a "garish and arresting picture" of the fate of the sinner.[29]

---

and the altar, mediated by the priest by means of a sacrificial animal's flesh and blood. . . . [B]y creating the unbroken chain of physical touch between the offerer and the altar, *YHWH* forgives the offerer and his anger is appeased" ("Assessment").

27 Notice that in the case of communal sin the elders are to lay their hands on the bull to be sacrificed as a sin offering (Lev 4:15). This cannot be construed as a sign of ownership.

28 See Jay Sklar, *Sin, Impurity, Sacrifice, Atonement: The Priestly Conceptions*, Hebrew Bible Monographs 2 (Sheffield: Sheffield Phoenix Press, 2005), 11–12, who shows, against those who think of death as merely the natural consequence of sin, that the consequence of sin is a punitive judgment from the divine. See more broadly the classic treatment in Jonathan Edwards, *The Works of Jonathan Edwards*, vol. 1, *The Great Christian Doctrine of Original Sin Defended* [1834] (Peabody, Mass.: Hendrickson, 1998), 146–233.

In commenting on the story of man's disobedience to God in the Garden of Eden and God's subsequent judgment, Kenneth Matthews points out that the words "you shall surely die" (*môt_ tāmût_*) occur repeatedly in the legal collections of the Pentateuch condemning criminals to death (Kenneth A. Matthews, *Genesis 1–11:26*, The New American Commentary 1A [Nashville: B&H, 1996], 211). Victor Hamilton adds that all of the *môt_ tāmût_* passages in the OT deal with either a punishment for sin or an untimely death as the result of punishment, so that here the expression clearly conveys the announcement of a death sentence by divine or royal decree (Victor P. Hamilton, *The Book of Genesis: Chapters 1–17*, The New International Commentary on the Old Testament [Grand Rapids: Eerdmans, 1990], 173–74). Umberto Cassuto discerns a number of trial motifs in the story (Umberto Cassuto, *A Commentary on the Book of Genesis*, part 1, *From Adam to Noah: Genesis I–VI. 8* [1944], trans. Israel Abrahams [Skokie, Ill.: Varda Books, 2005], 156–58).

29 Sir Walter Moberly, *The Ethics of Punishment* (Hamden, Conn.: Archon Books, 1968), 207. Moberly has an interesting discussion of ritual punishment, which he

Following the slaughter of the animal, the priest carries out a blood rite, which involves splashing or applying the blood in some way, depending on what type of sacrifice were offered and for whom. The meaning of this blood rite is disputed. The key text in this regard is Leviticus 17:11: "The life of the flesh is in the blood; and I have given it to you for making atonement for your lives on the altar; for, as life, it is the blood that makes atonement." According to Sklar, "It is commonly agreed that the atonement referred to by the verb [*kippēr*] in this verse is characterized by ransom."[30] For the expression translated "making atonement for your lives" (*le kappēr 'al napšōtêkem*) is found elsewhere in the OT only twice, where it has the meaning "to ransom your lives":

> "You shall take the atonement money from the Israelites and shall designate it for the service of the tent of meeting; before the LORD it will be a reminder to the Israelites of the ransom given for your lives." (Exod 30:16; cf. v. 12: "all of them shall give a ransom for their lives to the LORD")

> "We have brought the LORD's offering, what each of us found, articles of gold, armlets and bracelets, signet rings, earrings, and pendants, to make atonement for ourselves before the LORD." (Num 31:50)

The use of money or valuables as payment in these passages clearly indicates the ransoming function of *kippēr*. Accordingly, Leviticus 17:11 may be rendered, "For the life of the flesh is in the blood, and I have assigned it to you on the altar to ransom your lives; for it is the blood that ransoms by means of life."[31] In Leviticus 4–5 the blood rite involves sprinkling or pouring the animal's blood upon the altar, in line with

---

believes characterizes all punishment.

30 Sklar, "Sin and Impurity," 28; see extended discussion in idem, *Sin, Impurity, Sacrifice, Atonement*, 163–82.

31 This is Milgrom's translation in Jacob Milgrom, *Leviticus 17–22*, Anchor Yale Bible 3A (New Haven, Conn.: Yale University Press, 2000). The life referred to in v. 11c is not some mysterious life force but the animal's life that is forfeited; as Averbeck says, "The blood of the animal was accepted as the ransom for human life because the blood was identified with the life of the animal" (Richard E. Averbeck, "kpr [4105/4106]," *New International Dictionary of Old Testament Theology and Exegesis*, ed. Willem A. VanGemeren [Grand Rapids: Zondervan, 1997], 695). Notice the instrumental understanding of the word "*be*" in Milgrom's translation of v. 11c. According to Wenham, "The proposal with the fewest problems takes 'life' to refer to the animal's life and *be* to mean 'through.' It is thus the animal's life, united to its blood, that makes atonement for human lives

Leviticus 17:11, indicating that the sacrificial blood serves to ransom the life of the offerer.[32]

Some have claimed that what is important here is not the animal's death but the life force represented by or contained in the blood. Wright, for example, asserts, "In the ancient Hebrew scriptures the death of the sacrificial animal was not the heart of the ritual; it was only the preliminary event. What mattered was that the blood, symbolizing the life which would 'cover' all impurities of whatever sort, would then be presented on the altar."[33]

[souls] on the altar. The principle of substitution is at work. Animal life takes the place of human life" (Wenham, "Theology of Old Testament Sacrifice," 82).

32 According to Sklar, Milgrom's attempt to limit v. 11 to the peace offering "has not gained widespread acceptance" (Sklar, "Sin and Impurity," 25); how much less his idiosyncratic interpretation that one's life must be ransomed for having committed murder of the sacrificial animal itself (Milgrom, *Leviticus 17–22*, 1473). For a critique of this curious interpretation see Averbeck, "kpr [4105/4106]," 694–95.

33 Wright, *Day the Revolution Began*, 177. Wright rejects the view that "the sacrificial animals were being killed in the place of the worshipper," which he equates with "substitutionary punishment." He explains:

> The killing of the sacrificial animals was not, in ancient Israel, the important part of the ritual. The killing did not take place on the altar (an important difference from much pagan ritual). Cutting the animal's throat was simply the prelude to the release of blood, symbolizing the animal's life, which was then used as the all-important agent for purging or cleansing the worshippers and also the sacred place and its furniture, thus enabling the all-holy God to meet with his people without disastrous results. And that meeting took place precisely on the *kappōreth*, the place of cleansing or purgation. There is nothing here about punishment. (329)

But, as we have seen, one should not equate substitutionary death with substitutionary punishment. Rather, the animal suffers the fate that would have been the worshipper's punishment had it happened to him instead. Nor should one equate substitution with sin-bearing. The hand-laying ceremony does plausibly indicate symbolic identification of the offerer with the animal, but it need not indicate transference of sin (Hartmut Gese, "The Atonement," in *Essays on Biblical Theology*, trans. Keith Crim [Minneapolis: Augsburg, 1981], 106; Janowski, *Sühne als Heilsgeschehen*; Otfried Hofius, "Sühne und Versöhnung: Zum paulinischen Verständnis des Kreuzestodes Jesu," in *Paulusstudien*, 2nd rev. ed, edited by Otfried Hofius, WUNT 1/51 (Tübingen: J. C. B. Mohr [Paul Siebeck], 1994), 33–49; Richard H. Bell, "Sacrifice and Christology in Paul," *Journal of Theological*

What shall we make of this claim? In Lev 17:11, which governs the use of *kippēr* in sacrificial contexts, *kippēr* has the sense of "to ransom," in the sense "to rescue" or "to redeem." Milgrom thinks that the ransoming function of *kippēr* involves substitution,[34] in which case the animal's death would be of crucial importance, since it dies in the place of the offerer. It is not clear, however, that the concept of ransom per se implies substitution. In cases involving monetary forms of ransoming, it seems more appropriate to conceive of the ransom in terms of payment rather than substitution. (Such a financial form of ransom may, indeed, be a substitute for an animal sacrifice by the worshipper, but that is not to say that the financial payment is a substitute for the worshipper himself.) Nonetheless, in cases of animal sacrifice, the ransoming function of *kippēr* does seem to involve substitution.[35] The animal's life is given instead of the sinner's. The key difference between the cases lies in the fact that, in contrast to monetary payments, the animal's life is forfeited. Thus, the animal's death is of vital importance.

This conclusion is confirmed by the centrality of death in other Pentateuchal atonement narratives, such as Moses' offer to die to make atonement for the sin of the people (Exod 30:30-34), Phineas' making atonement for Israel's sin by killing the malefactors (Num 25:7-13),

---

Studies 53, no. 1 [2002]: 4; Simon Gathercole, *Defending Substitution: An Essay on Atonement in Paul* [Grand Rapids: Baker Academic, 2015], 18–19).

34 He speaks of "the substitute or ransom notion of *kippēr*," commenting, "There exists a strong possibility that all texts that assign to *kippēr* the function of averting God's wrath have *kōper* in mind: innocent life spared by substituting for it the guilty parties or their ransom" (Milgrom, *Leviticus 1–16*, 1081; cf. Averbeck, "kpr [4105/4106]," 698). Oddly, because Milgrom restricts Lev 17:11 to a peace offering given for the murder of the sacrificial animal, he rejects "the substitutionary theory of sacrifice, based largely on this verse and championed by so many in the scholarly world" (Milgrom, *Leviticus 17–22*, 1477). He says that such a theory should have been dismissed on the simple grounds that "if the death of an animal is so important, why is it performed by a layman not a priest?" I find this retort astonishing because it is precisely because the offerer kills the animal himself after laying his hand upon it rather than giving it over to the priest to do the work that the animal comes to stand in for the offerer. Milgrom's position thus hinges upon his implausible explanation of the hand-laying ceremony.

35 Here again we come back to the hand-laying ritual, whereby the worshipper identifies with the animal in its fate. As Gese emphasizes, we have as a result an inclusive substitution in which the offerer is represented (Gese, "Atonement," in *Essays on Biblical Theology*, 106), something impossible in the case of mere monetary payment.

and the prescription to make atonement for an unsolved murder in open country by breaking the neck of a heifer in the vicinity of the corpse (Deut 21:1-8).[36] Sklar summarizes, "In short, the animal's lifeblood was accepted as the ransom payment in place of the offeror's: it served as a mitigated penalty on the offeror's behalf, graciously accepted by the Lord (the offended party), in this way rescuing the offeror (the offending party) from due punishment and restoring peace to the relationship between the sinner and the Lord."[37]

Finally, Wright's claim that the public slaughter of a goat or bull was just "a preliminary event" strains credulity.[38] The blood rite carried out by the priest following the slaughter is more plausibly regarded not as the heart of the ritual but as the presentation to God of the animal's life, symbolized by the blood, given in place of the offerer's. On Wright's view, if ancient Israel had practiced bloodletting of animals rather than

---

36 Notice, too, how in Num 35:33 expiation "by blood" is equated with the death of the offender.

37 Jay Sklar, "Pentateuch," in *Companion to the Doctrine of Sin*, ed. Keith L. Johnson and David Lauber (London: T&T Clark, 2016), 6. I would demur only in Sklar's characterizing a ransom as a kind of commutation of sentence to a lesser penalty. Construing a ransom payment in penal terms is gratuitous. Morris' conclusion is better: "When a sacrifice was offered we should see it as a killing of the animal in place of the worshipper and the manipulation of the blood as the ritual presentation to God of the evidence that a death has taken place to atone for sin" (Morris, *Atonement*, 62).

38 Similarly, Moffit's claim that because Leviticus gives no instructions on how the animal is to be killed but gives detailed descriptions about how it is to be butchered and its blood distributed, the killing of the sacrificial animal is of minor importance and without atoning significance (David M. Moffitt, *Atonement and the Logic of Resurrection in the Epistle to the Hebrews*, Supplements to Novum Testamentum 141 [Leiden: Brill, 2013], 258–59, 271). The absence of instructions as to how to kill the animal shows at most that how the knife was wielded is of little importance for the ritual, not that the animal's death is of little importance. Based on the detail of instructions, the center of sacrifice would be the butchering of the animal, which seems absurd. Moffit also appeals to the fact that the atoning result of the sacrifice is never directly linked with the act of killing the animal but is often correlated with the application of blood to various items. But this shows only that the presentation of the animal's blood as an offering to God was a vital element in the ritual of atonement, without which the killing alone (which then could have been carried out anywhere!) would have been incomplete and inefficacious. The fundamental failing of those who would minimize the animal's death in the process of atonement, it seems to me, is their trying to divide up and separate elements that cohere together in a unified process.

sacrifice, merely drawing some of their blood and presenting it to God on the altar would have sufficed to atone for Israel's sins.

However we decide the meaning of the blood rite, the priest's distribution of the blood of the sacrificial animal on the altar indicates minimally that the animal's life has been offered to God as a sacrifice to expiate the offerer's sin and so to save his life.

Yom Kippur Sacrifices

The expiatory ritual par excellence was the annual sacrifices on Yom Kippur (Day of Atonement), which was performed on behalf of the whole nation and covered a wider range of sins than did the personal sacrifices (Lev 16). The totality of sins, expressed by the trifold description "iniquities, transgressions, and sins" (Exod 34:7) are removed from the people (Lev 6:21). An indication of this day's extraordinary power is the fact that only on Yom Kippur could sins committed with a high hand be sacrificially atoned for.

This day featured an extraordinary ritual involving the presentation of a pair of goats, one of which was sacrificially killed and the other (the so-called scapegoat)[39] driven out into the desert, bearing away the sins of the people, which had been symbolically laid on the goat through a hand-laying ritual performed by the priest. The priestly actions involving the pair of goats are best seen as two aspects of the same ritual rather than as separate rituals.[40] The high priest is said to receive not three animals but rather two goats for a sin offering and one ram. The two goats form a unit. In a similar ritual involving two birds offered for the cleansing of impurity, the blood of the slain bird cleanses the person while the release of the other bird symbolizes the removal of his impurity:

> This shall be the ritual for the leprous person at the time of his cleansing:
>
>> He shall be brought to the priest; the priest shall go out of the camp, and the priest shall make an examination. If the disease is

---

39 What "Azazel" (scapegoat) designates is uncertain. According to Milgrom, the most plausible explanation is that "Azazel" was the name of a demon who has now been eviscerated of his erstwhile demonic powers. In the priestly ritual he is no longer a personality but just a name designating the place to which impurities and sins are banished (Milgrom, *Leviticus 1–16*, 1021).

40 Nicole Ruane, "Constructing Contagion on Yom Kippur: Reflections on the Scapegoat as Hatta't" (paper presented to the "Ritual in the Biblical World" section of the Society of Biblical Literature, San Antonio, Tex., November 21, 2016).

healed in the leprous person, the priest shall command that two
living clean birds and cedarwood and crimson yarn and hyssop
be brought for the one who is to be cleansed. The priest shall
command that one of the birds be slaughtered over fresh water in
an earthen vessel. He shall take the living bird with the cedarwood and the crimson yarn and the hyssop, and dip them and the
living bird in the blood of the bird that was slaughtered over
the fresh water. He shall sprinkle it seven times upon the one who
is to be cleansed of the leprous disease; then he shall pronounce
him clean, and he shall let the living bird go into the open field.
(Lev 14:2-7)

The case of the two goats is analogous. The one goat is sacrificed and the
other released, symbolically carrying away the people's sins. The blood
sacrifice is essential. If sin could be expiated simply by laying it on a goat
and driving it away into the desert, then the whole sacrificial system
would become pointless. Rather, as we have seen, a sacrificial death is
necessary: "For the life of the flesh is in the blood; and I have given it for
you upon the altar to make atonement for your souls; for it is the blood
that makes atonement, by reason of the life" (Lev 17:11 RSV).

The description of the Yom Kippur ritual differentiates between
"mak(ing) atonement for the sanctuary, and . . . for the tent of meeting
and for the altar" and "mak(ing) atonement for the priests and for all
the people" (Lev 16:33). Making atonement for inanimate objects is to
purge them of ritual uncleanness; making atonement for persons is
to expiate their sins. "For on this day shall atonement be made for
you, to cleanse you; from all your sins you shall be clean before the
LORD" (v. 30). The sprinkled blood of the goat, along with the blood of
the bull sacrificed by the priest, shall not only "make atonement for the
sanctuary" but also make "atonement for himself and for his house and
for all the assembly of Israel" (vv. 16-17). Once the altar has also been
suitably purged, the priest may then "offer his burnt offering and the
burnt offering of the people, and make atonement for himself and for the
people" (v. 24). Thus, the blood of the sacrificial goat atones for the sins of
the people, while the driving out of the other symbolizes the efficacy of
the sacrifice in expiating their sin.[41]

---

41 According to Milgrom, *kippēr* here takes on the more abstract meaning "to expiate." "In effect, the original purpose of the scapegoat, to eliminate the impurities
removed from the sanctuary, has been altered to accommodate a new theological
notion—once a year, on the tenth of Tishri, the purgation rites of the sanctuary

JESUS' DEATH AS SACRIFICE

The construal of Jesus' death as a sacrificial offering pervades the NT. As mentioned,[42] the Greek *hilas-* equivalents of the Hebrew atonement words appear in the NT. In 1 John 2:2, we read that Jesus Christ "is the atoning sacrifice [*hilasmos*] for our sins, and not for ours only but also for the sins of the whole world." Two chapters later we read again that God "sent his Son to be the atoning sacrifice [*hilasmos*] for our sins" (1 John 4:10). In Hebrews the author characterizes Jesus as "a merciful and faithful high priest in the service of God, to make a sacrifice of atonement [*hilaskesthai*] for the sins of the people" (2:17). And Paul in his exposition of his doctrine of justification through faith states that God put Christ forward as "a sacrifice of atonement[43] [*hilastērion*] by his blood" (Rom 3:25). Averbeck makes the interesting observation that if we take this last verse to refer to a place of atonement, then in these passages we have Jesus represented as a vicarious sacrifice, a vicarious sacrificer, and a vicarious place of sacrifice—a "combination of motifs which bears a great deal of meaning for Christian theology."[44]

As we look at the NT authors' employment of the motif of sacrifice with respect to Jesus' death, it is worth bearing in mind that what ultimately matters for the Christian doctrine of the atonement is not how the sacrifices may have been originally understood but how the NT authors understood them. For example, the author of Hebrews says flatly, "It is impossible for the blood of bulls and goats to take away sins" (Heb 10:4). He thereby reveals his understanding of the OT sacrifices as expiatory in intention, if not in reality, and his view of Christ's self-sacrifice as truly expiatory. The NT authors did not think of Christ on the analogy of a bloodless scapegoat or grain offering but focused on the

---

also remove Israel's sins, provided the people show their remorse through acts of self-denial and cessation from labor" (*Leviticus 1–16*, 1023). See further Baruch J. Schwartz, "The Bearing of Sin in the Priestly Literature," in *Pomegranates and Golden Bells: Studies in Biblical, Jewish, and Near Eastern Ritual, Law, and Literature in Honor of Jacob Milgrom*, ed. David P. Wright, David Noel Freedman, and Avi Hurvitz (Winona Lake, Ind.: Eisenbrauns, 1995), 3–21, who emphasizes, "The text indicates clearly that a *double* purgation is described: one that removes *both* impurities and sins. . . . [O]n Purgation Day *both* are expunged by the blood of the goat of purification" (7).

42 See chap. 1, n. 2.
43 Or place of atonement.
44 Averbeck, "kpr [4105/4106]," 709.

animal sacrifices, the author of Hebrews going so far as to say that "without the shedding of blood there is no forgiveness of sins" (Heb 9:22).

The NT writers think of Christ's death as both expiatory and propitiatory. With regard to the expiation of sin, the author of Hebrews hammers home the point that in contrast to the OT sacrifices, which "can never take away sins" (10:11), Christ, "having been offered once to bear the sins of many" (9:28), "remove[d] sin by the sacrifice of himself" (9:26), so that "we have been sanctified through the offering of the body of Jesus Christ once for all" (10:10). John presents Christ as a Passover lamb whose death, in contrast to the original Passover sacrifice,[45] is expiatory: "Behold, the Lamb of God, who takes away the sin of the world!" (John 1:29). Paul uses technical Levitical terminology to refer to Christ as "a sin offering" (*peri hamartias*) (Rom 8:3; cf. Heb 10:6, 8; LXX Isa 53:10; Lev 4:35; 5:6; 6:10), the function of which, as we have seen, was expiatory. Those who have believed in Christ, he says, "have been justified by his blood" (Rom 5:9). Christ's righteous act of obedience "leads to justification and life for all. For . . . by the one man's obedience the many will be made righteous" (5:18-19). Through Christ's blood our guilt has been expunged.

With regard to propitiation, Christ's atoning death delivers us from the judgment of God. John presents Christ in legal terms as our advocate before the divine Judge: "If anyone does sin, we have an advocate with the Father, Jesus Christ the righteous; and he is the atoning sacrifice for our sins" (1 John 2:1-2; cf. 4:10). Christ expiates our sin and thereby carries our case before the divine tribunal, as if to answer the question,

---

45 Is it possible that by the first century the Passover sacrifice had come to be understood, at least in popular thinking, as expiatory? After the initial Passover, the sacrificial rites no longer took place in Jewish homes but in a central sanctuary (Deut 16:5-7). When Hezekiah reinstituted the Passover festival in the Temple in Jerusalem, expiation was necessary, for "there were many in the assembly who had not sanctified themselves; therefore the Levites had to slaughter the passover lamb for everyone who was not clean, to make it holy to the LORD" (2 Chron 30:17). Jub. 49:19-21 says, "In the days when the house has been built in the name of the LORD in the land of their inheritance, they shall go there and slay the Passover in the evening, at sunset, at the third part of the day. And they shall offer its blood on the threshold of the altar, and shall place its fat on the fire which is upon the altar, and they shall eat its flesh roasted with fire in the court of the house which has been sanctified in the name of the Lord." What else could this be but expiatory sacrifice? Josephus seems to take the Passover sacrifices to be expiatory, for he says that the blood of the Passover lambs in Egypt purified the homes of the Israelites (Josephus, *Antiquities of the Jews* 2.312).

"Who will come before You to plead as an advocate for the unrighteous?" (Wis 12:12). The answer is Jesus Christ the righteous.

Paul similarly holds that Christ delivers us from the judgment and wrath of God. The protracted debate over the linguistic meaning of *hilastērion* in Romans 3:25, "whom God put forward as a *hilastērion* in his blood," has unfortunately diverted attention from the conceptual necessity of propitiation in Paul's thinking.[46] We shall return to this debate in chapter 4 when we treat the motif of divine justice. For now we note merely that whatever word Paul might have used here—had he written, for example, *peri hamartias*, as in Romans 8:3, instead of *hilastērion*—the context would still require that Christ's death provide the solution to the problem described in chapters 1–3. Paul's crowning statement concerning Christ's atoning death (Rom 3:21-26) comes against the backdrop of his exposition of God's wrath upon and condemnation of mankind for its sin. Something in Paul's ensuing exposition of Christ's death must solve this problem, averting God's wrath and rescuing us from the death sentence hanging over us. The solution is found in Christ, "whom God put forward as a *hilastērion* in his blood" (3:25).

For Paul Christ's death is conceived to be both expiatory and propitiatory: "Since, therefore, we are now justified by his blood, much more shall we be saved by him from the wrath of God" (5:9). The first clause expresses expiation, the second propitiation.[47] Given the manifold effects of Christ's blood, *hilastērion* is doubtlessly a multivalent metaphor in Paul's usage, connoting both expiation and propitiation, so that a vague translation capturing the metaphor, for example, "place of propitiation," is about the best one can give.[48]

---

46 For an overview of the debate, see Daniel P. Bailey, "Biblical and Greco-Roman Uses of *Hilastērion* in Romans 3:25 and 4 Maccabees 17:22 (Codex S)," in *Biblical Theology of the New Testament*, by Peter Stuhlmacher, trans. and ed. Daniel P. Bailey with the collaboration of Jostein Ådna (Grand Rapids: Eerdmans, 2018), 824–68.

47 Wright's attempt to avoid propitiation in this verse on the grounds that the wrath in question is eschatological (Wright, *Day the Revolution Began*, 273, 330) is unavailing, for if Christ's death serves to shelter us from God's eschatological wrath, it is obviously propitiatory. Wright seems to understand propitiation as God's wrath being vented on Jesus, and, hence, he does find propitiation expressed in Isaiah 53 (where it does not seem to exist) but not in Rom 5:9 (where it does).

48 See discussion in chap. 4. In a recent study Stephen Hultgren concludes, "Biblical 'atonement' is multifaceted, comprehending expiation and forgiveness, as

CONCLUDING REMARKS

The table of the gem that is the biblical doctrine of the atonement is the motif of sacrifice. It predominates among all other biblical motifs used to interpret Jesus' death and features in the way Jesus saw his own death. Christ's death is interpreted by NT authors in terms of OT sacrifices such as the Passover sacrifice; the Levitical personal, animal, sacrifices; and the Yom Kippur sacrifices. These sacrifices served the fundamental purposes of expunging sin/impurity and of appeasing God's wrath. By securing divine forgiveness of sins, they served to reconcile God and sinners. Any biblically adequate theory of the atonement must, then, make good sense of Christ's death as an expiatory and propitiatory sacrifice to God the Father.

---

well as removal of divine wrath. In the LXX the ἱλάσκομαι word group is also complex, retaining propitiatory overtones from classical usage (although it is often better to speak of God removing his own wrath), while taking on the additional meaning of expiation and forgiveness. The Pentateuchal ἱλαστήριον is a 'place' for such 'atonement.' Amidst many proposals, 'the place of atonement' with allusion to the כַּפֹּרֶת remains the most likely meaning for ἱλαστήριον in Rom. 3:25. Christ is the 'place' where divine justice and mercy meet" (Stephen Hultgren, "*Hilastērion* [Rom. 3:25] and the Union of Divine Justice and Mercy. Part II: Atonement in the Old Testament and in Romans 1–5," *Journal of Theological Studies* [forthcoming]; cf. idem, "*Hilastērion* [Rom. 3:25] and the Union of Divine Justice and Mercy. Part I: The Convergence of Temple and Martyrdom Theologies," *Journal of Theological Studies* 70, no. 1 [April 2019]: 69–109). I prefer Bailey's suggested "place of propitiation" as better capturing the range of the metaphor.

Chapter 3

Isaiah's Servant of the Lord

INTRODUCTION

A second significant motif employed throughout the NT to interpret Christ's death is Isaiah's Servant of the Lord. NT authors saw Jesus as the suffering Servant described in Isaiah 52:13–53.12:[1]

52

13 See, my servant shall prosper;
    he shall be exalted and lifted up,
        and shall be very high.
14 Just as there were many who were astonished at him
      —so marred was his appearance, beyond human semblance,
      and his form beyond that of mortals—
15 so he shall startle many nations;
    kings shall shut their mouths because of him;
for that which had not been told them they shall see,
    and that which they had not heard they shall contemplate.

53

Who has believed what we have heard?
And to whom has the arm of the Lord been revealed?

---

1 For convenience's sake I shall adopt the customary convention of referring to this entire passage as Isaiah 53.

2 For he grew up before him like a young plant,
    and like a root out of dry ground;
he had no form or majesty that we should look at him,
    nothing in his appearance that we should desire him.
3 He was despised and rejected by others;
    a man of suffering and acquainted with infirmity;
and as one from whom others hide their faces
    he was despised, and we held him of no account.

4 Surely he has borne our infirmities
    and carried our diseases;
yet we accounted him stricken,
    struck down by God, and afflicted.
5 But he was wounded for our transgressions,
    crushed for our iniquities;
upon him was the punishment that made us whole,
    and by his bruises we are healed.
6 All we like sheep have gone astray;
    we have all turned to our own way,
and the LORD has laid on him
    the iniquity of us all.
7 He was oppressed, and he was afflicted,
    yet he did not open his mouth;
like a lamb that is led to the slaughter,
    and like a sheep that before its shearers is silent,
    so he did not open his mouth.
8 By a perversion of justice he was taken away.
    Who could have imagined his future?
For he was cut off from the land of the living,
    stricken for the transgression of my people.
9 They made his grave with the wicked
    and his tomb with the rich,
although he had done no violence,
    and there was no deceit in his mouth.

10 Yet it was the will of the LORD to crush him with pain.
When you make his life an offering for sin,
    he shall see his offspring, and shall prolong his days;
through him the will of the LORD shall prosper.
11 Out of his anguish he shall see light;
he shall find satisfaction through his knowledge.
    The righteous one, my servant, shall make many righteous,
    and he shall bear their iniquities.

12 Therefore I will allot him a portion with the great,
    and he shall divide the spoil with the strong;
because he poured out himself to death,
    and was numbered with the transgressors;
yet he bore the sin of many,
    and made intercession for the transgressors.

Ten of the twelve verses of the fifty-third chapter of Isaiah are quoted in the NT, which also abounds in allusions to and echoes of this passage. I have already mentioned the Synoptic Gospels' accounts of Jesus' words at the Last Supper, whereby he identified himself as the Servant of Isaiah 53.[2] In Acts 8:30-35, Philip, in response to an Ethiopian official's question concerning Isaiah 53, "About whom does the prophet speak?" shares "the good news about Jesus."[3] First Peter 2:22-25 is a reflection on Christ as the Servant of Isaiah 53, who "bore our sins in his body on the tree." Hebrews 9:28 alludes to Isaiah 53:12 in describing Christ as "having been offered once to bear the sins of many." The influence of Isaiah 53 is also evident in Romans, 1 and 2 Corinthians, Galatians, Philippians, 1 Timothy, and Titus. William Farmer concludes, "This evidence indicates that there is an Isaianic soteriology deeply embedded in the New Testament which finds its normative form and substance in Isaiah 53."[4]

---

2 See chap. 2, pp. 17–18.

3 In Luke's resurrection narrative of the appearance of Jesus to the Emmaus disciples, the risen Christ rebukes them, saying, "'Oh, how foolish you are, and how slow of heart to believe all that the prophets have declared! Was it not necessary that the Messiah should suffer these things and then enter into his glory?' Then beginning with Moses and all the prophets, he interpreted to them the things about himself in all the scriptures" (Luke 24:25-27). In Acts Peter similarly declares, "The God of our ancestors has glorified his servant Jesus, whom you handed over and rejected in the presence of Pilate. . . . In this way God fulfilled what he had foretold through all the prophets, that his Messiah would suffer" (3:13, 18). Apart from Isaiah 53 there is no place in the prophets that could plausibly be interpreted as being about Messiah's suffering the unjust death described by Luke and his subsequent victory.

4 William R. Farmer, "Reflections on Isaiah 53 and Christian Origins," in *Jesus and the Suffering Servant: Isaiah 53 and Christian Origins*, ed. William H. Bellinger Jr. and William R. Farmer (Harrisburg, Penn.: Trinity Press International, 1998), 267; cf. also Rikki E. Watts, "Jesus' Death, Isaiah 53, and Mark 10:45: A Crux Revisited," in Bellinger and Farmer, *Jesus and the Suffering Servant*, 125–51; and Daniel P. Bailey, "Concepts of *Stellvertretung* in the Interpretation of Isaiah 53," in Bellinger and Farmer, *Jesus and the Suffering Servant*, 223–50.

SUBSTITUTIONARY ATONEMENT IN ISAIAH 53

The Servant's Vicarious Punishment

While the identity of the Servant of the LORD in Isaiah 53 has been much discussed, our interest is not in the person of the Servant, who he is, but rather in his work, what he does. What is remarkable, even startling, about the Servant as described in Isaiah 53 is that he suffers vicariously for the sins of others. Moreover, his suffering is not only vicarious; it is punitive. Otfried Hofius calls the Servant's substitutionary punishment the "*dominant and central theme*" of the chapter.[5]

R. N. Whybray demurs, claiming that the Servant merely shares in the punitive suffering of the Jewish exiles.[6] But Whybray's interpretation does not make as good sense of the shock expressed at what Yahweh has done in afflicting His righteous Servant (Isa 52:14–53:1, 10) and is less plausible in light of the strong contrasts, reinforced by the Hebrew pronouns, drawn between the Servant and the persons speaking in the first person plural (Isa 53:4-6). H.-J. Hermisson translates verse 4 as

---

5   Otfried Hofius, "The Fourth Servant Song in the New Testament Letters," in *The Suffering Servant: Isaiah 53 in Jewish and Christian Sources*, ed. Bernd Janowski and Peter Stuhlmacher (1996), trans. Daniel P. Bailey (Grand Rapids: Eerdmans, 2004), 164.

6   R. N. Whybray, *Thanksgiving for a Liberated Prophet: An Interpretation of Isaiah Chapter 53*, Journal for the Study of the Old Testament Supplement Series 4 (Sheffield: JSOT, 1978), 30. For a critique see Steve Jeffery, Michael Ovey, and Andrew Sach, *Pierced for Our Transgressions: Rediscovering the Glory of Penal Substitution* (Wheaton, Ill.: Crossway Books, 2007), 54–61. Whybray's interpretation has not to my knowledge generated any following. Interestingly, however, the notion of joining people in their suffering is, in effect, Janowski's revisionary interpretation of *Stellvertretung* (usually translated "substitution" but literally "place-taking") not as taking the place of someone but as joining him in the place where he is (Bernd Janowski, *Stellvertretung: Alttestamentliche Studien zu einem theologischen Grundbegriff*, Stuttgarter Bibelstudien 165 [Stuttgart: Verlag Katholisches Bibelwerk, 1997], 19, 98; cf. Bernd Janowski, "He Bore Our Sins: Isaiah 53 and the Drama of Taking Another's Place," in *The Suffering Servant*, 53, where he seems to admit that this is not the biblical sense of place-taking). See also the similar view of M. D. Hooker, "Interchange in Christ," *Journal of Theological Studies* 22, no. 2 (1971): 349–61.

Surely our infirmities—*he* bore them
and our diseases—*he* carried them.[7]

and Hofius renders verse 11:

The righteous one, my servant, makes righteous the many,
for their iniquities—*he* bears them.[8]

Moreover, the people's suffering in the exile was entirely just, in contrast to the suffering of God's Servant, which is a perversion of justice (v. 8).[9] The Servant is doing something more than participating in the exiles' suffering, for he endures a suffering far beyond that of the exiles in order to restore them.

Notice that the Servant is said to bear the sins (*nāśā' ḥēṭ'*), or equivalently, carry the iniquities (*sābal 'awōn*) of many. In the OT the expression "to bear sin," when used of sinners, typically means "to be held liable to punishment" or "to endure punishment" (e.g., Lev 5:1; 7:18; 19:8; 24:15; Num 5:31; 9:13; 14:34).[10] The Servant, however, does not bear his own sins

---

7 Hermisson comments, "Regardless of whether one literally reads the emphatic pronoun 'he' (הוא) in the second line (with Hebrew MSS; Syr.; Vulg.) as in the first, there is an emphasis on the *Servant's* bearing of suffering in the first line that carries over into the second" (Hans-Jürgen Hermisson, "The Fourth Servant Song in the Context of Second Isaiah," in *The Suffering Servant*, 30).

8 Hofius, "Fourth Servant Song," 165.

9 David Peterson, "Atonement in the Old Testament," in *Where Wrath and Mercy Meet: Proclaiming the Atonement Today*, ed. David Peterson, Oak Hill School of Theology Series (Carlisle, Cumbria, U.K.: Paternoster, 2001), 21.

10 See Jay Sklar, *Sin, Impurity, Sacrifice, Atonement: The Priestly Conceptions*, Hebrew Bible Monographs 2 (Sheffield: Sheffield Phoenix Press, 2005), 20–23. By contrast, when "God" is the subject, the expression means "to forgive sins" (Exod 34:6-7). Schwartz challenges "this reigning scholarly consensus" by pointing out that *considered alone* the verb never means "suffer" or "forgive," nor does the word for sin mean "punishment" (Baruch J. Schwartz, "The Bearing of Sin in the Priestly Literature," in *Pomegranates and Golden Bells: Studies in Biblical, Jewish, and Near Eastern Ritual, Law, and Literature in Honor of Jacob Milgrom*, ed. David P. Wright, David Noel Freedman, and Avi Hurvitz [Winona Lake, Ind.: Eisenbrauns, 1995], 8–9). This argument fails to reckon with the meaning of the idiomatic expression as a whole. Curiously, Schwartz recognizes the expression as a figure of speech in which wrongdoing is conceived of as an object. But he holds that "the phrase has two *uses*, but only one *meaning*" (9). Schwartz's distinction represents an untenable bifurcation between an expression's meaning and use. He seems to equate the figurative expression's meaning with the words'

but the sins of others (vv. 4, 11-12). Intriguingly, the Levitical priests can be said to bear others' sins by making atonement for them (e.g., Lev 10:17: "that you may bear the iniquity of the congregation, to make atonement for them before the LORD"). But the priests, unlike the Servant, do not do so by vicarious suffering. The punitive nature of the Servant's suffering is clearly expressed in phrases like "wounded for our transgressions," "crushed for our iniquities," "upon him was the punishment that made us whole," "the LORD has laid on him the iniquity of us all," and "stricken for the transgression of my people" (Isa 53:5, 6, 8). This fact also serves to distinguish the Servant's sin-bearing from that of the Levitical scapegoat, which was merely the symbolic vehicle for the removal of sin on Yom Kippur. The scapegoat carried away Israel's sins into the desert, but it was not held to be liable for their sins or to endure the punishment due them for their sins.

We may profitably compare the LORD's punishment of His Servant in Isaiah 53 with the LORD's symbolically laying the punishment of Israel and Judah upon the prophet Ezekiel, such that he could be said to "bear their punishment":

Lie on your left side, and place the punishment of the house of Israel upon it; you shall bear their punishment for the number of the days that you lie there. For I assign to you a number of days, three hundred ninety days, equal to the number of the years of their punishment; and so you shall bear the punishment of the house of Israel. When you have completed these, you shall lie down a second time, but on your right side, and bear

---

literal meaning and its use with its figurative sense. But since use determines meaning, the expression has two meanings, since it has two metaphorical uses:

When the sinner himself "bears" his sin, he *may* suffer its consequences if such there be. In this usage, the phrase is a metaphor for the sinner's unrelieved guilt. It is at most an oblique way of saying that the sinner deserves punishment; it is never indicative of punishment per se. However, when and if another party—most often, but not necessarily, God—"bears" the sinner's burden, it no longer rests on the shoulders of the wrongdoer; the latter is relieved of his load and of its consequences, once again if such there be. In this second usage, the "bearing" of the sin by another is a metaphor for the guilty party's release from guilt. (9)

This explication of the two uses of "to bear sin" is not significantly different from the scholarly consensus. God's relieving a sinner of his guilt and its consequences just *is* forgiveness, and a sinner's being guilty and so deserving punishment just *is* to be held liable to punishment.

the punishment of the house of Judah; forty days I assign you, one day for each year. (Ezek 4:4-6)[11]

Ezekiel bore the people's punishment symbolically, but in Isaiah 53 the Servant's bearing the punishment for Israel's sins is not symbolic but real. Hofius observes, "Here in Isaiah 53 . . .—and only here—there is talk of one person 'bearing' *substitutionarily* the guilt of *other* persons; he thus suffers the penal consequences of *alien* guilt."[12]

The Servant as a Guilt Offering

The idea of substitutionary suffering for sin is, as we have seen in chapter 2, already implicit in the animal sacrifices prescribed in Leviticus. Death is the consequence of sin, and the animal dies in the place of the sinner. By the hand-laying ritual that precedes the sacrifice, the worshipper symbolically indicates his identification with the animal that he will sacrifice. This identification should not be thought of in terms of a magical penetration of the worshipper's soul into the animal[13] but in substitutionary terms. The animal's death is symbolic of the sinner's death. Thus, the animal "shall be accepted for him to make atonement for him" (Lev 1:4). Similarly, in Isaiah 53 the Servant is said "to make himself an offering for sin ['āšām, the so-called guilt offering]" (v. 10).

Some scholars have rejected the translation of 'āšām as "guilt offering" in favor of "the means of wiping out guilt (or the obligation arising from guilt)."[14] The claim is that the term stems originally not from the

---

11 Hermann Spieckermann rightly draws our attention to how surprising it is that sin-bearing should be said to be the subject of a symbolic prophetic act, given Ezekiel's radical emphasis on individual responsibility (18:20). Isaiah 53's idea of real, vicarious suffering overcomes even the radically heightened doctrine of individual retribution in the book of Ezekiel (Hermann Spieckermann, "The Conception and Prehistory of the Idea of Vicarious Suffering in the Old Testament," in *The Suffering Servant*, 15).

12 Hofius, "Fourth Servant Song," 166. For a syntactical analysis and comparison with other passages, see J. Alan Groves, "Atonement in Isaiah 53," in *The Glory of the Atonement: Biblical, Historical, and Practical Perspectives*, ed. Charles E. Hill and Frank A. James III (Downers Grove, Ill.: InterVarsity, 2004), 71–80.

13 As alleged by Jacob Milgrom, *Leviticus 1–16*, The Anchor Bible (New York: Doubleday, 1991), 151.

14 Preeminently, Bernd Janowski; see, e.g., Janowski, "He Bore Our Sins," 48, 66–69. Groves seems to agree that a cultic context is missing in Isaiah 53 but

cultic context but from a legal context (e.g., Gen 26:10; 1 Sam 6:3-4, 8, 17). One cannot suppose that Isaiah 53 borrowed the term after its integration into the priestly sacrificial context because 'āšām in verse 10 has no cultic connotations whatsoever. There is no mention of the shed blood of the Servant, nor does the Servant take on the role of a sacrificial animal ritually slaughtered by a priestly official. The verb "crush" is not a sacrificial term, and cultic vocabulary is lacking. Moreover, the uniqueness of the wiping out of guilt in Isaiah 53 is said to stand in contradiction to the thought of sacrifice, which requires repetition.[15] Rather, "verse 10aβ therefore says that the Servant made his life the means of 'discharging' or 'wiping out guilt.' . . . Through substituting his existence for that of others, the Servant clears the guilty of guilt. He secures them the acquittal that makes possible their continued life (53:11b) and therefore the 'healing' of their broken relationship with God, the restoration of their שלום (53:5b)."[16]

Congenial as this interpretation might be to the Christian atonement theorist, it seems that these objections to a (penultimate) cultic provenance of 'āšām are quite weak.[17] While atonement vocabulary (kpr) is not used in Isaiah 53, the concept is clearly present. The Servant "pours out himself to death" and gives "his life" as a sacrificial offering (cf. Lev 17:11). It is hard to see how the comparison of the Servant to "a lamb that is led to the slaughter" (v. 7) could be plausibly interpreted in any other

---

rightly challenges the assumption that atonement belongs exclusively to a cultic context (see Num 16:46-49; 25:1-13) (Groves, "Atonement in Isaiah 53," 66).

15 Janowski, "He Bore Our Sins," 68; Spieckermann, "Conception and Prehistory," 3.
16 Hofius, "Fourth Servant Song," 167–68.
17 No positive evidence exists for taking the provenance to be purely legal or, for that matter, for taking the 1 Sam passages to be devoid of cultic connotations. The offering by the Philistines could obviously not be offered in the Tabernacle! There seems, in any case, to be a false dichotomy assumed here. Is not the guilt offering precisely a "means of wiping out guilt"? See comments of Averbeck, who charges that Janowski "has driven an uncalled for diachronic and conceptual wedge between the narrative passages and the cultic ones" (Richard E. Averbeck, "Christian Interpretations of Isaiah 53," in *The Gospel According to Isaiah 53: Encountering the Suffering Servant in Jewish and Christian Theology*, ed. Darrell L. Bock and Mitch Glaser [Grand Rapids: Kregel, 2012], 46). The problem with Janowski's claim that the background of 'āšām is not cultic but from contexts in which guilt-incurring encroachments and their reparation are the theme is, according to Averbeck, that the guilt offering in the priestly material was also all about guilt-incurring encroachments and their reparation.

way than in terms of the sacrificial cult. As for the thought that the sacrifices require repetition, the reason that repetition is necessary is obviously because sinning and uncleanness are ongoing, thus requiring new sacrifices. It is not as though the sacrifices needed to be offered for old failings once atoned for! Those have been forgiven or cleansed. Therefore, the benefits of expiation of guilt, continued life, and the restoration of relationship with God are precisely what is thought to be achieved through sacrificial offering.[18]

Human Sacrifice

Groves has observed, "The problem in Isaiah 53 is not the absence of the language of the cult. 'Bearing guilt' is itself the language of atonement, whether the cult is mentioned or not. The problem instead is the humanness of the one making atonement with his sacrifice and death."[19] It is sometimes said that the idea of offering a human substitute is utterly foreign to Judaism and so could not have been contemplated by Isaiah; but that claim is, in fact, not true. The idea of substitutionary punishment is clearly expressed in Moses' offer to the LORD to be killed in place of the people, who had apostatized, to "make atonement" for their sin:

> On the next day Moses said to the people, "You have sinned a great sin. But now I will go up to the LORD; perhaps I can make atonement for your sin." So Moses returned to the LORD and said, "Alas, this people has sinned a great sin; they have made for themselves gods of gold. But now, if you will only forgive their sin—but if not, blot me out of the book that you have written." But the LORD said to Moses, "Whoever has sinned against me I will blot out of my book. But now go, lead the people to the place about which I have spoken to you; see, my angel shall go in front of you. Nevertheless, when the day comes for punishment, I will punish them for their sin." (Exod 32:30-34)

---

18 Averbeck thinks that just as the skin-diseased person who had been expelled from the Israelite camp and needed a guilt offering in order to be restored to the camp and the Tabernacle presence of the LORD, so the Servant in Isaiah 53 offers himself as a guilt offering to make reparation and atonement on behalf of Israel for its sin and corruption so that they could come out of exile and be restored to their holy land and to their holy servant status (Averbeck, "Christian Interpretations of Isaiah 53," 53).

19 Groves, "Atonement in Isaiah 53," 87; cf. 67.

Yahweh's response to Moses shows that Moses is not merely asking Yahweh to put him out of his misery, so to speak, if He will not forgive Israel's sin but rather is offering to bear the punishment due to the Israelites for their apostasy. Although Yahweh rejects Moses' offer of a substitutionary atonement, saying that "when the day comes for punishment, I will punish them for their sin" (v. 34), the offer is nonetheless clear, and Yahweh simply declines the offer but does not dismiss it as absurd or impossible. Similarly, while in the OT Yahweh consistently rejects human sacrifice, in contrast to the practice of pagan nations, the story of God's commanding Abraham to sacrifice his son Isaac (whom the NT treats as a type of Christ) shows that such a thing is not unthinkable (Gen 22:1-19). In Isaiah 53, moreover, the idea of the Servant's substitutionary punishment is treated as extraordinary and surprising. The LORD has inflicted on His righteous Servant the suffering that He refused to inflict on Isaac and Moses.

Summation

By bearing himself the punishment the people deserved, the Servant reconciles them to God. The Servant by his suffering brings wholeness and healing (v. 5), he "shall make many righteous" (v. 11), and he makes "intercession for the transgressors" (v. 12). Spieckermann draws attention to five features of the Servant's vicarious suffering:

(1)   One person suffers for the sins of others.[20]
(2)   The one who intercedes for the sins of the others is himself sinless and righteous (vv. 9, 11).[21]
(3)   The vicarious act of the one occurs once for all with ramifications for the future (vv. 10-11).

---

20 Better, one person is punished for the sins of others. As we have seen, even an animal offered in sacrifice suffers for the sins of others, but it is not punished for the sins of others. But in Isaiah 53 we have the extraordinary affirmation of penal substitution with respect to the LORD's Servant.

21 These verses more plausibly imply the Servant's innocence rather than his sinlessness. More significant is the expression "exalted and lifted up" (52:13) used to describe the Servant. This expression is used three other times in Isa (6:1; 33:10; 57:15) and nowhere else in the OT. In every other case the expression refers to Yahweh. See Groves, "Atonement in Isaiah 53," 81.

(4) One intercedes for the sins of others of his own will (vv. 4-5).[22]

(5) God intentionally brings about the vicarious suffering of the one for the sins of the others, which displays the unity of will of the LORD and His Servant (vv. 6-10).[23]

On the basis of these five features of Isaiah 53, Spieckermann concludes that "the main idea behind [the Servant's] vicarious suffering is the close community of will between God and the Servant with the intention of wiping out guilt for the many."[24]

DEPLOYMENT OF ISAIAH'S SERVANT OF THE LORD IN THE NT

Returning to the NT, we find Christian authors interpreting Jesus to be the sin-bearing Servant of Isaiah 53. Citing LXX Isaiah 53:9b, 1 Peter 2:21-24 states:

Christ also suffered for you, leaving you an example, so that you should follow in his steps.

"He committed no sin,
    and no deceit was found in his mouth."

When he was abused, he did not return abuse; when he suffered, he did not threaten; but he entrusted himself to the one who judges justly. He himself bore our sins in his body on the cross, so that, free from sins, we might live for righteousness; by his wounds you have been healed.

These verses constitute a brief meditation on Isaiah 53 in application to Christ. Isaiah 53:7 is reflected in the sentence, "When he was abused, he

---

22 Again, at least as significant in this regard is the fact twice repeated in v. 7 that "he did not open his mouth" to protest his maltreatment; also v. 12 "he poured out himself to death."

23 Hofius comments, "It is important to notice that *Yahweh* is ultimately the one at work behind the Servant's fate. *He 'caused* to fall (hiphil) on him the iniquity of us all' (53:6b); it was *his* plan—that is, *his* will—'to crush him' (53:10a). Yahweh himself thus redirects the due punishment from the guilty by discharging it upon the innocent Servant. At the same time it is true that the Servant submitted himself to Yahweh's plan in free obedience and therefore in deliberate self-surrender 'gave up his life to death' (53:12b)" ("Fourth Servant Song," 167).

24 Spieckermann, "Conception and Prehistory," 8.

did not return abuse; when he suffered, he did not threaten." Isaiah 53:8a is echoed in Christ's trusting in a just God despite the injustice of what he suffered. Echoing Isaiah's words concerning the Servant's bearing sin in 53:4a, 11d, 12b, the author affirms Christ's substitutionary punishment on our behalf, with the result that we are now liberated from sin and able to live righteously (cf. 53:11c). We have been healed by his suffering (cf. 53:5).

Sin-bearing derived from Isaiah 53 is also evident in Hebrews 9:26b-28:

> But as it is, he has appeared once for all at the end of the age to remove sin by the sacrifice of himself. And just as it is appointed for mortals to die once, and after that the judgment, so Christ, having been offered once to bear the sins of many, will appear a second time, not to deal with sin, but to save those who are eagerly waiting for him.

Here Christ is described as a voluntary, expiatory sacrifice, offered, in the language of Isaiah 53, to bear the sins of many (53:12c). Again, Christ's substitutionary punishment for humanity's sins is in view.

Other NT texts echo Isaiah 53 more subtly. In light of Isaiah 53, texts like "Christ died for our sins in accordance with the Scriptures" (1 Cor 15:3), ambiguous when taken in isolation, become pregnant with meaning.[25] For there is no other passage in the Jewish Scriptures that could be construed as even remotely about Messiah's dying for people's sins. The formulaic expression "died for our sins," so prominent in the Pauline corpus, thus refers to substitutionary, punitive suffering. This meaning of "for" (*hyper*) is made clear by expressions like "delivered up for our trespasses" (Rom 4:25), where "for" translates *dia* + the accusative, meaning "on account of," and along with "delivered up" and "trespasses" recalls LXX Isaiah 53:12; similarly, Mark 10:45, where "for" translates *anti*, "instead of," "in exchange of."

Paul's summary statement in 2 Corinthians 5:21, "For our sake he made him to be sin who knew no sin, so that in him we might become the righteousness of God," is seen to echo in all its parts Isaiah 53. "Who knew no sin" recalls "the righteous one, my servant," in whose mouth was no deceit (vv. 9, 11); "for our sake he made him to be sin" recalls "the Lord has laid on him the iniquity of us all" (v. 6); "in him we might become the righteousness of God" recalls "the righteous one, my servant,

---

25 See comments by Simon Gathercole, *Defending Substitution: An Essay on Atonement in Paul* (Grand Rapids: Baker Academic, 2015), 67.

[shall] make many to be accounted righteous" (v. 11). Again, no other OT passage remotely approaches the content of this sentence. However we more closely interpret Paul's sentence, the affirmation that Christ is the sin-bearing Servant of Isaiah 53 is clear.

CONCLUDING REMARKS

The NT authors, then, following Jesus in his own self-understanding, saw Christ as the righteous Servant of Isaiah 53, who suffered in the place of sinners, bearing the punishment they deserved, that they might be reconciled to God. As we saw in chapter 2, Jesus understood his death, like that of the Servant (Isa 42:6; 49:6), to be on behalf of Gentiles as well as Jews. Christ's death was thus understood to be nothing less than a vicarious punishment for humanity's sins.

Chapter 4

DIVINE JUSTICE

INTRODUCTION

A third important atonement motif, prominent in the letters of Paul, is divine justice. We are interested not in Paul's doctrine of justification by faith, since that concerns not the atonement itself but rather the appropriation of its benefits. We want to inquire rather about the role of divine justice in the act of atonement. Paul's exposition of the way in which Christ's death achieves reconciliation with God is suffused with forensic terminology rooted in Jewish notions of law and justice.

OT JUSTICE MOTIFS

In the OT God is addressed with the legal title "Judge" (Gen 18:25) and acts rightly in that capacity. Words deriving from the root *sedek* (righteousness) occur 523 times in OT. The nominal forms fall mainly into three groups: legal righteousness (123 times), ethical righteousness (114 times), and correctness (26 times). As we shall see, when it is God's righteousness that is at stake, almost all cases are related some way to legal righteousness within a judicial context. Moreover, God is not only the Judge, He is also the lawgiver. The heart of OT Judaism was the divine Torah (law) that governed all of life and man's relationship to God. Leon Morris reckons that of the 220 uses of *tôrah* in the OT only 17 are clearly not about God's law. Of the 127 occurrences of *hōq* (statute), 87 are linked with the LORD; *huqqah*, another word for statute, is similarly linked in 96 out of 104 cases. *Mishpāt*, which is linked with the LORD about 180 times, is the usual term for "judgment" and in its participial form is used to refer to God as Judge. It may also mean "law." Even the notion of a covenant (*berith*) is the notion of a legal contract. It is intriguing how OT writers often prefer legal to any other imagery when they are referring to what God does (e.g., Mic 6:1-2; Isa 3:13; 41:21). The use of legal categories with respect to God in the OT, says Morris, "is frequent, so frequent indeed that it is plain that it corresponds to something deep-seated in Hebrew thinking. Law and the LORD went together."[1] In fact, it would be difficult to find a religion more wedded to legal categories than OT Judaism.

NT JUSTICE MOTIFS

So the NT is filled with judicial language reflective of its Jewish background. By Morris' count the NT has ninety-two examples of the noun *dikaiosynē* (justice or righteousness), thirty-nine of the verb *dikaioō* (to justify or reckon righteous), ten of the noun *dikaiōma* (ordinance or sentence of justification), eighty-one of the adjective *dikaios* (just or righteous), and five of the adverb *dikaiōs* (justly or righteously).

In a key atonement passage Paul blends cultic and judicial terminology in characterizing Christ's death:

> [21] But now, apart from law, the righteousness of God has been disclosed, and is attested by the law and the prophets, [22] the righteousness of God through faith in Jesus Christ for all who believe. For there is no distinction, [23] since all have sinned and fall short of the glory of God; [24] they are now justified by his grace as a gift, through the redemption that is in Christ Jesus, [25] whom God put forward as a sacrifice of atonement by his blood, effective through faith. He did this to show his righteousness, because in his divine forbearance he had passed over the sins previously committed; [26] it was to prove at the present time that he himself is righteous and that he justifies the one who has faith in Jesus. (Rom 3:21-26)

The NRSV translation alternates between righteousness terminology and justice terminology. One could have used righteousness terminology throughout by adopting Paul's expression "reckon righteous" from

---

1   Leon Morris, *The Atonement: Its Meaning and Significance* (Downers Grove, Ill.: InterVarsity, 1983), 181.

Romans 4:3, 23-24 instead of "justify," so as to read in verse 24: "They are now reckoned righteous by his grace." On the other hand, using justice terminology throughout would make clear Paul's wordplay in verse 26: God is both "just and the justifier."

There are ten interpretive turning points in this passage:[2]

1. The significance of the preceding passage (Rom 1:18–3:20). As we have already seen in chapter 2, the human predicament described in the opening chapters of Romans is the universality of human sin and mankind's consequent condemnation before a just God. Jew and Gentile alike are said to stand under the wrath of God. "For the wrath of God is revealed from heaven against all ungodliness and wickedness of those who by their wickedness suppress the truth" (1:18). Gentiles as well as Jews know the requirements of the law (2:15), "so that every mouth may be silenced, and the whole world may be held accountable to God. For 'no human being will be justified in his sight' [Ps 143:2] by deeds prescribed by the law, for through the law comes the knowledge of sin" (3:19-20). Not one of us, as lawbreakers, will be acquitted before the bar of God's justice; the verdict of "guilty" is pronounced over every human being. Any adequate interpretation of the succeeding passage must find therein Paul's solution to the problem of man's condemnation before a just Judge and the attendant dissolution of divine wrath.

2. "But now" (*nuni de*) (Rom 3:21). The contrast is temporal, not logical, as the remainder of the passage makes clear. God has broken into human history in the person of Jesus Christ, so as to inaugurate a new era, in which justification is now available through faith in Jesus.

3. "Apart from law" (*chōris nomou*) (Rom 3:21). The NRSV, reflecting the majority view, takes this phrase to modify "has been disclosed," but it could instead be taken to modify "the righteousness of God." But that might imply that there was once a righteousness of God through law that was obtainable, which is precisely what Paul wants to rule out. Elsewhere Paul does speak of a righteousness through the law, but this is not a "righteousness from God" but a "righteousness of my own" (Phil 3:6-9). Taking the manifestation of righteousness to be apart from the law is in keeping with the turn of the era signaled by "but now."

4. "The righteousness of God" (*dikaiōsynē theou*) (Rom 3:21). This represents the most significant turning point in the interpretation of

---

2 As identified by D. A. Carson, "Atonement in Romans 3:21–26," in *The Glory of the Atonement: Biblical, Historical, and Practical Perspectives*, ed. Charles E. Hill and Frank A. James III (Downers Grove, Ill.: InterVarsity, 2004), 119–39.

the passage. Classically, there has been a debate whether the expression *dikaiōsynē theou* (righteousness or justice of God) refers to an attribute of God Himself or to the righteousness that He reckons to believers. Lutheran theologians were especially insistent on the latter understanding. This is a righteousness that is from God and given to us, not a property inhering in God Himself.

It is clear, I think, that the expression *dikaiōsynē theou* is multivalent. "The righteousness of God through faith" (v. 22) clearly refers to reckoned righteousness, since God's attribute is not "through faith" nor is it "for all who believe." God's inherent righteousness, like His power or wisdom, is an essential property of God that He has objectively and independently of whether any human beings at all exist, much less have faith in Him. So the righteousness referred to in verse 22 is a righteousness from God that believers possess. But then just as clearly, "he himself is righteous" (v. 26) designates a property God Himself has. Here we do have reference to a property possessed not by believers but by God, akin to His wisdom or power. At least three times in the Pauline corpus, Paul uses *dikaiōsynē theou* to refer to God's inherent righteousness (Rom 3:5, 25-26); the remaining seven uses may be taken to refer to the righteousness that humans have as a result of justification (Rom 1:17; 3:21, 22; 10:3 [2x]; 2 Cor 5:21; Phil 3:9). In addition there are in Paul's letters a couple of dozen occurrences of *dikaiōsynē* without the genitive modifier *theou* where the righteousness belongs to human persons now justified.

Recently, a new debate about the expression *dikaiōsynē theou* has arisen as a result of the so-called new perspective on Paul, some proponents of which construe God's righteousness to be His covenant faithfulness. This construal is not itself new but goes back to German theologians like Hermann Cremer in the late nineteenth century.[3] Cremer believed that the righteousness of God is not a normative concept but rather a relational concept involving persons. He claims, moreover, that God's righteousness has only to do with God's saving activity. He does not deny that God's salvation of the righteous entails His punishment of the wicked, but he insists that God's righteousness finds expression only in His saving action. Proponents of the new perspective

---

3   See brief background in Mark A. Seifrid, "Righteousness Language in the Hebrew Scriptures and Early Judaism," in *Justification and Variegated Nomism: A Fresh Appraisal of Paul and Second Temple Judaism*, 2 vols., ed. D. A. Carson, Peter T. O'Brien, and Mark A. Seifrid, vol. 1, *The Complexities of Second Temple Judaism*, WUNT 2/140 (Tübingen: Mohr Siebeck, 2001), 417–19.

have followed Cremer in thinking God's righteousness to be a relational, not a normative, concept and have identified it with God's being faithful to His covenant people.

The claim here seems to be implausible on its face, for it amounts to nothing less than the claim that teams of English translators, not to mention non-English translators, have for generations actually mistranslated the expression *dikaiōsynē theou*, since the English word "righteousness" just does not mean "faithfulness."[4] Proponents of the new perspective would have us believe that the meaning of NT Greek *dik-* words, under the influence of the LXX, has been fundamentally changed so as to introduce covenantal ideas not present in extrabiblical Greek. The Hebrew word *sedek* (also, in effect, mistranslated as "righteousness") is also said not to express a normative concept like "goodness" but rather a relational concept like "faithful to."

If one reduces God's righteousness to His covenant faithfulness, this will radically impact one's understanding of Paul's atonement doctrine. For then justification is not about God's reckoning us to be guiltless by the standard of divine justice but about God's reckoning to us covenant faithfulness, which makes dubious sense and in any case would not avail for salvation. When Paul declares his desire for a righteousness "that comes through faith in Christ, the righteousness from God based on faith," he is not longing for faithfulness to the covenant, for he was already "blameless" in that respect and it availed him nothing (Phil 3:6-9).[5]

---

4 See Carson's incredulity that that anyone should think that the *dik-* words have nothing to do with justice or righteousness (D. A. Carson, "The Vindication of Imputation: On the Fields of Discourse and Semantic Fields," in *Justification: What's at Stake in the Current Debates*, ed. Mark Husbands and Daniel J. Treier [Downers Grove, Ill.: InterVarsity, 2004], 51). Henri Blocher draws attention to the combination of such words in 2 Thess 1:5-9: "Apart from 2 Timothy 4:8 (recompense awarded by the Righteous Judge), 2 Thessalonians 1:5-9 is most remarkable: the unfolding of God's 'righteous judgment' (v. 5, *dikaias kriseōs*) implies that it is 'just' (v. 6, *dikaion*) for God to requite (*antapodounai*) persecutors, thereby achieving 'vengeance' or satisfaction of justice (v. 8, *ekdikēsin*) in flaming fire, the punishment (v. 9, *dikēn*) of everlasting ruin" (Henri Blocher, "Justification of the Ungodly (*Sola Fide*): Theological Reflections," in *Justification and Variegated Nomism*, vol. 2, *The Paradoxes of Paul*, WUNT 2/181 [Tübingen: Mohr Siebeck, 2004], 475).

5 Notice that Paul here desires a righteousness *from* God (*dikaiōsunē ek theou*), a monadic property bestowed by God. Given the parallel of Phil 3:9 and Rom 10:3,

The implausibility of the new perspective's reductionism is per-haps best seen by asking what the opposite of righteousness—that is, unrighteousness—is said by Paul to be. It is not unfaithfulness, but wick-edness and ungodliness (Rom 1:18) or lawlessness (2 Cor 6:14).[6] Faithless-ness is but one of the litany of sins listed by Paul that result in God's just condemnation (Rom 1:29-31; 2:2). Righteousness is a broad moral prop-erty that entails faithfulness, since to break one's word is wrong, but is not reducible to it. As Mark Seifrid puts it, "All 'covenant-keeping' is righ-teous behavior, but not all righteous behavior is 'covenant-keeping.' It is misleading, therefore, to speak of 'God's righteousness' as his 'covenant-faithfulness.'"[7] Seifrid points out that righteousness language in the OT has primarily to do with God's role as Judge and Ruler of creation. As such it is normative, having to do with God's establishing right moral order in the world.[8] It takes on a positive or salvific sense because the

---

it is doubtful that Paul means by *dikaiōsunē theou* something different than this. Since Rom 10:3 reflects Rom 3:21, the earlier passage should also be understood in terms of a monadic property given human persons by God.

6   Since righteousness is the opposite of wickedness and ungodliness, it should become obvious, if it is not already, that "righteousness" is the nominalization of a property *righteous*, just as "wisdom" is the nominalization of *wise* and "power" of *powerful*. Righteousness is not, therefore, as is often asserted, an activity of God. Those who say that God's righteousness is His "eschatological justifying or vindicating activity" (Carson, "Atonement in Romans 3:21-26," 124) or "the justifying activity of God," including "his eschatological intervention to vindi-cate and deliver his people" (Douglas J. Moo, *The Epistle to the Romans*, New International Commentary on the New Testament [Grand Rapids: Eerdmans, 1996], 222) are speaking ungrammatically. Moo compounds the confusion when he says that "from the human side it includes the status of acquittal acquired by the persons so declared just" (222). Such status may be an *effect* of God's saving activity, but what sense does it make to speak of such a status as included in God's saving activity? See as well, from the new perspective, the inconsis-tent characterization by Onesti and Brauch of the righteousness of God as both God's "relation-restoring love" (a divine property) and "God's saving deed" (a divine act) (*Dictionary of Paul and His Letters*, ed. Gerald F. Hawthorne et al., s.v. "Righteousness, Righteousness of God" by K. L. Onesti and M. T. Brauch [Downers Grove, Ill.: InterVarsity, 1993], 836).

7   Seifrid, "Righteousness Language," 424.

8   Seifrid explains:

> Righteousness language in the Hebrew Scriptures (as in the Ancient Near East generally) has its basis in creational theology rather than in the framework of covenantal ideas. This assessment is especially relevant

biblical writers expect God to intervene to reinstate right order when it is usurped by evil in the world. It takes on a negative or punitive sense because the biblical writers expect reinstatement of right order to involve the punishment of the wicked. As Seifrid so aptly puts it, "Retribution remains on the 'backside' of divine acts of righteousness."[9] So while there are sixty-four instances of God's saving righteousness in the OT, Seifrid counts as well fifteen cases in which God's righteousness is conceived in retributive or punitive terms (Exod 9:27; Pss 7:10; 7:12; 11:5-7; 50:6; Isa 1:27; 5:15-16; 10:22; 28:17; Lam 1:18; 2 Chron 12:1-6; Neh 9:33; Dan 9:7; 9:14; 9:16). God's righteousness comprises both aspects.

Moreover, although the intention of proponents of the new perspective is to explain God's "justification" of the Gentiles as His declaring them to be "righteous" (= faithful to the covenant), in fact the new perspective, by reducing God's righteousness to His covenant faithfulness, does not make sense of God's relations to Gentiles, since they stand outside the covenant made with Israel. If unrighteousness is unfaithfulness to the covenant, then Gentiles cannot be said to be unrighteous, which Paul has expressly said (Rom 1:18). Nor could a Gentile like Job be said to be righteous, as Yahweh Himself affirms, since he was not faithful to the covenant. In point of fact, no connection between justification and covenant faithfulness seems to exist. Seifrid observes that of the 283 occurrences of "covenant" and the more than 500 occurrences of "righteousness" in the OT, in only 7 instances do the two terms come into any significant semantic contact.[10] One generally does not

---

with respect to those passages that have to do with the administration of justice, and the divine administration of justice in particular. It is these which serve as the background for Paul's announcement of the revelation of God's righteousness and his further statements on the justifying work of God in Christ. In such settings, God appears as the ruling king who effects justice (or "righteousness") in (and for) the world that he has made. This conclusion, which finds broad acceptance in the relevant literature, calls for a fundamental revision of current readings of Paul that have been based upon the largely unexamined assumption that "righteousness" (in the context of God's relationship with Israel) is to be interpreted as "covenant faithfulness" (Mark A. Seifrid, "Paul's Use of Righteousness Language against Its Hellenistic Background," in *The Paradoxes of Paul*, 40).

9 Seifrid, "Paul's Use of Righteousness Language," 44. Or more accurately, of God's saving acts of righteousness.

10 Seifrid, "Righteousness Language," 423.

act righteously or unrighteously with respect to a covenant. Rather, one "keeps," "remembers," or "establishes" a covenant, or, conversely, one "breaks," "transgresses," or "despises" it. In thinking of righteousness as covenant faithfulness, proponents of the new perspective seem to be guilty of a category mistake.

In any case, the reductionistic interpretation of *dikaiōsynē theou* as covenant faithfulness has been shown to be lexicographically untenable. Charles Irons' *The Righteousness of God* (2015) is the definitive work on this expression and a convincing refutation of the reductionistic interpretation of the new perspective.[11] Irons conducts a thorough examination of righteousness language in the Hebrew OT, the Septuagint, and extrabiblical Jewish writings and concludes:

> In all three corpora—extra-biblical Greek, the Old Testament, and Jewish literature—the term "righteousness" . . . can be used in two primary ways: ethically and judicially. . . . When used judicially in the OT and in Jewish writings, "righteousness" primarily denotes distributive justice. When used ethically . . . , "righteousness" primarily denotes that behavior or conduct which is in accordance with God's law and which is approved by God in his sight. The judicial element comes into play insofar as God, as the divine Judge, recognizes the righteousness of humans and deems it to be pleasing in his sight. This shows that ultimately the two broad categories of usage are integrated theologically.[12]

With respect to the use of *sedek* in the OT, Irons finds that the word does not have a relational meaning like "faithfulness." "Almost all instances of 'the righteousness of God' can be interpreted as in some way related to legal righteousness within a judicial context in which God is figuratively seated on his throne as the great judge who executes justice by punishing the wicked and vindicating his people."[13] In the OT "righteousness is a

---

11 Charles Lee Irons, *The Righteousness of God: A Lexical Examination of the Covenant-Faithfulness Interpretation*, WUNT 2/386 (Tübingen: Mohr Siebeck, 2015). See also the earlier critique of Moo, *Epistle to the Romans*, 79–90.

12 Irons, *Righteousness of God*, 272.

13 Irons, *Righteousness of God*, 112. Notice that both vindication and punishment are expressions of divine righteousness. Proponents of the new perspective have focused solely on the positive role of God's righteousness in vindicating and saving His people, when in fact the flip side of that vindication is the punishment of the wicked who are oppressing God's people and opposing God. Irons counts forty-one examples in the OT and thirty-five in the Dead Sea Scrolls where God's righteousness is used in the sense of God's judicial activity that results

Normbegriff [normative concept], and the norm is God's own moral law, which is grounded in his unchanging nature as a God of perfect holiness, justice, and truth."[14] Righteousness in the context of a covenant does entail being faithful to keep one's promises, but that does not imply that the meaning of "righteousness" is "faithfulness." Faithfulness is but one manifestation of righteousness.

With respect to extrabiblical Greek no essential differences emerge from OT usage: "The Hebraic/relational theory of righteousness operates with a false contrast between Greek and Hebrew thought. Even extrabiblical Greek recognizes that keeping one's promises is a subset of 'righteousness.' Conversely, Hebraic usage is just as judicially stamped by the concept of *iustitia distributiva* as extrabiblical Greek, if not more so."[15]

With respect to the Septuagint, Irons recognizes the importation of Hebrew meanings into NT Greek via the Septuagint but finds no good evidence that *dikaiosynē* is a Greek word with a Hebrew meaning (that is, a calque). Moreover, the imported nuances of the term are judicial, not relational. He finds that *dikaioō* in the NT "may mean (1) to vindicate someone, or (2) to declare someone to be righteous and to treat them [*sic*] as righteous. . . . For Paul it is a soteriological term that denotes God's act of forgiving sins and accounting sinners as righteous in his sight."[16] He

---

in the punishment of Israel's enemies, thereby delivering and vindicating His people (296).

14 Irons, *Righteousness of God*, 340. Seifrid explains, "Biblical usage of righteousness language is distinct from Greek thought *not* in the lack of the idea of a norm, but in that it does not *define* the norm it presupposes in terms of the *idea* of the good. . . . The Hebrew Scriptures operate with the simple but profound assumption that 'righteousness' in its various expressions is ultimately bound up with God and his working" (Seifrid, "Paul's Use of Righteousness Language," 43–44). Moo comments that even more basic than the idea of covenant is God's always acting in accordance with the norm of his own purpose and promises. "God's *dikaiosynē* in the OT can denote God's character as that of a God who will always do what is right, God's activity of establishing right, and even, as a product of this activity, the state of those who have been, or hope to be, put right" (Moo, *Epistle to the Romans*, 84).

15 Irons, *Righteousness of God*, 84.

16 Irons, *Righteousness of God*, 76. Seifrid draws attention to the difference between Paul and Josephus' use of *dikaioō*. Under the influence of biblical usage, the verb for Paul has the positive, forensic connotation "to vindicate," whereas for Josephus the word means "to punish" (Seifrid, "Paul's Use of Righteousness Language," 52). Moo comments that the thoroughly forensic flavor of the word is

comments, "Now it is generally agreed that this new usage came about because of the influence of the Septuagint mediating a Hebraic context and connotation to the word *dikaioō*. . . . Since the Hebrew verb is used in a positive, judicial sense, that meaning has been introduced into the Greek word among Greek-speaking Jews."[17] Still, "Paul's 'righteousness' language is largely understandable in terms of standard Greek usage, albeit with some biblical theological content drawn from the LXX (especially Gen 15:6 and Hab 2:4), but without any need for recourse to knowledge of Hebrew usage."[18]

A final observation, says Irons, puts the matter to rest. When Paul does speak of God's covenant faithfulness, he does not use *dik*-words but instead words such as *pistis* (faith), *aletheia* (truth), *bebaioō* (to

---

clear from Paul's addition of the phrase "before God" (Rom 2:13; 3:20) and from the contrast with *katakrinō* (condemn) in Rom 8:33. He reports that it is now generally agreed that *dikaioō* in Paul means to "declare righteous" or "acquit" on the analogy of the verdict pronounced by a judge. The term signifies to acquit a guilty one and declare him or her righteous (Moo, *Epistle to the Romans*, 86; cf. 227, 266, 297, 345). Moo's characterization of the term, while on track, is not sufficiently nuanced. Justifying sinners is, as we shall see in the sequel, more akin to pardoning than it is to acquitting, since the verdict of condemnation is not, as it were, overturned on appeal. Andrew Lincoln is more accurate when he comments:

> The imagery of the lawcourt predominates through the language of justification. God's righteousness is the power by which those unable to be justified on the criterion of works are set right with him and being set in a right relationship with God involves his judicial verdict of pardon. It is not that people are deemed innocent of the charges in the indictment against them. Their unrighteousness has been clearly depicted in Paul's argument. But he believes the righteous judge has acted ahead of time in history and in his grace has pronounced a pardon on those who have faith in Christ, so that their guilt can no longer be cited against them. (Andrew T. Lincoln, "From Wrath to Justification: Tradition, Gospel, and Audience in the Theology of Romans 1:18–4:25," in *Pauline Theology*, vol. 3, *Romans*, ed. David M. Hay and E. Elizabeth Johnson [Minneapolis: Fortress, 1995], 148)

—though he, like Moo, misconstrues pardon as a judicial prerogative, when it is, in fact, an executive, not a judicial, function. Moo alludes to pardon in *Epistle to the Romans* (87) but fails to distinguish it from acquittal.

17 Irons, *Righteousness of God*, 77.
18 Irons, *Righteousness of God*, 339.

establish).[19] For example, in Romans 11, where Paul addresses the question of God's covenant faithfulness, he does not use *dikaiōsynē theou*. This fact confirms that the translation "the covenant faithfulness of God" is incorrect.

Fortunately, proponents of the new perspective have backed away from the overly simplistic, reductive conception of God's righteousness.[20] For example, J. D. G. Dunn, in response to his critics, acknowledges that the Hebrew concept of righteousness cannot be reduced to covenant faithfulness or salvation. Righteousness language in the Hebrew Scriptures also involves punitive divine justice, according to which righteousness is "understood as measured by a norm, right order, or that which is morally right," with the qualification that "the norm is not seen as some abstract ideal . . . , but rather as a norm concretised in relation" between God and creatures.[21] So when we come to Romans, "that God's

---

19 Irons, *Righteousness of God*, 296.
20 N. T. Wright, while doubling down on his claim that the righteousness of God is His faithfulness to the covenant, acknowledges, "First, there is the underlying issue of idolatry, injustice, and plain old 'sin.' That is clear. It hasn't gone away. It hasn't, as some suppose, been displaced by all this talk of the covenant. . . . But, second, there is the problem of God's faithfulness to the covenant" (N. T. Wright, *The Day the Revolution Began: Reconsidering the Meaning of Jesus' Crucifixion* [San Francisco: HarperOne, 2017], 313). He qualifies his position by affirming that "God's 'righteousness' is not *simply* God's status of being morally upright. . . . Paul is not, then, talking about God's moral uprightness in general. He is referring more particularly to his faithfulness to his covenant purposes, enacted through the faithful Messiah, Jesus, through which he brings his putting-right purposes (his 'justice') to the world" (303, 305 [emphasis added]). He affirms that "people of all sorts—Jew and Gentile alike—were now free, free from past sins, free to come into the single covenant family. They were 'freely declared to be in the right' . . ." (348). Wright fails to appreciate that the necessity of God's being faithful to His covenant due to His inherent righteousness does not imply anything about the meaning of the expression "the righteousness of God." He insists that "nothing vital in traditional Western understandings has been lost through this approach. What has been lost is the paganized vision of an angry God looming over the world and bent upon blood" (349). We thereby glimpse not merely Wright's affirmation of the traditional understanding of justification but also his unfortunate misunderstanding of traditional atonement theories such as Anselm's and the Reformers'.
21 James D. G. Dunn, "The New Perspective: Whence, What and Whither?" in *The New Perspective on Paul*, rev. ed. (Grand Rapids: Eerdmans, 2008), 63–64; cf. Wright, *Day the Revolution Began*, chap. 13.

righteousness towards the peoples he has created includes wrath and judgment as well as faithfulness and salvation is clearly implicit in the sequences Rom. 1.16–18 and 3.3–6."[22] Those who deny that *dikaiōsynē* is a forensic term pay insufficient attention to Rom 4:4-5, "where the forensic background is clear in the allusion to the legal impropriety of a judge 'justifying the ungodly' . . . , and where again the thought is entirely of attributing a righteous status to one who is unrighteous."[23]

5. **"Through faith in Jesus Christ"** (*dia pisteos Iēsou Christou*) (Rom 3:22). Although this phrase might be taken to be a subjective genitive meaning "through the faithfulness of Jesus Christ," it is usually understood as an objective genitive with Christ as the object of faith, as per the NRSV. Paul almost always uses *pistis* to mean "faith," and no contextual support exists here for construing it otherwise. The expression "for all who believe" serves to emphasize the universality of the gift of righteousness obtainable through faith. Paul thus prepares the way for his doctrine of justification by faith (Rom 3:27).

6. **"Through the redemption"** (*dia tēs apolytrōseōs*) (Rom 3:24). It is odd that Carson leapfrogs the key phrase *dikaioumenoi dōrean tē chariti* ("justified by his grace as a gift") (Rom 3:24); but he rightly comments that people's being justified or set right with God "involves his judicial verdict of pardon. . . . the righteous judge . . . in his grace has pronounced a pardon on those who have faith in Christ, so that their guilt can no longer be cited against them."[24] We have already seen that *dikaioō* in Paul's usage is a soteriological term that denotes God's act of forgiving sins and accounting sinners as righteous in his sight.

---

22 Dunn, "New Perspective," 64–65.

23 Dunn, "New Perspective," 64. Dunn's point is that Paul's referring to God as "him who justifies the ungodly" (Rom 4:5) recalls the OT description of the unjust judge who justifies the wicked (Prov 17:15), an abomination in the LORD's sight. Blocher remarks on "the staggering audacity of Paul's combination of words: God who *justifies* the *ungodly* (Rom 4:5)! Have new perspective (and other scholars) measured the shocking magnitude of this paradox? God is doing what he expressly forbids (Deut 25:1; Isa 5:23; Prov 17:15), God is doing what he said he would *not* do (Exod 23:7)! And the implication, in context, is that the term, *asebēs*, applies to our Father Abraham. Can one iron out this way of speaking, and thinking, as if it were a mere revision of Judaism's belief and piety?" (Blocher, "Justification of the Ungodly," 490).

24 Carson, "Atonement in Romans 3:21–26," 128. N.B. the caveat in note 16 that pardon is not a judicial but rather an executive prerogative.

Although "redemption" can mean simply "liberation," it is frequently connected with the buying back of slaves or prisoners of war from captivity and so involves a ransom price.[25] We have already encountered in chapter 2 the notion of ransoming in the Levitical animal sacrifices, which are said to ransom the lives of those who offer them by means of the shed blood (Lev 17:11). Significantly, Paul proceeds to make the sacrificial context explicit by mentioning the *hilastērion* "through his blood" (*en tō autou haimati*) in verse 25. This suggests that in speaking of the redemption that is Christ Jesus, Paul is thinking of the ransoming power of Christ's blood given as a sacrificial offering to God.[26] Elsewhere Paul says, "you were bought with a price" (1 Cor 6:20; 7:23), and here we see that that price is the blood of Christ, which like the OT sacrifices cleanses us of sin and frees us from its bondage.

7. **"Propitiation"** (*hilastērion*) (Rom 3:25). The NRSV translates this word as "sacrifice of atonement" or alternatively, "place of atonement." C. H. Dodd famously argues that while the *hilas-* words of the LXX convey the idea of expiation of sin, they do not convey the idea of propitiation of God's wrath, and so *hilastērion* does not have here the meaning that the *hilaskesthai* word group does in extrabiblical literature.[27]

---

25 On the Hebrew words translated by Greek redemption words like *lytrōsis*, see Morris, *Atonement*, chap. 5: "Redemption." Although Morris presses rather too hard the idea that redemption always costs God something, e.g., effort expended, the relevant sense of "redemption" in Rom 3:24 is, I think, *kpr*, which does involve the payment of a price, as we have seen.

26 Smeaton observes that wherever redemption words are found in connection with the death, blood, or sufferings of Christ, the reference is sacrificial; and that supplementary expression contains an allusion to ransom (Gal 3:13; Eph 1:7; 1 Pet 1:19; Rev 5:9) (George Smeaton, *The Doctrine of the Atonement, as Taught by the Apostles* [Edinburgh: T&T Clark, 1870]; repr. ed.: *The Apostles' Doctrine of the Atonement* [Grand Rapids: Zondervan, 1957], 135).

27 C. H. Dodd, "Ἱλασκεσθαι, Its Cognates, Derivatives, and Synonyms, in the Septuagint," *Journal of Theological Studies* 32, no. 128 (1931): 352–60. Daniel P. Bailey points out to me that Dodd, as well as his most famous early critics Leon Morris and Roger Nicole (cf. the next note), erred in analyzing the entire *hilaskesthai* word group in order to pour its distilled essence into Paul's use of the very particular term *hilastērion* in Rom 3:25. All three concurred in rejecting the idea of Jesus as the mercy seat. Dodd himself considers two options, which he takes to be theologically equivalent: Paul understands Jesus to be a *hilastērion* in the sense of either (1) being an abstract, merely functional means of "expiation" of sin without any concrete metaphor; or (2) being himself "expiatory" toward sin. The latter is a syntactical innovation that goes back to the RV marginal note

Although Carson says that today it is widely recognized that Dodd was wrong "in his central contentions,"[28] Carson tacitly acknowledges that we find quite different meanings of *hilastērion* in the LXX and in extrabiblical Greek literature, including the literature of Hellenistic Judaism. What is disputed is which is the relevant meaning of *hilastērion* as used by Paul on this one occasion.

On the one hand, Paul might be using *hilastērion* with the predominant meaning in extrabiblical literature, including Hellenistic Jewish literature. According to Bailey there are now nine known concrete referents of the term *hilastērion* in Hellenistic or Greco-Roman sources.[29] These are concrete, inanimate propitiatory offerings to God or the gods,

---

at Rom 3:25, although it uses the competing adjective "propitiatory," i.e., "whom God set forth *to be* propitiatory."

28 Carson, "Atonement in Romans 3:21–26," 130. As noted above, Morris and Nicole, though analyzing the entire *hilaskesthai* group and Hebrew equivalents, as Dodd did, were nevertheless sharply critical of his method and argumentation (Leon Morris, "The Meaning of ἱλαστήριον in Romans III.25," *New Testament Studies* 2, no. 1 [1955]: 33–43; and Roger Nicole, "C. H. Dodd and the Doctrine of Propitiation," *Westminster Theological Journal* 17, no. 2 [1955]: 117–57, esp. 122–54). Dodd argues that because *kpr* is sometimes translated by words other than *hilas-* words, the *hilas-* words and these other words are synonymous, an obvious non sequitur given the wide range of meanings of *kpr*. He makes a similar argument based on the fact that *hilas-* words are sometimes used to translate words other than *kpr*, an argument which falsely presupposes that the *hilas-* words have only a single meaning. Perhaps the most curious of Dodd's claims is that while in Zech 7:2; 8:22; and Mal 1:9, we have "unmistakeable examples of the ordinary classical and Hellenistic sense" of *eksilaskisthai* = "to propitiate," the LXX translators reject this meaning as unworthy of the God of Israel. Such a rejection does not deny but actually presupposes that the term can and sometimes does have the meaning "to propitiate" in the LXX. Propitiation of God is also found by means of the verb *hilaskesthai* in *Sibylline Oracles* 1.167; 3.625, 628; 7.138; and 8.333.
29 These range in time from a drinking or libation bowl called a *hilatērion* (Doric spelling) in *The Lindos Chronicle* B49 of 99 B.C. through Dio Chrysostom's application in the second century of *hilastērion* to the Trojan horse (*Orations* 11.121; cf. 11.123). Bailey in his "Biblical and Greco-Roman Uses of *Hilastērion* in Romans 3:25 and 4 Maccabees 17:22 (Codex S)," in *Biblical Theology of the New Testament*, by Peter Stuhlmacher, trans. and ed. Daniel P. Bailey with the collaboration of Jostein Ådna (Grand Rapids: Eerdmans, 2018), 827–29, counts eight referents of the term *hilastērion* in ancient primary sources but now says that Apollo's tripod, a votive offering mentioned in the *Scholion* on Apollonius of Rhodes 4.1549 (829–30) should be added as a ninth, where a rare term for the offering is explained in part by *hilastērion* (in the plural).

but the term with this meaning can be used metaphorically. Especially noteworthy are the deaths of the Maccabean martyrs, which allayed God's wrath upon Israel (2 Macc 7:38) and thus served as "a propitiatory offering [*hilastērion*]" (4 Macc. 17:22 codex S).[30] The Hellenized heroes of 4 Maccabees 17:22 dedicate their lives in death as a *hilastērion*, much as a Greek hero might dedicate a sacred object as a *hilastērion* or "propitiatory gift."[31]

In Romans 1–3 Paul has expounded at some length on God's wrath, so that it would be natural for him then to say, "But God has put forward Christ as a propitiatory offering," thereby completing his argument.[32] Greco-Roman *hilastēria* were publicly displayed, as was the crucified Christ, but it would be extraordinary to say that God has publicly displayed the mercy seat hidden in the Holy of Holies. The objection that it makes no sense for Paul to say that God gives Christ as a gift to Himself is undercut by the fact that that is exactly the way in which the Levitical

---

30 David deSilva has translated 4 Macc 17:22 for the ESV Apocrypha, "And through the blood of those devout ones and their death as a propitiatory offering (*hilastērion*), divine Providence preserved Israel that previously had been afflicted."

31 DeSilva claims that "the gain of the reading of ἱλαστήριον as 'propitiatory offering' is the connection between the martyrs' deaths and their continuing, durable existence in the realm of God (Bailey 1999:134–135)" (David deSilva, *4 Maccabees: Introduction and Commentary on the Greek Text in Codex Sinaiticus* [Leiden: Brill, 2006], 251). DeSilva's reference is to Daniel P. Bailey, "Jesus as the Mercy Seat: The Semantics and Theology of Paul's Use of *Hilasterion* in Romans 3:25" (Ph.D. dissertation, University of Cambridge, 1999), 134–35, https://doi.org/10.17863/CAM.17213.

32 The idea that Christ's being put forward as a *hilastērion* in Rom 3:25 is comparable in its effect to that of an inanimate "propitiatory offering" (*Sühnemal*) or a "propitiatory votive offering" (*versöhnendes Weihegeschenk*) has been defended by Alexander Weiss, "Christus Jesus als Weihegeschenk oder Sühnemal? Anmerkungen zu einer neueren Deutung von hilasterion (Röm 3,25) samt einer Liste der epigraphischen Belege," *Zeitschrift für die Neutestamentliche Wissenschaft* 105, no. 2 (2014): 294–302; Stefan Schreiber, "Weitergedacht: Das versöhnende Weihegeschenk Gottes in Röm 3,25," *Zeitschrift für die Neutestamentliche Wissenschaft* 106, no. 2 (2015): 201–15. Both scholars stress the notion of propitiation involved in the typical Hellenistic or Greco-Roman *hilastērion*. Schreiber further notes that propitiation leads to reconciliation: "The metaphor of the 'propitiatory votive offering' allows the function of the death of Jesus to come to the fore: God himself is active in it, he takes the initiative and effects reconciliation with humanity" (213). (Once again, I am grateful to Daniel Bailey for these references.)

sacrifices were conceived (Lev 17:11)! God *gave* the people the blood on the altar to ransom their lives. So He could give Christ as a means or instrument of propitiation.

On the other hand, Paul might be using *hilastērion* as the LXX most often does, to refer to the *kappōret*, or top of the ark of the covenant, where the blood of the Yom Kippur sacrifice was sprinkled or, more widely, to altar faces where sacrificial blood was smeared (Ezek 43:14, 17, 20; Amos 9:1). We have already seen how Paul's use of *dikaioō* reflects the Septuagintal usage in contrast to that of extrabiblical Greek, and so it may be here. On this interpretation Christ is said to be the place where atonement is made for sin. God does do something extraordinary in displaying Christ as the mercy seat.

Carson does not opt for the extrabiblical meaning. Rather, observing that the only other NT occurrence of *hilastērion* (Heb 9:5) certainly refers to the *kappōret*, or mercy seat, as do twenty-one of the twenty-seven occurrences in the LXX, Carson believes that Paul is presenting Jesus as the ultimate mercy seat, the ultimate place of atonement, and so derivatively as the ultimate sacrifice.[33] Such a view is entirely consistent with Morris' claim that when one looks at the contexts in which *hilaskōmai* is used in the LXX, one frequently finds a reference to divine anger. "Again and again we find that, however the word is translated, there is the thought of the divine wrath in the context."[34] Carson would see propitiation as part of the derivative connotations of Paul's use of *hilastērion*.

Douglas Moo claims that the Pentateuchal *hilastērion* "*means* 'propitiation,'" but it *refers to* the cover of the ark,"[35] and that Paul's use of *hilastērion* similarly "'refers to' the atonement cover of the ark and 'means' sacrifice of atonement."[36] Moo would illustrate the difference between meaning and reference by words like "Waterloo" and "Watergate." The term "Waterloo" may refer to the historic battle in 1815 but often means a decisive defeat. Similarly, "Watergate" may refer to an office building but also mean a political cover-up. Moo cautions, "To insist that a word can

33 Carson, "Atonement in Romans 3:21–26," 129.
34 Morris, *Atonement*, 161.
35 Douglas J. Moo, *Encountering the Book of Romans* (Grand Rapids: Zondervan, 2002), 84.
36 Douglas J. Moo, *Romans*, NIV Application Commentary (Grand Rapids: Zondervan, 2000), 132.

only function in one way or the other is to miss the flexibility of language both to 'refer' and to 'mean.'"[37]

While I think that Moo is onto something important here, nonetheless, not being a linguistic philosopher, he misexpresses his point by appealing to the distinction between meaning and reference. The distinction between meaning and reference, as originally explained by Gottlob Frege, involved expressions like "the morning star" and "the evening star," for example, which have different meanings but the same referent, namely, Venus. The referent is what the speaker is talking about, even if linguistic expressions with different meanings are used to pick out the referent. Obviously, that is not the relevant distinction to be made concerning *hilastērion*. If anything, Moo gets things backward: the LXX meaning of the Greek word *hilastērion* is "mercy seat" or "place of atonement," but Paul allegedly uses it to refer to propitiation. In fact, however, the distinction between meaning and reference is not the relevant distinction here. Rather, the distinction to be drawn in this case is between literal meaning and figurative meaning. For example, the literal meaning of "There's a bee in her bonnet" has to do with an insect in someone's hat, but the figurative meaning is that she is angry or irritable. Although in this example the statement may be literally false while figuratively true, on other occasions a statement may be true whether interpreted literally or figuratively, as "No man is an island." So with respect to Moo's examples, words like "Waterloo" and "Watergate" have become metaphors for expressing things far beyond what is conveyed by their literal meaning.

Now if Paul is describing Jesus as the mercy seat, then he is obviously using *hilastērion* metaphorically, and so the question arises as to the meaning of the metaphor. Taken metaphorically rather than literally, the expression could convey a rich variety of connotations associated with sacrifice and atonement, so that the sort of dichotomistic reading forced by literal meanings becomes inappropriate, and the force of propitiation can be present.[38] Intriguingly, Philo explains the biblical use of the term

---

37 Moo, *Romans*, 132.
38 Bailey observes that both the Septuagint lexicon of T. Muraoka and Danker's BDAG distinguish the biblical sense of *hilastērion* as a place and the Greco-Roman sense of a propitiatory offering. Muraoka and Danker give as the biblical sense *"Place where cultic rites for appeasing a divine being are performed"* (applicable to the mercy seat and the *hilastēria* of Ezek 43.15 and Amos 9.1) and *"place of propitiation"* (applicable only to the mercy seat), respectively (Daniel P. Bailey,

as "a symbol, in a theological sense, of the merciful power of God and, in the human sense, of a mind which is merciful to itself."[39] Paul could similarly use the word metaphorically to carry a range of connotations.

Paul was a Hellenistic Jew, and he might have expected that his Gentile Roman readers would have understood *hilastērion* in the customary Greco-Roman sense.[40] Bailey thinks that any confusion concerning the term, whether it should be understood to allude to the mercy seat or a Hellenistic votive offering, could have been cleared up by Paul's letter carrier, in this case Phoebe (Rom 16:1-2), whom Longenecker calls "the first commentator" on the letter to the Romans:[41]

> Phoebe had been Paul's patron during his ministry at Corinth, had most likely heard from his own lips the contents of the letter as it was being formulated, and must have had some part in discussing with Paul and other Christians of that area at least a few portions of the letter—and therefore would have been in a position to explain to the Christians at Rome (1) what Paul was saying in the various sections of his letter, (2) what he meant by what he proclaimed in each of those sections, and (3) how

---

"Biblical and Greco-Roman Uses of *Hilastērion* in Romans 3:25 and 4 Maccabees 17:22 [Codex S]," in *Biblical Theology of the New Testament*, by Peter Stuhlmacher, trans. and ed. Daniel P. Bailey with the collaboration of Jostein Ådna [Grand Rapids: Eerdmans, 2018], 848). If they are right, then the biblical sense does, indeed, carry a connotation of propitiation. Averbeck wisely remonstrates, "The debate has generally been overwrought with false dichotomies and a lack of willingness to see the broader picture, apparently because of previous doctrinal commitments" (Richard E. Averbeck, "kpr [4105/4106]," *New International Dictionary of Old Testament Theology and Exegesis*, ed. Willem A. VanGemeren [Grand Rapids: Zondervan, 1997], 708). Bailey himself says, "Paul's application of ἱλαστήριον to Jesus involves a spatial metaphor, which cannot simply be reduced to juristic categories" (Bailey, "Biblical and Greco-Roman Uses of *Hilastērion*," 824).

39 Philo, *On the Life of Moses* 2.95.

40 Bailey advises that none of the new -τήριον place-nouns invented for the translation of the Septuagint "ever experienced widespread borrowing by the Gentile world or took on an instrumental sense. . . . Therefore, students can be assured that ἱλαστήριον as applied to the mercy seat is a special word, historically unrelated to the Greco-Roman use, and that non-Jews did not encounter it on the streets, but only in connection with a Jewish community and Scripture readings of the relevant passages in Exodus, Leviticus, and Numbers" ("Biblical and Greco-Roman Uses of *Hilastērion*," 863).

41 Bailey, "Biblical and Greco-Roman Uses of *Hilastērion*," 837.

he expected certain important sections of his letter to be worked out in practice in the particular situations at Rome.[42]

By borrowing an image from the Day of Atonement rituals, Paul would also convey to his hearers the OT notion of an atoning blood sacrifice. Thomas Hiecke comments that already in the OT "by means of abstraction, the ritual itself turns into a metaphor," thus building "the basis and starting point for multiple transformations and further abstractions as well as metaphorical charging in Judaism . . . and Christianity (Rom 3:25: Christ as *hilasterion*—expiation or sacrifice of atonement, etc.)."[43] Propitiation would also be one of the many connotations of the metaphor.[44]

8. "In his blood" (*en tō autou haimati*) (Rom 3:25). This phrase probably modifies *hilastērion* and serves to construe Christ's death as a sacrificial offering for sin akin to the Yom Kippur sacrifices, the blood of which was sprinkled on the altar. In so construing Christ's death, Paul agrees with the author of Hebrews that Christ has superseded the Levitical sacrifices and, in effect, put an end to them because of the final efficacy of his atoning death. The Temple with its *hilastērion* is now obsolete and seen to be merely provisional, a temporary arrangement set up until God's ultimate sacrificial offering should be set forth. Indeed, like the author of Hebrews, Paul will go on to imply that these OT sacrifices were not really effectual at all in expiating sins, which were not finally dealt with until Christ's atoning sacrifice. The demands of God's justice were not really satisfied by the elaborate sacrificial system; rather, God in His forbearance just overlooked the sins of previous generations until He

---

42 R. N. Longenecker, *The Epistle to the Romans*, The New International Greek Testament Commentary (Grand Rapids: Eerdmans, 2016), 1064.

43 Thomas Hiecke, "Participation and Abstraction in the Yom Kippur Ritual according to Leviticus 16" (paper presented to the "Ritual in the Biblical World" section of the Society of Biblical Literature, San Antonio, Tex., November 21, 2016).

44 When a theologian like Otfried Hofius asserts that "nowhere in the New Testament is there talk of a satisfactory and propitiatory sacrifice of atonement" brought by Christ, one needs to understand that he means a sacrifice brought "to achieve the satisfaction demanded by a God who is insulted by sin and deadly angry with sinners and to render him gracious" (*Theologische Realenzyklopädie*, ed. Gerhard Müller, vol. 32, *Spurgeon-Taylor* [Berlin: Walter de Gruyter, 2001], s.v. "Sühne IV: Neues Testament," by Otfried Hofius), a caricature of the notions of satisfaction and propitiation by Hofius, who himself recognizes the need of sinners to escape God's just condemnation for their sin.

set forth Christ as a *hilastērion*. Christ having been offered, the demands
of God's justice are forever satisfied, even with respect to future sins, so
that no further satisfaction need be made.

9. "To demonstrate etc." (*eis endeiksin ktl.*) (Rom 3:25b-26). Having said that God put Christ forward as a sacrifice of atonement, Paul
claims that God did this in order to show His righteousness, since in
His forbearance (*anochē*) He had passed over the sins of previous generations, the point being, presumably, that God's failure to punish previous sins called into question that aspect of His righteousness that
is His retributive justice. But now through Christ's sacrificial death,
God's justice has been vindicated. How so? Paul does not say. But the
almost inescapable implication is that these sins have now received their
due; no longer can they be considered overlooked or unpunished. Like
the Servant of Isaiah 53, Christ has borne the punishment instead.
Punitive justice, God's justice, has been discharged in Christ, thereby
vindicating God's righteousness.

It is uncontroversial that Paul is asserting here that God has graciously not given sinners of previous generations their just desert. Earlier
Paul had spoken of God's "forbearance" (*anochē*) toward the unrighteous,
explaining that "God's kindness is meant to lead you to repentance"
(2:4), thereby implying that God had graciously stayed His just judgment (cf. Acts 17:30). Proponents of the new perspective on Paul have,
however, challenged the interpretation that God has now vindicated His
justice though Christ's sacrificial death. Rather, Paul is saying that God
demonstrates His covenant faithfulness by forgiving or simply overlooking former sins.[45]

---

45 Some scholars have taken *paresis* to indicate that God has forgiven former sins;
   but this interpretation is less plausible than the interpretation that God has
   overlooked the former sins, since *paresis* does not mean "forgiveness" but "passing over." So Wright, for example, claims:

   > Paul is not here saying . . . that God has *punished* former sins, whether
   > of Israel or the Gentiles, certainly not that he has punished them in
   > Jesus. . . . Paul says, rather, that God has chosen to overlook the "former
   > sins." . . . The assumption here must be, I think, that Paul is referring
   > to Israel's former sins. God is faithful in the Messiah to the covenant
   > *through Israel for the world*, and to that end he has pushed the "former
   > sins" to one side. (*Day the Revolution Began*, 331)

   Paresis in a legal context involves a reprieve of punishment until a later time, in
   which case God's justice must finally be satisfied.

The new perspective interpretation is, however, implausible.[46] In the first place, it depends on taking God's righteousness to be His faithfulness to His covenant, which notion has been exploded by Irons' work, as we have seen. Moreover, the interpretation of *dia tēn paresin* as "by passing over" depends on taking *dia* + the accusative to mean "by" rather than "because of," which is an extremely rare usage lacking any contextual justification. Finally, the interpretation makes dubious sense. It seems a non sequitur to say that because God had overlooked previous sins, He now puts forth Christ as a sacrificial offering as a demonstration of His faithfulness. If the sins have been simply overlooked, there is just no rationale for a sacrificial offering. It is very hard to see what Christ's death actually atones for or accomplishes.

By contrast, the traditional interpretation makes the rationale of Christ's death perspicuous: it atones for those previous sins that did not receive their just desert and were not effectually expiated. Since God's righteousness comprises retributive justice as one of its elements, Christ's atoning death proves God's righteousness. By offering a final, decisive sacrifice of atonement that truly expiates sins, God is shown to be both just and the justifier of him who has faith in Jesus (v. 26), a wordplay that makes sense only on the traditional interpretation.

10. Significance of the succeeding passages (Rom 3:27–31; 4:1ff). Paul proceeds to explain what it means that God justifies him who has faith in Jesus (v. 26). Justification entails the forgiveness of sins:

> David speaks of the blessedness of those to whom God reckons righteousness apart from works:

> "Blessed are those whose iniquities are forgiven,
>   and whose sins are covered;
> blessed is the one against whom the Lord will not reckon sin." (Rom 4:6-8)

The Levitical system of sacrificial offerings in the Tabernacle and Temple, offerings that Paul took to prefigure Christ's own death as the ultimate sacrificial offering, aimed, as we have seen, not merely at the cleansing of consecrated objects from impurity but more fundamentally at the expiation of the sins of the people and their forgiveness. Again and again the promise is given, "the priest shall make atonement

---

46 See not only Carson's comments but also those of Moo, *Romans*, 238–39.

on your behalf for the sin that you have committed, and you shall be forgiven" (Lev 4:35; cf. 4:20, 26, 31; 5:10, 13, 16, 18; etc.). Christ's atoning death is truly expiatory. In short, in Christ "we have redemption, the forgiveness of sins" (Col 1:14; cf. Eph 1:7).

It is noteworthy that the object of divine forgiveness is said by Paul to be sins, not just sinners. Not only are people forgiven for their sins, but their sins are forgiven. This fact makes it evident that divine forgiveness is not (merely) a change of attitude on God's part toward sinners. The word *aphiēmi* carries the connotation of nullifying or canceling and can be used of the remission of debts. Paul says that God will "take away" (*aphaireō*) sins (Rom 11:27). Divine forgiveness has as its effect not (merely) God's laying aside feelings of anger or indignation (or what have you, according to one's favorite analysis of forgiveness), but rather the removal of the liability to punishment that attends sin. As a result of divine forgiveness, a person who formerly deserved punishment now no longer does so. Because of the forgiveness that is to be found in Christ, those who are united with him through faith are no longer held accountable for their sins. "There is therefore now no condemnation for those who are in Christ Jesus" (Rom 8:1). It is evident, then, that divine forgiveness is much more akin to legal pardon than to forgiveness as typically understood.

This is not to say that divine forgiveness is just a legal pardon issued to those who have faith in Christ.[47] For a pardon might be issued by an official who is personally indifferent or even hostile to the condemned (cf. Pontius Pilate's exercise of executive clemency in pardoning Barabbas [Mark 15:6-15]). As we have seen, God's wrath is also put away by Christ's atoning death. God's pardon is motivated by compassion for sinners, and ongoing wrath directed against a justified believer is

---

47 As is implied by Hofius' view that the wrath of God is not an emotion of God but God's eschatological justice that condemns the sinner to death (Otfried Hofius, "Sühne und Versöhnung: Zum paulinischen Verständnis des Kreuzestodes Jesu," in *Paulusstudien*, 2nd rev. ed., WUNT 1/51 [Tübingen: J. C. B. Mohr (Paul Siebeck), 1994], 36). I. H. Marshall rightly cautions, "To deny that God feels some kind of negative feelings about sin is a denial of a personal character of God who reacts to the evil that ruins his creation and destroys his relationship with his creatures" (I. Howard Marshall, *Aspects of the Atonement: Cross and Resurrection in the Reconciling of God and Humanity* [London: Paternoster, 2007], 21). Just as God is a loving and compassionate personal being, so He has feelings of anger occasioned by sin. It seems that too many scholars forget what every parent knows: one can be angry with those whom one loves.

inconceivable. Legal pardon does not, then, exhaust divine forgiveness; nevertheless, it does lie at its heart in taking away our liability to punishment.[48]

Those who have faith in Christ are not merely pardoned and forgiven, however. According to Paul, the righteousness of God is credited to all who believe in Jesus.[49] Recalling the case of Abraham, to whom God reckoned righteousness apart from works of the law, Paul says, "Now the words, 'it was reckoned to him,' were written not for his sake alone, but for ours also. It will be reckoned to us who believe in him who raised Jesus our Lord from the dead, who was handed over to death for our trespasses and was raised for our justification" (Rom 4:23-25). Notice that the gift of righteousness is accorded by means of "reckoning" (*logizomai*), in the sense in which a merchant would settle accounts.[50] Here,

---

48 For much more on pardon see chaps. 12, 13.

49 It is of little consequence whether the righteousness is God's, as Robert Gundry insists (see following note), or Christ's, as Reformation theologians typically maintained. What matters is that it is an alien righteousness first exemplified by a perfect person. See comments by Michael F. Bird, "Progressive Reformed View," in *Justification: Five Views*, ed. James K. Beilby and Paul Rhodes Eddy, assoc. ed. Steven E. Eenderlein (Downers Grove, Ill.: IVP Academic, 2011), 148–52, who, while expressing reservations concerning the imputation to us of Christ's righteousness won by his active obedience during his lifetime, nonetheless holds that "the consistent point is that *by faith* and *in Christ* we experience the status of 'righteous'" (149), which is just to affirm imputation. He calls imputation "a necessary *implicate* of the biblical materials": "Something like 'imputation' sounds like a logical necessity of describing the application of salvation for those who are 'in Christ'" (151). Moreover, despite Bird's reservations as a strictly biblical theologian, it is certainly open to the atonement theorist to propose a theory of the atonement according to which the alien righteousness imputed to us is that of Christ's active obedience, thereby securing an emphasis on Christ's life as well as his death.

50 There is some dispute as to how righteousness is reckoned to us, viz., is faith the means by which we receive the gift of God's righteousness or is our faith itself taken by God to be righteousness? See, e.g., Robert H. Gundry, "The Nonimputation of Christ's Righteousness," in Husbands and Treier, *Justification*, 17–45; D. A. Carson, "The Vindication of Imputation: On the Fields of Discourse and Semantic Fields," in Husbands and Treier, *Justification*, 46–79.

On the one hand, over and over Paul says that it is by means of our faith (in Christ) that God's righteousness is reckoned to us: "the righteousness of God through faith in Jesus Christ for all who believe" (Rom 3:22); "effective through faith" (Rom 3:25); "we hold that a person is justified by faith (*pistei*) apart from works" (Rom 3:28); "he will justify the circumcised on the ground of faith (*ek*

however, the context is not commercial but legal. The relevant legal category is imputation. The now-justified believer does not have righteousness infused into him so that he suddenly becomes a virtuous person, exemplifying selflessness, compassion, veracity, fidelity, and so on. Rather, he is accorded a new legal status. He moves from a state of legal condemnation before God to a state of fully meeting the law's requirements: "that the just requirement (*dikaiōma*) of the law might be fulfilled in us" (Rom 8:4).

Although it is sometimes said that justification involves merely acquittal and not a positive ascription of righteousness, nothing in the text warrants so diluting the righteousness of God that is reckoned to

---

pisteōs) and the uncircumcised through that same faith (*dia tēs pisteōs*)" (Rom 3:30); "we are justified by faith (*ek pisteōs*)" (Rom 5:1); "much more surely will those who receive the abundance of grace and the free gift of righteousness exercise dominion in life" (Rom 5:17); "Gentiles, who did not strive for righteousness, have attained it, that is, righteousness through faith (*dikaiōsynēn tēn ek pisteōs*); but Israel, who did strive for the righteousness that is based on the law, did not succeed in fulfilling that law. Why not? Because they did not strive for it on the basis of faith (*ek pisteōs*)" (Rom 9:30-32).

On the other hand, in Rom 4 Paul says several times that Abraham's faith was "reckoned to him as righteousness" (vv. 5, 9, 22). Gundry interprets these statements to mean that God considers Abraham's faith to be something that it is not, namely, righteousness and so reckons Abraham to be righteous. Here faith serves as an *Ersatz* for righteousness. It is difficult to understand why Gundry denies that in so doing God adopts the legal fiction that faith is righteousness. We seem to have here a paradigm of a legal fiction: the divine Judge declares that for the purposes of this action He will adopt the assumption that Abraham's faith = righteousness, even though He knows full well that it is not. It is similar to a case in which the court adopts the fiction that Minorca is part of London, so that a resident of Minorca is, for the purposes of the action, a resident of London (see the sequel). Just as residency of London is reckoned to the plaintiff, so righteousness is reckoned to Abraham.

How one adjudicates this debate will probably depend upon whether one interprets the former passages through the lens of the latter or the latter through the lens of the former. For my part, I suspect that Paul would be surprised at Gundry's attribution to him of so wooden a reading of "his faith was reckoned to him as righteousness." The many statements about how righteousness is acquired through faith probably govern the others and are meant to explicate the OT quotation, rather than vice versa. Moreover, the view of faith as a means makes better sense of Paul's not seeing faith as something meritorious in the believer. Ultimately, the dispute is of little consequence for the doctrine of the atonement, since in either case righteousness is imputed to the person of faith.

believers. Even a stone can be said to be not guilty, and justified believers are certainly more righteous than a stone. Biblically, the righteousness of God is, as we have seen, a rich property, not a bare absence of guilt. *Prima facie* God's righteousness in its full moral rectitude is reckoned to believers. That the righteousness reckoned by God to believers is a rich, positive property is evident in Paul's rapturous words to the Philippians:

> I regard everything as loss because of the surpassing value of knowing Christ Jesus my Lord. For his sake I have suffered the loss of all things, and I regard them as rubbish, in order that I may gain Christ and be found in him, not having a righteousness of my own that comes from the law, but one that comes through faith in Christ, the righteousness from God based on faith. (Phil 3:8-9)

The righteousness that Paul here extols, next to which everything else is like dung, could not possibly be equated with a mere absence of guilt. It is, in fact, the same property that God Himself exemplifies that is imputed to us. No wonder Paul is in rapture! That God's righteousness is imputed to us seems clearly expressed in 2 Cor 5:21b: "that in him we might become the righteousness of God." There is no exegetical warrant for diluting this statement or trying to explain it away: in Christ our legal status is that we are righteous, as God is righteous.

The reflex of the imputation of Christ's righteousness to believers is the imputation of their sins to Christ. We have already seen in chapter 3 that NT authors, including Paul, identified Christ with the suffering Servant of Isaiah 53, who "bore the sins of many" (Isa 53:12), a phrase employing a customary Semitic idiom for being held liable to or enduring punishment. Isaiah 53 does not make clear whether the Servant merely endured the punishment that was the just desert of the people or whether he was imputed their guilt and liability to punishment. One could administer vicarious punishment to a person who did not deserve it, to whom no guilt or liability to punishment was imputed.[51] Such a person's legal status would be the same as that of any person who was innocent of a crime. But if sins are imputed to the penal substitute, then that person's legal status is the same as that of a person convicted and condemned for the crimes. He may be personally virtuous

---

51 For examples in classical literature, see Simon Gathercole, *Defending Substitution: An Essay on Atonement in Paul* (Grand Rapids: Baker Academic, 2015), chap. 3: "The Vicarious Death of Christ and Classical Parallels."

and without fault, but he is reckoned to be legally guilty and liable to punishment. Is there any reason to think that in Paul's view Christ was not merely punished for people's sins but that people's sins were imputed to Christ? I think there is.

First, in Galatians 3:10-14 Paul makes the shocking affirmation that Christ actually became accursed of God on our behalf:

> For all who rely on the works of the law are under a curse; for it is written, "Cursed is everyone who does not observe and obey all the things written in the book of the law." Now it is evident that no one is justified before God by the law; for "The one who is righteous will live by faith." But the law does not rest on faith; on the contrary, "Whoever does the works of the law will live by them." Christ redeemed us from the curse of the law by becoming a curse for us—for it is written, "Cursed is everyone who hangs on a tree"—in order that in Christ Jesus the blessing of Abraham might come to the Gentiles, so that we might receive the promise of the Spirit through faith.

People who look to works of the law for their justification are said to be accursed. This is the severest of language. Earlier in the letter Paul had called down God's curse on those false apostles who were preaching a counterfeit gospel (Gal 1:8-9). Those who rely on the law are now said to be similarly accursed. That is because they are lawbreakers and so cannot fulfill its requirements. This is the same desperate situation that Paul describes in the early chapters of his letter to the Roman church. And as in Romans, Christ is here said to have redeemed us from this accursed state. But how? *By becoming a curse for us.* Though he was not a lawbreaker, he became accursed on our behalf. It is hard to understand this in any other way than the imputation to Christ of our sins and consequent condemnation before the righteous Judge. He accepts as his own our legal status of condemned criminals and then endures our punishment to liberate us from such a state of condemnation.

Second, in 2 Corinthians 5:21a Paul says that God made Christ to be sin on our behalf: "For our sake he made him to be sin who knew no sin." Though Christ was not merely personally virtuous but even sinless, God made him to become sin for our sake. How else can this startling statement be plausibly understood than as the affirmation that God imputed our sins to Christ, so that despite his perfect goodness, he was legally guilty before God for our wrongdoing? There is no exegetical warrant for trying to dilute the force of this statement by taking it to mean that God made Christ to become a sin offering for our sake. For Paul does not use the phrase *peri hamartias*, and the evident parallelism between verses 21a and b militates strongly against any interpretation that breaks the parallelism. Notice, too, that in verse 19 Paul says that in Christ God did not count (*logizomai*) our trespasses against us. Our sins are not imputed to us; rather, they are imputed to Christ. Any plausible interpretation must make sense of the contrast between verses 19 and 21, as well as the parallelism of verses 21a and b.

So I think that there are good grounds to see the imputation of our sins to Christ and of his righteousness to us as an entailment of Paul's doctrine of the atonement.

CONCLUDING REMARKS

Forensic terminology pervades both the OT and NT, especially Paul's epistles. God's righteousness is both an ethical and legal normative concept, a rich property of God Himself indicating His moral rectitude. Before Him, as before a supreme and righteous Judge, every human being finds himself justly condemned due to his violation of God's laws. By Christ's atoning death, God has made possible our pardon, so that we may escape condemnation and punishment. God legally imputed our sins to Christ, and he vicariously bore the just desert of those sins. Divine justice satisfied, God offers us the gift of His righteousness, that is to say, the imputation to us of that same property that He essentially exemplifies. Those who place their faith in Christ receive God's pardon and the imputation of a new legal status of righteousness in the place of condemnation.

These legal motifs are blended with an array of motifs drawn from other spheres such as the Levitical cult. Christ's death is seen as a sacrificial offering to God that ransoms us from sin's bondage. Our sins are expiated by Christ's death, and God is propitiated. Through faith in Christ we are not merely pardoned but forgiven, as God's wrath is dissolved. These motifs supplement or express in other categories the truths that are legally expressed. Sacrifice is analogous to vicarious punishment; expiation is the analogue of divine pardon; propitiation of the satisfaction of divine justice; redemption of our undeserved change of legal status. Obviously, we have here rich materials for a substantive doctrine of the atonement.

Chapter 5

REPRESENTATION AND
REDEMPTION

INTRODUCTION

Two further facets of the biblical doctrine of the atonement, to which we have already alluded and so which may be treated more briefly here, are representation and redemption.

REPRESENTATION

In Paul's theology Christ serves as our representative before God. But already in some of the Levitical sacrifices, the motif of representation is present.

Levitical Sacrifices

If I am correct that the hand-laying ceremony that featured in all the personal animal sacrifices was meant to symbolize the offerer's identification with the animal and its fate, then the animal in some sense represents the offerer before God. The animal is not just a substitute for the offerer, something killed instead of the worshipper, much less a payment of some sort akin to a monetary ransom. By identifying himself symbolically with the sacrificial animal, the offerer comes to share in the animal's fate of dying and being offered to God. Because the offerer has identified himself symbolically with the animal, the animal's death represents the offerer's death, the just desert for his sins, and the animal's being offered to God represents the offering of the worshipper's life to God.

In addition, while the daily sacrifices were killed by the offerer himself, on the Day of Atonement access to the Tabernacle was permitted to the high priest alone, who therefore had to act as the people's representative before God, bringing the sacrifice for them and then confessing their sins over the scapegoat (Lev 16:17). Here we have the priest acting as a personal representative on behalf of the people. We should not think of the scapegoat as a representative of the people, for it is merely the symbolic vehicle for carrying away their sins, out of the community into the desert. Its being driven out does symbolize and in that sense represent the removal of the people's sins, but it is not a representative of the people themselves, as though they were being symbolically driven from the camp. But personal representation is clearly present in the high priest's acting on the people's behalf in doing what they were not authorized to do, to approach the place of atonement in the innermost sanctum of the Tabernacle with the atoning blood.

Christ Our Representative

Paul characterizes Christ as our personal representative before God in two ways. First, there is the corporate solidarity of all mankind with Christ, who is the antitype of the first man, Adam. In the fifth chapter of Romans Paul states, "As one man's trespass led to condemnation for all, so one man's act of righteousness leads to justification and life for all. For just as by the one man's disobedience the many were made sinners, so by the one man's obedience the many will be made righteous" (Rom 5:18-19). Notice that Christ's atoning sacrifice is here conceived as universal in its scope. There is no exegetical basis for thinking that Christ died only for the elect. The representative nature of Christ's death becomes clear in Paul's statement "we are convinced that one has died for all; therefore all have died" (2 Cor 5:14). Christ did not simply die in my place; rather what my representative did, I did. Christ's death was representatively our death.[1]

---

1   This may also be the import of the author of Hebrews' words: "that by the grace of God he might taste death for every one" (2:9). In Hebrews Christ is not only the high priest who represents us before God but he is also the sacrificial victim

Paul thus makes an advance over Isaiah 53 by clarifying that the Servant suffers not merely substitutionally for the many but representatively. Some biblical scholars have mistakenly claimed that the sort of substitution (*Stellvertretung*) envisioned in Isaiah 53 is exclusionary (*exkludierende*) rather than inclusionary (*inkludierende*).[2] But this is a

---

who dies our death. The substitutionary nature of Christ's death is neglected by David M. Moffitt, *Atonement and the Logic of Resurrection in the Epistle to the Hebrews*, Supplements to Novum Testamentum 141 (Leiden: Brill, 2013), 42, who sees Jesus' death as merely initiating the process that will lead to atonement and that serves as an example of righteous suffering. Moffit is setting up a straw man when says that Jesus' death can be seen as "the first element in the larger process of blood sacrifice, without being conflated or collapsed by the author [of Hebrews] into the central act of offering that effects atonement. In the author's schema, Jesus' death is therefore necessary, though not by itself sufficient, for the atonement he procured" (285). No one is suggesting such a collapse or conflation or trying to isolate Jesus' death from his offering his blood to God. The majority view of Hebrews is that the author describes Christ's death and ascension as the analogues to the killing of a sacrificial animal and the presentation of its blood in the Holy of Holies. One can appreciate Moffit's emphasis on Jesus' resurrection as an entailment of his ascension to heaven without denying the atoning significance of Christ's death.

2   See, e.g., Otfried Hofius, "The Fourth Servant Song in the New Testament Letters," in *The Suffering Servant: Isaiah 53 in Jewish and Christian Sources*, ed. Bernd Janowski and Peter Stuhlmacher (1996), trans. Daniel P. Bailey (Grand Rapids: Eerdmans, 2004), 170. Hofius adopts the distinction made by Hartmut Gese between *einschliessende* and *ausschliessende Stellvertretung* (Hartmut Gese, "The Atonement," in *Essays on Biblical Theology*, trans. Keith Crim [Minneapolis: Augsburg, 1981], 106). Critical of Hofius' exclusionary interpretation of Isaiah 53 is Bernd Janowski, *Stellvertretung: Alttestamentliche Studien zu einem theologischen Grundbegriff*, Stuttgarter Bibelstudien 165 (Stuttgart: Verlag Katholisches Bibelwerk, 1997), 91. For discussion see Daniel P. Bailey, "Concepts of *Stellvertretung* in the Interpretation of Isaiah 53," in *Jesus and the Suffering Servant: Isaiah 53 and Christian Origins*, ed. William H. Bellinger Jr. and William R. Farmer (Harrisburg, Penn.: Trinity Press International, 1998), 223–50.

Hofius defines *exkludierende Stellvertretung* as "one party taking the place of another in such a way that the guilty party is *excluded* from that obligation or fate" ("Fourth Servant Song," 170). He regards such a notion as untenable:

> Just as it is impossible for people to die the death of others, so it is impossible for them, being sinners *themselves*, to make the sin of others their own. When this is acknowledged it also forces a conclusion about the fourth Servant Song. What this song says about the Servant's substitutionary death is theologically incomprehensible as it stands and as it is

meant. . . . we must conclude: being freed up from sin and guilt through *human* substitution is theologically simply unthinkable! (172)

Hofius maintains that the NT authors did not simply take up the fourth Servant song and apply it to Jesus; rather, they completely reinterpreted it as Christ's taking our place in such a way as to include us. "Christ takes the place of sinners in such a way that he does not displace them (as in the substitutionary model) but rather encompasses them as *persons* and affects them in their very being" (173). This rather fuzzy characterization of "inclusive place-taking" is said to involve four essential aspects: (1) God Himself, not a mere man, has taken our place; (2) the meaning and goal of Christ's coming into the world is his vicarious death for sinners; (3) Christ is himself the saving presence of God; (4) Christ has not simply come alongside the sinner in order to take away guilt and sin; he has rather become identical with the sinner, in order through the surrender of his life to lead sinners into union with God. Hofius concludes that what is at issue in inclusive place-taking is the fundamental recognition that only God is able to free sinners from their sin.

As we have seen in chapter 3, Hofius' assumption that Isaiah 53 precludes the divinity and sinlessness of the Servant is not only gratuitous but even contrary to the evidence. Moreover, it is unclear that divinity is on Hofius' view a necessary condition of inclusionary place-taking, for Hofius agrees with Gese that the Levitical animal sacrifices were inclusionary! And even if we agree that Christ's divinity and sinlessness are a necessary condition of his vicariously bearing the sins of others, why think that they suffice to render his vicarious suffering inclusionary? Hofius says nothing to show that divinity and sinlessness are the determining factors in rendering place-taking inclusionary rather than exclusionary. In his encyclopedia article, Hofius plausibly contends that the universality and finality of Christ's sacrifice are grounded in the fact that it is God Himself who acts in Christ, but he gives no clue as to why divinity renders Christ's *Stellvertretung* inclusionary (*Theologische Realenzyklopädie*, ed. Gerhard Müller, vol. 32, *Spurgeon-Taylor* [Berlin: Walter de Gruyter, 2001], s.v. "Sühne IV: Neues Testament," by Otfried Hofius). Hofius' point (4), if taken literally, would be absurd, for then only human sinners would exist. Taken figuratively, however, (4) seems to me an effort to capture the idea of representation in contrast to mere substitution by means of the unfortunate dichotomy between inclusionary and exclusionary place-taking. Intriguingly, Hofius elsewhere explains, "God has identified Christ with the sinner and the sinner with Christ. Or in other words: the crucified Christ, who represents [*repräsentiert*] the holy God, has bound himself inextricably with godless humanity and thereby bound godless humanity inextricably with himself" (Otfried Hofius, "Sühne und Versöhnung: Zum paulinischen Verständnis des Kreuzestodes Jesu," in *Paulusstudien*, 2nd rev. ed., WUNT 1/51 [Tübingen: J. C. B. Mohr (Paul Siebeck), 1994], 46). Would it not be more accurate to say that Christ represents sinners to God and that humanity is therefore bound up with what Christ suffers?

false dichotomy. The Servant's suffering may not be described in inclusionary terms, but that does not imply that it is exclusionary. It would be very natural to take the Servant of the LORD to be a representative of the many before God, rather than a mere whipping boy, and so to include them representatively in his suffering. Indeed, this is precisely the move that Paul made.

Second, there is the union of believers with Christ, whereby they become the beneficiaries of his atoning death. In Romans 6 Paul describes the means by which we appropriate the benefits of Christ's atoning death on our behalf:

> Do you not know that all of us who have been baptized into Christ Jesus were baptized into his death? Therefore we have been buried with him by baptism into death, so that, just as Christ was raised from the dead by the glory of the Father, so we too might walk in newness of life. For if we have been united with him in a death like his, we will certainly be united with him in a resurrection like his. We know that our old self was crucified with him so that the body of sin might be destroyed, and we might no longer be enslaved to sin. For whoever has died is freed from sin. But if we have died with Christ, we believe that we will also live with him. We know that Christ, being raised from the dead, will never die again; death no longer has dominion over him. The death he died, he died to sin, once for all; but the life he lives, he lives to God. So you also must consider yourselves dead to sin and alive to God in Christ Jesus. (vv. 3-11)

No universalist, Paul believed that "those who receive the abundance of grace and the free gift of righteousness will reign in life through the one man Jesus Christ" (Rom 5:17). The way in which we appropriate the benefits of Christ's atoning death is by faith culminating in baptism. We thereby come to identify with his death and resurrection.

This section of Paul's letter is thus not about Christ's representing us on the cross but about our faith union with him as Christians. Paul says that "all of us who have been baptized into Christ Jesus were baptized into his death" (Rom 6:3); therefore "we have died with Christ" (v. 8), "crucified with him" (v. 6). Similarly, by his resurrection we "have been brought from death to life" (v. 13). Because of our union with him, his death and resurrection are ours as well (cf. Col 2:12, 20; Gal 2:19-20). God appointed Christ as our human representative, but we benefit from his atoning death only insofar as we are "in Christ." "There is therefore now no condemnation for those who are in Christ Jesus" (Rom 8:1). We are in Christ through faith culminating in baptism, by which we identify with his death and resurrection. We, in effect, thereby accept his representation of us. Those who reject Christ reject his representation of them and so are not united with him and do not share in the benefits of his atoning death.

It is in this light that we should understand the ministry of reconciliation which Paul describes in 2 Corinthians 5:11-21. In verses 14 and 19 he speaks of the universal scope of Christ's atoning death: "For the love of Christ urges us on, because we are convinced that one has died for all; therefore all have died. . . . God was in Christ reconciling the world to himself, not counting their trespasses against them, and entrusting the message of reconciliation to us." But in verses 17-18 and 20 he speaks more narrowly of those who are "in Christ" and so have become new creations: "So if anyone is in Christ, there is a new creation: everything old has passed away; see, everything has become new! All this is from God, who reconciled us to himself through Christ, and has given us the ministry of reconciliation. . . . So we are ambassadors for Christ, since God is making his appeal through us; we entreat you on behalf of Christ, be reconciled to God." This appeal to be reconciled to God and become a new creation different from the world makes no sense if we think that Christ's death on the cross accomplishes everything pertaining to salvation and does not need to be applied or its benefits received through faith. Paul clearly believes that there are people in the world who are as yet unreconciled to God, despite Christ's death on their behalf, and so need to hear the message of reconciliation and respond to it.[3]

Thus, Paul's atonement doctrine has a strong representational aspect to it. Like Adam, Christ represents every human being before God and dies for him. Additionally, those who by faith receive God's forgiveness

---

3   I cannot therefore agree with Hofius when he comments, "The New Testament witness is then fundamentally distorted, when we view the Christ event as merely God's securing the *possibility* of reconciliation and the proclamation of the Gospel as just the *offer* of reconciliation and above all the reception of reconciliation as the *realization* of reconciliation by faith" (*Theologische Realenzyklopädie*, ed. Gerhard Müller, vol. 35, *Vernunft III–Wiederbringung aller* [Berlin: Walter de Gruyter, 2003], s.v. "Versöhnung: Neues Testament," by Otfried Hofius [emphasis added]). Even if we hold that the reception of the Gospel is not a free act of the will on the part of those who believe, it is indisputable that those who have not yet come to faith are unreconciled to God and so under divine condemnation until God produces in them saving faith (Eph 2:3). On Hofius' view Paul's appeal to be reconciled to God, and, hence, his entire ministry, is pointless and superfluous.

and gift of righteousness thereby become the actual beneficiaries of Christ's death and resurrection on their behalf. Christ's atoning death is thus offered on behalf of all mankind, represented by Christ before God, thereby making divine pardon and justification available to all, but actual redemption of various individuals takes place over time throughout history as people come to place their faith in Christ and receive God's gift of righteousness.[4] The universality of Christ's representation and the particularity of its efficacy is best explained by understanding atonement as achieved potentially at the cross and actualized historically through individual acts of faith.

REDEMPTION

While there are many other facets of the NT doctrine of the atonement, we shall mention but one more: redemption. In the ancient world the notion of redemption had to do with the buying of prisoners of war out of captivity or the manumission of slaves out of slavery. The payment could be called a ransom (*lytrōsis*). NT writers prefer the unusual compound word *apolytrōsis* for Christ's redemption of us from sin, perhaps as a way of underlining its extraordinary nature.

As we have seen, ransom was implicit in the blood sacrifices' liberating people from their sins. "For the life of the flesh is in the blood, and I have given it to you on the altar to ransom your lives; for it is the blood that ransoms by means of the life" (Lev 17:11). Moreover, for certain sacrifices a monetary ransom might be substituted for an animal sacrifice as a means of atonement. It is noteworthy in passing that the ransom is paid to God to gain forgiveness and cleansing. God both supplies and receives the ransom that redeems us.

In the LXX *lytrōsis* words translate Hebrew words from three different groups: *g'l*, *pdh*, and *kpr*.[5] The first word group has to do with discharging familial obligations such as securing the release of persons

---

4 This bears out the truth of Dunn's remark: "Some who have overreacted against the traditional Reformation focus on justification have sought instead to replace it with a focus on participation. . . . however, what has been too quickly passed over is the fact that Paul held *together* these two ways of conceptualizing the process of salvation" (James D. G. Dunn, "New Perspective View," in *Justification: Five Views*, ed. James K. Beilby and Paul Rhodes Eddy, assoc. ed. Steven E. Eenderlein [Downers Grove, Ill.: IVP Academic, 2011], 176–201).

5 See discussion in Leon Morris, *The Atonement: Its Meaning and Significance* (Downers Grove, Ill.: InterVarsity, 1983), 11–18.

or property by means of a payment. The second group has to do with nonfamilial situations in which money is freely paid to redeem a person or animal. The third group is used for ransom payments that anyone might make for his deliverance, such as the blood sacrifices. All three word groups are used with respect to God's redemption of His people (e.g., Exod 6:6; Neh 1:10; Isa 43:3-4). The LORD is called Israel's Redeemer, and His great redemptive act in the OT is the Exodus signaled by the Passover. In the case of God's redemptive activity, no ransom payment seems to be involved. Although Morris tries to find the analogue of a ransom price in God's case in the effort it costs Him to liberate Israel, he is probably straining too hard to import a ransom price into the picture. God is, after all, almighty, and He does not pay anything to anyone for Israel's manumission. In the case of Christ's redeeming us, however, a price is very clearly present: our liberation comes at the cost of his blood, his life.

As we have seen, Jesus described his mission as giving his life as "a ransom for many" (Mark 10:45). His life served as a payment for our liberation from sin's captivity. Similarly, NT authors did not think of our redemption as costless: "you were ransomed . . . with the precious blood of Christ, like that of a lamb without blemish" (1 Pet 1:18-19); "In him we have redemption through his blood" (Eph 1:7); Christ offered "his own blood, thus securing an eternal redemption" (Heb 9:12). Paul could therefore remind the Corinthians, "You were bought with a price" (1 Cor 6:20; 7:23).

The author of Hebrews echoes Jesus' words at the Last Supper in seeing his redemptive death as inaugurating a new covenant and forgiveness of sins: "he is the mediator of a new covenant, . . . since a death has occurred which redeems them from the transgressions under the first covenant" (Heb 9:15). In Revelation 5:9-10 John describes his vision of worship of the exalted sacrificial lamb:

> "You are worthy to take the scroll
>   and to open its seals,
> for you were slaughtered and by your blood you ransomed for God
>   saints from every tribe and language and people and nation;
> you have made them to be a kingdom and priests serving our God,
>   and they will reign on earth."

Thus is fulfilled the frustrated intention of the old covenant: "You shall be for me a priestly kingdom and a holy nation" (Exod 19:6).

A biblically adequate atonement theory must therefore include as one facet the way in which Christ's death serves to set us free from sin and its consequences. Christ's life, sacrificed on our behalf, will be that which serves to ransom us from bondage.

CONCLUDING REMARKS

In part 1 of this work, we have surveyed some of the principal motifs that constitute the biblical doctrine of the atonement. We have seen that the most important motif is sacrifice, the interpretation of Jesus' death as a sacrificial offering to God. On the pattern of the Passover and Levitical sacrifices described in the OT, Christ's death serves the twin purposes of expiating our sin and propitiating God. Divine forgiveness is thus won by Christ's sacrificial death on our behalf. We are cleansed and God is satisfied. More than that, the NT writers see Christ's sacrifice as truly efficacious and final. Animal sacrifices need no longer be offered. Indeed, they were not really efficacious to begin with but were a provisional arrangement graciously instituted by God until Christ should come. His decisive sacrifice is now sufficient for the sins of all persons throughout history.

Scarcely less important is the NT identification of Jesus with the suffering Servant of the LORD described in Isaiah 53. Here Christ's substitutionary suffering, already implicit in the Levitical animal sacrifices, comes sharply to the fore. Christ, though innocent and righteous, becomes our sin-bearer, that is at least to say, he endures the punishment that is our just desert for sin. The death that we deserve he suffers, that we might be freed from our liability to punishment and be constituted righteous by him. In dying in our place to pay the penalty of our sin, he inaugurates a new covenant between God and man, a universal covenant replete with the knowledge of God and the forgiveness of sins.

Christ's bearing the suffering that was our just desert satisfies God's justice. Propitiation of God's righteous wrath is at bottom a matter of the satisfaction of divine justice. As the righteous Judge and King, God does not blink at sin, even if in His mercy He stays for a time His judgment; rather, every sin receives its just desert. On the basis of Christ's satisfaction of the demands of divine justice, God can not merely forgive sinners but legally pardon them and declare them righteous before Him. Just as our sins are imputed to Christ, so God's righteousness is graciously imputed to us.

Finally, Christ acts as our representative before God. What he suffers we suffer because he acts on our behalf. His representation is universal in its scope but must be individually appropriated by personal faith in order to be efficacious. By placing our faith in him we come to appropriate the benefits of his death on our behalf. His life given in sacrifice to satisfy the demands of divine justice redeems us from sin's bondage and perdition and sets us free. Grace does not come cheap; it is costly.

Any adequate theory of the atonement, if it is to commend itself to us as a Christian atonement theory, must make peace with these biblical motifs. As we turn to survey the history of dogma regarding the doctrine of the atonement, we therefore do well to keep in mind Farmer's comment: "Some exegetes appear to . . . think of Christian doctrine as having come into being largely through church councils later in the history of the church. The truth is that Christian doctrine begins with biblical texts and with the earliest interpretations of those texts, which we find in the New Testament itself."[6] The adequacy of dogmatic theories of the atonement will need to be evaluated by those very biblical texts.

---

6   William R. Farmer, "Reflections on Isaiah 53 and Christian Origins," in Bellinger and Farmer, *Jesus and the Suffering Servant*, 275.

II

Dogmatic History of the Doctrine of the Atonement

Chapter 6

PATRISTIC THEORIES

INTRODUCTION

In part 2 of this work, we want to survey briefly some of the historically most influential theories of the atonement. We do not pretend to
survey adequately the history of the development of this doctrine; comprehensive histories have already been written.[1] Rather our aim is simply
to highlight some of the principal theories of the atonement that have
been offered throughout church history up until the modern period. An
understanding of these various accounts of the atonement will be helpful
to us as we seek in part 3 to articulate a philosophically coherent and
biblically adequate theory (or theories) of the atonement.

Embroiled as they were in Trinitarian and Christological controver-
sies concerning the *person* of Christ, the Church Fathers devoted little

---

1 Albrecht Ritschl, *A Critical History of the Christian Doctrine of Justification and Rec-
onciliation* (1870), trans. John S. Black (Edinburgh: Edmonton and Douglas, 1872);
Jean Rivière, *The Doctrine of the Atonement: A Historical Essay*, 2 vols., trans. Luigi
Cappadelta (London: Kegan Paul, Trench, Trübner, 1909), 1:27; Robert S. Franks,
A History of the Doctrine of the Work of Christ in Its Ecclesiastical Development, 2 vols.
(London: Hodder & Stoughton, 1918), 2:364–65; L. W. Grensted, *A Short History
of the Doctrine of the Atonement*, Theological Series 4 (Manchester: Manchester
University Press, 1920); Joseph F. Mitros, "Patristic Views of Christ's Salvific
Work," *Thought* 42, no. 3 (1967): 415–47; Gunther Wenz, *Geschichte der Versöhnung-
slehre in der evangelischen Theologie der Neuzeit*, 2 vols. (Munich: Chr. Kaiser, 1984).

time to reflection upon what later theologians were to call the *work* of Christ (e.g., his achieving atonement). The doctrine of the atonement therefore never occasioned the sort of controversy aroused by the Trinity and incarnation, with the result that no ecumenical council ever pronounced on the subject of the atonement, leaving the church without conciliar guidance.

When the Church Fathers did mention the atonement, their comments were brief and for the most part unincisive. Indeed, during this period there was no treatise of any Church Father devoted to the subject of the atonement. The church had to wait until Anselm's *Cur Deus homo?* in the eleventh century for a systematic exploration of the atoning significance of Christ's death. What remarks the Church Fathers did make on the subject of the atonement have to be culled from their biblical commentaries, where brief comments on the death of Christ are made, or from treatises devoted to wider topics like the incarnation, where asides might be made concerning the atonement.

The remarks of the Fathers on the atonement tend to reflect the multiplicity and diversity of the NT motifs concerning the atonement that the Fathers had inherited from the biblical authors. Hence, it would be inappropriate to ascribe to the Church Fathers any unified or developed theory of the atonement. All the NT motifs concerning atonement—sacrifice, substitutionary punishment, ransom, satisfaction, and so on—may be found in their pages.

EUSEBIUS

To illustrate the point, consider the description of Christ's passion given by Eusebius (260/5–339/40) in his *Demonstration of the Gospel*:

> The Lamb of God . . . was chastised on our behalf, and suffered a penalty He did not owe, but which we owed because of the multitude of our sins; and so He became the cause of the forgiveness of our sins, because He received death for us, and transferred to Himself the scourging, the insults, and the dishonour, which were due to us, and drew down on Himself the apportioned curse, being made a curse for us. And what is that but the price of our souls? And so the oracle says in our person: "By his stripes we were healed," and "The Lord delivered him for our sins." (10.1)

Echoing Isaiah 53 and Galatians 3:13, Eusebius employs the motifs of sacrifice, vicarious suffering, penal substitution, satisfaction of divine justice, and ransom price.

Eusebius rightly emphasizes Christ as a sacrificial offering to God for sins on the pattern of the OT Levitical animal sacrifices. In chapter 10 of book 1 he explains:

> While then the better, the great and worthy and divine sacrifice was not yet available for men, it was necessary for them by the offering of animals to pay a ransom for their own life, and this was fitly a life that represented their own nature. Thus did the holy men of old, anticipating by the Holy Spirit that a holy victim, dear to God and great, would one day come for men, as the offering for the sins of the world, believing that as prophets they must perform in symbol his sacrifice, and shew forth in type what was yet to be. But when that which was perfect was come . . . the former sacrifices ceased at once because of the better and true Sacrifice. (1.10)

Notice that Eusebius correctly construes the ransom as a sacrifice offered to God for sins. Christ is the sacrifice to end all sacrifices that was symbolized by the animal sacrifices. Eusebius also sees these sacrificial victims as substitutes for those who offer them. Quoting Leviticus 17:11, Eusebius comments that Moses

> says clearly that the blood of the victims slain is a propitiation in the place of human life. And the law about sacrifices suggests that it should be so regarded, if it is carefully considered. For it requires him who is sacrificing always to lay his hands on the head of the victim, and to bear the animal to the priest held by its head, as one offering a sacrifice on behalf of himself. Thus he says in each case: "He shall bring it before the Lord. And he shall lay his hands on the head of the gift." Such is the ritual in every case, no sacrifice is ever brought up otherwise. And so the argument holds that the victims are brought in place of the lives of them who bring them. (1.10)

Eusebius plausibly interprets the hand-laying ritual as indicative of the substitution of the animal for the offerer in its death. In the same way Christ is offered to God as a substitute for us, taking the death we deserve: "The great and precious ransom has been found for Jews and Greeks alike, the propitiation for the whole world, the life given for the life of all men, the pure offering for every stain and sin, the Lamb of God" (1.10). Eusebius even seems to affirm the imputation of our sins to Christ:

> The Lamb of God is made thus both sin and curse—sin for the sinners in the world, and curse for those remaining in all the things written in Moses' law. And so the Apostle says: "Christ has redeemed us from the

curse of the law, being made a curse for us"; and "Him that knew no sin, for our sakes he made sin." (1.10)

Eusebius' proof texts are, appropriately, Galatians 3:13 and 2 Corinthians 5:21. Christ therefore suffers the punishment for our sins:

> He then . . . branded on Him all our sins, and fastened on Him as well the curse that was adjudged by Moses' law, as Moses foretells: "Cursed is every one that hangeth on a tree." This He suffered "being made a curse for us; and making himself sin for our sakes." And then "He made him sin for our sakes who knew no sin," and laid on Him all the punishments due to us for our sins, bonds, insults, contumelies, scourging, and shameful blows, and the crowning trophy of the Cross. (1.10)

We thus find in Eusebius a faithful exposition of the multifaceted biblical teaching concerning Christ's atonement. Rivière observes that the two ideas of penal substitution and of expiatory sacrifice are conjoined in Eusebius, who in consequence is able to give the outlines of a legal theory of penal expiation. Although medieval scholastics will press deeper into the problem and will seek the reason for this substitution in the demands of divine justice, even in the early fourth century the doctrinal foundations were already laid.[2]

ORIGEN

Indeed, those foundations are already to be found in Origen (184/5–253/4), one of the most influential and seminal atonement theorists. His statements concerning Christ's atoning death also involve a rich mélange of motifs, including penal substitution and expiatory sacrifice. Like Eusebius after him, he interprets Christ's death as a sacrificial offering foreshadowed by the Levitical animal sacrifices. In his *Homilies on Numbers* he portrays Christ as a sacrificial lamb who not only propitiates God but also purifies mankind of sin (24.1.6–8). For sin is expiated through death, which is the prescribed penalty for sin: "Death which is inflicted as the penalty of sin is a purification of the sin itself for which it was ordered to be inflicted. Therefore, sin is absolved through the penalty of death and nothing remains which the day of judgment . . . will find for this offense" (*Homilies on Leviticus* 14.4.2). Animal victims, however, could not avail to cleanse mankind from sin; Christ alone "is one 'lamb' who was able to

---

2   Rivière, *Doctrine of the Atonement*, 1:196.

take away the sin of the entire world" (*Homilies on Numbers* 24.1.8). It is Christ's deity that makes his sacrifice uniquely efficacious for the expiation of the sins of mankind.

> But, what has never been related in any history, is that one suffered death for the whole world and that the whole world was cleansed by this sacrifice, whereas without such a sacrifice it must perforce have perished. Christ only could receive on the cross the burden of the sins of all; to carry this burden nothing short of His Divine might was required. (*Commentary on the Gospel of John* 28.18.19.[14])[3]

Notice that, according to Origen, apart from Christ's sacrifice the world would have necessarily perished. Origen, indeed, seems to think that the incarnation and sacrifice of Christ were necessary conditions of salvation from sin:

---

3   I cite Rivière's translation of the Greek text, which may be found in *Origines Werke*, vol. 2, *Der Johanneskommentar*, ed. Erwin Preuschen (Leipzig: J. C. Heinrich'sche Buchhandlung, 1903), 413. Cyril of Jerusalem (313–386) states the point even more forcefully in terms of Christ's righteousness:

> Christ took our sins "in his body upon the tree; that we, having died to sin," by His death "might live to justice." He who died for us was of no small worth; He was no material sheep; He was no mere man; He was more than an angel, He was God made man. The iniquity of sinners was not as great as the justice of Him who died for them; the sins we committed were not as great as he justice he wrought, who laid down His life for us. (*Catechesis* 13.33)

According to Rivière, we have here the first theological statement of the infinite superabundance of the satisfaction made by the God-man (Rivière, *Doctrine of the Atonement*, 1:200).

By contrast Basil (329/30–379) connects the necessity of Christ's deity not to the need to satisfy divine justice for sin but to the need of an unrefusable ransom offered the devil to purchase the release of his human captives:

> You stand in need of redemption. You have lost your freedom, being vanquished by the devil who holds you captive and will not let you loose save for a fitting ransom. Hence the ransom must be of a different kind and of much greater worth to compel the tyrant to yield up his captives. For this reason no one of your brothers could redeem you, for no man is able to make the devil deliver up what has once fallen into his hands. (*Homily on Psalm xlviii*.3; Rivière's translation)

> If there had not been sin, it had not been necessary for the Son of God
> to become a lamb, nor had need been that he, having become incarnate,
> should be slaughtered, but he would have remained what he was, God
> the Word; but since sin entered into this world, whilst the necessity of sin
> requires a propitiation, and a propitiation is not made but by a victim, it
> was necessary that a victim should be provided for sin. (*Homilies on Num-
> bers* 24.1.6)

According to this statement, God the Word would have remained in his
preincarnate state and would not have become a sacrificial victim had not
propitiation for sin been necessary (for salvation).

Notice that Christ's sacrificial death serves both to expiate sin by
discharging the penalty due for sin and to propitiate God by satisfying
the demands of divine justice:

> "God pre-determined him as a propitiation through faith in his blood."
> This means of course that through the sacrifice of himself he would make
> God propitious to men. . . . For God is just, and the one who is just could
> not justify the unjust; for that reason he wanted there to be the mediation
> of a propitiator so that those who were not able to be justified through
> their own works might be justified through faith in him. (*Commentary on
> the Epistle to the Romans* 3.8.1)

At the foundation of Origen's atonement doctrine lie the demands of
divine justice, which prescribed the just desert for sin and which must
be satisfied if forgiveness of sin is to be available.

Since the prescribed punishment for sin is death and God's justice
must be satisfied, Christ, like the Servant of Isaiah 53, bears in our place
the punishment that was our just desert:

> He bared His back to the scourges and gave His cheeks to be buffeted, nor
> did He recoil before being spat upon; we it was who had deserved these
> outrages; He delivered us by Himself suffering for us. He did not die to
> withdraw us from death, but that we might not have to die for ourselves.
> He allowed Himself to be buffeted for us that we who had deserved such
> handling might not suffer this for our sins, but that suffering all things for
> justice sake we might receive them all with joy. (*Commentary on the Gospel
> of Matthew*, Series 113)[4]

---

4 This reference is to the Latin translation of Origen's *Commentary on the Gospel
of Matthew*, which extends beyond the extant Greek text. These Latin editions
have not been divided into books but into 140 chapters or "series." The English

Christ could be punished for our sins because our sins were imputed to him. Origen expressed with shocking boldness the imputation of our sins to Christ. Explaining in his *Commentary on the Gospel of John* that "darkness is brought upon men by their evil deeds," Origen denies that 1 John 1:5 "God is light, and in Him there is no darkness" can be truly said of Christ the Savior.

> Could it not be said of Him also that He is light, and that there is no darkness in Him? . . . [I]f God made Christ who knew no sin to be sin for us, then it could not be said of Him that there was no darkness in Him. For if Jesus was in the likeness of the flesh of sin and for sin, and condemned sin by taking upon Him the likeness of the flesh of sin, then it cannot be said of Him, absolutely and directly, that there was no darkness in Him. We may add that He took our infirmities and bare our sicknesses, both infirmities of the soul and sicknesses of the hidden man of our heart. On account of these infirmities and sicknesses which He bore away from us, He declares His soul to be sorrowful and sore troubled, and He is said in Zechariah to have put on filthy garments, which, when He was about to take them off, are said to be sins. Behold, it is said, I have taken away your sins. Because He had taken on Himself the sins of the people of those who believed in Him, he uses many such expressions as these: Far from my salvation are the words of my transgressions, and You know my foolishness, and my sins were not hid from You. (2.21)

Since our sins are imputed to Christ, there is darkness in Christ after all, despite his deity. Origen quickly adds, "Let no one suppose that we say this from any lack of piety towards the Christ of God; for as the Father alone has immortality and our Lord took upon Himself, for His love to men, the death He died for us, so to the Father alone the words apply, 'In Him is no darkness,' since Christ took upon Himself, for His goodwill towards men, our darknesses" (2.21). Our sins imputed to him, Christ bears the punishment that our sins deserve, thereby expiating sin and propitiating God, satisfying divine justice and obtaining for us God's forgiveness of our sins.

---

translation cited is from Rivière; the Latin text may be found in *Origenes Werke: Die Griechischen Christlichen Schriftsteller der ersten drei Jahrhunderte*, vol. 11, *Origenes Matthäuserklärung*, ed. Ernst Benz and Erich Klostermann (Leipzig: J. C. Heinrich'sche Buchhandlung, 1933), 235. I am indebted to Ronald Heine for guidance through the maze of Origen texts.

Origen was not alone in affirming the imputation of our sins to Christ and his substitutionary punishment for our sins. No clearer statement is to be found among the Church Fathers of the imputation of sin and substitutionary punishment than that of John Chrysostom (349–407). "For all the outrages which we heaped on Him in return for His benefits, He not only did not punish us, but gave us His Son. He made Him to be sin for us—that is, He allowed Him to be condemned as a sinner and die as one accursed. He made Him to be a sinner and sin, who, far from having committed sin, knew no guile" (*Homilies on II Corinthians*, homily 11).[5] Christ was punished, then, for our sins: "God was about to punish them, but He forbore to do it. They were about to perish, but in their stead He gave His own Son" (*Homilies on I Timothy*, homily 7.3). Chrysostom provides this striking illustration: "A king, beholding a robber and malefactor under punishment, gave his well-beloved son, his only-begotten and true, to be slain; and transferred the death and the guilt as well, from him to his son, (who was himself of no such character), that he might both save the condemned man and clear him from his evil reputation" (*Homilies on II Corinthians*, homily 1). Notice that both the guilt itself and the penalty for it (death) are laid on Christ.

Along with the motif of sacrifice, Origen wants to include the motif of redemption in his doctrine of the atonement. But instead of thinking of redemption in terms of a sacrificial offering, Origen thinks of it as a ransom payment to the enemy who held us captive.

> Let us look carefully at the meaning of "redemption which is in Christ Jesus." The term "redemption" refers to that which is given to enemies for those whom they are keeping in captivity, in order that they might restore them to their original freedom. Captives conquered by sin, as if by war, were being held fast, then, by the enemies of the human race. The Son of God . . . gave himself as the redemption price, that is to say, he handed himself over to the enemies and, what is more, poured out his own blood to those thirsting for it. (*Commentary on the Epistle to the Romans* 3.7.14)

Origen thinks that Christ's human soul was a ransom payment made to Satan to gain our release:

> But to whom did he give his soul a ransom for many? Certainly not to God. Was it perhaps, then, to the evil one? For he had power over us until the soul of Jesus was given to him as our ransom. He was deceived of

---

5   I cite Rivière's translation.

course and imagined that he could have power over it. He did not see that he could not apply torture to constrain it. Therefore, "death," although it thought it had power over "him, no longer had power" over him who alone was free "among the dead" and stronger than the power of death [Rom 6:9; Ps 87:5]. He was so much stronger that all those held by death who wished to follow him were able to be free. Death no longer had any power against them at all, for death cannot assail anyone who is with Jesus. (*Commentary on the Gospel of Matthew* XVI. 8)[6]

Origen never integrated these motifs of ransom and sacrifice into a systematic unity. In his commentary on Romans, after speaking of Christ as a ransom payment, Origen does proceed to speak of Christ as not only ransom but sacrifice, saying:

> For above [Paul] had said that Christ had given his very self as the redemption price for the entire human race so that he might redeem those who were being held in the captivity of their sins. . . . Now he has added something even more profound and says, "God pre-determined him as a propitiation through faith in his blood." This means of course that through the sacrifice of himself he would make God propitious to men and through this he would manifest his own righteousness as he forgives them their past sins. (*Commentary on the Epistle to the Romans* 2.8.1)

A long, interesting discussion of the mercy seat follows. Origen concludes that Christ is at once "the propitiatory and priest and sacrifice which is offered for the people." Because "he is a sacrifice, propitiation

---

6 Book 16 has not yet been published in English, but a provisional translation has recently been posted online (https://reseminary.academia.edu/JustinGohl). I cite here with gratitude from Ronald Heine's translation of the entire commentary (*The Commentary of Origen on the Gospel of St. Matthew*, 2 vols., Oxford Early Christian Texts [Oxford: Oxford University Press, 2018]), which he allowed me to read in manuscript. The Greek text may be found in *Origenes Werke: Die Griechischen Christlichen Schriftsteller der ersten drei Jahrhunderte*, vol. 10, *Origenes Matthäuserklärung*, ed. Ernst Benz and Erich Klostermann (Leipzig: J. C. Heinrich'sche Buchhandlung, 1935), 498–99.

    Again:

> If then we have been bought at a price, as Paul also confirms, undoubtedly we were bought from someone whose slaves we were, who also demanded the price he wanted so that he might release from his authority those whom he was holding. Now it was the devil who was holding us, to whom we had been dragged off by our sins. Therefore he demanded the blood of Christ as the price for us. (*Commentary on the Epistle to the Romans* 2.13.29)

is effected by the shedding of his own blood for the forgiveness of past sins" (2.8.11). How this fits with Christ as a ransom paid to Satan remains obscure. They appear as two largely independent aspects of Origen's multifaceted atonement theory.

Underlying Origen's ransom approach is a view stemming from Irenaeus (d. 202) that Satan had certain legal rights over man in virtue of his sinning that God, as perfectly just, had to respect. Though God could have ripped man from Satan's clutches by force, says Irenaeus, He freed man instead by rational persuasion, offering Christ in exchange for man.

> The Word, who is perfect in all things, as the mighty Word, and very man, who, redeeming us by His own blood in a manner consonant to reason, gave Himself as a redemption for those who had been led into captivity. And since the apostasy tyrannized over us unjustly, and, though we were by nature the property of the omnipotent God, alienated us contrary to nature, rendering us its own disciples, the Word of God, powerful in all things, and not defective with regard to His own justice, did righteously turn against that apostasy, and redeem from it His own property, not by violent means, as the [apostasy] had obtained dominion over us at the beginning, when it insatiably snatched away what was not its own, but by means of persuasion, as became a God of counsel, who does not use violent means to obtain what He desires; so that neither should justice be infringed upon, nor the ancient handiwork of God go to destruction. (*Against Heresies* 5.1)

What Satan did not realize was that Christ, as the second person of the Trinity, could not be held by him. Raising Christ from the dead, God defeated Satan, leaving him without captives. Irenaeus explains:

> But inasmuch as God is invincible and long-suffering, He did indeed show Himself to be long-suffering in the matter of the correction of man and the probation of all, as I have already observed; and by means of the second man did He bind the strong man, and spoiled his goods, and abolished death, vivifying that man who had been in a state of death. For at the first Adam became a vessel in his [Satan's] possession, whom he did also hold under his power, that is, by bringing sin on him iniquitously, and under colour of immortality entailing death upon him. For, while promising that they should be as gods, which was in no way possible for him to be, he wrought death in them: wherefore he who had led man captive, was justly captured in his turn by God; but man, who had been led captive, was loosed from the bonds of condemnation. (3.23)

Gregory of Nyssa (335–395), who followed Origen closely in matters of the atonement, went even further by emphasizing that men had freely sold themselves into slavery to Satan; hence, Satan's right over man must be respected (*Catechetical Oration* 22). Still, Satan was a deceiver, and so it was just of God to deceive Satan in return. By his incarnation the Son appeared an attractive hostage in exchange for the human beings under Satan's sway. Gregory offered a popular illustration of God's clever deception of Satan: "In order to secure that the ransom in our behalf might be easily accepted by him who required it, the Deity was hidden under the veil of our nature, that so, as with ravenous fish, the hook of the Deity might be gulped down along with the bait of flesh" (24). Only after the captives had been freed did the Son manifest his divine power by rising from the dead, breaking the bonds of death and hell and escaping from Satan's power.

In expressing Christ's triumph over the forces of evil, Origen echoes the apostle Paul:

> He . . . blotted out the written bond that was against us by His own blood, and took it out of the way, so that not even a trace, not even of our blotted-out sins, might still be found, and nailed it to His cross; who having put off from Himself the principalities and powers, made a show of them openly, triumphing over them by His cross. And we are taught to rejoice when we suffer afflictions in the world, knowing the ground of our rejoicing to be this, that the world has been conquered and has manifestly been subjected to its conqueror. (*Commentary on the Gospel of John* 6.37)

This emphasis on Christ's achieving victory over sin, death, and the devil has come to be known as the *Christus Victor* theory of the atonement.[7] Modern scholars have tended to focus on this facet of the Fathers' teaching, doubtless because of its peculiarity and curiosity. According to this theory the sacrifice of Christ's life served to deliver mankind from bondage to Satan and from the corruption and death that are the consequences of sin. Sometimes, as in Origen's case, the Fathers interpreted Jesus' ransom saying very literally to mean that Christ's life was a payment to Satan in exchange for human beings.

---

7   Gustaf Aulén, *Christus Victor: An Historical Study of the Three Main Types of the Idea of the Atonement*, trans. A. G. Herbert (New York: Macmillan, 1969).

But not everyone agreed with Origen's ransom model.[8] A different version of the *Christus Victor* theory is to be found, especially among the Latin Fathers, according to which Christ was not given as a ransom to Satan but rather was the victim of Satan's unjust and deadly attack. Often confused with the ransom model, this so-called political model of *Christus Victor* attributes Satan's undoing to an overreach of authority on the devil's part. As on the ransom model, Satan was conceived to have, by God's permission, right of bondage over sinners. Thinking Christ to be vulnerable human flesh, Satan attacked and killed Christ. But unlike the sinners under Satan's authority, who deserved the punishments inflicted by him, Christ was entirely guiltless and therefore undeserving of death. Satan had thus acted unjustly in slaying Christ, so that God was justified in liberating those who are united with Christ by faith.

---

8   Gregory Nazianzus (329–390), for example, sharply denounces the notion that Christ's death is a ransom paid either to Satan or to God. "Now, since a ransom belongs only to him who holds in bondage, I ask to whom was this offered, and for what cause? If to the Evil One, fie upon the outrage! If the robber receives ransom, not only from God, but a ransom which consists of God Himself, and has such an illustrious payment for his tyranny, a payment for whose sake it would have been right for him to have left us alone altogether. But if to the Father, I ask first, how? For it was not by Him that we were being oppressed" (*Orations* 45.22). Rather, the motif of ransom should be interpreted to mean that Christ offered himself as a sacrifice to God, "so as to snatch us from him who had us in his power, so that, in exchange for him who fell, he might take the Christ" (*Against Apollinarius* 69–72).

Gregory has a strong emphasis on both the imputation of our sins to Christ and on the inclusionary nature of Christ's suffering:

> But look at it in this manner: that as for my sake He was called a curse, Who destroyed my curse; and sin, who taketh away the sin of the world; and became a new Adam to take the place of the old, just so He makes my disobedience His own as Head of the whole body. . . . It was not He who was forsaken either by the Father, or by His own Godhead, as some have thought, as if It were afraid of the Passion, and therefore withdrew Itself from Him in His Sufferings (for who compelled Him either to be born on earth at all, or to be lifted up on the Cross?) But as I said, He was in His own Person representing us. For we were the forsaken and despised before, but now by the Sufferings of Him Who could not suffer, we were taken up and saved. Similarly, He makes His own our folly and our transgressions. (*Orations* 30.5)

AUGUSTINE

Augustine (354–430) is a paradigmatic proponent of this political version of the *Christus Victor* theory, which, in Augustine's hands, integrates, in a way not found in Origen, the motifs of sacrifice and redemption. In his treatise *On the Trinity* Augustine explains:

> He made a show of principalities and powers, openly triumphing over them in Himself. For whereas by His death the one and most real sacrifice was offered up for us, whatever fault there was, whence principalities and powers held us fast as of right to pay its penalty, He cleansed, abolished, extinguished; and by His own resurrection He also called us whom He predestinated to a new life; and whom He called, them He justified; and whom He justified, them He glorified. And so the devil, in that very death of the flesh, lost man, whom he was possessing as by an absolute right, seduced as he was by his own consent, and over whom he ruled. (4.13.16)

We see here the affirmation of the devil's right over man, in consequence of man's freely chosen sins.[9] So Augustine emphasizes repeatedly that Christ's victory over Satan was won not through an exercise of raw power but by righteousness. "It pleased God, that in order to the rescuing of man from the grasp of the devil, the devil should be conquered, not by power, but by righteousness" (13.13.17). To be sure, the devil is also conquered by the power of Christ's resurrection, but Christ's conquering through righteousness is first and foremost: "He conquered the devil first by righteousness, and afterwards by power: namely, by righteousness, because He had no sin, and was slain by him most unjustly; but by power, because having been dead He lived again, never afterwards to die" (13.14.18).

This raises the question, "What, then, is the righteousness by which the devil was conquered?" The answer: "What, except the righteousness

---

9 Our bondage in sin is connected especially to Adam's original sin, in virtue of which we his progeny stand condemned. "By the justice of God in some sense, the human race was delivered into the power of the devil; the sin of the first man passing over originally into all of both sexes in their birth through conjugal union, and the debt of our first parents binding their whole posterity" (*On the Trinity* 13.12.16). Augustine adds, "The way in which man was thus delivered into the power of the devil, ought not to be so understood as if God did this, or commanded it to be done; but that He only permitted it, yet that justly" (13.12.16). Cf. Augustine, *Enchiridion* 14.48.

of Jesus Christ?" (*On the Trinity* 13.14.18). The further question then arises: "And how was he conquered?" Augustine answers:

> Because, when he found in Him nothing worthy of death, yet he slew Him. And certainly it is just, that we whom he held as debtors, should be dismissed free by believing in Him whom he slew without any debt. In this way it is that we are said to be justified in the blood of Christ. For so that innocent blood was shed for the remission of our sins. (13.14.18)

The initial answer, more superficial, seems to be that Christ conquered through righteousness in that he, being righteous, was unjustly treated by Satan. But this answer would not suffice to explain how we are freed from our just desert and forgiven of our sins by believing in him. The deeper answer is therefore that "innocent blood was shed for the remission of our sins."

Here we connect with a second motif in the passage cited above, that Christ was "the one and most real sacrifice offered up for us."[10] The principalities and powers could justly demand our death as the "penalty" for sin. But Christ's innocent death was undeserved and could therefore serve as a sacrifice that removes sin and obviates its penalty: "We, indeed, came to death through sin; He through righteousness: and, therefore, as our death is the punishment of sin, so His death was made a sacrifice for sin" (*On the Trinity* 4.12.15). God's love is proved in that Christ should, "without any evil desert of His own, bear our evils" (13.10.13).

In his treatise *Against Faustus* Augustine makes explicit his affirmation of Christ's being substitutionally punished. He says, "Christ, though guiltless, took our punishment, that He might cancel our guilt, and do away with our punishment" (14.4). He interprets Galatians 3:13 to mean by "curse" the punishment of death that is due for sin:

> As He died in the flesh which He took in bearing our punishment, so also, while ever blessed in His own righteousness, He was cursed for our offenses, in the death which He suffered in bearing our punishment. . . . The believer in the true doctrine of the gospel will understand that Christ is not reproached by Moses when he speaks of Him as cursed, not in His divine majesty, but as hanging on the tree as our substitute, bearing our punishment. (14.6–7)

---

10 See further *On the Trinity* 4.14.19 on sacrifice.

Augustine says, "The curse is pronounced by divine justice, and it will be well for us if we are redeemed from it. Confess then that Christ died, and you may confess that He bore the curse for us" (14.7). So in *On the Trinity* Augustine characterizes Christ's atoning death as "a hidden and exceeding mysterious decree of divine and profound justice" (4.12.15).

It is interesting that Augustine seems to affirm Christ's penal substitution without imputation of sin to Christ. In *Against Faustus* he says to his opponent, "Confess that he died, and you may also confess that he, without taking our sin, took its punishment" (14.7). Perhaps he is here speaking *ex concessis*. But elsewhere he says, "By taking on your punishment, while not taking on your guilt, he canceled both guilt and punishment."[11] But he seems to be of two minds on the issue, for he qualifies his statement by adding, "and if he did take it on, he took it on in order to cancel it, not to commit it" (*Sermons* 171.3). Since everyone would agree that Christ did not commit sin, Augustine's *prima facie* claim that Christ assumed punishment but not guilt would seem to imply a doctrine of penal substitution without imputation.

As a result of Christ's sacrificial death, we are delivered from Satan: "If, therefore, the commission of sins through the just anger of God subjected man to the devil, doubtless the remission of sins through the merciful reconciliation of God rescues man from the devil" (*On the Trinity* 13.12.16).[12] Therefore, "he who even slew Christ for a time by a death which was not due, can as his due detain no one who has put on Christ, in the eternal death which was due" (13.16.20).[13]

Comparing the conquering of Satan by power and by righteousness, Augustine reflects:

---

11 According to Franks, the sentence "Suscipiendo poenam et non suscipiendo culpam et culpam delevit et poenam" is frequently repeated with slight variations in Augustine's writings (Robert S. Franks, *A History of the Doctrine of the Work of Christ in Its Ecclesiastical Development*, 2 vols. [London: Hodder & Stoughton, 1918], 1:126). See, e.g., Augustine, *The Merits and Forgiveness of Sins* 1.61, where he says that Christ transferred to his own flesh death but not sin.

12 "He, being Himself put to death, although innocent, by the unjust one acting against us as it were by just right, might by a most just right overcome him, and so might lead captive the captivity wrought through sin, and free us from a captivity that was just on account of sin, by blotting out the handwriting, and redeeming us who were to be justified although sinners, through His own righteous blood unrighteously poured out" (Augustine, *On the Trinity* 4.13.16).

13 By contrast anyone who has not put on Christ remains subject to damnation (Augustine, *Enchiridion* 14.51).

> It is not then difficult to see that the devil was conquered, when he who
> was slain by Him rose again. It is something more, and more profound of
> comprehension, to see that the devil was conquered when he thought him-
> self to have conquered, that is, when Christ was slain. For then that blood,
> since it was His who had no sin at all, was poured out for the remission of
> our sins; that, because the devil deservedly held those whom, as guilty
> of sin, he bound by the condition of death, he might deservedly loose them
> through Him, whom, as guilty of no sin, the punishment of death unde-
> servedly affected. (*On the Trinity* 13.15.19)

Here we find that integration of the motifs of redemption and penal
substitution that was wanting in Origen. Christ bore undeservedly the
punishment of sin that we deserved, namely, death, so that by his death
our sins are remitted. This is how he through righteousness achieves victory over the devil. Augustine muses that God's power is more greatly
manifested by raising Christ from death than by preventing his death;
but that is not the reason why God permitted Satan to so afflict Christ.
"But the reason is really a different one why we are justified in the blood
of Christ, when we are rescued from the power of the devil through
the remission of sins: it pertains to this, that the devil is conquered by
Christ by righteousness, not by power" (13.14.18). Thus, Augustine won-
derfully confesses Christ as "both Victor and Victim, and therefore Victor, because the Victim" (*Confessions* 10).

Augustine also interacts with an interesting objection to his view.
On the one hand, prior to sending the Son, God is wrathful with us and
needs to be reconciled to us by the death of His Son; on the other hand,
it is through the Father's love that the Son is sent in the first place. "In
the one, the Son dies for us, and the Father is reconciled to us by His
death; in the other, as though the Father first loved us, He Himself on
our account does not spare the Son, He Himself for us delivers Him up
to death" (*On the Trinity* 13.11.15). How is this paradox to be resolved?
Augustine's answer serves to underline the importance of the satisfaction
of divine justice. He explains that the wrath of God "is nothing else but
just retribution. For the wrath of God is not, as is that of man, a perturbation of the mind" (13.16.20).[14]

---

14 Cf. Augustine's statement:

> Since men are in this state of wrath through original sin—a condition
> made still graver and more pernicious as they compounded more and
> worse sins with it—a Mediator was required; that is to say, a Reconciler
> who by offering a unique sacrifice, of which all the sacrifices of the Law

If, therefore, the just retribution of God has received such a name, what can be the right understanding also of the reconciliation of God, unless that then such wrath comes to an end? Neither were we enemies to God, except as sins are enemies to righteousness; which being forgiven, such enmities come to an end, and they whom He Himself justifies are reconciled to the Just One. And yet certainly He loved them even while still enemies, since He spared not His own Son, but delivered Him up for us all, when we were still enemies. (13.16.20)

The wrath of God is not hatred but retributive justice. God loves even those who are justly condemned before Him and so sends His Son to redeem them.

One of the most interesting features of the *Christus Victor* theory espoused by Augustine is his conviction, shared by many Fathers, that Christ's incarnation and death were not necessary for man's redemption. God could have liberated mankind by a simple exercise of divine power. Not everyone agreed, however. Origen, as we have seen, seemed to think the satisfaction of God's justice necessary for man's redemption and salvation.[15] Gregory of Nyssa connected the necessity of Christ's passion

---

and the Prophets were shadows, should allay that wrath. Thus the apostle says, "For if, when we were enemies, we were reconciled to God by the death of his Son, even more now being reconciled by his blood we shall be saved from wrath through him." However, when God is said to be wrathful, this does not signify any such perturbation in him as there is in the soul of a wrathful man. His verdict, which is always just, takes the name "wrath" as a term borrowed from the language of human feelings. (*Enchiridion* 10.33)

15 Similarly, Cyril of Alexandria holds that in virtue of His goodness, God would necessarily save man from sin and death:

For it was necessary that God, who is also good, come to the aid of those who had been utterly ruined, and reveal the malice of the devil as powerless. . . . [W]hat, therefore, was it then necessary for the creator of all things to do? To allow impure demons to rule those on earth, and the malice of the devil to overpower God's wishes? To not save those into danger? To fail to extend his salvific hand to those brought to the ground? To not transfer to a better state those seized by great shame? To not illuminate the mind from things in darkness? To not turn back what went astray? Then how would he be good, if, though it was possible for him to do these things—and with no effort at all!—he decided to pay no heed to us? For why, in short, did he even bring us into being and life in the first place, if he was not going to have mercy on us who have undergone sufferings without any hope and who acted so wretchedly?

not to the need to satisfy divine justice but to the need of a ransom offered the devil to purchase the release of his human captives. Gregory discusses at some length the following objection:

> For if . . . there is such power in Him that both the destruction of death and the introduction of life resides in Him, why does He not effect His purpose by the mere exercise of His will, instead of working out our salvation in such a roundabout way, by being born and nurtured as a man, and even, while he was saving man, tasting death; when it was possible for Him to have saved man without subjecting Himself to such conditions? (*Catechetical Oration* 17)

Gregory's response appeals crucially to God's justice, which required His payment of a ransom to the one who rightly held men in bondage, if they were to be freed:

> What, then, under the circumstances is justice? It is not exercising any arbitrary sway over him who has us in his power, nor, by tearing us away by a violent exercise of force from his hold, thus leaving . . . a just complaint to him who enslaved men. . . . [T]hey who have bartered away their freedom for money are the slaves of those who have purchased them. . . . [I]f any one out of regard for the person who has sold himself should use violence against him who has bought him, he will clearly be acting unjustly in thus arbitrarily rescuing one who has been legally purchased as a slave, whereas,

---

(*Contra Julianum* 8.36–37. My citation of this work is courtesy of Brad Boswell, whose translation of the work is unpublished; for the Greek, see Wolfram Kinzig and Thomas Brüggemann, eds., *Kyrill von Alexandrien: Werke*, vol. 1, *Gegen Julian*, book 2, *Buch 6–10 und Fragmente*, Die Griechischen Christlichen Schriftsteller der ersten Jahrhunderte, Neue Folge 21 [Berlin: Walter de Gruyter, 2017], 581–83)

Salvation in turn necessitated Christ's incarnation and death: "The Savior's object was to die for us, and to do this in order to destroy death. As the destruction of death was above the power of human nature it was necessary that the Word of God should take flesh" (*Ad reginas de recta fide, Oratio altera* 31. My citation of this untranslated work is from Rivière, *Doctrine of the Atonement*, 1:227; for the Greek, see J.-P. Migne, ed., *Patrologia Græca* [Paris, 1859], vol. 76, col. 1376). "By shedding his blood for us, Christ destroyed death and corruption. . . . Had he not died for us we should never have been saved and the cruel sovereignty of death would never have been abolished" (*Glaphyrorum in Exodum* 2.2. My citation of this untranslated work is also from Rivière, *Doctrine of the Atonement*, 1:226; for the Greek see J.-P. Migne, ed., *Patrologia Græca* [Paris: 1864], vol. 69, col. 437).

if he wishes to pay a price to get such a one away, there is no law to prevent that; on the same principle, now that we had voluntarily bartered away our freedom, it was requisite that no arbitrary method of recovery, but the one consonant with justice should be devised by Him Who in His goodness had undertaken our rescue. Now this method is in a measure this; to make over to the master of the slave whatever ransom he may agree to accept for the person in his possession. (22)

What ransom would induce Satan to relinquish his captives? The offer of Christ himself:

Therefore it was that the Deity was invested with the flesh, in order, that is, to secure that he [Satan], by looking upon something congenial and kindred to himself, might have no fears in approaching that supereminent power; and might yet by perceiving that power, showing as it did, yet only gradually, more and more splendour in the miracles, deem what was seen an object of desire rather than of fear. Thus you see how goodness was conjoined with justice, and how wisdom was not divorced from them. (23)

As Gregory's final comment makes clear, the redemption of mankind via the passion of Christ exhibits God's goodness, justice, and wisdom. "His choosing to save man is a testimony of His goodness; His making the redemption of the captive a matter of exchange exhibits His justice, while the invention whereby He enabled the Enemy to apprehend that of which he was before incapable, is a manifestation of supreme wisdom" (23).[16]

In contrast to this necessitarian perspective, Augustine speaks of "the other innumerable ways which He who is omnipotent could have employed to free us" (On the Trinity 13.16.20; cf. 13.10.13). Augustine asserts bluntly, "They are fools who say the wisdom of God could not

---

16 Since in Gregory's view these divine attributes are essential to God, if God in His goodness deigns to free man, He must do so in a way that is just and so respects the devil's rights over man. Gregory goes on to address explicitly the objection that the clever plan to deceive Satan, which God in His wisdom has chosen, is itself unjust in virtue of its being "in some measure a fraud" (Catechetical Oration 26). He also addresses the further objection that even if it were "absolutely necessary" for Christ to die, still he should not have been subjected to so ignominious a death as crucifixion, to which Gregory responds by citing not the need of an enticing ransom to the devil but the need of the healing of our nature (Catechetical Oration 32).

otherwise free men than by taking human nature, and being born of a woman, and suffering all that he did at the hands of sinners" (*On the Christian Struggle* 100.11). Given His omnipotence, God could have freed man from Satan's power directly. But God preferred to conquer Satan not by sheer power alone but by just means that respected Satan's "rights." The entire arrangement was freely chosen by God as most fitting. So the defense of Christ's passion as God's chosen means of salvation requires one to show "not indeed that no other mode was possible to God, to whose power all things are equally subject, but that there neither was, nor need have been, any other mode more appropriate for curing our misery" (*On the Trinity* 13.10.13). Augustine believes that no other mode of salvation would more effectively demonstrate how greatly God loves us, thereby giving us hope of immortality beyond our just deserts (13.10.13; cf. 13.14.18).

George Smeaton suggests that because the Church Fathers focused on the consequences of sin, principally death, rather than sin itself, they held that God in His omnipotence could redeem us without atonement. God freely chose to take on human nature in Christ as an appropriate way to deal with human mortality and death. But Christ's death was not required to satisfy the demands of God's inherent justice. "They separated God's free-will from the moral perfections of His nature—rectitude, wisdom, and goodness."[17] The statement needs to be qualified, however. As we have seen, when concerns of justice did come into play, it was often the devil's rights that were in the forefront, not the demands of God's retributive justice. In virtue of the necessity of dealing justly with the devil, *Christus Victor* theories of the atonement could be just as necessitarian in nature as Anselm's later satisfaction theory.

CONCLUDING REMARKS

The thoughts of the Church Fathers on the subject of Christ's atonement, sketchy and scattered as they are, exhibit that diversity of motifs found in the NT. The notion that the Fathers were singularly committed to a *Christus Victor* theory of the atonement is a popular misimpression generated by the secondary literature. A reading of the primary sources makes it clear that they were equally committed to the understanding

---

17 George Smeaton, *The Doctrine of the Atonement, as Taught by the Apostles* (Edinburgh: T&T Clark, 1870); repr. ed., *The Apostles' Doctrine of the Atonement* (Grand Rapids: Zondervan, 1957), 509.

of Christ's death as a sacrificial offering to God for human sins. Indeed, according to Joseph Mitros, by the fourth and fifth centuries in both the Latin West and the Greek East, "the sacrificial theory of salvation combined with the idea of penal substitution constituted the main stream of thinking."[18]

Rarely were these motifs integrated. In Augustine's poignant slogan *Victor quia Victima* we find the best expression of a systematic view of these diverse motifs. Christ conquers by his self-giving sacrifice. Augustine's synthesis illustrates effectively the truth that *Christus Victor* is not a stand-alone theory but an aspect or facet of a fuller account. Taken alone, *Christus Victor* not only ignores important NT atonement motifs, but it also fails of explanatory sufficiency, for it offers nothing to explain how God's vanquishing Satan achieves forgiveness of sin and reconciliation with God.

The *Christus Victor* theory or motif persisted for about nine hundred years, from Irenaeus and Origen until the time of Anselm. The medieval critique of the view was directed primarily against the notion of Satan's having rights over man. But it might be questioned whether that feature of the theory is essential. Fallen man's lying within Satan's power is certainly a biblical teaching (2 Tim 2:26; 1 John 5:19) and does not depend upon Satan's having any legitimate right over us. Already in the patristic period, versions of *Christus Victor* existed that did not center on payment of a ransom to Satan to gain sinners' release but on God's vanquishing Satan by means of Christ's passion, again a biblical teaching that is independent of Satan's having legitimate rights over fallen human beings (2 Cor 2:8; Col 2:15).

Modern critics, however, generally dismiss any role whatsoever for the devil in one's atonement theory. Since Satan is in modern thinking a mythological figure, obviously we cannot have been freed from bondage to him.[19] In any case, *Christus Victor* can still be a valuable facet of an atonement theory even without the devil. For redemption from our bondage to sin, death, and hell does not depend upon the reality of a

---

18 Mitros, "Patristic Views of Christ's Salvific Work," 437–38.

19 Insofar as such a dismissal is rooted in anti-supernaturalism, however, it is a prejudice of modernity to which the Christian theologian need not yield. See Alvin Plantinga's remarks on the plausibility of the existence of Satan and his cohorts with reference to Plantinga's Free Will Defense against the problem of evil in "Self-Profile," in *Alvin Plantinga*, ed. James E. Tomberlin and Peter van Inwagen, Profiles 5 (Dordrecht: D. Reidel, 1985), 43.

personal devil. Of course, the modern mind-set may be equally averse to notions of personal immortality and especially hell, but such compromises of biblical teaching can be resisted.[20] Anyone aspiring to articulate a biblically adequate atonement theory will want to include *Christus Victor* as a facet of that theory.

---

20 For a brief response to objections to the doctrine of eternal punishment, see J. P. Moreland and William Lane Craig, *Philosophical Foundations for a Christian Worldview*, 2nd ed. (Downers Grove, Ill.: InterVarsity, 2017), 631–33.

Chapter 7

Medieval Theories

INTRODUCTION

In turning to the medieval period, we remind ourselves that our aim is not to survey even the most prominent medieval thinkers regarding the atonement but to highlight theories of the atonement that came to prominence during this period. The most important of these is undoubtedly the so-called satisfaction theory of the atonement broached by Anselm of Canterbury.

SATISFACTION THEORY

Anselm's *Cur Deus homo* (1098) was the first systematic exploration of the doctrine of the atonement, a work of unsurpassed importance in the history of the doctrine and a watershed between the patristic and medieval periods. Although Anselm's comprehensive atonement theory incorporates major elements of the *Christus Victor* theory, including God's victory over Satan and even a rationale for His not achieving this victory directly (1.23; 2.19), the fundamental thrust of Anselm's theory is very different.

Anselm's main complaint about the *Christus Victor* theory is that it is on its own inadequate to explain why God would take the extraordinary step of sending His Son to suffer and die in order to redeem mankind. In contrast to *Christus Victor* theorists, Anselm argues that the salvation of mankind is about much more than defeating Satan. It is about making satisfaction to God for man's sins. And that necessitated the incarnation and suffering of Christ.

Anselm's satisfaction theory is unfortunately often misrepresented in the secondary literature. It is typically said by detractors that Anselm's fundamental concern is the restoration of God's honor, which has been besmirched by man's sin. Anselm is said to portray God as a sort of feudal monarch, whose wounded ego demands some satisfaction before the insult is forgiven. Since God would be all the greater if He magnanimously forgave the insult without demanding satisfaction, Anselm's theory fails to show that Christ's atoning death was necessary.[1]

---

1   This construal of Anselm's theory is intimately connected to the critique of Anselm leveled by classical liberal theologians like Adolf von Harnack and Albrecht Ritschl to the effect that Anselm thinks of God on the analogy of a private person involved in a personal legal dispute (Albrecht Ritschl, *A Critical History of the Christian Doctrine of Justification and Reconciliation*, trans. John S. Black [Edinburgh: Edmonston and Douglas, 1872], 30–31; Adolf Harnack, *Lehrbuch der Dogmengeschichte*, 4th ed., vol. 3, *Die Entstehung des kirchlichen Dogmas II, III* [Tübingen: J. C. B. Mohr, 1909], 408, who goes so far as to say that Anselm has turned the patristic devil into the Father!). This critique seems to have been inspired by Hugo Grotius' similar indictment of Faustus Socinus, to be discussed in the sequel, applied now to Anselm. The claim of the liberal theologians was that insofar as legal concepts are a part of Anselm's theory, they concern notions of private law, not public law, for example, a civil action brought by a creditor against a debtor. Since justice does not require the creditor to demand payment of the debt, he could simply forgive it if he wished. But Anselm's God demands payment.

   It is certainly true that Anselm speaks frequently of the infinite debt we humans owe to God, so that we do stand to Him in the relationship of debtor to creditor. But it is clear that for Anselm God is not like a private party to a personal dispute. God is the Ruler of a kingdom, and "it is not fitting for God to pass over anything in his kingdom undischarged" (*Cur Deus homo* 1.12). The just order of the universe would be disrupted were neither punishment of sin nor satisfaction for sin to occur. That is why God necessarily imposes punishment for sin in the absence of compensation: unlike a private person He cannot do otherwise, lest He be unjust. So with regard to the debate over whether God's honor is to be construed in terms of private law or public law categories, Gunther Wenz judges that the latter interpretation captures more adequately Anselm's intention "to uphold the public order of justice" (Gunther Wenz, *Geschichte der Versöhnungslehre in der evangelischen Theologie der Neuzeit*, 2 vols. [Munich: Chr. Kaiser, 1984], 2:47).

However, a careful reading of Anselm reveals that his fundamental concern is with God's essential justice and its moral demands. Sin is materially bringing dishonor to God, but the reason God cannot just overlook the offense is that it would be unjust to do so and thus would contradict God's very nature.

Anselm defines sin as the failure to render to God His due. What is God's due? It is that "Every wish of a rational creature should be subject to the will of God." Anselm says, "This is justice, or uprightness of will, which makes a being just or upright in heart, that is, in will; and this is the sole and complete debt of honor which we owe to God, and which God requires of us." So the honor we owe to God is to be just or upright in will. "He who does not render this honor which is due to God, robs God of his own and dishonors him; and this is sin" (*Cur Deus homo* 1.11).

So given the moral character of dishonoring God, Anselm asks "whether it were proper for God to put away sins by compassion alone,

---

Although the interpretation of Anselm in classical liberal theology still persists, Dietrich Korsch reports in a standard theological encyclopedia that it is now disfavored:

> The criticism of Anselm's doctrine of satisfaction has been multifaceted. Above all it has had to do with the legal relationship by which God knows Himself to be connected with the world and which He is, apparently, neither willing nor able to change. This criticism is mistaken, as more recent studies have shown (Kessler; Greshake; Steindl; Plasger). God is not thought of as an infinitely powerful but also arbitrary private person; rather, the legal relationship between God and man is public and encompasses the entire world and, therefore, cannot be changed at will. (*Theologische Realenzyklopädie*, ed. Gerhard Müller, vol. 35, *Vernunft III–Wiederbringung aller* [Berlin: Walter de Gruyter, 2003], s.v. "Versöhnung: Theologiegeschichtlich und dogmatisch," by Dietrich Korsch, 27)

Korsch's references are Hans Kessler, *Die theologische Bedeutung des Todes Jesu: Eine traditionsgeschichtliche Untersuchung* (Düsseldorf: Patmos-Verlag, 1970); Gisbert Greshake, *Gnade als konkrete Freiheit* (Mainz: Matthias-Grünewald-Verlag, 1972); Helmut Steindl, *Genugtuung: Biblische Versöhnungsdenken—eine Quelle für Anselms Satisfaktionstheorie?* Studia Friburgensia, NS 71 (Freiburg, Switzerland: Universitätsverlag, 1989); Georg Plasger, *Die Notwendigkeit der Gerechtigkeit: Eine Interpretation zu* "Cur Deus homo" *v. Anselm v. Canterbury*, Beiträge zur Geschichte und Philosophie des Mittelalters, NF 38 (Münster: Aschendorff, 1993).

Since we have not yet come to discuss Socinus and Grotius, we are getting rather ahead of ourselves in handling this interpretation of Anselm on the part of liberal theologians, and so our brief notice is confined to a footnote.

without any payment of the honor taken from him?" Anselm responds negatively: "To remit sin in this manner is nothing else than not to punish; and since it is not right [*recte*] to cancel sin without compensation or punishment; if it be not punished, then it is passed by undischarged" (*Cur Deus homo* 1.12). The concern here is not merely with propriety but with its being wrong to leave sin unpunished. The concern is justice. "Truly such compassion on the part of God is wholly contrary to the Divine justice, which allows nothing but punishment as the recompense of sin" (1.24). The fundamental problem, then, is not honor but justice. Anselm's primary concern, then, is ethical and not merely with insulted dignity.

It is intriguing that Anselm sees the relevance of a Divine Command Theory of ethics to his concern with justice. For on a Divine Command Theory, God does not have any duties to fulfill, since duties are constituted by divine imperatives, and God, presumably, does not issue commands to Himself. But if God is not bound by any moral duties, it makes no sense to speak of His acting unjustly. So, Anselm asks, since God is subject to no law and His will determines what is right, why does He, being supremely merciful, not just ignore the injury done to Him (*Cur Deus homo* 1.12)? In reply Anselm gives the correct response to the Euthyphro Dilemma: "There is nothing more just than supreme justice, which . . . is nothing else but God himself" (1.13). God is not at liberty to do "anything improper for the Divine character." Since "the nature of God" sets limits to divine liberty, "it does not belong to his liberty or compassion or will to let the sinner go unpunished" (1.12). "Therefore, as God cannot be inconsistent with himself, his compassion cannot be of this nature" (1.24). The character or nature of God Himself necessitates that He punish sin.

Anselm allows, in fact, two ways of meeting the demands of God's justice: punishment or compensation (*satisfactio*). Anselm defines compensation or satisfaction as "voluntary payment of the debt" (*Cur Deus homo* 1.19). There has been considerable scholarly debate about the roots of Anselm's notion of satisfaction.[2] Some detect the influence of Germanic law, which allowed for crimes to be pardoned in consideration of a voluntary pecuniary compensation which was not considered punitive. Other historians of doctrine have found the distinction between compensation and punishment already in Roman law and trace Anselm's

---

2 For literature and brief discussion see Wenz, *Geschichte der Versöhnungslehre*, 2:45–54.

notion of satisfaction to the sacrament of penance in the early church, where a satisfaction was required as a condition of reconciliation. However one decides this historical question, what is clear is that in Anselm's theory a satisfaction is not any kind of punishment. "Despite the divergent judgments of the tradition-historical provenance and character of the satisfaction concept," writes Wenz, "one can still establish an essential agreement that the background of the Anselmian doctrine of satisfaction displays the conception of a substitutionary work wrought by meritorious effort [*Vorstellung eines durch verdienstliche Leistung zu erbringenden Ersatzwerkes*] which is independent of the thought of bearing punishment."[3]

Anselm's theory ought therefore properly to be called the compensation theory of the atonement, since that is what a *satisfactio* was. It is natural for English-speaking readers to think that Anselm's theory is a satisfaction theory in the sense that a precondition of divine forgiveness of sins is the satisfaction of the demands of divine justice. But while that characterization fits Anselm's theory, it fails to state a sufficient condition for a theory's being correctly classified as a satisfaction theory in the Anselmian sense. For the Reformers also typically held that human salvation requires the satisfaction of divine justice, but this was achieved through substitutionary punishment, not compensation (*satisfactio*), so that their and Anselm's theories are quite distinct. What makes a theory a satisfaction theory in the Anselmian sense is the way in which the demands of divine justice are satisfied, namely, by compensation. The label "satisfaction theory" is now too deeply entrenched to change, so we must simply exercise care in using it and in speaking of the satisfaction of divine justice.

Anselm thus presents the atonement theorist with a choice: since the demands of divine justice must be met, there must be either punishment of or compensation for sin. Anselm chose the second alternative, since he naturally assumed that punishment would result in mankind's eternal damnation. By contrast, the later Protestant Reformers chose the first alternative, holding that Christ bore the punishment we deserved. Anselm and the Reformers are therefore on the same footing: for salvation to be possible, the demands of divine justice must somehow be met.

Anselm insists on compensation being made to God for the injustice done Him. But how can we render compensation to God? The difficulty

3 Wenz, *Geschichte der Versöhnungslehre*, 2:53–54; cf. 2:46.

we face in paying our debt, Anselm explains, is that there is nothing we can give to God by way of compensation for our sin, since we already owe Him total obedience. Our situation is compounded by the fact that in order to compensate God we need to give back more than we owed originally and by the gravity of our offense, having dishonored God, so that the debt we have incurred is of infinite proportion. So no one but God could pay a debt of such magnitude, but no one but man is obliged to pay it. It follows that our salvation requires that God become man. "If it be necessary, therefore, . . . that the heavenly kingdom be made up of men, and this cannot be effected unless the aforesaid satisfaction be made, which none but God can make and none but man ought to make, it is necessary for the God-man to make it" (*Cur Deus homo* 2.6).

Anselm affirms that in the incarnation of the second person of the Trinity, two complete natures are united in one person (*Cur Deus homo* 2.7). The gift that the incarnate Christ presents to God can be found in nothing other than him, and so he must give himself to God. Since Christ was sinless, he was under no obligation to die. By voluntarily laying down his life, he gives to God a gift of infinite value that he did not owe (2.11). On Anselm's view Christ does not die in our place or pay the penalty for our sins; rather, he offers a compensation to God on our behalf. When Anselm affirms that Christ "allowed himself to be slain for the sake of justice" (2.18b), one must keep in mind that the demands of justice can be satisfied by either punishment or compensation. Christ offers compensation.

How, then, does the gift of Christ's life win our salvation? Anselm says that divine justice requires God the Father to reward the Son for the gift of his life. But how can a reward be bestowed on someone who needs nothing and owes nothing? The Son therefore gives the reward to those for whose salvation he became incarnate. He remits the debt incurred by their sins and bestows on them the beatitude they had forfeited (*Cur Deus homo* 2.19). Anselm suggests that we become the beneficiaries of Christ's reward through "faith in the Gospel" and by making the Son an offering for ourselves with the love that he deserves (2.20).

Anselm's satisfaction theory was to exert a profound and enduring influence upon Christian theology, making it all the more remarkable that the Protestant Reformers were able to shake themselves loose from it. Subsequent medieval thinkers typically thought of Christ's atonement in terms of his making compensation to God on our behalf for the debt we had incurred through sin. Thomas Aquinas, for example, takes up Anselm's satisfaction theory as a part of his omnibus account of the atonement.[4] Christ's passion, he says, has a threefold effect: insofar as it frees us from the servitude of guilt, it acts by way of *redemption*; insofar as it reconciles us to God, it acts by way of *sacrifice*; and insofar as it liberates us from the debt of punishment, it acts by way of *satisfaction* (*Summa theologiae* 3.48.6 *ad* 3). In discussing whether Christ's passion brought about our salvation by way of satisfaction (*per modum satisfactionis*), Aquinas affirms that this is indeed the case: "He properly atones for an offense [*proprie satisfacit pro offensa*] who offers something which the offended one loves equally, or even more than he detested the offense. But by suffering out of love and obedience, Christ gave more to God than was required to compensate for the offense of the whole human race [*Deo exhibuit quam exigeret recompensatio totius offensae humani generis*]" (3.48.2). Though he quotes Isaiah 53:4, Aquinas does not explicate Christ's passion in terms of substitutionary punishment; rather, Christ's passion delivers us from the debt of punishment in that it was the "sufficient and superabundant satisfaction for the sins of the whole human race: but when sufficient satisfaction has been paid, then the debt of punishment is abolished" (3.49.3).[5]

---

4 Eleonore Stump attempts to differentiate Aquinas' doctrine of satisfaction from Anselm's, claiming that Aquinas did not see satisfaction as a precondition for God's forgiveness. But her interpretation is based on a conflation of Aquinas' views on the role of satisfaction in the sacrament of penance and its role in Christ's atonement. When it comes to atonement, Aquinas' view is the same as Anselm's:

> God's "severity" (cf. Rm. 11:22) is thereby shown, for He would not remit sin without penalty: and the Apostle indicates this when (Rm. 8:32) he says: "God spared not even His own Son." Likewise His "goodness" (Rm. 11:22) shines forth, since by no penalty endured could man pay Him enough satisfaction: and the Apostle denotes this when he says: "He delivered Him up for us all": and, again (Rm. 3:25): "Whom"—that is to say, Christ—God "hath proposed to be a propitiation through faith in His blood." (*Summa theologiae* 3.47.3; cf. 3.48.4)

In his discussion, Aquinas refers to Christ's passion as an expiatory sacrifice, a propitiation, a compensation for sin, a payment of the penalty for sin, as well as a satisfaction for sin, all preconditions of forgiveness. For a critique of Stump's interpretation of Aquinas' doctrine of satisfaction, see Nikolaus Breiner, "Punishment and Satisfaction in Aquinas's Account of the Atonement: A Reply to Stump," *Faith and Philosophy* 35, no. 2 (2018): 237–56.

5 As Breiner points out, Aquinas is quite willing to affirm that Christ bore the entire penalty for our sin and took upon himself the punishment we deserved (*Compendium theologiae* 227, 231; *Summa contra gentiles* 4.55.22), so that Breiner

Where Aquinas departs significantly from Anselm is with respect to the necessity of rendering satisfaction for our debt of punishment as a precondition of divine forgiveness and salvation. Aquinas reverts to the view of many of the Church Fathers that God could have simply remitted men's sins without satisfaction, had He so wished. Not merely that some other means of meeting the demands of divine justice could have been found apart from compensation—more radically, the demands of divine justice might simply have been waived. There is no necessity that God observe the order of divine justice that He has established requiring satisfaction for sin. "Even this justice depends on the Divine will, requiring satisfaction for sin from the human race. But if He had willed to free man from sin without any satisfaction, He would not have acted against justice" (*Summa theologiae* 3.46.2 *ad* 3).[6] God's choosing to save us by means of rendering satisfaction for the debt of punishment we owe was God's contingent choice.

God's contingent choice of requiring satisfaction for sin and of Christ's passion in particular as the means of satisfaction was not arbitrary but well motivated as the best way of achieving human salvation. Aquinas lists the numerous benefits of God's achieving salvation via Christ's passion:

------

takes Aquinas to endorse a theory of penal substitution (Breiner, "Punishment and Satisfaction," 252–53). But Aquinas never unites these motifs into a coherent theory; as a compiler he tends to adopt all the various motifs of his predecessors. According to Rivière, "Satisfaction always consists in a penalty—not of course in the penalty deserved by the guilty, but in a work which is troublesome to him who undertakes it" (Jean Rivière, *The Doctrine of the Atonement: A Historical Essay*, 2 vols., trans. Luigi Cappadelta [London: Kegan Paul, Trench, Trübner, 1909], 2:35). On this view Christ satisfies divine justice by offering a compensation to God that is (more than) equivalent to the harsh treatment which is the just desert of sinners. Aquinas' defense of one person's satisfying for another especially suggests this interpretation (*Summa contra gentiles* 4.55.22). Breiner suggests a synthesis according to which Christ bore the suffering which would have been our punishment, had it been inflicted on us (Nikolaus Breiner, "Penal Substitution, but Not Substitutionary Punishment: Aquinas on the Atonement" [paper presented at the Eastern Regional Meeting of the Society of Christian Philosophers, Wilmore, Ky., September 28–30, 2017]).

6   N.B. that such a statement is quite consistent with Aquinas' affirmations elsewhere that "the order of divine justice . . . requires that God should not remit sin without satisfaction" (*Summa contra gentiles* 4.54.9) and that "if God had decided to restore man solely by an act of His will and power, the order of divine justice would not have been observed" (*Compendium theologiae* 200). For that order is contingent.

Many other things besides deliverance from sin concurred for man's salvation. In the first place, man knows thereby how much God loves him,
and is thereby stirred to love Him in return. . . . Secondly, because thereby
He set us an example of obedience, humility, constancy, justice, and the
other virtues displayed in the Passion, which are requisite for man's salvation. Thirdly, because Christ by His Passion not only delivered man from
sin, but also merited justifying grace for him and the glory of bliss. . . .
Fourthly, because by this man is all the more bound to refrain from
sin. . . . Fifthly, because it redounded to man's greater dignity, that as man
was overcome and deceived by the devil, so also it should be a man that
should overthrow the devil; and as man deserved death, so a man by
dying should vanquish death. . . . It was accordingly more fitting that we
should be delivered by Christ's Passion than simply by God's good-will
[*Dei voluntatem*]. (*Summa theologiae* 3.46.3; cf. 3.1.2)

So Aquinas can consistently affirm that the order of divine justice
requires satisfaction for sin but that this requirement is contingent.

Anselm and Thomas thus offer two versions of the satisfaction theory,
which we may characterize as necessitarian and non-necessitarian,
respectively. On a necessitarian account, forgiveness and salvation are
not possible without the satisfaction of divine justice, whereas on a non-
necessitarian account, forgiveness and salvation depend only contingently
upon the satisfaction of divine justice. This differentiation is not unique
to satisfaction theories. As we shall see, both necessitarian and non-
necessitarian versions of penal substitution also eventually developed.

MORAL INFLUENCE THEORY

The other theory of the atonement that emerged during the Middle Ages
and that eventually became enormously influential was the so-called
moral influence theory. According to theories of this type, Christ's death
achieved our reconciliation with God not by offering some compensation to God or ransoming us from the devil but by moving our hearts
to contrition and love as we contemplate Christ's voluntarily embracing
horrible suffering and death. Nothing actually transpired between God
and man at Jesus' crucifixion. No debt was paid, no sins were punished.
The entire power of the cross to achieve reconciliation lies in its exem-
plary force to produce a subjective impact on us.

The thinker traditionally associated with the moral influence theory
of the atonement is the twelfth-century logician and theologian Peter
Abelard. In his comments on Romans 3:24-26, Abelard seeks to explain

how Christ's death achieves reconciliation. He follows Anselm in rejecting the ransom theory on the grounds that Satan has no right over human
beings that God must respect. This raises the question, "What need was
there, I say, for the Son of God, for the sake of our redemption, when
he received flesh to endure so many great fasts, reproaches, lashings,
spitting, and finally the most violent and shameful death of the cross?"
This is the same question that drove Anselm's inquiry. But Abelard does
not seem to be persuaded by Anselm's answer that Christ's death is a
compensatory gift to God. He exclaims, "How very cruel and unjust it
seems that someone should require the blood of an innocent person as a
ransom, or that in any way it might please him that an innocent person
be slain, still less that God should have so accepted the death of his
Son that through it he was reconciled to the whole world!" (*Commentary
on the Epistle to the Romans* 2).

Anselm had met this same objection by insisting that "God the
Father . . . did not compel him to suffer death, nor even allow him to
be slain against his will, but of his own accord he endured death for the
salvation of man" (*Cur Deus homo* 1.8). Anselm's reply corrects the misimpression that God demanded the blood of an innocent person, but it
remains the case that on the satisfaction theory God is pleased with the
Son's free gift of his life and so is reconciled to the world.

Abelard's answer to the objection is quite different:

> Nevertheless it seems to us that in this we are justified in the blood of
> Christ and reconciled to God, that it was through this matchless grace
> shown to us that his Son received our nature, and in that nature, teaching
> us both by word and by example, persevered to the death and bound us to
> himself even more through love, so that when we have been kindled by so
> great a benefit of divine grace, true charity might fear to endure nothing
> for his sake. (*Commentary on the Epistle to the Romans* 2)

Here Abelard seems to suggest that atonement is accomplished by
Christ's igniting in us a flame of love by means of his teaching and
example, persevering even unto death. Abelard even suggests that persons prior to Christ's advent were similarly moved by looking forward to
the manifestation of God's love in Christ. Still, "each one is also made
more righteous after the Passion of Christ than before; that is, he loves
God more, because the completed benefit kindles him in love more than
a hoped-for benefit." Abelard concludes, "Therefore, our redemption is
that supreme love in us through the Passion of Christ, which not only

frees us from slavery to sin, but gains for us the true liberty of the sons of God, so that we may complete all things by his love rather than by fear" (*Commentary on the Epistle to the Romans* 2).

Noteworthy is the fact that whereas the view that Abelard found objectionable was that God needed to be reconciled to the world by Christ's death, Abelard's view is that we need to be reconciled to God by Christ's death. Albrecht Ritschl nicely captures this difference between Abelard and Anselm's theories by distinguishing a God-ward and a man-ward function of Christ's work. "The part of Christ's work that relates to God is ranked by Anselm above that which relates to men. But, in Abelard's view, God's love towards men as displayed in Christ—in His incarnation, in His teaching, and His passion—is the leading thought upon which depends the effect of the intercession directed to God by the incarnate God."[7] Since the rise of classical liberal theology, it has become almost an axiom among contemporary theologians that God does not need to be reconciled to sinners; the entire obstacle lies on our side. Our hearts need to be changed so that our hostility to God evaporates and we embrace His love. So Abelard sees atonement with God achieved as Christ's passion enkindles our hearts and inspires love for God within us. We are liberated from sin as we come to love God more and so become more righteous.

Now, taken in isolation, the moral influence theory might seem far too thin an account to do justice to the NT data concerning God's wrath, Christ's substitutionary death, justification, and so on. It seems to amount to little more than moral self-improvement inspired by Christ's example. Bernard of Clairvaux, Abelard's contemporary, saw clearly the inadequacy of a pure moral influence theory: Absent the redemptive death of Christ, his humility and charity "are as if you were to paint on the air. A very great and most necessary example of humility, a great example of charity, and one worthy of all acceptation, has He set us; but they have no foundation, and, therefore, no stability, if redemption be wanting."[8]

However, scholars have recently called into question the assumption that the above, oft-quoted passage from Abelard's commentary

---

7   Ritschl, *A Critical History of the Christian Doctrine of Justification and Reconciliation*, 39.

8   Bernard of Clairvaux, "Letter to Pope Innocent, Against Certain Heads of Abaelard's Heresies," in *Some Letters of Saint Bernard, Abbot of Clairvaux*, trans. Samuel J. Eales (London: John Hodges, 1904), 292.

represents Abelard's full atonement theory rather than one facet of it. In his comment on Romans 4:25 Abelard writes:

> He is said to have died *on account of our transgressions* in two ways: at one time because we transgressed, on account of which he died, and we committed sin, the penalty of which he bore; at another, that he might take away our sins by dying, that is, he swept away the penalty for sins by the price of his death, leading us into paradise, and through the demonstration of so much grace . . . he drew back our souls from the will to sin and kindled the highest love of himself. (*Commentary on the Epistle to the Romans* 2)

In this passage Abelard appears to endorse a vague sort of penal substitution on Christ's part. Abelard affirms that Christ bore the punishment for our sins, thereby removing the punishment from us. The moral influence of Christ's death mentioned in the final clause of the sentence is now seen to be but a part of a more comprehensive theory—just as it was for Anselm, who also speaks of the influence of Christ's example of voluntary suffering (*Cur Deus homo* 2.11.18b).[9]

Aquinas, even more than Anselm, also stressed the man-ward function of Christ's passion in reconciling us to God. As one facet of a more complex theory, the moral influence theory makes a valuable contribution to understanding how the benefits won by Christ's death come to be appropriated.

CONCLUDING REMARKS

The satisfaction theory came to stamp indelibly Catholic theology, while the moral influence theory has, since the rise of classical liberalism in Protestant theology, come to exert an influence on thinking about the atonement that is perhaps even more far reaching. We turn our attention next to the Protestant Reformers, who in their commitment to *sola Scriptura* sought to enunciate a theory of the atonement more reflective of biblical teaching.

---

9 Rivière is skeptical: "Such passing inconsistencies and unconscious concessions to popular language are not sufficient to correct, still less to contradict, Abelard's formal statements. . . . Hence it is certain that Abelard, though he sometimes, from force of habit, used traditional expressions, denied all objective value to the Passion, and reduced its saving efficaciousness to a merely subjective impression, and that liberal Protestants are uttering no calumny when they speak of him as their forerunner" (Rivière, *Doctrine of the Atonement*, 1:59, 61).

Chapter 8

Reformation and Post-Reformation Theories

INTRODUCTION

The theological revolution wrought by the Protestant Reformers brought to full bloom the theory of the atonement that has come to be known as penal substitution. Though anticipated by the Church Fathers and approximated by Aquinas, the theory found its full expression and defense in the work of the Reformers and their scholastic progeny.

PENAL SUBSTITUTION THEORY

The Reformers

The Protestant Reformers, while appreciative of Anselm's satisfaction theory and recognizing that Christ's death satisfied God's justice, interpreted the satisfaction of God's justice in terms of penal substitution. That is to say, Christ voluntarily bore the suffering that we were due as the punishment for our sins. There is therefore no longer any punishment due to those who are the beneficiaries of Christ's death. God's wrath is propitiated by Christ's substitutionary death, for the demands of divine justice have been met.

More than that, our sins themselves having been imputed to Christ, our sin is expiated by Christ's substitutionary death. Although the imputation of our sin to Christ is purely forensic, Martin Luther could speak of it in very colorful terms:

> Being the unspotted Lamb of God, Christ was personally innocent. But because He took the sins of the world His sinlessness was defiled with the sinfulness of the world. Whatever sins I, you, all of us have committed or shall commit, they are Christ's sins as if He had committed them Himself. Our sins have to be Christ's sins or we shall perish forever. . . . Our merciful Father in heaven . . . therefore sent His only Son into the world and said to Him: "You are now Peter, the liar; Paul, the persecutor; David, the adulterer; Adam, the disobedient; the thief on the cross. You, My Son, must pay the world's iniquity." The Law growls: "All right. If Your Son is taking the sin of the world, I see no sins anywhere else but in Him. He shall die on the Cross." And the Law kills Christ. But we go free.[1]

Moreover, just as our sins are imputed to Christ, his righteousness is imputed to us through faith in him. Luther writes, "Believe in Christ and your sins will be pardoned. His righteousness will become your righteousness, and your sins will become His sins."[2]

Similarly, John Calvin, to motivate a deeper appreciation of what Christ has done on our behalf, strikingly summarizes both the calamity from which Christ has delivered us and the means by which he does so:

> Let [a person] be told, as Scripture teaches, that he was estranged from God by sin, an heir of wrath, exposed to the curse of eternal death, excluded from all hope of salvation, a complete alien from the blessing of God, the slave of Satan, captive under the yoke of sin; in fine, doomed to horrible destruction, and already involved in it; that then Christ interposed, took the punishment upon himself, and bore what by the just judgment of God was impending over sinners; with his own blood expiated the sins which rendered them hateful to God, by this expiation satisfied and duly propitiated God the Father, by this intercession appeased his anger, on this basis founded peace between God and men, and by this tie secured the Divine benevolence toward them; will not these considerations move him the more deeply, the more strikingly they represent the greatness of the calamity from which he was delivered? (*Institutes of the Christian Religion* 2.16.2)[3]

---

1   Martin Luther, *Commentary on St. Paul's Epistle to the Galatians*, trans. Theodore Graebner (Grand Rapids: Zondervan, 1939), 63–64.
2   Luther, *Epistle to the Galatians*, 54–55.
3   Lest he be misunderstood, Calvin goes out of his way to emphasize that God did not begin to love us as a result of Christ's work. He cites with approval

We find here the affirmation of expiation of sins and propitiation of God's wrath through Christ's satisfaction of divine justice by means of substitutionary punishment. The efficacy of penal substitution depends upon the imputation of our sin and guilt to Christ: "Our acquittal is in this—that the guilt which made us liable to punishment was transferred to the head of the Son of God (Is. liii.12). . . . [A]s he was to wash away the pollution of sins, they were transferred to him by imputation" (*Institutes of the Christian Religion* 2.16.5, 6). Our sins imputed to him, Christ satisfies divine justice by bearing the punishment for those sins.

Penal substitution is thus intimately connected with the Reformers' forensic view of justification.[4] Justification is understood as a legal act of God whereby we are declared not guilty and even righteous before Him. Justification is not the infusion of Christ's righteousness into us, making us suddenly virtuous people. Such sanctification will be the result only of a lifelong process of moral transformation. But in virtue of our union with Christ, believers are legally declared righteous by God. Indeed, one of the chief advantages of a penal substitutionary theory of the atonement is that no other atonement theory connects so well with the NT doctrine of forensic justification.[5]

Faustus Socinus

The Reformers' theory of penal substitution came under withering attack by the Unitarian theologian Faustus Socinus in his *On Jesus Christ Our Savior* (1578).[6] In part 1 of this work Socinus lays out his own atonement

---

Augustine's words: "Our being reconciled by the death of Christ must not be understood as if the Son reconciled us, in order that the Father, then hating, might begin to love us, but that we were reconciled to him already, loving, though at enmity with us because of sin" (*Institutes of the Christian Religion* 2.16.4). It is God's "gratuitous love" that prompts Him to receive us into favor (2.16.3).

4 See inter alia Alister E. McGrath, *Iustitia Dei: A History of the Christian Doctrine of Justification*, 3rd ed. (Cambridge: Cambridge University Press, 2005); James K. Beilby and Paul Rhodes Eddy, eds., *Justification: Five Views* (Downers Grove, Ill.: IVP Academic, 2011).

5 A connection rightly emphasized by Steve Wellum, "Penal Substitution as the Ground for Forensic Justification and Imputation" (paper presented at the annual meeting of the Evangelical Theological Society, Providence, R.I., November 15–17, 2017).

6 Remarkably, an English translation of this epochal work has never been published. The works of Socinus are included in Andreas Wissowatius, ed.,

theory. Socinus holds that Jesus Christ is our Savior "because he announced to us the way of eternal life, and, in his own person, both by the example of his life and by rising from the dead, he manifestly disclosed this, and that he is going to give eternal life to us, who have faith in him" (*On Jesus Christ Our Savior* 1.1; cf. 1.8).[7] Socinus reveals himself to be a genuine advocate of a moral influence theory, one that does not require the deity of Christ, which he denies. Christ is God's appointed messenger announcing His forgiveness of all who have faith and trust in Him. Nothing really happens at the cross; Christ's death, like his miracles and resurrection, merely serves as confirmation to us of God's favor. Christ's death can be said to be expiatory in the sense that it helps to awaken faith and trust in God, which results in our appropriating divine forgiveness.[8]

While Socinus' own atonement theory is today of only historical interest, his attack on penal substitution remains remarkably contemporary. Even critics who evince no firsthand acquaintance with Socinus' work bear the unmistakable imprint of his influence, and their criticisms pale by comparison. Indeed, I should say that Socinus' critique of penal substitution remains today unsurpassed in terms of its depth and breadth. In part 2 of his treatise he deals extensively with the alleged exegetical basis for satisfaction and penal substitution theories. Then in part 3, which will be the focus of our interest, he presents philosophical objections to such theories. He argues that it was neither necessary nor even possible for Christ to make satisfaction for our sins to divine justice. We shall consider his principal arguments only.

Bibliotheca Fratrum Polonorum quos Unitarios vocant (Irenopoli [Amsterdam]:1668). Alan Gomes, to whom I am indebted, has translated the crucial part 3 of Socinus' *De Jesu Christo Servatore* in his unpublished doctoral dissertation, "Faustus Socinus' *De Jesu Christo Servatore*, Part III, with a Historical Introduction, Translation, and Critical Notes" (Ph.D. diss., Fuller Theological Seminary, 1990). A detailed summary of the argument of the entire work is available in John Charles Godbey, "A Study of Faustus Socinus' *De Jesu Christo Servatore*" (Ph.D. diss., University of Chicago Divinity School, 1968).

7 Noteworthy is how easily the death of Christ is passed over in this statement. Although the cross is elsewhere said to confirm to us Christ's message of divine forgiveness, it is completely overshadowed in this respect by the resurrection, for which Christ' death is a prerequisite. For a full exposition of Socinus' theory see Godbey, "Faustus Socinus' *De Jesu Christo Servatore*."

8 Christ's expiatory work actually takes place only after Christ's exaltation to heaven and consists in his reminding us of God's love and moving us to embrace it.

Socinus assails the contention that satisfaction of divine justice is a necessary condition of the remission of sins (*On Jesus Christ Our Savior* 3.1). He asserts that we must not think of God as a Judge "who acts according to an external legal authority and who may not deviate from the letter of the law." Rather, God should be considered a "Lord and Ruler" (*dominus et princeps*), whose will alone is "the law in everything and is the absolutely perfect standard." Anselm would, of course, have agreed but insisted that justice is essential to God's nature. Socinus, however, replies that punitive justice (or vengeance) is not an essential property of God any more than is His mercy. If punitive justice were an attribute of God, then God could under no circumstances forgive sins; likewise, were mercy a divine attribute, God could under no circumstances punish sins. Rather what is essential to God is His uprightness (*rectitudo*) or fairness (*aequitas*). But whether He punishes sin is up to His free will. Similarly, mercy (*misericordia*) is an essential property of God only in the sense that God is loving. But whether God chooses to pardon sinners is up to His free will. Drawing on the analogy of the creditor and the debtor, Socinus says, "God is our creditor and we are His debtors by virtue of our sins. But every creditor has the absolute right to forgive the debtor his debt—either in whole or in part—without receiving satisfaction."

It is worthwhile to pause at this point to compare Socinus' view of the satisfaction of divine justice with Aquinas' view. Both reject the Anselmian position that God's justice necessitates His punishing sin. For both Aquinas and Socinus, God is no less just if He chooses to forgive rather than punish sin. Moreover, it is noteworthy that both agree that God has, in fact, chosen to punish rather than remit the sins of the impenitent. For Socinus only those who place their faith and trust in God are forgiven of their sins. God's severity and vengeance are visited upon those who are unrepentant. Where Aquinas and Socinus differ is not with respect to the particularity of God's freely exercising His forgiveness but with respect to how that forgiveness is achieved. For Aquinas, as for Anselm and the Reformers, God satisfies the demands of retributive justice through Christ; but for Aquinas He does so contingently. By contrast, Socinus thinks that God's contingent choice to forgive sinners is independent of justice's demands. God gratuitously extends to repentant sinners forgiveness of their sins and reserves His punitive justice for the unrepentant. Just as Socinus opposed Anselm's view that satisfaction of divine justice is necessary, he would be equally opposed to Aquinas' view that God through Christ contingently satisfies divine justice.

So, in the next chapter, Socinus proceeds to argue that satisfaction is actually logically incompatible with the remission of sins, which would rule out the Thomistic as well as the Anselmian doctrine (*On Jesus Christ Our Savior* 3.2). Remission, by definition, entails that the creditor forgo satisfaction of the debt and that the debtor is forgiven of his obligation. Hence it is logically incoherent to affirm that a creditor has both forgiven the debtor and accepted satisfaction of the debt. If the advocate of satisfaction answers that satisfaction of the debt can be made by one person and remission be given to another, Socinus will reply that because satisfaction has been made, nothing is remitted to the debtor. "There is no need for remission—indeed, remission is an impossibility—where the debt no longer exists." So it is an impossibility that a debt be both satisfied and remitted at the same time.

Socinus then presses an objection against the morality of penal substitution: a bodily punishment like eternal death cannot be endured by anyone other than the sinner himself (*On Jesus Christ Our Savior* 3.3). Admittedly, monetary penalties can be assumed legally by another person, since one person's money is just as effective as another's. But to release the guilty and to punish the innocent in their place "is not only completely opposed to any standard of justice: it is worse than inhuman and savage." If God wanted to punish our sins, then to demand the penalties from someone other than us would be contrary to justice properly so-called, namely, to uprightness and fairness, which are essential to His nature. Socinus later acknowledges that there are circumstances in which an innocent person can be afflicted without being wronged. For example, the innocent person could be under the authority of another who wishes to afflict him in order to achieve a higher purpose. "But," Socinus insists, "such affliction should not at all be regarded as penalty or punishment" (3.10).

In the case of Christ, from Socinus' Unitarian perspective, God did "not take violent action against himself: he harmed an innocent man instead" (*On Jesus Christ Our Savior* 3.3). Moreover, this innocent man was not "associated with the guilty in such a way that the guilty can be said to have undergone those penalties." Christ had "no other connection" with other human beings "except that this person, like them, is a human being." This remark raises the question whether Socinus' objections to the morality of substitutionary punishment would fail if Christ were taken to represent sinners in some way. As Socinus sees it, the provision of Christ (that is, handing him over to death) "should be called an act of sheer cruelty and violence rather than generosity" (3.2).

Socinus later asserts that it is "ridiculous and wicked" to claim that the sins of others could be imputed to an innocent person (*On Jesus Christ Our Savior* 3.10). He concedes that the sins of others can be imputed to someone, but only if (1) that person is connected to those persons in such a way that he should appear to partake of their transgressions solely because of that connection and (2) that person has also sinned and imitated the wickedness of the others. He thinks neither condition is met in Christ's case.

Finally, Socinus argues that even if Christ's rendering satisfaction for our sins were possible, he did not in fact do so (*On Jesus Christ Our Savior* 3.4). For the penalty each of us faces is eternal death, but Christ did not literally endure this. If the penal substitution theorist says that the dignity of Christ's divine person makes his sufferings of higher value, Socinus will reply that he "would regard as unjust a law that avenges the same crime more lightly on an eminent person than it does on a common one." If it be said that God reckons the light punishments of Christ as equivalent to the punishments due us, Socinus will respond that if that were true, then Christ need not have suffered such bitter tortures and so horrible a death. "God could have made full satisfaction to his justice by exacting some extremely light penalty from Christ."

The only basis on which one could legitimately ascribe infinite value to Christ's sufferings, Socinus grants, would be that Christ is eternal God. But the divine nature is impassible, so that Christ could not have suffered in any way. Moreover, even if Christ could have suffered in his divine person, his sufferings were transitory and therefore not of infinite value. Again, even if Christ's sufferings were of infinite value, they would have sufficed to satisfy the debt of one person alone, for we each face infinite sufferings for our sins. If one rejoins that Christ's suffering encompasses all of these infinities of punishment, then any suffering at all on his part should have sufficed to satisfy God's justice. Instead, He chose to inflict a horrible and accursed death on him.

There is much more in Socinus' wide-ranging and incisive work, but the foregoing objections to penal substitutionary theories are the most important. Socinus' broadside against penal substitution elicited a flood of responses from Protestant thinkers in defense of their theory. Among the many who sought to defend the theory, the Swiss Reformed theologian Francis Turretin stands out as one of the most important.

Francis Turretin

Francis Turretin's *Institutes of Elenctic Theology* (1685) is his systematic exposition of Reformed doctrine in conversation with opposing views. In questions 10–14 of topic 14, "The Mediatorial Office of Christ," he treats the doctrine of the atonement. As with Socinus, we shall pass over Turretin's extensive survey of the exegetical basis for his claim that Christ satisfied God's justice by being substituted in our place and suffering the punishment due to us.

The foundations of Turretin's atonement doctrine are laid in his treatment of divine justice (*Institutes of Elenctic Theology* 3.19). In contrast to Socinus, Turretin holds that punitive justice is essential to God. There are two principal virtues of God: justice and goodness. While goodness "is that by which he is conceived as the supreme good and the giver of all good," justice is "that by which God is in himself holy and just and has the constant will of giving to each his due." Although "justice" can be used as a universal term comprising all God's virtues, justice in a particular sense "gives to each his due and is occupied with the distribution of rewards and punishments and is called distributive justice." Distributive justice may be either punitive (inflicting punishment) or premiative (bestowing rewards). God's right to punish may be said to be either supreme and rigorous (called accurate right) or to be tempered by a certain moderation. The former is exercised when God imposes punishment not only on sin but also on the very person of the sinner. The latter is exercised when God grants a moderation in the imposition of punishment either in time (by delaying it) or in person (by transferring it) or in degree (by mitigating it). Justice demands necessarily that all sin should be punished but does not equally demand that it should be punished in the very person sinning or at a certain time and in a certain degree.

Turretin takes cognizance of Socinus' claim that punitive justice is merely the result of God's free will. Turretin acknowledges a diversity of opinion among Christian theologians with respect to whether God must exercise punitive justice and, hence, a diversity of views concerning the necessity of satisfaction with respect to the remission of sins. But the common opinion among the orthodox, and one he shares, is that "God neither has willed, nor could have willed to forgive sins, without a satisfaction made to his justice" (*Institutes of Elenctic Theology* 10.14). In support of his view that God must exercise punitive justice, Turretin offers four arguments: (1) Scripture teaches that God detests sin and is a just Judge; (2) conscience and the consent of nations testify to the necessity of punishment for evil; (3) if sins could be expiated merely by God's will, then it is not true that it is impossible that the blood of goats and bulls should take away sin; and (4) apart from the necessity of satisfaction no lawful reason could be devised for God's subjecting His Son to such an accursed and cruel death (cf. 14.10). So on Turretin's view, retributive justice, broadly conceived, is essential to God, but its exercise requires the determination of God's free will as to the time, the degree, and the persons upon whom it is inflicted.

It is also worth noting that Turretin holds to a sort of Divine Command Theory of ethics, according to which God is not bound by some external natural law. Rather, natural law is founded on God, the supreme lawgiver. The natural law is not arbitrary because God's commands are founded on the very holiness and wisdom of God Himself (*Institutes of Elenctic Theology* 11.1).

Turning to the doctrine of the atonement, Turretin explains that sin may be regarded as either (1) a debt which we owe to divine justice or (2) a mutual enmity between us and God or (3) a crime for which we deserve everlasting death before God, the supreme ruler and judge of the world (*Institutes of Elenctic Theology* 14.10). Satisfaction for sin must therefore involve (1) payment of the debt, (2) appeasement of divine wrath, and (3) expiation of our guilt. This multifaceted character of satisfaction is important because the right to punish is not the private right of a creditor, though sins are sometimes compared to debts, for sins are also crimes that cannot remain unpunished without prejudice to the laws (1.19). In the case of pecuniary debt, the creditor, upon receiving satisfaction, is not said to act with indulgence because he is paid exactly what was due to him. But in a penal or criminal debt, the act of a judge is required if the guilty person is to be freed without strict enforcement of the law. This judicial act is known as *relaxation*. In such a case the very thing that is owed is not paid (namely, the criminal's undergoing punishment), but in the judge's forbearance something else is allowed.

So with respect to our sin, God can be regarded as (1) the creditor or as (2) the offended party or as (3) the judge. The "capital error" of Socinus is neglecting the last role. God "has the claims not only of a creditor or Lord (which he can assert or remit at pleasure), but also the right of government and of punishment (which is natural and indispensable)."[9] So "God can relax his right, but not absolutely. He can do it only in so

---

9 Here Turretin undoubtedly evinces the influence of Hugo Grotius, whose theory we shall treat in the next section.

far as his justice will allow (to wit, he cannot act unjustly)." In God's role as judge a certain forbearance can be admitted, either in relation to the time by the delay of punishment or in relation to the degree by mitigation of the punishment or in relation to persons by a substitution. As the supreme judge, God can exempt sinners from the due punishment and transfer it to a substitute. In the satisfaction rendered by Christ, there is a relaxation of the law in God's admission and acceptance of a substitute. Christ thus plays a threefold role as well: (1) a surety who can pay the debt for us, (2) a mediator who takes away enmity and reconciles us to God, and (3) a priest and victim who substitutes himself in our place for a penal satisfaction.

Under what conditions can such a substitution of the innocent for the guilty be lawfully made? Necessary conditions include (1) a common nature of sinner and substitute so that sin may be punished in the same nature that is guilty, (2) the free consent of the substitute's will, (3) the substitute's having power over his own life so that he may rightfully determine what is done with it, (4) the substitute's having power to bear all the punishment due to us and take it away as much from himself as from us, and (5) the substitute's sinlessness so that he need not offer satisfaction for himself. These conditions are jointly sufficient for penal substitution. Since Christ fulfilled all these conditions, it was not unjust for Christ to substitute himself for us. "For thus no injury is done to anyone," not to Christ himself, or to God, or to the sinner, or to the law, or to the government of the universe.

Against Socinus' arguments that Christ's sufferings did not in fact satisfy the demands of divine justice, Turretin maintains that while Christ's punishment was not infinite as to duration, still it was equivalent as to value on account of the infinite dignity of the person suffering (*Institutes of Elenctic Theology* 14.11). Christ not only suffered a violent and bitter death but was forsaken by God the Father by His withdrawing from him the beatific vision and by suspending the joy and comfort and sense and fruition of full felicity. The law required no less to answer to the demands of justice. Although a death of infinite value was due for every individual sinner, the dignity of an infinite person swallows up and absorbs all the infinities of punishment due to us. We cannot doubt the infinite value of Christ's satisfaction, for although his human nature was finite, the satisfaction is infinite, since it is relative to the person, who is the efficient cause and to whom the obedience and suffering are to be attributed (14.12).

On Turretin's view Christ did not merely suffer the punishment due us for our sins. Our sins themselves were imputed to Christ (*Institutes of Elenctic Theology* 14.13). In turn Christ's righteousness was imputed to us. Justification consists in the imputation of righteousness, not merely a righteousness of innocence but a righteousness of perseverance. The remission of sins brings the righteousness of innocence by taking away the guilt of sins, but it does not therefore bring with it the righteousness of perseverance. That righteousness is won by the lifelong obedience of Christ, whereby he completely fulfilled the law. In the same way that the sins we committed in violation of the law are imputed to Christ, so the righteous actions by which he completely fulfilled the law for us are imputed to us. By the righteousness of Christ, Turretin does not mean the essential righteousness of God (16.3). That righteousness, he believes, could not be communicated to us without our becoming God also. The righteousness of Christ imputed to us is the obedience of his life and the suffering of his death by which he answered the demands of the law. This is called the righteousness of God because it belongs to a divine person and so is of infinite value. By this righteousness is understood the entire obedience of Christ—of his life as well as of his death, active as well as passive.

Turretin emphasizes that such imputation is a purely forensic notion and does not involve either an infusion of sin into Christ or an infusion of Christ's righteousness into us (*Institutes of Elenctic Theology* 14.16). While agreeing that by the grace of Christ inherent righteousness is infused into us, Turretin insists that it plays no role in justification: "For the righteousness of Christ alone imputed to us is the foundation and meritorious cause upon which our absolutary sentence rests, so that for no other reason does God bestow the pardon of sin and the right to life than on account of the most perfect righteousness of Christ imputed to us and apprehended by faith" (16.1). Similarly, Christ was made sin for us, not inherently or subjectively (since he knew no sin), but imputatively because God imputed to him our sins (16.3).

The word "impute," explains Turretin, properly means "to hold him who has not done a thing as if he had done it," whereas "not to impute" means "to hold him who has done a thing as if he had not done it" (*Institutes of Elenctic Theology* 16.3). Socinus in part 4.1 of *On Jesus Christ Our Savior* had inveighed against the doctrine of the imputation of Christ's righteousness to believers as a sort of sham righteousness that substituted for genuine holiness of life. But Turretin distinguishes between "imputed" and "fictitious." For imputation is no less real in its own order (judicial and forensic) than infusion is in a moral or physical order. Someone legally declared debt-free, for example, is really delivered from his creditor.

One of Socinus' complaints against penal substitution, it will be remembered, is that Christ has no connection with us so as to be punishable for our sins. Relevant to this criticism is an intriguing but underdeveloped aspect of Turretin's atonement theory, namely, our union with Christ. He states, "The curse and punishment of sin which he received upon himself in our stead secures to us blessing and righteousness with God in virtue of that most strict union between us and him by which, as our sins are imputed to him, so in turn his obedience and righteousness are imputed to us" (*Institutes of Elenctic Theology* 16.3). This relation is not one of simple substitution; there is a union here that is the basis of the imputation of our sins to Christ and his righteousness to us. According to Turretin, so long as Christ is outside of us and we are out of Christ we can receive no benefit from his righteousness. But God has united us with Christ by means of a twofold bond, one natural (namely, communion of nature by the incarnation), the other mystical (namely, the communion of grace by Christ's mediation), in virtue of which our sins might be imputed to Christ and his righteousness imputed to us. It is evident that imputation depends upon our union with Christ. "Having been made by God a surety for us and given to us for a head, he can communicate to us his righteousness and all of his benefits." Our union with Christ is the "cause and foundation" of our sharing in all his benefits, including justification (remission of sins and adoption as sons) (16.6).

Unfortunately, Turretin has almost nothing to say by way of explanation of what this union actually is or how it comes to be. But he thinks of it as a historical event. Prior to a person's birth, his sins cannot be said to have been remitted because nonentities have no properties and, hence, no sin and guilt to be remitted (*Institutes of Elenctic Theology* 16.5). Such a person is not yet in union with Christ and so not yet justified. Justification, though eternally decreed, takes place in this life in the moment of God's effectual calling, by which the sinner is transferred from a state of sin to a state of grace and is united to Christ, his head, by faith. "For hence it is that the righteousness of Christ is imputed to him by God, by whose merit apprehended by faith he is absolved from his sins and obtains a right to life" (16.9). Faith is thus "the instrumental cause of our justification" (16.7) and by implication of our union with Christ. Hence, believers have "immediate and absolute union" with Christ (18.25).

In virtue of our union with Christ, his righteousness is imputed to us (*Institutes of Elenctic Theology* 16.4). The imputation of his righteousness brings two benefits: the remission of sins and the bestowal of a right to life (in which two benefits the whole of justification is comprised). In Turretin's view, the imputation of righteousness is explanatorily prior to the remission of sins. If we wish to philosophize correctly, he advises, we must not say that God first remits our sins and afterward imputes Christ's righteousness to us; rather, God first imputes Christ's righteousness and afterward on account of that imputed righteousness remits our sins. Turretin explains that a satisfaction must necessarily intervene in order that remission may be granted by God without detriment to His justice and that it may be the foundation of the absolving sentence.

Thus, Turretin's atonement theory has a peculiar explanatory structure: first, we are through faith united with Christ as our head by nature and by his mediatorial office; next, in virtue of our union with Christ, his righteousness is imputed to us; finally, in virtue of his imputed righteousness, our sins are remitted, since God's justice has been satisfied by Christ's vicarious suffering and death, and we are given the right to life, adoption as sons.

THE GOVERNMENTAL THEORY

The final atonement theory we shall survey is the governmental theory usually associated with Hugo Grotius, a famous international jurist who published a treatise in response to Socinus on the doctrine of the atonement entitled *A Defense of the Catholic Faith concerning the Satisfaction of Christ, against Faustus Socinus* (1617). Just as Aquinas defended a non-necessitarian version of the satisfaction theory, so Grotius is a defender of a non-necessitarian penal substitutionary theory.

Unfortunately, Grotius' theory is today widely misrepresented in the secondary literature. He is even accused of capitulating to Socinus and betraying the Reformers' theory of penal substitution, offering in its place a quite different theory, yclept the governmental theory. According to this theory, as typically presented, God is to be conceived as the sovereign Ruler of the world. As such, it lies entirely within His discretion to remit sins without satisfaction. God has not chosen to punish Christ substitutionally for our sins. Rather, God chose to inflict terrible suffering on him as an example to us of what sin deserves, so that we shall be motivated to live holy lives before God. God's freely choosing to thus afflict Christ is done for the sake of the moral governance of the world. On this view Grotius' theory is a combination of the moral influence theory with a consequentialist view of punishment for the sake of deterrence.

By contrast, Grotius expressly presents his treatise as a defense of penal substitution:

> The catholic doctrine, then, is as follows: God was moved by his own goodness to bestow considerable blessings upon us, but our sins, which deserved punishment, were an obstacle to this; so he decided that Christ, willingly and because of his love for mankind, should pay the penalty for our sins by undergoing the most severe tortures and a bloody and disgraceful death. Thus, the demonstration of divine justice would remain unaffected, and we, through the intervention of true faith, might be liberated from the punishment of eternal death. (*Defense* 1.2)

After a fairly impressive exegesis of the biblical text in both Greek and Hebrew, Grotius concludes that Christ's death was, indeed, a punishment:

> So, to sum up what has been said up to this point: since Scripture says that Christ was "chastised" by God (i.e., punished), that "Christ bore our sins" (i.e., the punishment of sins), "was made sin" (i.e., subjected to the punishment of sins), "was made a curse in the eyes of God" or "into a curse," i.e., liable to the penalty of the law; since, furthermore, the suffering of Christ itself, full of tortures, bloody, ignominious, is a most appropriate matter of punishment; since, moreover, Scripture says that this was inflicted on him by God "on account of our sins" (i.e., our sins so deserving), since death itself is said to be the "wages," i.e., the punishment of sin, certainly it can by no means be doubted that with regard to God the suffering and death of Christ had the character of a punishment. (1.39)

Grotius conceives of divine justice as retributive and of Christ's death as a punishment for our sins.

God's purpose in Christ's death was twofold: first, to demonstrate divine retributive justice with respect to sin, which had so long been postponed, and, second, to exempt us from punishment by remission of our sins. Grotius ridicules Socinus' moral influence theory, according to which the death of Christ is meant to persuade us to exercise faith in hope of eternal life: "What is more widely removed from the truth, than that the death of a perfectly innocent man, so bloody, should of itself have power to persuade us that the greatest joys are prepared by God for those who live holily?" (*Defense* 1.52).

Grotius concedes to Socinus that we should not think of God as a judge placed under the law, for such a judge could not liberate the guilty from punishment (*Defense* 2.3). But neither should we think of God as Socinus often does, as an offended party in a personal dispute. For such a private person has no right to punish another or even to demand punishment of another.[10] Certainly, God is offended by sin, but He does not act as merely the offended party in punishing it. Rather, God should be considered to act as a Ruler. "For to inflict punishment, or to liberate from punishment . . . is the exclusive prerogative of the ruler as such, as it is of the father in a family, of the king in a state, and of God in the universe" (2.1).

Grotius contrasts a creditor governed by private law with a ruler who administers public law:

> For with regard to debt, a right which has been created for the advantage of the creditor, everyone is completely free in making a decision, and the less he demands, the more liberal he is; but in demanding [payment] he performs no act of virtue. With regard to punishment, however, which pertains to the common good and to order, a ruler certainly does have power, but not without limits. And when he exacts punishment, he exercises a kind of virtue which is called *antapodotike,* "retributive," justice. (*Defense* 4.19)

Grotius thinks it would be unjust in a ruler, even in God, to let certain sins go unpunished, such as sins of the unrepentant, and so it is inconsistent with the justice of God that He should remit all punishment whatsoever.

Grotius appeals to the notion of relaxation to explain God's act of punishing Christ in the place of sinners: "The act of God with which we are dealing will be the punishment of one in order to obtain the impunity of another. . . . [T]he act itself will be a means of indulgence or of moderation of this law, an indulgence which today we call 'dispensation'; it may be defined as an act of a superior by which the obligation imposed by a law remaining in force is removed with regard to certain persons or things" (*Defense* 3.2). Although some laws are not relaxable because their opposite involves immutable wickedness, all positive laws are relaxable.

---

10 He later explains, "For God is a judge, and we are private persons. It is fitting for a judge to be concerned with the effect of an example; this care does not apply to private persons. The office of a judge comprises the power of punishment; this power has been taken away from private persons" (6.19). God is, then, both Judge and Ruler.

Grotius thus combines a view of justice as retributive with the possibility of relaxation of the law by an authority.

> That, therefore, someone who has committed a delict deserves punishment and is thus liable to punishment, this necessarily follows from the very relation of sin and the sinner to the superior and is properly natural. But that every sinner must be punished with a punishment such that it corresponds to his guilt, this is not simply or universally necessary nor properly natural, but to some degree in accordance with nature. From this it follows that nothing prevents the law which prescribes this from being relaxable. (3.10)

So on Grotius' view retributive justice permits but does not require punishment. God had a very weighty reason for relaxing the law so as not to punish us but Christ in our stead, namely, had He not done so, the entire human race would have been destroyed.

As with Augustine, imputation seems to play no role in Grotius' theory. Christ's bearing our sin is interpreted to mean that Christ bore the punishment for our sin. Justification is taken to be a declaration of innocence rather than to include the imputation of Christ's righteousness to us. On Grotius' view Christ was thus completely innocent, both personally and even legally. God chose to punish him for our sins so that our debt of punishment might be remitted and we be liberated.

Grotius next takes up three objections to substitutionary atonement. First is the objection that it was unjust to punish Christ in our place (*Defense* 4). Socinus acknowledges that it was not unjust that God should afflict Christ with suffering, but he denies that such suffering could effect anything to obtain our pardon. Grotius maintains to the contrary that it was neither unjust nor contrary to the nature of punishment that someone should be punished for another's sins. With respect to the nature of punishment, Grotius makes the astute observation that "innocence does not prevent punishment any more than it does affliction" (4.7)— a person might be punished *though* innocent. As to the justice of God's punishing an innocent person, Grotius maintains that scriptural prohibitions against punishing children for the sins of their fathers is, in part, a positive law imposed by God upon humanity, but God Himself "is not bound, as he never imposed it upon himself, and cannot, in fact, be bound by any law" (4.6).

Socinus claims that there ought to be some connection between the guilty party and the person who is punished in his place. Grotius agrees but points out that Christ was designated by God Himself as the head of the body of which we are members (*Defense* 4.8). God has the right to afflict Christ, and Christ has freely assented to the same, and so nothing prevents God's ordaining that that affliction be the punishment for the sins of others connected to him.

The second objection concerns whether God had sufficient reason to punish Christ in our place (*Defense* 5). Socinus errs in thinking that the reason for Christ's substitutionary death must show that his death was necessary. Appealing to the Church Fathers, Grotius argues that God had good reasons for not remitting our sins without punishing Christ, though He might have done so. God was unwilling to pass over so many and such heinous sins without testifying by some act how greatly displeased He is with sin. The act most suitable for this is punishment. Moreover, to neglect to punish sin altogether leads to a lower estimation of sin, whereas the best means of preventing sin is the fear of punishment. Not only so, but in Christ's voluntary self-sacrifice God declares in a marked way His great love for us. Thus, God in His most perfect wisdom chose that way of redemption by means of which He could manifest both His hatred of sin and His love of mankind (5.7).

The third objection concerns whether God did in fact punish Christ in our place (*Defense* 6). Here Grotius responds to Socinus' allegation that satisfaction for sins and remission of those same sins are logically incompatible. Grotius distinguishes between the strict performance of a debt or punishment and satisfaction for the same. If a debt or punishment is discharged by the performance of the very thing required, then there is no remission granted by the creditor or ruler. But when anything other than what one is obligated to perform is done instead, then "it is necessary that some act of the creditor or the ruler be added, which act is properly and usually called remission." This substitution for strict performance, when accepted by the creditor or ruler, has "a special name in law, viz. satisfaction, which is sometimes contrasted with performance in the stricter sense of the word" (6.11). In civil law the discharge of a debt without any sort of performance is called "acceptilation." "But with regard to punishment it has no proper name . . . but is commonly called grace, pardon, indulgence or abolition" (6.13).

In the case of the remission of sins, it is remission with antecedent satisfaction. Socinus errs in thinking that these two notions are in conflict, for all satisfaction is allowed on the condition that there is opportunity for remission by the creditor or ruler. The creditor or ruler may accept or reject the substitute for strict performance, and if he does accept it, it is deemed satisfactory. Socinus' claim that "by satisfaction a debt is altogether and immediately extinguished . . . is not true, unless satisfaction, contrary to legal usage, is taken to refer to the performance by the debtor of the very thing which was due" (*Defense* 6.16). But when someone else performs instead of the debtor and something else is performed instead of what was due, then the creditor or ruler must act to accept the substitute.

Grotius makes the interesting observation that the virtue God exhibits in remitting sins is not liberality but clemency (*Defense* 6.25). God pardons sins as rulers pardon crimes (6.3). God's beneficence was shown to us in that "when God was moved with great hatred against sin, and could refuse to spare us altogether . . . , yet, in order to spare us, he accepted a performance such as he was not bound to accept, but, he also devised it himself, of his own accord. . . . So, the clemency of God is not overthrown by the performance of the punishment, since the acceptance of such a performance, and much rather the devising of it, sprang from clemency alone" (6.26).

Grotius' rich treatise, from which we have but sampled, remains essential reading for any atonement theorist today. Unfortunately Grotius' so-called governmental theory has been widely misunderstood. It is true that he thought that God as Ruler could remit sins without satisfaction while preserving His essential justice and holiness. But against Socinus, Grotius thinks that God had powerful reasons, namely, setting an example for us, for a merely partial relaxation of the law, so that another might satisfy divine justice by bearing the punishment we deserved. As the supreme Ruler He had the right to do this. "There is, therefore, no injustice in this, that God, who has the highest power with regard to all things not in themselves unjust and who is himself not subject to any law, wanted to use the sufferings and death of Christ in order to set a serious example against the immense guilt of us all, with whom Christ was very closely connected by his nature, reign and suretyship" (*Defense* 4.23).

CONCLUDING REMARKS

I trust that our all too superficial survey has given us some accurate understanding of traditional atonement theories along with considerable food for thought. Unfortunately, the traditional thinkers whom we have discussed have been misrepresented and even pilloried in the secondary literature.[11] Such caricatures not only do a disservice to contemporary theology, which may as a result miss the insights that traditional thinkers have to offer, but also impugn the reputations of godly men like Anselm who deserve our respect and admiration.

Although Grotius, Turretin, and many others wrote able replies to Socinus' work, Socinus was in step with the skepticism of the coming European Enlightenment concerning traditional Christian doctrines. The erosion of belief in traditional atonement theories was the result. Nowhere is this more poignantly illustrated than in the life of Friedrich Schleiermacher, the father of modern theology. As a theology student at the University of Halle, which by the late eighteenth century had become infected with German rationalism, the young Schleiermacher

---

11 The most unfortunate example in my acquaintance is the impression given by N. T. Wright in his *The Day the Revolution Began: Reconsidering the Meaning of Jesus' Crucifixion* (San Francisco: HarperOne, 2017) that traditional atonement theories are "paganized" theories of the atonement. Parodying John 3:16, Wright characterizes the neo-pagan view as holding that "God so hated the world that He killed His only Son." Wright erects this straw man to serve as a foil for the presentation of his own account of the atonement (which turns out, ironically, to be fairly traditional). Remarkably, Wright is unable to furnish a single example of either a scholar or a popular writer who espouses this supposedly widespread neo-pagan theory of the atonement. The closest he comes is the example of a minister who said, "Someone had to die," an expression of a necessitarian view of satisfaction which hardly merits Wright's horrified disapprobation. The words of P. T. Forsyth, written more than a generation ago, take on a new poignancy:

> The Christian idea of atonement is identified offhand with the pagan idea of atonement, as a Hyde Park lecturer might. And when you have done that at the outset, it is the simplest thing to show how false and absurd and pagan such theology is. It is said further, that the whole Church has become paganised in this way, and has spoken as though God could be mollified by something offered to Him. The criticism is sometimes ignorant, sometimes ungenerous, sometimes culpable. If such language has ever been held, it has only been by sections of the Church, sections that have gone wrong in the direction of unqualified extremes. You have extravagancies, remember, even in rational heresy. Has the Church on the whole ever really forgotten that it is in the mercy of God that all our hopes begin and end? (*The Work of Christ*, 2nd ed. [London: Independent Press, 1938], 91–92)

The answer is, of course not, and the thinkers we have surveyed have not espoused paganized atonement theories.

wrote to his father, a Reformed chaplain, to announce his abandonment of the orthodox faith:

> Alas! dearest father, if you believe that without this faith no one can attain to salvation in the next world, nor to tranquility in this—and such, I know, is your belief—oh! then pray to God to grant it to me, for to me it is now lost. I cannot believe that he who called himself the Son of Man was the true, eternal God; I cannot believe that his death was a vicarious atonement.[12]

With the Enlightenment came a proliferation of atonement theories, as theologians abandoned the traditional approaches. Not only would it be impossible to survey here the bewildering variety of atonement theories characteristic of modernity, but our interest lies in building upon the foundation of traditional atonement theories in line with biblical parameters. The challenge we face is to articulate and defend an account of the atonement that will do justice to the biblical data we have surveyed in a philosophically coherent and plausible way.

---

12 From B. A. Gerrish, *A Prince of the Church: Schleiermacher and the Beginnings of Modern Theology* (Philadelphia: Fortress Press, 1984), 25.

III

Philosophical Reflections on
the Doctrine of the Atonement

Chapter 9

PENAL SUBSTITUTION
Its Coherence

INTRODUCTION

We come at length to reflect philosophically upon issues raised by atonement theories. We want to explore what options are open to a biblically faithful atonement theorist. Essential to any biblically adequate theory of the atonement, it seems to me, is penal substitution. No atonement theory that neglects penal substitution can hope to account adequately for the biblical data we have surveyed, particularly Isaiah 53 and its NT employment. Moreover, penal substitution, if true, could not be a merely tangential, minor facet of an adequate atonement theory, for it is foundational, as we shall see, to so many other aspects of the atonement, such as satisfaction of divine justice, redemption from sin, and the moral influence of Christ's example. So a biblically adequate atonement theory must include penal substitution at its center.

Penal substitution in a theological context may be defined as the doctrine that God inflicted upon Christ the suffering that we deserved as the punishment for our sins, as a result of which we no longer deserve punishment. Notice that this explication leaves open the question whether Christ was punished for our sins. Some defenders of penal substitution recoil at the thought that God punished His beloved Son for

147

our sins. For example, John Stott advises, "We must never make Christ the object of God's punishment."[1] Even in their ringing defense of penal substitution, Steve Jeffery, Michael Ovey, and Andrew Sach do not define penal substitution in such a way as to imply that Christ was punished in our place. Rather, they offer the more subtle explication: "The doctrine of penal substitution states that God gave himself in the person of his Son to suffer instead of us the death, punishment, and curse due to fallen humanity as the penalty for sin."[2] If we take the definite description "the punishment due to fallen humanity" referentially,[3] it refers to the withdrawal of God's fellowship and blessing.[4] This Christ suffered

---

1   John Stott, *The Cross of Christ* (Leicester, UK: InterVarsity, 1986), 151. Cf. I. Howard Marshall: "It is not a case of God punishing Christ but of God in Christ taking on himself the sin and its penalty. Indeed, at some point the challenge needs to be issued: where are these evangelicals who say that God punished Christ? Name them!" ("The Theology of the Atonement," in *The Atonement Debate*, ed. Derek Tidball, David Hilborn, and Justin Thacker [Grand Rapids: Zondervan, 2008], 63).

2   Steve Jeffery, Michael Ovey, and Andrew Sach, *Pierced for Our Transgressions: Rediscovering the Glory of Penal Substitution* (Wheaton, Ill.: Crossway Books, 2007), 21. Similarly, David Hilborn, in describing the recent controversy over penal substitution among British evangelicals, offers this characterization: "Penal substitution presents Jesus' crucifixion as a vicarious sacrifice which appeased or 'propitiated' God's wrath towards sin by paying the due 'penalty' for that sin, which is suffering, death, and condemnation" ("Atonement, Evangelicalism and the Evangelical Alliance: The Present Debate in Context," in Tidball, Hilborn, and Thacker, *The Atonement Debate*, 19). The use of "scare quotes" with the word "penalty" suggests some diffidence about the word, which may accordingly be understood referentially by those who, like Stott, deny that God punished Christ. Hilborn reports that the Evangelical Alliance preferred the more straightforwardly biblical imagery of Christ's "paying the price" of our sin (1 Cor 6:20; 7:23) and allowed this to carry the implication of penal substitutionary sacrifice.

3   That is, we consider the referent or denotation of the description, however it may be described. On the difference between an expression understood referentially and attributively, see Keith Donnellan, "Reference and Definite Descriptions," *Philosophical Review* 75, no. 3 (1966): 281–304.

4   Jeffery, Ovey, and Sach, *Pierced for Our Transgressions*, 301. Cf. Francis Turretin's characterization of Christ's dereliction on the cross as God the Father's withdrawing from him the beatific vision and suspending the joy and comfort and sense and fruition of full felicity (*Institutes of Elenctic Theology*, 3 vols., trans. George Musgrave Giger, ed. James T. Dennison Jr. [Phillipsburg, N.J.: P&R, 1992], 14.11).

on the cross instead of us. Indeed, for many of these theorists, God did not even inflict on Christ the harsh treatment that we deserved; rather, Christ voluntarily took upon himself the suffering that we deserved as the punishment for our sins.

On such an understanding, Christ bore the suffering that, had it been inflicted upon us, would have been our just desert and, hence, punishment. In other words, Christ was not punished but he endured the suffering that would have been our punishment had it been inflicted on us. We should not exclude by definition such accounts as being penal substitutionary theories, since Christ on such accounts suffers as our substitute and bears what would have been our punishment, thereby freeing us from punishment.[5] Accordingly, penal substitution in a theological context ought to be understood as the doctrine that Christ endured the suffering that we deserved as the punishment for our sins, as a result of which we no longer deserve punishment. This explication leaves open the question of whether God punished Christ for our sins.

The doctrine of penal substitution, ever since the time of Socinus, has faced formidable, and some would say insuperable, philosophical challenges. A discussion of such challenges takes us into lively contemporary debates over issues in the philosophy of law, the subdiscipline of philosophy where questions about the theory of punishment are most thoroughly treated. Unfortunately, most theologians, and in fact most Christian philosophers, have little familiarity with these debates. The doctrine of penal substitution is usually dismissed by its critics in a single paragraph, even a single sentence, to the effect that it would be unjust of God to punish an innocent person for others' sins, end of discussion. More deserves to be said.

A cautionary word is, however, in order at this point. The punishment that is discussed by legal theorists and philosophers of law is almost invariably legal punishment in the context of criminal law. Even when discussing penalties that are mandated by civil law rather than criminal law, the framework is still legal. One is discussing punishment as administered by the state as part of a system of justice. While analogous to divine justice, human systems of justice will also have features that are

---

5   These features serve to distinguish such an account from satisfaction theories. On such an account the harsh treatment deserved for wrongdoing is still administered, even if it is not punishment because of the absence of condemnation. I think the important question remaining about such accounts is whether divine justice would thereby be satisfied, a question we shall take up in chapter 11.

significantly disanalogous to divine justice. To give an obvious example, the state may be forced not to administer punishment as a result of lack of prison space, due to overcrowding and lack of resources. God is evidently not so hampered. Still, legal theorists and philosophers of law have for several centuries poured an enormous amount of thought into the theory of punishment, and so, given the widespread presence of forensic and judicial motifs in the biblical texts pertinent to the atonement, we may expect to learn a great deal from them.[6]

A theory of punishment should treat both the *definition of punishment* and the *justification of punishment*, aspects of the theory of punishment that legal philosophers have teased apart only in recent decades. A definition of punishment will enable us to determine whether some act counts as punishment, while a justification of punishment will help us to determine whether a punitive act is permitted or even required, depending on one's theory. Both aspects of the theory of punishment are relevant to the doctrine of penal substitution. In this chapter we shall consider challenges to the coherence of penal substitution, especially challenges arising from the definition of punishment.

THE ALLEGED INCOHERENCE
OF PENAL SUBSTITUTION

What is punishment? Punishment involves, first, harsh treatment, as is obvious from typical cases of punishment. Theorists prefer the term

---

6 Adonis Vidu defends the provocative and not initially implausible thesis that there exists a cross-fertilization between atonement theories and developments in legal theory (*Atonement, Law, and Justice: The Cross in Historical and Cultural Contexts* [Grand Rapids: Baker, 2014]). Unfortunately, he is unable to demonstrate any tight connections between atonement theories and developments in philosophy of law, drawing only the most general of parallels. Indeed, it is striking how widely divergent atonement theories emerge in the same cultural context. The only attempt in legal literature that I have encountered to connect the doctrine of the atonement with theory of law is Jerome Hall, "Biblical Atonement and Modern Criminal Law," *Washington University Law Quarterly* 65 (1987): 694–710. I am indebted to Francis Beckwith for this reference. But while Hall gives a very responsible survey of the history of the doctrine of the atonement, he has little to say by way of integration with criminal law. Vicarious liability (to be discussed in the sequel) does get a passing mention on p. 708, and he closes with some reflections on the inevitability of retributive justice in any adequate theory.

"harsh treatment" to "suffering" because the latter is subjective and, hence, person relative—the masochist might enjoy being treated harshly and so would not be "punished"! Harsh treatment is not sufficient for punishment, however. As Socinus recognized, God may inflict suffering on some person without its being punishment. So what transforms harsh treatment into punishment? This where the debate begins.

No consensus in fact exists concerning the conditions sufficient for punishment. But consider Alec Walen's characterization of some of the necessary conditions of punishment in a standard philosophical encyclopedia:

> For an act to count as punishment, it must have four elements.
>
> First, it must impose some sort of cost or hardship on, or at the very least withdraw a benefit that would otherwise be enjoyed by, the person being punished.
>
> Second, the punisher must do so intentionally, not as an accident, and not as a side-effect of pursuing some other end.
>
> Third, the hardship or loss must be imposed in response to what is believed to be a wrongful act or omission.
>
> Fourth, the hardship or loss must be imposed, at least in part, as a way of sending a message of condemnation or censure for what is believed to be a wrongful act or omission.[7]

Most theorists would also want to require that the hardship or loss be imposed by a recognized authority, so as to distinguish punishment from personal vengeance or vigilantism.

Walen's characterization is a version of what is called an expressivist theory of punishment, made popular by legal philosopher Joel Feinberg, according to which the harsh treatment imposed must express condemnation or censure in order to count as punishment.[8] Some critics of penal substitution such as Mark Murphy have claimed that given an expressivist theory of punishment, it is conceptually impossible that God punish

---

7 *Stanford Encyclopedia of Philosophy*, edited by Edward N. Zalta. Summer 2014 ed., s.v. "Retributive Justice," by Alec Walen, June 28, 2014, http://plato.stanford .edu/entries/justice-retributive/.

8 Joel Feinberg, *Doing and Deserving: Essays in the Theory of Responsibility* (Princeton, N.J.: Princeton University Press, 1970). Sometimes expressivist theories may be divided into two versions: the communicative version, which communicates to the offender a message of condemnation, and the denunciatory version, which denounces to the world at large the wrong committed.

Christ for our sins.[9] Murphy sets the familiar moral objections to penal substitution to the side in order to argue that "the problem is not that penal substitution is immoral, but that it is conceptually defective."[10] For God could not condemn or censure Christ, since he did no wrong. The point is not that it would be immoral for God to punish Christ for others' wrongs, but that any such harsh treatment inflicted on him by God for those wrongs would not count as punishment because it would not express condemnation or censure. A necessary condition of punishment is that "punishment *expresses condemnation* of the wrongdoer, of the wrongdoer as performer of the wrong."[11]

If this necessary condition of punishment is correctly formulated, Murphy concludes, then punishment expresses condemnation of the person punished. If that is right, then one cannot punish a person whom one does not take to be worthy of condemnation. And one cannot regard a person as worthy of condemnation unless he has actually done the act for which he is condemned. "Punishing presupposes that the object of punishment has failed in particular respects. . . . If (non-defective) punishment is essentially condemning of the agent who failed to live up to the standard the violation of which justifies the punishment, then penal substitution is unintelligible. We know that attempts to justify it will founder not for moral reasons but for prior conceptual reasons."[12]

---

9   Mark C. Murphy, "Not Penal Substitution but Vicarious Punishment," *Faith and Philosophy* 26 (2009): 255–59.

10 Murphy, "Not Penal Substitution," 255.

11 Murphy, "Not Penal Substitution," 256. Murphy's view actually differs somewhat from Feinberg's, as we shall see. Murphy thinks that "if punishment condemns only the act, it is hard to see why we are so set on ascertaining the precise identity of the wrongdoer. . . . The best way to characterize the condemnation, then, is that it is of *the wrongdoer in a certain respect*, that is, as a performer of the wrongful action" (256).

12 Murphy, "Not Penal Substitution," 257. Oddly, Murphy allows that "perhaps one can [express condemnation of someone whom one does not take to be worthy of condemnation], but then the punishing act will be defective" (256). There is a genuine tension in Murphy's exposition in this respect. Sometimes he speaks as though punishment entails that the person punished be worthy of condemnation, just as honoring entails that the person honored be worthy of praise. From this characterization the counterintuitive consequence follows that the undeserving cannot be punished or praised, an ironic consequence in light of Murphy's unfortunate illustration of Lance Armstrong's being honored for winning the Tour de France! Other times Murphy speaks as though punishment entails that the person inflicting the punishment *regard* the person being

Murphy concludes flatly, "The classic penal substitution view of the Atonement is incoherent."[13]

The crucial premises of this argument seem to be the following:

(1) If Christ was sinless, God could not have condemned Christ.
(2) If God could not have condemned Christ, God could not have punished Christ.
(3) If God could not have punished Christ, penal substitution is false.

Thus, it follows from the sinlessness of Christ that penal substitution is false.

RESPONSES TO THE ALLEGED INCOHERENCE OF PENAL SUBSTITUTION

It seems to me that there are a number of ways in which the proponent of penal substitution might plausibly respond to Murphy's coherence objection.

Penal Substitution without Punishment

A penal substitution theorist who holds that God did not punish Christ denies (3) and so will be unfazed by and perhaps even welcome Murphy's objection. Such a theorist, if he wishes, may simply use a different word than "punishment" to characterize Christ's suffering. Feinberg, for example, distinguishes *penalties*, such as parking tickets, offside penalties in sports, firings at work, flunkings in school, and so on, from *punishments* technically so-called, which always express condemnation. Borrowing this distinction, the defender of penal substitution may say

---

punished as worthy of condemnation, which would allow for the innocent to be mistakenly punished. This characterization still has the counterintuitive consequence that a tyrant, say, cannot punish a person whom he knows to be innocent. Murphy seems to sense the difficulties here and so backpedals to the position that such harsh treatment is punishment, but it is defective punishment. Unfortunately, Murphy does not explain what it means for punishment to be defective, other than saying that when a case of punishing fails to meet the necessary conditions he lists, we have "a case of *defective* punishment" (255). It had better not mean *unjust*, or the coherence objection collapses to the moral objection. I therefore take it that defective punishment is not truly punishment.

13 Murphy, "Not Penal Substitution," 260.

that God penalized Christ for our sins, that Christ paid the penalty for our sins. If God's harsh treatment of Christ did not express condemnation, then God did not punish Christ for our sins, but He may still be said to have penalized him for our sins. Feinberg recognizes that inflicting penalties on an innocent person may be even worse than inflicting punishments on an innocent person.[14] The debate will then move on to the familiar question of the morality of afflicting an innocent person with the suffering that we deserved as the punishment for our sins.

Seen in this light, Murphy is employing what the eminent legal theorist H. L. A. Hart famously called "a definitional stop" to short-circuit debate.[15] Anthony Quinton had previously argued that for harsh treatment to be punishment, the person afflicted with harsh treatment had to deserve that treatment.[16] The problem with Quinton's definition was that it made it logically impossible to punish the innocent. Yet it is indisputable that innocent people are often found guilty and subjected to harsh treatment for crimes they did not commit. Quinton was forced to say that such persons, though sentenced and treated harshly, were not really punished, technically speaking. Hart's complaint was that ruling out their treatment as punishment by mere definition was just a semantic maneuver that masked important questions about punishment. Murphy employs a similar definitional stop regarding substitutionary punishment. Historically, substitutionary punishment, like punishment of the innocent, apparently does take place.[17] Debate over the justifiability of penal substitution should not be brought to a halt by a definitional stop.

---

14 Feinberg, *Doing and Deserving*, 112.

15 H. L. A. Hart, *Punishment and Responsibility* (Oxford: Oxford University Press, 1968), 5.

16 A. M. Quinton, "On Punishment," *Analysis* 14 (1954): 133–42.

17 See below, n29. Some atonement theorists have also pointed to plausible examples involving punishment of everyone in a group for wrongs done by only some members of that group (Steven L. Porter, "Swinburnian Atonement and the Doctrine of Penal Substitution," *Faith and Philosophy* 21, no. 2 [2004]: 236; Daniel J. Hill and Joseph Jedwab, "Atonement and the Concept of Punishment," in *Locating Atonement: Explorations in Constructive Dogmatics*, ed. Oliver D. Crisp and Fred Sanders [Grand Rapids: Zondervan, 2015], 144–45). I see no non-question-begging reason that we must agree with Leo Zaibert that in every such case the non-culprits are being either victimized or punished for other wrongs (Leo Zaibert, *Punishment and Retribution* (Aldershot, UK: Ashgate, 2006), 42). Again, we must be careful to avoid confusing the question of

Murphy rejects the comparison with Quinton, claiming that his objection is not that substitutionary punishment is logically impossible but that it is conceptually incoherent. For the person who is punishing the substitute is committed to holding that the substitute is innocent but worthy of condemnation.[18] I take this to mean that the punisher must regard the substitute as both worthy of condemnation and not worthy of condemnation, which he cannot do. Whether this aporia involves a logical impossibility or a conceptual incoherence, it seems to me that the maneuver is still the same: one has just put a definitional stop to substitutionary punishment by defining "punishment" in such a way that the harsh treatment authoritatively inflicted for the violation of a norm on a substitute will not count as punishment. If we simply replace the term "punishment" with "penalty" with respect to God's harsh treatment of Christ, then the alleged incoherence vanishes.

David Lewis responds to the definitional stop as an attempt to short-circuit debate over penal substitution by acquiescing to the expressivist's definition of "punishment" but insisting, "I trust that the reader will understand: I mean that the volunteer undergoes something that would have constituted punishment if it had happened instead to the guilty offender."[19] Discussion of the justice of such treatment may then proceed. Lewis' counterfactual characterization is, in fact, in accord with penal substitution as we have defined it.

Punishment without Expressivism

If the penal substitution theorist does hold that God punished Christ for our sins, then it is open to him to deny (2). Hart maintained that to avoid the definitional stop, we must recognize certain secondary forms of

---

whether, e.g., a teacher punishes a whole class for deeds done by some members of the class with the question of whether the teacher's so doing is justifiable.

18 Murphy, "Not Penal Substitution," 258n10.

19 David Lewis, "Do We Believe in Penal Substitution?" *Philosophical Papers* 26, no. 3 (1997): 209n1. In his discussion of Lewis, Murphy ignores Lewis' response to the attempted definitional stop. Instead, Murphy claims that the person paying a fine on behalf of someone else is not punished because that person is not condemned. But Lewis has already said that he will acquiesce to saying that the substitute is not "punished"; however, he avoids Murphy's definitional stop by construing penal substitution to mean that the substitute bears the harsh treatment which would have been punishment had it been inflicted on the person deserving it.

punishment, such as punishment of persons who neither are in fact nor supposed to be offenders.[20] Accordingly, on Hart's view, substitutionary punishment is one kind of punishment. On this view an expression of condemnation of the person punished is not a necessary condition of punishment.

Murphy does not consider the possibility that the penal substitution theorist might reasonably reject an expressivist theory of punishment. Though popular, it is not as though the theory has overwhelming arguments in support. Murphy lists two virtues of Feinberg's theory: (1) It carves the cases properly. In contrast to criminal cases, sports penalties and tort awards do not typically involve expression of condemnation. Only in criminal cases are defendants found guilty. (2) It makes intelligible the fact that crimes have guilty mind (*mens rea*) conditions as essential elements. In criminal law one is not found guilty simply for wrongdoing (*actus reus*) if one performed the act unknowingly or without a blameworthy volitional state (e.g., intentionally, recklessly, or negligently) and so lacked a *mens rea*. It also explains the defense strategies of showing that the accused had some excuse or justification for the wrongdoing and so is not to blame.

Consider, first, Murphy's claim that the expressivist theory carves the cases properly. This is, in fact, not true. One of the problems with the theory is that the line between punishments and mere penalties in the law does not coincide with the line between condemnatory and non-condemnatory harsh treatment.

Penalties plausibly often express society's "resentment" and "stern judgment of disapproval" for the wrong done.[21] This seems undeniable in cases involving torts such as assault and battery, defamation, fraud, and wrongful death. Arthur Ripstein explains that tort law articulates certain norms of acceptable conduct, and if the plaintiff is to recover damages from the defendant, he must show that the defendant has violated those norms. "The entire proceeding is structured by questions of whether defendant behaved unacceptably towards plaintiff, and whether plaintiff's injury is appropriately related to defendant's mistreatment of her. The structure of a tort action thus expresses the way in which it answers questions about whose problem it is when things go wrong by

---

20 Hart, *Punishment and Responsibility*, 5.
21 The fusion of resentment and reprobation (stern disapproval) is what Feinberg calls condemnation.

considering the ways in which people treat each other."[22] The judgment of the unacceptability of the defendant's conduct may often be so severe as to express condemnation. Indeed, some torts are also crimes, in which case the act for which compensatory damages are awarded is also the object of condemnation in a criminal verdict. And even for torts that are not crimes, sometimes the damages awarded are actually punitive damages, which exceed the aims of merely corrective justice. Very large awards, in particular, plausibly often express society's strong disapproval of the wrong done to the plaintiff. Even in sports, penalties imposed for fouls like unsportsmanlike conduct and taunting seem to carry censure with them. While these infractions are not crimes, since they are not violations of criminal law, still the penalties imposed for such infractions plausibly express condemnation.

By the same token, there are crimes that are punishable, even though such punishments do not seem to express condemnation. For example, crimes involving so-called *mala prohibita* are punishable, even though such punishments may not express resentment or stern disapproval, such as punishment for violation of U.S. federal laws against marijuana possession.[23] Moreover, there are, in the criminal law, cases of so-called strict liability in which crimes are committed without fault and yet are punishable. Murphy acknowledges these, but insists that "these are unusual, severe outliers in the criminal law."[24] These cases are, in fact, far from unusual, there being many thousands of statutory offenses involving elements of strict liability, including crimes like possession of narcotics or firearms and the selling of mislabeled foods or of prescription

---

22 Arthur Ripstein, "Philosophy of Tort Law," in *The Oxford Handbook of Jurisprudence and Philosophy of Law*, ed. Jules Coleman and Scott Schapiro (Oxford: Oxford University Press, 2002), 658. "Tort law," says Ripstein, "decides whose problem something is by looking at how people are allowed to treat each other" (686).

23 *Mala prohibita* are distinguished from *mala in se*, in that they are not inherently wrong, independent of criminal law, but are wrong only in virtue of being proscribed by criminal law. For discussion see Douglas Husak, "*Malum Prohibitum* and Retributivism," in *Defining Crimes: Essays on the Special Part of the Criminal Law*, ed. R. A. Duff and Stuart P. Green, Oxford Monographs on Criminal Law and Justice (Oxford: Oxford University Press, 2005), 65–90. Despite the lack of condemnation of violators, such laws are often taken to serve a useful purpose and so are not repealed.

24 Murphy, "Not Penal Substitution," 256.

drugs without a prescription.[25] Punishments for crimes of strict liability often seem to involve no condemnation of the person involved and yet are still punishments in our criminal justice system.

Crimes of strict liability also go to undermine Murphy's second alleged virtue of the expressivist theory, for no *mens rea* of any sort is required for conviction. Mere wrongdoing suffices, and the law permits no excuses or justification. Indeed, David Ormerod and Karl Laird point out that "where an offence is held to be one of strict liability, not only is it unnecessary for the prosecution to tender evidence of mens rea as to the matter of strict liability . . . , they *must* not adduce evidence of D's mens rea as to that aspect of the offence," lest D be found to be at fault.[26] Consider, for example, the case of *Pharmaceutical Society of Great Britain v. Storkwain Ltd.* (1986) 2 All ER 635. A certain pharmacist D sold some prescription drugs on the basis of what, unbeknownst to him at the time, turned out to be a forged prescription. He was convicted of violating the Medicines Act of 1968, which prohibits the retail sale of certain drugs without a prescription by an appropriate medical practitioner. This was a strict liability offense, which involved no *mens rea*. Ormerod and Laird report, "There was no finding that D acted dishonestly, improperly or even negligently in acting on that prescription and providing X with the medicines."[27] Summarizing a number of similar cases, they reflect, "In each of these cases D was not even negligent. He intended the conduct element of offence—to sell medicine or meat or liquor or to possess tobacco—but he was blamelessly unaware of the crucial circumstance element in the actus reus—that the tobacco was adulterated, that the meat was contaminated, that the person was drunk, etc. In each case he was criminally liable despite not having been at fault in relation to this material element of the offence."[28]

Thus, it is simply not true, as Murphy claims, that the line between condemnatory and non-condemnatory harsh treatment coincides with the line between punishments and mere penalties in the law.

In fact, penal substitution in a secular context furnishes itself a powerful counterexample to the claim that punishment inherently expresses

---

25 See David Ormerod and Karl Laird, *Smith, Hogan, and Ormerod's Criminal Law*, 15th ed. (Oxford: Oxford University Press, 2018), chap. 5: "Crimes of Strict Liability," for many examples.

26 Ormerod and Laird, *Smith, Hogan, and Ormerod's Criminal Law*, 145.

27 Ormerod and Laird, *Smith, Hogan, and Ormerod's Criminal Law*, 143.

28 Ormerod and Laird, *Smith, Hogan, and Ormerod's Criminal Law*, 145.

an attitude of condemnation toward the person punished. As Hugo Grotius documents, the punishment of a substitute was well understood and widely accepted in the ancient world.[29] Not only so, but those who voluntarily stepped forward to die as a substitute for someone else were universally admired as paradigms of nobility. We moderns may regard such a practice as immoral and ourselves as more enlightened for renouncing it, but it would be an example of cultural imperialism to claim that these ancient societies did not really endorse and even practice substitutionary punishment. To think that because it was unjust, it was not punishment is to confuse the definition of punishment with the justification of punishment, an error made by theorists who similarly held that punishment of the innocent is not really punishment. Just as most theorists today recognize that it is coherent to punish the innocent, so we should acknowledge the coherence of punishing a substitute.

An expressivist theory of punishment is thus by no means incumbent upon the penal substitution theorist. In fact, Leo Zaibert considers Feinberg's expressivist theory to be actually dangerous for a democratic society because what are clearly punitive measures can be rationalized by the state as mere penalties. Zaibert warns, "Pragmatically speaking, the most problematic aspect of Feinberg's view is that it opens up the possibility for the State to inflict painful treatment upon its citizens, a treatment which is 'much worse than punishment,' but for which the citizens have fewer defenses than they would if they had been 'merely' punished. 'Even floggings and imposed fastings,' Feinberg continues, 'do not constitute punishments, then, where social conventions are such that they do not express public censure.'"[30] The U.S. Supreme Court, Zaibert notes, has had considerable difficulty in interpreting the Eighth Amendment's prohibition of cruel and unusual punishment because it is unclear what actions count as punishment. One notorious example is the court's

---

29 Hugo Grotius, *A Defence of the Catholic Faith concerning the Satisfaction of Christ, against Faustus Socinus* trans. Frank Hugh Foster (Andover, Mass.: Warren F. Draper, 1889), chap. 4. See further Simon Gathercole, *Defending Substitution: An Essay on Atonement in Paul* (Grand Rapids: Baker Academic, 2015), chap. 3. According to Gathercole, the preeminent example of substitutionary death in classical literature is Euripides' Alcestis, who was willing to die in place of her husband, Admetus. In Rom 5:7-8 Paul compares the death of Jesus with other heroic deaths that his Roman readers might have known. Gathercole thinks that Alcestis may well be the example that Paul had in mind.

30 Zaibert, *Punishment and Retribution*, 113. The embedded quotations are from Feinberg.

decision in *Flemming v. Nestor*, 363 U.S. 603 (1960) that deportation is merely an administrative matter and not punishment, despite the fact that deportation in that (and other cases) seems to be punitive.[31] "The widespread standard account makes it easy for the state to abuse its punitive power by masquerading punitive measures as if they were not really punitive, labeling certain governmental acts as merely administrative, as if this label would *deus ex machina* obscure the fact that some such acts are clearly punitive."[32]

A defender of penal substitution could avoid the coherence objection, then, by denying Murphy's claim that the expressive function of punishment is part of the definition of punishment.

Expressivism without Condemnation of Christ

But the penal substitution theorist need not reject expressivism outright in order to deny (2). For expressivism as typically formulated is wholly consistent with penal substitution. Consider, once again, Walen's account given above. His fourth condition does not require that the person punished be condemned or censured for the act or omission believed to be wrong. Censure could be either of the person who did the act or of the act itself. Similarly, on Feinberg's account "punishment expresses the community's strong disapproval of *what the criminal did*. Indeed it can be said that punishment expresses the judgment of the community that *what the criminal did* was wrong."[33] Even Murphy's own formulation, intended to show the incoherence of penal substitution, namely, that punishment expresses condemnation of the wrongdoer as the performer of the wrong, does not rule out penal substitution, for it does not require that condemnation be directed toward the person bearing the punishment. Hence, Murphy's inference "if this . . . condition is correctly formulated, then punishment expresses condemnation of the person punished" is a non sequitur.[34]

---

31 Zaibert, *Punishment and Retribution*, 48, 54.

32 Zaibert, *Punishment and Retribution*, 4.

33 Feinberg, *Doing and Deserving*, 100 (emphasis added). An even stronger attitude or judgment of condemnation may be directed as well toward *what the criminal did*.

34 Murphy, "Not Penal Substitution," 256. This same jump in Murphy's argument has been pointed out by Hill and Jedwab, "Atonement and the Concept of Punishment," 139–53. They observe, "It is not a feature of Murphy's definition that

In fact, it needs to be asked whether critics of the coherence of penal substitution have not fundamentally misunderstood expressivism with regard to punishment. Expressivism holds that there is a certain stigma attached to punishment, in the absence of which the harsh treatment is not punishment. It is no part of expressivism that the censure expressed by punishment target a particular person. Expressivist theories of punishment, as typically formulated, are perfectly consistent with penal substitution—which is just as it should be, given the attitudes of those in societies endorsing or practicing penal substitution. Hence, (2) is undercut.

Condemnation of Christ without Personal Sin and Guilt

But suppose one adopts an expressivist theory of punishment that does require that condemnation be directed toward the person punished. Would such a theory rule out penal substitution? Not necessarily, for one might espouse a theory of penal substitution that includes the imputation of sin, such as the Reformers articulated and Turretin defended. On such a theory, Christ, though personally without moral fault, is legally guilty and so condemned by God for our sins. Hence, (1) is denied. Murphy admits that given the doctrine of the imputation of sins, his charge of incoherence fails.

Unsurprisingly, however, critics of penal substitution are unlikely to be sympathetic to the doctrine of imputation. But reservations about that doctrine are even more rarely unfolded than the standard moral objection to penal substitution. Murphy cursorily dismisses the doctrine of imputation with the observation that we have no experience of the *transfer* either of moral responsibility for actions or of guilt in isolation from actions from one person to another.[35] We shall take up that issue in the next chapter when we discuss the justification of penal substitution. For now we note merely in passing that given the doctrine of the imputation of our sin to Christ, the objection to the coherence of penal substitution is a self-confessed failure.

---

the one punished has to be the one that failed to measure up to the binding standard; nor does his definition specify that the one punished has to be the one condemned. . . . Of course, this could be added as a fifth condition, but, in the absence of argument, this would simply beg the question."

35 Murphy, "Not Penal Substitution," 259.

Summary

We may thank Murphy for alerting Christian philosophers to the relevance of debates over the definition of punishment in the philosophy of law to the doctrine of the atonement, particularly to penal substitution. But his discussion of the coherence of penal substitution is not sufficiently nuanced. Not all advocates of penal substitution hold that Christ was punished for our sins. Murphy's attempted definitional stop to substitutionary punishment is a mere semantic maneuver that can be adroitly circumvented, if one wishes, by affirming that Christ was penalized for our sins. It is not, in any case, incumbent upon Christian or legal philosophers to adopt an expressivist definition of punishment. But if we do, the typical articulations of expressivist theories are perfectly compatible with penal substitution, which is just as it should be, given the attitudes expressed toward penal substitutes in societies recognizing the justice of such a practice. Finally, even if we adopt a definition of punishment that is so narrowly construed as to rule out normal cases of penal substitution, that does not, by Murphy's own admission, subvert the Reformers' doctrine of penal substitution, predicated as it is on the doctrine of imputation, a doctrine that, as we shall see, is not without legal analogies in our own experience. Thus, multiple responses to the coherence objection are available to the penal substitution theorist, depending on how many of the critic's premises one accepts. Therefore, the charge of philosophical incoherence has not been sustained.

THE ALLEGED THEOLOGICAL INCOHERENCE OF PENAL SUBSTITUTION

Murphy's challenge to the coherence of penal substitution arose from considerations pertinent to the definition of punishment. Eleonore Stump, however, challenges the theological coherence of penal substitution. She charges that such a theory of the atonement "is incompatible with God's love."[36] Since penal substitutionary theories affirm God's love, it follows that any such theory is incoherent and therefore unsalvageable.[37] Stump

---

36 Eleonore Stump, *Atonement* (Oxford: Oxford University Press, 2018), 80.
37 Stump, *Atonement*, 33.

calls this "the central and irremediable problem" with penal substitution-ary atonement theories.[38]

How are penal substitutionary atonement theories incompatible with God's love? The problem Stump sees in such theories is that they require satisfaction of God's justice as a precondition of God's forgive-ness. Stump thinks that such a precondition is incompatible with God's unconditional love and forgiveness. She provides this pithy summary of her argument:

> God's forgiveness, like God's love, is unilateral and unconditional. It does not depend on anything; rather, it is a function of God's nature, which is perfectly good and therefore also perfectly loving. God's love and forgive-ness, and God's acceptance of reconciliation with human wrongdoers, are there for every human person, even those who are unrepentant wrongdo-ers. And so the Anselmian kind of interpretation of the doctrine of the atonement, in all its variants, is wrong.[39]

"Anselmian" is Stump's rather misleading label for any atonement theory that sees the satisfaction of divine justice as a necessary condition of salvation. It is meant to comprise not only satisfaction theories but penal substitutionary theories as well.

Stump's argument seems to be based on three simple premises:

(1)   God is perfectly loving.
(2)   If God is perfectly loving, He is perfectly forgiving.
(3)   If God is perfectly forgiving, His forgiveness has no preconditions.

---

38 Stump, *Atonement*, 79. Her indictment is directed at satisfaction theories of the atonement as well, but our concern is with penal substitutionary theories.

39 Stump, *Atonement*, 101. We should note that on Stump's view an "acceptance of reconciliation" no more implies actual reconciliation than does love and forgiveness. It just means that the offended party is ready to reconcile with the wrongdoer and will do so once the obstacle to reconciliation is removed from the wrongdoer (433n1). So in Stump's view God's anger with and even hatred of unrepentant sinners is compatible with His acceptance of reconcilia-tion with them. On the compatibility of necessitarian atonement theories with God's unconditional acceptance of reconciliation with sinners, see Hayden C. Stephan, "Is the God of Anselm Unloving? A Response to Eleonore Stump," *Religious Studies* (August 23, 2019), published online.

According to "Anselmian" atonement theories, however, God's forgiveness does have preconditions, namely, the satisfaction of God's justice. Accordingly,

> (4) If any "Anselmian" atonement theory is true, God's forgiveness has preconditions.

From these premises it follows that

> (5) No "Anselmian" atonement theory is true.

RESPONSE TO THE ALLEGED THEOLOGICAL INCOHERENCE OF PENAL SUBSTITUTION

Stump's argument for the incompatibility of penal substitutionary theories of the atonement with God's love and forgiveness is predicated on a number of questionable assumptions. In view of her argument's much more fundamental problems, however, I relegate these difficulties to a footnote.[40]

---

40 Stump's argument is predicated on the connection between love and forgiveness. She affirms, "Because love is necessary and sufficient for forgiveness, God . . . forgives each human being. A perfectly loving God can and does forgive unconditionally and unilaterally, just as he can and does love unrequitedly" (Stump, *Atonement*, 109–10).

But is love truly a necessary condition of forgiveness? Victims of crimes like sexual assault have often remarked that it is necessary for them to forgive their offender in order to break the emotional tie with him and so be rid of him and find healing. Their forgiveness is not due to a desire for the good of the offender but for their own good. Thus, forgiveness is not a sufficient condition of love.

Moreover, is love always a sufficient condition of forgiveness, as Stump's argument assumes? If a loved one, say, one's son, has committed a truly heinous act, such as a mass killing of innocent schoolchildren, does a parent's love for the son require him to forgive his son for what he has done? Does the argument against the coherence of penal substitution depend on so uncertain a premise as this?

In any case, given that love is sufficient for forgiveness, God's loving every person implies His forgiving every person. But on "Anselmian" theories, Stump says, satisfaction of God's justice is a precondition of God's forgiveness. Therefore, Anselmian theories, which hold that God's forgiveness is conditional on the satisfaction of divine justice, are incompatible with the doctrine that God is perfectly loving.

A curious feature of Stump's argument is that it applies not only to necessitarian accounts of the atonement like Anselm's and Turretin's but also to non-necessitarian accounts like Aquinas' and Grotius'. For if the consequent of (4) is true on necessitarian accounts of the atonement, it is also true on non-necessitarian accounts, howbeit by God's free choice rather than by His nature. God has freely chosen to punish Christ for our sins because of the great advantages to be won thereby. But this leads to a bizarre conclusion. Suppose, for example, that God knew that free pardon without satisfaction would have taken on the appearance of "cheap grace" and so would have been far less effective in winning people to salvation. Therefore, He has freely chosen to make Christ's satisfaction of divine justice a precondition of His pardon of sinners. It would seem absurd to think Him less loving for preferring a costly grace that implied enormous self-sacrifice for God in Christ if by such a means multitudes more would freely find salvation. Thus, it seems incredible that such accounts could be indicted for being incompatible with God's love. In that case (3) is plausibly false, and it is hard to see why (3) would not also be false if God's decision were demanded by His nature rather than contingently chosen. God's forgiveness is, indeed, unconditional in the sense that it requires nothing of sinners,[41] but that does not imply that it is not based on Christ's satisfaction of divine justice on behalf of sinners.

This inference is too quick. How is the universality of God's love and forgiveness incompatible with there being preconditions of forgiveness, like the satisfaction of God's justice? After all, another precondition of forgiveness is wrongdoing, but that precondition does not preclude God's universal forgiveness. If God provides satisfaction for all persons, then the precondition of universal forgiveness is met. Stump fails to appreciate that what unconditional forgiveness requires is that there be no conditions "that *the wrongdoer* must satisfy" in order to be forgiven (Karen D. Hoffman, "Forgiveness without Apology: Defending Unconditional Forgiveness," *Proceedings of the American Catholic Philosophical Association* 82 [2008]: 135, emphasis added), not that forgiveness has no preconditions. From God's universal love and forgiveness, all that follows is that any preconditions for universal forgiveness have been met: God has provided satisfaction for every human being. Stump's is really an argument against limited atonement, not penal substitution.

41 See again Hoffman, "Forgiveness without Apology," 135. Stump's argument thus relies on an equivocal use of the word "unconditional."

Love and Forgiveness on Penal Substitutionary Theories

But let that pass. There are, it seems to me, two fundamental problems with Stump's argument. The first fundamental problem is, *given Stump's definitions of love and forgiveness, it is not true that God, as characterized by penal substitutionary atonement theories, fails to be perfectly loving and forgiving.* That is to say, given Stump's definitions, (4) is false. God's love and forgiveness, given Stump's definitions, are unconditional on penal substitutionary atonement theories. Stump's explications of love and forgiveness are so thin that God as described by penal substitutionary atonement theories meets the conditions sufficient for being perfectly loving and forgiving.

On Stump's view love involves both a desire for the good of the beloved and a desire for union with him. Just as a person can love unrequitedly, so he can forgive unilaterally, despite the wrongdoer's rejection of that forgiveness. So, Stump says, "God can forgive a wrongdoer unilaterally and unconditionally, in the sense that, even without any repentance on the wrongdoer's part, God can still desire the good for her and union with her."[42] Stump even goes so far as to argue that an attitude of hatred and aversion toward the wrongdoer, as well as anger with the wrongdoer, are compatible with love and forgiveness of him, so long as one's ultimate desire remains for the good of the wrongdoer.[43] So long as one would not be disappointed and grieved if the wrongdoer were to repent and change for the better, then hatred and anger toward the wrongdoer are compatible with love.

---

42 Stump, *Atonement*, 84.

43 Stump, *Atonement*, 85–88. She later explains:

> A morally perfect God can forgive a wrongdoer unconditionally and unilaterally, in the sense that God can desire the good for the wrongdoer and union with him no matter what the state of the wrongdoer is. Even the anger and hatred God has towards some people are the kind of anger and hatred that are compatible with love. These reactive attitudes coexist in God with an acceptance of reconciliation with those people for whom God has anger or hatred, and they come with a continual offer of divine grace that would produce goodness and closeness to God in any wrongdoer who did not reject that grace. What God ultimately desires for every person, even those with whom he is angry or those whom he hates, is union with them. (111–12)

These affirmations are wholly compatible with penal substitutionary accounts of the atonement.

It should be obvious that there is nothing in penal substitutionary theories that precludes that wholly apart from the satisfaction of God's justice, God both wills the good of every person and desires union with him. If Reformed and Lutheran theologians deny that God so wills and desires, that denial stems not from their atonement theory but from their doctrine of election. Arminian and Molinist defenders of penal substitution affirm that God wills the good of and desires union with all persons, even in their fallen condition. Hence, on Stump's definition God forgives them unilaterally and, hence, unconditionally. Therefore, (4) is false, given Stump's understanding of forgiveness.

Stump's characterization of forgiveness has the odd implication that the exercise of God's retributive justice in punishing wrongdoers is compatible with His also forgiving those wrongdoers. Biblically speaking, people whose sins have been forgiven will not be punished by God for those sins. But on Stump's account God may both forgive their sins and yet punish them for those sins! Stump thinks that retributive justice can be seen as a good for the person punished, in which case God in punishing wrongdoers still wills their good and desires union with them, that is to say, He forgives them.[44] So on her account of love and forgiveness, she concludes, "It is possible to hold that imposing warranted retributive punishment on a wrongdoer is at least sometimes obligatory, and still to maintain that love and forgiveness are always obligatory, even love and forgiveness for wholly unrepentant wrongdoers."[45] Now if it seems odd that a person can be both forgiven for his sins and punished for those sins, this oddity ought to make us question whether something has not gone wrong with Stump's account of divine forgiveness. That forms a nice segue to the second fundamental failing of her argument against the coherence of penal substitutionary atonement theories.

God as Judge and Ruler

The second fundamental problem with Stump's objection is that *her entire approach to the doctrine of the atonement is based on construing God on the analogy of a private party involved in various personal relationships rather than as a Judge and Ruler.* She frequently compares God and human persons with two friends, Paula and Jerome, who have to deal with wrongs committed by one against the other. Hugo Grotius already identified

---

44 Stump, *Atonement*, chap. 3, 89–92.
45 Stump, *Atonement*, 91–92.

this same construal as the fundamental failing of Socinus' critique of penal substitutionary atonement theories. Grotius maintains that we should not think of God as merely a private party in a personal dispute. Rather, God should be considered to act as a Ruler and Judge.

On the contemporary scene legal philosopher Jeffrie Murphy has made a similar distinction between the private and public spheres in an effort to carve out conceptual space for exercises of mercy consistent with the demands of retributive justice. Distinguishing between a judge in a criminal case and a creditor in a civil lawsuit, Murphy maintains that as a litigant in a civil lawsuit, the creditor occupies a "private role" and so does not have "an antecedent obligation, required by the rules of justice, to impose harsh treatment" by demanding repayment of the debt owed.[46] He is therefore free to show mercy without prejudice to justice. By contrast a judge in a criminal case "has an *obligation* to do justice—which means, at a minimum, an obligation to uphold the rule of law. Thus if he is moved, even by love or compassion, to act contrary to the rule of law—to the rules of justice—he acts wrongly."[47] Murphy thinks that the judge qua judge cannot, like the creditor, act mercifully without prejudice to the demands of justice. Like Grotius he thinks that the executive power can exercise mercy but only within the limits of individualized justice.[48]

The overriding lesson is that God should not be thought of merely as a private party to a personal dispute but as Judge and Ruler of the world

---

46 Jeffrie Murphy, "Mercy and Legal Justice," in *Forgiveness and Mercy*, ed. Jeffrie G. Murphy and Jean Hampton (Cambridge: Cambridge University Press, 1988), 175–76.

47 Murphy, "Mercy and Legal Justice," 175. See also H. R. T. Roberts, "Mercy," *Philosophy* 46, no. 178 (1971): 352–53, in response to Alwynne Smart, "Mercy," *Philosophy* 43, no. 166 (1968): 345–59. Roberts criticizes Smart for confining her attention to the courtroom, which leaves her unable to provide any examples of genuine mercy. That is because cases of so-called judicial mercy are really cases of determining that exaction of the full penalty allowed by law would not be just. "Whereas in ordinary life a person could weigh every relevant factor and yet properly say, 'In all justice x owes me A, but it is *mine* to exact and I choose not to,' a judge, though perhaps required to decide on a debt due to an individual, is never required to pronounce on one due to himself and so can never exercise real mercy" (353).

48 See also comments by Samuel T. Morison, "The Politics of Grace: On the Moral Justification of Executive Clemency," *Buffalo Criminal Law Review* 9, no. 1 (2005): 89–90.

and therefore responsible for administering justice. Indeed, as we have seen in chapter 4, the Bible portrays God as at once Lawgiver and Judge and Ruler. In contrast to Western systems of government, God embodies in one individual the legislative, judicial, and executive functions of government. He is clearly not a merely private individual. He is a public person responsible for the administration of justice in the world.

Like far too many contemporary atonement theorists, Stump neglects legal analogies of the atonement and turns instead to private, personal relationships to motivate or criticize theories of the atonement, thereby overlooking God's status as Ruler and Judge. She takes God to be like the offended party in a personal dispute and so extends Anselm's insistence on our need to satisfy the demands of God's justice (whether by compensation or punishment) to two private parties in a personal friendship. This sort of extension is illegitimate, both for Anselm and for the Reformers, who see us as sinners who have violated God's law and so stand condemned before the bar of His justice.[49]

On penal substitutionary theories God is like a judge who must administer justice whatever his personal feelings toward the accused.[50] It is perfectly possible for a judge to love and forgive a personal friend brought before his bar, even as he declares him guilty and sentences him to severe punishment. As Stump herself recognizes, God can personally will the good of sinners and desire their union with him without waiving the demands of retributive justice.

Rather than thinking of God's forgiveness of sins on the analogue of human friendships, Stump ought to be thinking of divine forgiveness in terms of legal analogies like pardon or commutation of punishment.[51] As we shall see, pardon is a legal act that removes the criminal's liability to

---

49 Stump's treatment generally neglects legal aspects of the atonement and ignores forensic motifs in the NT. Her doctrine of justification, for example, is non-forensic, being a matter of God's infused righteousness into the believer, not a legal pardon granted by God. By contrast, as we have seen (chap. 4, n17), the forensic nature of justification is Pauline. See further chap. 10, n29.

50 As dramatically illustrated at the murder trial of Dallas police officer Amber Guyger. After pronouncing sentence on Guyger, Judge Tammy Kemp emotionally embraced and comforted Guyger. https://www.washingtonpost.com/nation/2019/10/03/judge-botham-jeans-brother-hugged-amber-guyger-igniting-debate-about-forgiveness-race/.

51 See provocative discussions of pardon by Henry Weihofen, "The Effect of a Pardon," *University of Pennsylvania Law Review* 88 (December 1939): 177–93;

punishment and restores his civil rights. God's pardon of us is based on Christ's fully discharging substitutionally our sentence and so satisfying divine justice.

The failing of Stump's argument as I have formulated it, then, lies in an equivocal use of the word "forgiveness" in (3) and (4). On penal substitutionary atonement theories, God is perfectly forgiving in Stump's sense and so provides satisfaction for undeserving sinners, but His forgiveness of sins in the sense of pardoning those sins is based on the precondition of Christ's satisfaction of divine justice. In the penultimate draft of her book (graciously provided me in preprint), Stump uses the word "pardon" only once, in a subheading. But in the final draft pardon is introduced at several junctures. Unfortunately, Stump tends to conflate it with forgiveness in her sense and fails to differentiate it as a legal notion. For example, she speaks of a case in which "Paula has pardoned Jerome, but her pardon is insufficient to produce in Jerome the kind of state necessary for him to return to company with her."[52] Stump is evidently using "pardon" here in the sense of "forgiveness," since Paula as a private person has no authority to issue a legal pardon. Or again, we find this interesting characterization of "Anselmian" atonement theories:

> There are then two claims central to all the variants on the Anselmian kind of interpretation of the doctrine of the atonement. First, without Christ's making amends to God, God would not forgive human wrongdoers or accept being reconciled with them. And, second, the main (or only) point of Christ's atonement is to satisfy a condition needed for God's forgiveness and reconciliation. Oliver Crisp, who is in this tradition of interpretation, likens God's acceptance of reconciliation with human beings to the pardon of a monarch. On the Anselmian kind of interpretation, it is a pardon that is won for human beings by the atonement of Christ and that would not be given without that atonement. God's forgiveness and reconciliation with human beings, God's granting the pardon, is conditional on God's receiving what human sin owes God in the atonement of Christ.[53]

Samuel Williston, "Does a Pardon Blot Out Guilt?" *Harvard Law Review* 28, no. 7 (May 1915): 647–63.

52 Stump, *Atonement*, 445n106.

53 Stump, *Atonement*, 74. It should be evident that Crisp does not mean by "acceptance of reconciliation" what Stump means (see n39 above). Cf. 101–2 for the same conflation:

> God's forgiveness of human beings and acceptance of reconciliation with them is thus dependent on Christ's making satisfaction to God. . . .

As we have seen, penal substitutionary theorists regard both claims as false, unless forgiveness is understood not as Stump understands it but as legal pardon. Citing Crisp in the quotation above, Stump suddenly introduces the notion of pardon and rightly says that it would not be given without Christ's atonement. But then in the final sentence she lapses back into conflating God's granting a pardon with His forgiveness and reconciliation as she understands them.

On penal substitutionary theories (whether necessitarian or non-necessitarian) God as Ruler (while willing our good and desiring union with us) does not merely pardon us but exacts the punishment demanded by retributive justice. He does not exact it from us but from Himself in Christ. We who accept Christ's substitutionary sacrifice are thereby freed from our liability to punishment and therefore declared "not guilty." Seeing that Christ has vicariously satisfied the demands of divine retributive justice on our behalf, God can, in turn, pardon us of our sins. It is in that sense that God can be said to have forgiven our sins. "And you, who were dead in your trespasses . . . , God made alive together with [Christ], having forgiven us all our trespasses, by canceling the record of debt that stood against us with its legal demands. This he set aside, nailing it to the cross" (Col 2:13-14 ESV). Forgiveness in this legal sense is the declaration that the penalty has been fully paid and therefore we are free.

There are fascinating questions to be explored here, and my point is that progress is more apt to be made by conceiving of God along Grotian lines as Ruler and Judge than along Socinian lines as an offended party in a private dispute. When we do so consider God, then it seems obvious that God's being perfectly loving and forgiving are entirely compatible with legal condemnation of sinners and, indeed, may motivate God to provide the satisfaction for sinners requisite for His just pardon of them.

Summary

In summary, Stump's central objection to the theological coherence of penal substitutionary atonement theories is, I think, a fundamental failure because (1) given Stump's definitions of love and forgiveness, God, as characterized by such atonement theories, is perfectly loving and

---

[T]he point of Christ's satisfaction is to provide a perfectly good God with this needed condition for pardoning human beings. . . . [T]he point remains that God's forgiveness and acceptance of reconciliation depends on Christ's making satisfaction to God.

forgiving, and (2) Stump's entire approach to the doctrine of the atonement is based on misconstruing God as a sort of private person rather than as supreme Judge and Ruler.

CONCLUDING REMARKS

In conclusion, we have seen no good argument against the coherence of penal substitutionary atonement theories. The attempt to demonstrate an incoherence arising from the definition of punishment is based upon so many dubious assumptions that the alleged incoherence is not difficult to avoid. The attempt to show that penal substitutionary atonement theories are theologically incoherent is based on an equivocal use of "forgiveness" and the failure to construe divine forgiveness on the analogy of a legal pardon by an executive authority rather than on the model of reconciliation in private relationships. Consideration of such coherence objections has nonetheless proved to be profitable in view of the insights it has already yielded concerning penal substitution and divine punishment. With these insights in hand, we may now turn to the more important and pressing moral objection to the justice of penal substitution.

Chapter 10

Penal Substitution
Its Justification

INTRODUCTION

A lthough some persons have objected to the coherence of the doctrine of penal substitution, by far and away the most prevalent and
powerful objection to the doctrine is the Socinian claim that penal substitution is unjust and therefore immoral. For example, Eleonore Stump
complains:

> On the Anselmian kind of interpretation, it is a violation of God's . . .
> justice . . . not to punish the sins of a human person guilty of those
> sins. . . . But, according to interpretations of the Anselmian kind, what
> God does to act compatibly with his . . . justice is in fact to fail to
> punish the guilty. . . . Worse yet, instead of punishing the guilty . . . , God
> visits their merited punishment on the innocent. . . . How is justice . . .
> served by punishing a completely innocent person?[1]

---

1   Eleonore Stump, *Atonement* (Oxford: Oxford University Press, 2018), 124. The
    elisions have to do with satisfaction theories; our focus is on penal substitu-
    tionary theories. By "Anselmian" Stump designates theories that hold that,
    necessarily, divine justice must be satisfied as a precondition of divine pardon.
    Thus, she is able to classify both satisfaction theories and penal substitutionary

Notice how carefully Stump characterizes the so-called Anselmian position on divine retributive justice: it would be a violation of divine justice not to punish the sins of a guilty person. It does not follow from this that that very person must be punished for his sins; someone else might be punished in his place. The objection, then, is the familiar Socinian objection that it would be unjust of God to punish Christ, an innocent person, in our place. Detractors of penal substitution who press this objection almost never develop it in any depth, and Stump is no exception to the rule. There is nothing here to interact with apart from the single question: How is justice served by punishing a completely innocent person? We need to go deeper.

THE ALLEGED INJUSTICE OF
PENAL SUBSTITUTION

Critics of penal substitution frequently assert that God's punishing Christ in our place would be an injustice on God's part. For it is an axiom of retributive justice that it is unjust to punish an innocent person. But Christ was an innocent person. Since God is perfectly just, He cannot therefore have punished Christ. It does no good to say that Christ willingly undertook this self-sacrifice on our behalf, for the nobility of his selfless act does not annul the injustice of punishing an innocent person for deeds he did not do.

The crucial premises and inferences of this objection appear to be the following:

(1) God is perfectly just.
(2) If God is perfectly just, He cannot punish an innocent person.
(3) Therefore, God cannot punish an innocent person.
(4) Christ was an innocent person.
(5) Therefore, God cannot punish Christ.
(6) If God cannot punish Christ, penal substitution is false.

It follows that if God is perfectly just, then penal substitution is false.

One quick and easy way to deal with this objection would be to adopt a consequentialist theory of justice. Theories of justice may be classified as broadly *retributive* or *consequentialist*. Retributive theories of justice

---

theories as "Anselmian." A less misleading label would be, as I have suggested, "necessitarian."

hold that punishment is justified because the guilty deserve to be punished. Consequentialist theories of justice hold that punishment is justified because of the extrinsic goods that may be realized thereby, such as deterrence of crime, sequestration of dangerous persons, and reformation of wrongdoers. Retributive theories are often said to be retrospective, imposing punishment for crimes committed, whereas consequentialist theories are prospective, aiming to prevent crimes from being committed. It is common coin that on consequentialist theories of justice punishment of the innocent may be justified, in view, for example, of its deterrence value. In fact, one of the main criticisms of consequentialist theories of justice is precisely the fact that on such theories it may be just to punish the innocent. A consequentialist penal substitution theorist could fairly easily provide justification for God's punishing Christ for our sins, namely, so doing prevents the loss of the entire human race. So given a consequentialist understanding of (1), we have no reason to think that (2) is true.

But consequentialism seems ill suited to serve as a basis for divine punishment because God's judgment is described in the Bible as ultimately eschatological. The ungodly are "storing up wrath" for themselves for God's final day of judgment (Rom 2:5). Punishment imposed at that point could seemingly serve no other purpose than retribution. The Christian consequentialist could say that punishment in hell does have a consequentialist justification, namely, the sequestration of the wicked from the community of the redeemed, just as hardened criminals are removed from society. But since God could achieve this end by simply annihilating the damned, the consequentialist will need to find some non-retributive reason for God's preserving them in existence. In any case, the biblical view is that the wicked deserve punishment (Rom 1:32; Heb 10:29), and it ascribes to God retribution (*ekdikēsis*; *avtapodoma*) for sins (Rom 11:9; 12:19), so that God's justice must be in some significant measure retributive.

During the first half of the twentieth century, under the influence of social scientists, retributive theories of justice were frowned upon in favor of consequentialist theories. Fortunately, there has been over the past half century or so a renaissance of theories of retributive justice, accompanied by a fading of consequentialist theories,[2] so that we, working

---

2   See, e.g., Mark D. White, ed., *Retributivism: Essays on Theory and Policy* (Oxford: Oxford University Press, 2011); Michael Tonry, ed., *Retributivism Has a Past: Has It a Future?* Studies in Penal Theory and Philosophy (Oxford: Oxford

within the mainstream position, need not be diverted by justifying a retributive theory of justice. This change is due in no small part to the unwelcome implication of pure consequentialism that there are circumstances under which it is just to punish innocent people. Unfortunately, it is precisely the conviction that the innocent ought not to be punished that lies behind the claim that penal substitutionary atonement theories are unjust and immoral.

RESPONSES TO THE ALLEGED INJUSTICE
OF PENAL SUBSTITUTION

Penal Substitution without Punishment

It is not widely appreciated that the present objection has no purchase against penal substitution theorists who hold that God did not punish Christ for our sins, since they reject (6).[3] Christ may be said to have voluntarily taken upon himself the suffering that would have been the punishment for our sins, had it been inflicted on us. He may even be said to have willingly paid the penalty for our sins. Our justice system permits people to pay penalties like fines on behalf of other persons without moral protest.[4] Since Christ was not punished for our sins, his voluntarily suffering on our behalf cannot be said to be unjust on God's part. So the objection is pressing only for penal substitution theorists who hold that God did punish Christ for our sins.

University Press, 2011). One of the few legal theorists to connect retributivism and the doctrine of the atonement is Jerome Hall, "Biblical Atonement and Modern Criminal Law," *Washington University Law Quarterly* 65 (1987): 708–10. Ironically, some theologians, unaware of the sea change in theories of justice, denounce in the strongest terms a God of retributive justice (Stephen Finlan, *Options on Atonement in Christian Thought* [Collegeville, Minn.: Liturgical Press, 2007], 97–98), not realizing that their objection to the justice of penal substitution depends on a view of divine justice as retributive, lest God punish the innocent on consequentialist grounds. Kathleen Dean Moore, *Pardons: Justice, Mercy, and the Public Interest* (Oxford: Oxford University Press, 1989), chap. 5, gives a moving account of the horrendous results of consequentialism for our penal system.

3 Recall our discussion in chapter 9, pp. 148–49.
4 David Lewis, "Do We Believe in Penal Substitution?" *Philosophical Papers* 26, no. 3 (1997): 207.

Metaethical Contextualization

Suppose that we do accept that God punished Christ in our place. An assessment of (2) requires its contextualization within a metaethical theory about the grounding of objective moral values and duties. Who or what determines what is just or unjust? The Protestant proponents of penal substitution were, like Anselm, all advocates of some sort of Divine Command Theory of ethics, according to which moral duties are constituted by divine imperatives. There is no external law hanging over God to which He must conform. Since God does not issue commands to Himself, He literally has no moral duties to fulfill. He can act in any way consistent with His nature. He does not have the moral duties we have, and He will have unique prerogatives, such as giving and taking human life as He wills. He may usually act *in accordance with* duty, to borrow a Kantian phrase, but since He does not act *from* duty, He is free to make exceptions. This is the lesson of the astonishing story of God's commanding Abraham to sacrifice his son Isaac (Gen 22:1-19).

Now if such a metaethical theory is even coherent, not to say true, as able proponents like Robert Adams, William Alston, and Philip Quinn have argued it is,[5] then the present objection will have difficulty even getting off the ground.[6] As Hugo Grotius observed, even if God has established a system of justice among human beings that forbids the punishment of the innocent (and, hence, substitutionary punishment), He Himself is not so forbidden. He refused Moses' offer of himself as a substitutionary sacrifice (Exod 32:30-34), just as He refused the sacrificing of Isaac; but if He wills to take on human nature in the form of Jesus of Nazareth and give His own life as a sacrificial offering for sin, who is to forbid Him? He is free to do so as long as it is consistent with His nature. And what could be more consistent with our God's gracious nature than that He should condescend to take on our frail and fallen humanity and give His life to satisfy the demands of His own justice?

---

5 Robert Adams, *Finite and Infinite Goods: A Framework for Ethics* (Oxford: Oxford University Press, 1999); William P. Alston, "What Euthyphro Should Have Said," in *Philosophy of Religion: A Reader and Guide*, ed. William Lane Craig (Edinburgh: Edinburgh University Press, 2002), 283–98; Philip L. Quinn, *Divine Commands and Moral Requirements* (Oxford: Clarendon Press, 1978).

6 I have since discovered a forceful statement of this point by Alvin Plantinga, "Comments on 'Satanic Verses: Moral Chaos in Holy Writ,'" in *Divine Evil? The Moral Character of the God of Abraham*, ed. Michael Bergmann, Michael J. Murray, and Michael C. Rea (Oxford: Oxford University Press, 2011), 113–14.

The self-giving sacrifice of Christ exalts the nature of God by displaying His holy love.

Retributive Justice and the Divine Nature

Perhaps the best face that can be put on the present objection is to claim that, contrary to Socinus,[7] retributive justice is part of God's nature, and therefore it is impossible that He act contrary to the principles of retributive justice. Accordingly, (2) is true.

But that raises the question, What is retributive justice? The present objection does not sufficiently differentiate various accounts of retributivism. While a so-called *negative retributivism* holds that the innocent should not be punished because they do not deserve it, the essence of retributive justice lies in so-called *positive retributivism*, which holds that the guilty should be punished because they deserve it. What distinguishes retributivism as a theory of justice is the positive thesis that punishment of the guilty is an intrinsic good because the guilty deserve it. God is a positive retributivist "who will by no means clear the guilty" (Exod 34:7). But the penal theorist may maintain that God is only qualifiedly a negative retributivist, since even if He has prohibited human beings from punishing innocent persons (Deut 24:16), and even if He is too good to Himself punish innocent human persons (Gen 18:25), still He reserves the prerogative to punish an innocent divine person, namely, Christ, in the place of the guilty. This extraordinary exception is a result of His goodness, not a defect in His justice. Hence, (2) is false.

Lest positive retributivism be thought to be too thin a theory of retributive justice to ascribe to God, it should be noted how extraordinarily strong such a thesis is, so strong in fact that it has been criticized as utterly unrealistic on a human level. Leo Zaibert indicts Michael Moore's claim that just desert constitutes a sufficient condition of punishment (i.e., the guilty should be punished because they deserve it) as entailing legal moralism, which would require the state to punish every moral wrong. Legal moralism would require "an impossibly large criminal justice apparatus" which would be "utterly unmanageable and

---

7   Ironically, objectors to penal substitution need retributive justice to belong essentially to God, lest the Divine Command Theorist say that God freely determines that it is just to punish Christ, however innocent he may be.

unrealistic."[8] Even outside the context of the state the implausibility of punishing every immorality is so high that even the staunchest unbridled retributivist has to admit that such a suggestion must be rejected. It is arguably impossible to try to punish every wrong, Zaibert exclaims, without going crazy.[9] The theist can only smile at this secular theorist's huffing and puffing about a task for which God alone is qualified and capable of carrying out. But at least we see therein how robust is a positive retributive theory of justice, which can then be further augmented by taking God to be a qualified negative retributivist as well.

This response alone suffices to dispense with the objection, but even more can be said.

Prima Facie *vs.* Ultima Facie *Justification of Punishment*

The objection based on (2) also fails to reckon with the fact that the *prima facie* demands of retributive justice can be outweighed in specific cases by weightier moral considerations, so that punishment in such a case may be justified *ultima facie*. Theorists often make this point by distinguishing between justification of the *practice* of punishment and justification of an *act* of punishment. When positive retributivists claim that the guilty should be punished, they are talking about justification of the general practice of punishment, not about specific cases. In specific cases, the act of punishment may not be required in light of overriding considerations, for example, protecting the rights of others or securing a plea bargain in order that persons guilty of even more heinous crimes can be punished.[10] In such a case the *prima facie* demands of retributive justice are waived.

So Feinberg and Gross observe that there are occasions in which a person can be fully justified in voluntarily producing an unjust effect upon another person. Person *A* may be justified in violating person *B*'s rights when there is no third alternative open to him; but that justification does

---

8   Leo Zaibert, *Punishment and Retribution* (Aldershot, Hants: Ashgate, 2006), 161.

9   Zaibert, *Punishment and Retribution*, 183–85.

10 See Samuel T. Morison, "The Politics of Grace: On the Moral Justification of Executive Clemency," *Buffalo Criminal Law Review* 9, no. 1 (2005): 77–86. It is precisely on these grounds that the claim of the pure retributivists that pardons given out of any other reason than advancing justice are unjust and therefore unjustified is vulnerable. A pardon given out of mercy may be unjust in a *prima facie* sense but nonetheless justified *ultima facie* in view of overriding moral considerations.

not cancel the injustice done to *B*. Drawing upon Aristotle's distinction between the just/unjust *quality* of an act and the just/unjust *effect* of an act upon others, they state, "In that case, we can say that *B* was unjustly *treated* although *A*'s act resulting in that effect was not an instance of unjust *behavior*. For an act to have an unjust quality (whatever its effects) it must be, objectively speaking, the wrong thing to do in the circumstances, unexcused and unjustified, voluntarily undertaken, and deliberately chosen by an unrushed actor who is well aware of the alternatives open to him."[11]

Cases of strict liability,[12] in which a person having no *mens rea* (blameworthy mental state) is nonetheless found guilty and punished because of overriding moral concerns pertinent to public welfare, are good examples of instances in which the *prima facie* demands of negative retributive justice are waived. In fact, in cases of vicarious liability (see below), a person may be held criminally liable and punished even though he has neither an *actus reus* nor a *mens rea*! Such punishment seems *prima facie* unjustified but is justified *ultima facie* by overriding considerations.

Similarly, even if God's essential justice includes unqualified negative retributivism, the *prima facie* demands of negative retributive justice may be overridden in the case of Christ. In the case of the death of Christ, the penal theorist might claim that God is fully justified in waiving the demands of negative retributive justice for the sake of the salvation of mankind. Biblical scholar Donald Carson reminds us, "It is the *unjust* punishment of the Servant in Isaiah 53 that is so remarkable. Forgiveness, restoration, salvation, reconciliation—all are possible, not because sins have somehow been canceled as if they never were, but because another bore them *unjustly*. But by this adverb 'unjustly' I mean that the person who bore them was just and did not deserve the punishment, not that some moral 'system' that God was administering was

---

11 Joel Feinberg and Hyman Gross, eds., *Philosophy of Law*, 2nd ed. (Belmont, Calif.: Wadsworth, 1980), 286. Consider the example of the state's exercise of eminent domain. In such a case a homeowner may suffer the terrible injustice, which may be deeply felt and bitterly resented, of being stripped of his hearth and home, but the state does not act unjustly in bringing about this effect because of overriding justificatory reasons.

12 Recall chapter 9, pp. 157–58.

thereby distorted."[13] The penal substitution theorist might maintain that in the specific case of Christ's death, the demands of negative retributive justice were overridden by weightier moral considerations.

Even the staunchest of contemporary retributivists, Michael Moore, recognizes that the demands of retributive justice are *prima facie* demands that can be and are overridden in specific cases. That is why Moore is not committed, as Zaibert imagines, to legal moralism. Moore says that we must not confuse the intrinsic goodness of retribution with the categorical duty to carry out retributive justice on every possible occasion. He calls himself a "threshold deontologist," that is to say, he abides by the categorical norm of morality until doing so produces sufficiently bad consequences as to pass some threshold.[14] So in the extreme case where one must punish an innocent person or else the world will be totally destroyed, one should punish the person. The penal substitution theorist could similarly claim that God, by waiving the *prima facie* demands of negative retributive justice and punishing Christ for our sins, has mercifully saved the world from total destruction and was therefore acting compatibly with moral goodness.

Now it might be asked why, if there are weightier considerations prompting God to waive the demands of negative retributive justice in Christ's case, He did not instead waive the demands of positive retributive justice and offer everyone a general pardon for sin. In fact, many of the Church Fathers freely embraced this possibility, as did Aquinas and Grotius after them.[15] But these thinkers also held that God had good reasons for achieving atonement through Christ's passion. As Abelard and Grotius saw, so doing was a powerful display of both God's love of people and His hatred of sin, which has proved powerfully attractive throughout history in drawing people to faith in Christ, especially as they themselves face innocent suffering.

---

13 D. A. Carson, "Atonement in Romans 3:21–26," in *The Glory of the Atonement: Biblical, Historical, and Practical Perspectives*, ed. Charles E. Hill and Frank A. James III (Downers Grove, Ill.: InterVarsity, 2004), 133.

14 Michael Moore, *Placing Blame: A Theory of Criminal Law* (Oxford: Oxford University Press, 1997), 158.

15 For the most vigorous contemporary defense of a non-necessitarian penal substitution theory, see Blaine Swen, "The Logic of Divine-Human Reconciliation: A Critical Analysis of Penal Substitution as an Explanatory Feature of Atonement" (Ph.D. diss., Loyola University, Chicago, 2012).

God's pardoning sin without satisfaction does not, despite first appearances, imply universal salvation, for God's pardon may still require its free acceptance by people, and it is not at all implausible that a world in which the great demonstration of God's love and holiness in the vicarious suffering and death of Christ occurs is a world in which a more optimal number of people come freely to embrace salvation than a world in which free pardon without cost or consequence is offered men. The counterfactuals involved are too speculative to permit us to claim that a general pardon would have been more effective in accomplishing God's ends. Besides, substitutionary punishment of Christ permits God to relax far less His essential retributive justice for the sake of mercy than would be the case with a general pardon, thereby expressing more fully His essential character of holy love.

Punishment and the Imputation of Sins

But suppose that the *prima facie* demands of negative retributive justice are essential to God and cannot be overridden, so that (2) is true. Would God be unjust to punish Christ? Not necessarily, for consider (4). Up to this point we have acquiesced in the assumption that Christ was, indeed, innocent. But for penal theorists like the Protestant Reformers, who affirm the imputation of our sins to Christ, there is no question in Christ's case of God's punishing the innocent and so violating even the *prima facie* demands of negative retributive justice. For Christ in virtue of the imputation of our sins to him was legally guilty before God. Of course, because our sins were merely imputed to Christ and not infused in him, Christ was, as always, personally virtuous, a paradigm of compassion, selflessness, purity, and courage, but he was declared legally guilty before God. Therefore, he was legally liable to punishment. Thus, given the doctrine of the imputation of sins, the present objection to penal substitutionary theories is a nonstarter, being based on the false assumption of (4).

Of course, critics of penal substitution are apt to be unsympathetic to the claim that our sins were imputed to Christ. Mark Murphy, for example, distinguishes two possible imputation doctrines, both of which he deems unacceptable: the first holds that our sins, that is to say, our wrongful acts, were imputed to Christ, and the second holds that our guilt for our wrongful acts was imputed to Christ. Murphy's complaint in both cases is the same: we have no experience of the *transfer* either of moral responsibility for actions or of guilt in isolation from actions from one person to another.[16]

The force of Murphy's objection depends on the probability that if the doctrine of imputation is true, then we should have some experience of such a transfer in human affairs. But why think that? The proponent of penal substitution might plausibly respond that our want of such experience is hardly surprising, since imputation of sins or guilt is a uniquely divine prerogative.[17] In contrast to Western systems of justice, God embodies in one individual the legislative, judicial, and executive functions.[18] Arguably, God as supreme Lawgiver, Judge, and Ruler is in a unique position to impute the sins and guilt of one person to another. So it would be hardly surprising if imputation of sin, though a divine prerogative, failed to find an analogy in our system of justice.

But are we so utterly bereft of analogies to imputation as Murphy alleges? I think not.

Legal Fictions

Consider first the idea that our wrongful acts were imputed to Christ. On this view, although Christ did not himself commit the sins in question, God chooses to treat Christ *as if* he had done those acts. Such

---

16 Mark C. Murphy, "Not Penal Substitution but Vicarious Punishment," *Faith and Philosophy* 26 (2009): 259. This complaint is very common, both among philosophers (e.g., Philip L. Quinn, "Christian Atonement and Kantian Justification," *Faith and Philosophy* 3, no. 4 [1986]: 445, 456; Richard Purtill, "Justice, Mercy, Supererogation, and Atonement," in *Christian Philosophy*, ed. Thomas P. Flint [Notre Dame, Ind.: University of Notre Dame Press, 1990], 38; Eleonore Stump, *Aquinas* [New York: Routledge, 2003], 436) and theologians (Otfried Hofius, "The Fourth Servant Song in the New Testament Letters," in *The Suffering Servant: Isaiah 53 in Jewish and Christian Sources*, ed. Bernd Janowski and Peter Stuhlmacher [1996], trans. Daniel P. Bailey [Grand Rapids: Eerdmans, 2004], 168).

17 So John Owen, *A Dissertation on Divine Justice; Or, The Claims of Vindicatory Justice Asserted* (Latin version 1653) (London: L. J. Higham, n.d.), 157; cf. the "theological response" of Paul Jensen, "Forgiveness and Atonement," *Scottish Journal of Theology* 46, no. 2 (1993): 150–51.

18 Contrast the U.S. separation of powers, according to which Congress defines crimes and their punishments, the judiciary interprets and applies those laws and punishments, and the executive holds the power of pardon (Jeffrey Crouch, *The Presidential Pardon Power* [Lawrence: University Press of Kansas, 2009], 14). In God's case all these powers are vested in the same individual.

language is formulaic for the expression of legal fictions.[19] The nearly universal understanding of a legal fiction is that it is something that the court consciously knows to be false but treats as if it were true for sake of a particular action. The use of legal fictions is a long-established, widespread, and indispensable feature of systems of law.

Penal substitution theorists have typically been understandably leery of talk of legal fictions in connection with their views, lest our redemption be thought to be something unreal, a mere pretense.[20] But such a fear is misplaced. The claim is not that penal substitution is a fiction, for Christ was really and truly punished on such a view. Nor is his expiation of sin or propitiation of God's wrath a fiction, for his being punished for our sins removed our liability to punishment and satisfied God's justice. All these things are real. What is fictitious is that Christ himself did the wrongful acts for which he was punished. Every orthodox Christian believes that Christ did not and could not commit sins, but on the

---

19 The seminal treatment of contemporary discussions is L. L. Fuller, "Legal Fictions," *Illinois Law Review* 25 (1930): 363–99; no. 5 (1931): 513–46; no. 8 (1931): 877–910. The more distant progenitor is Hans Vaihinger, *The Philosophy of "As if"* (1911), trans. C. K. Ogden, 2nd ed., International Library of Psychology, Philosophy, and Scientific Method (London: Kegan Paul, Trench, Trübner, 1935).

20 As charged by Marcus Borg and John Dominic Crossan:

> If you misread the Justice of Paul's God as retributive, the only good news might be that God would pretend, as it were, that we were just, that God would impute to us a justice we did not have. Such an "as if" treatment would have horrified Paul. There is nothing, for example, about fictional imputation of justice, but everything about factual transformation by Justice in these claims from [Paul]. (Marcus J. Borg and John Dominic Crossan, *The First Paul: Reclaiming the Radical Visionary behind the Church's Conservative Icon* [San Francisco: HarperOne, 2009], 165)

Borg and Crossan are talking, of course, about the reflex imputation of Christ's righteousness to us, but they nicely illustrate how poorly legal imputation (not to mention retributive justice) is understood by many theologians.

By contrast, the Catholic theologian Gerald O'Collins clearly understands that a forensic transaction is not fictitious but real: "If a jury says at the end of a trial, 'we find the accused not guilty,' that statement *does* things and *transforms* the situation: the accused is free to walk away. Clearing someone in court is . . . a performative utterance, an utterance that effectively does something" ("Traditional Reformed View: Roman Catholic Response," in *Justification: Five Views*, ed. James K. Beilby and Paul Rhodes Eddy [Downers Grove, Ill.: IVP Academic, 2011], 127).

present view God adopts for the administration of justice the legal fiction that Christ did such deeds.

Penal substitution theorists will sometimes object to the employment of legal fictions in the doctrine of the atonement because God's legally justifying us has real, objective results. Someone whose debt has been legally remitted, for example, really becomes free of the burden of financial obligation to his former creditor. But such an objection is based upon a misunderstanding of the role of legal fictions in the achievement of justice. A legal fiction is a device that is adopted precisely in order to bring about real and objective differences in the world.

Take, for example, the classic case of a legal fiction employed in *Mostyn v. Fabrigas* (1774) 1 Cowp. 161. Mr. Fabrigas sued the governor of the Mediterranean island of Minorca, then under British control, for trespass and false imprisonment. Since such a suit could not proceed in Minorca without the approval of the governor himself, Mr. Fabrigas filed suit in the Court of Common Pleas in London. Unfortunately, that court had jurisdiction only in cases brought by residents of London. Lord Mansfield, recognizing that a denial of jurisdiction in this case would leave someone who was plainly wronged without a legal remedy, declared that for the purposes of the action Minorca was part of London! Frederick Schauer observes, "That conclusion was plainly false and equally plainly produced a just result, and thus *Mostyn v. Fabrigas* represents the paradigmatic example of using a fiction to achieve what might in earlier days have been done through the vehicle of equity."[21]

Or consider the legal fiction that a ship is a person.[22] The adoption of this fiction by U.S. federal courts in the early nineteenth century came about because of the efforts of ship owners to evade responsibility for violating embargo laws and carrying unlawful cargo, including slaves. When the ships were seized, the captains and crews passed on legal responsibility to the ship owners, who in turn produced innocent manifests while denying any knowledge of the illegal activity of the captains

---

21 Frederick Schauer, "Legal Fictions Revisited," in *Legal Fictions in Theory and Practice*, ed. Maksymilian Del Mar and William Twining, Law and Philosophy Library 110 (Cham, Switzerland: Springer Verlag, 2015), 122. By "equity," Schauer has reference to recourse to "an elaborate series of Chancellor's courts known as courts of equity, in order to gain equitable relief from the rigidity of law."

22 Described colorfully by Douglas Lind, "The Pragmatic Value of Legal Fictions," in Del Mar and Twining, *Legal Fictions in Theory and Practice*, 95–96.

and crews. The courts responded by making the ship itself (herself?) the
person against whom charges were brought. By the end of the century
this fiction became the settled view of ships in maritime law, so that the
"offending ship is considered as herself the wrongdoer, and as herself
bound to make compensation for the wrong done."[23] According to Lind,
the "ontologically wild" fiction of ship personification had profound and
beneficial results, facilitating the condemnation and forfeiture of offending vessels and producing a more just, coherent, and workable admiralty
jurisprudence.[24]

Holding that God, in His role as supreme Judge, adopts for the purposes of our redemption the legal fiction that Christ himself had done
the deeds in question in no way implies that our forensic justification
before His bar is unreal. Thus, through the device of legal fictions we
do, indeed, have some experience of how legal responsibility for acts can
be imputed to another person who did not really do the actions, thereby
producing real differences in the world outside the fiction.

Vicarious Liability

Consider now the second alternative, that God imputes to Christ the
guilt of our wrongdoing.[25] It is worth noting that the question does not,
pace Murphy, concern the *transfer* of guilt from one person to another, in

---

23 *The John G. Stevens*, 170 U.S. 113 (1898), 122, cited by Lind, "Pragmatic Value of
    Legal Fictions," 95.

24 Lind, "Pragmatic Value of Legal Fictions," 96.

25 Remarkably, the only theological work that I know of that has explored the legal
    notion of vicarious liability with respect to the atonement is the unpublished
    Th.M. thesis of Emmanuel Mwale, "Jesus Christ's Substitutionary Death:
    An Attempt to Reconcile Two Divergent Seventh-Day Adventist Teachings"
    (Th.M. thesis, University of South Africa, 2015), chaps. 5–6. This work came
    only lately to my attention, thanks to Francis Beckwith. Mwale provides a thor-
    ough and informative review of vicarious liability cases in criminal and civil law
    in Britain and elsewhere. He depends heavily on M. M. Botha and D. Millard,
    The Past, Present and Future of Vicarious Liability in South Africa (Pretoria: Preto-
    ria University Press, 2014), which I have not read, though I was able to consult
    their earlier article, Monray Marsellus Botha and Daleen Millard, "The Past,
    Present and Future of Vicarious Liability in South Africa," *De Jure Law Journal*
    45, no. 2 (2012): 225–53.

the sense that guilt is removed from one person and placed on another.[26] For the defender of the doctrine of imputation does not hold that when my guilt is imputed to Christ, it is thereby removed from me. Guilt is merely replicated in Christ, just as, according to the doctrine of original sin, Adam's guilt was replicated in me, not transferred from Adam to me. Adam remains guilty, as do I when my guilt is imputed to Christ. The entire rationale of penal substitution is, after all, the removal of guilt by punishment.

What is at issue, then, is whether we have any experience of the *replication* of guilt in a person different from the person who did the act. The question is not the removal of the primary actor's guilt but the imputation of guilt for his wrongdoing to another as well. So understood, we are not wholly without analogies in our justice system.[27]

---

26 Mwale is guilty of the same confusion. He complains that, vicarious liability notwithstanding, "it still remains a fact that the law of the land does not allow *transfer* of guilt from the guilty to the innocent" (Mwale, "Jesus Christ's Substitutionary Death," 179 [emphasis added]; cf. 81).

27 What follows could have also been said with respect to the vicarious liability of corporations as persons in the eyes of the law. David Ormerod and Karl Laird explain, "Corporations have a separate legal identity. They are treated in law as having a legal personality distinct from the natural persons—members, directors, employees, etc.—who make up the corporation. That presents the opportunity, in theory, of imposing criminal liability on the corporation separately from any liability which might be imposed on the individual members for any criminal wrongdoing" (David Ormerod and Karl Laird, *Smith, Hogan, and Ormerod's Criminal Law*, 15th ed. [Oxford: Oxford University Press, 2018], 245). In cases in which the law defines corporate crimes, the corporate directors are not found to be personally liable, but under the so-called identification doctrine the law regards the acts and states of mind of the corporate officers as the corporation's acts and state of mind, so that the corporation is held liable for what are deemed to be its own criminal acts. Since corporate persons might be thought by some to be legal fictions, however, I leave them aside to focus on the vicarious liability of human beings.

It is intriguing to note that the criminal liability of unincorporated associations seems to involve very different principles from those relating to corporations. In (2008) EWCA Crim 1970, (2009) Crim LR 381, the chairman and treasurer of a nine-hundred-member golf club, rather than the club itself, were prosecuted for the strict liability offense of polluting a stream by a heating oil leak caused directly by an independent contractor. The Court of Appeal held that personal liability for the offense arose as a result of club membership. Ormerod and Laird muse, "Personal criminal liability might result simply by virtue of a person's voluntary membership of a lawful association. Liability is not

In civil law there are cases involving what is called vicarious liability. In such cases the principle of *respondeat superior* (roughly, the master is answerable) is invoked to impute the liability of a subordinate to his superior, for example, a master's being held liable for acts done by his servant. On the contemporary scene this principle has given rise to a widespread and largely uncontroversial principle of vicarious liability of employers. An employer may be held liable for acts done by his employee in his role as employee or in close connection with his employment, even though the employer did not do these acts himself. Cases typically involve employers' being held liable for the illegal sale of items by employees but may also include torts like assault and battery, fraud, manslaughter, and so on. It needs to be emphasized that the employer is not in such cases being held liable for other acts, such as complicity or negligence in, for instance, failing to supervise the employee. Indeed, he may be utterly blameless in the matter. Rather, the liability incurred by his employee for certain acts is imputed to him in virtue of his relationship with the employee, even though he did not himself do the acts in question. The liability is not thereby transferred from the employee to the employer; rather the liability of the employee is replicated in the employer. In cases of vicarious liability, then, we have the responsibility for an act imputed to a person other than the actor.

It might be said that in such civil cases it is not guilt that is imputed to another person but mere liability. This claim may be left moot, for vicarious liability also makes an appearance in criminal law as well as civil law.[28] There are criminal as well as civil applications of *respondeat superior*. The liability for crimes committed by a subordinate in the discharge of his duties can also be imputed to his superior. Both the employer and the employee may be found guilty for crimes that only the employee committed.[29] For example, in *Allen v. Whitehead* (1930)

---

dependent on any personal fault. Where individual members of an unincorporated association are prosecuted, it is not on the basis of some form of vicarious liability. Nor, unlike corporations, does liability turn on the person holding a position of responsibility or office so that he might be regarded as a controlling officer" (261). We find in this case a different illustration of the imputation of the crimes of one person to an innocent third party.

28 See L. H. Leigh, *Strict and Vicarious Liability: A Study in Administrative Criminal Law*, Modern Legal Studies (London: Sweet and Maxwell, 1982).

29 Leigh notes that vicarious liability takes two forms. In one, a person is held liable for the acts of another who has a *mens rea*, while in the other, more typical case,

1 K.B. 211, the owner of a café was found to be guilty because his employee, to whom management of the café had been delegated, allowed prostitutes to congregate there in violation of the law. In *Sherras v. De Rutzen* (1895) 1 Q.B. 918, a bartender's criminal liability for selling alcohol to a constable on duty was imputed to the licensed owner of the bar. In such cases, we have the guilt of one person imputed to another person who did not do the act. Interestingly, vicarious liability is another case of strict liability, where the superior is held to be guilty without being found blameworthy, since no *mens rea* is required.[30] He is thus guilty and liable to punishment even though he is not culpable.

The two cases above illustrate two principles governing the determination of vicarious liability: the delegation principle and the attribution principle. According to the delegation principle a person may be held liable for the criminal acts of another person to whom he has delegated the performance of certain duties required of him by law. According to the attribution principle a person, typically an employer, may be held liable for criminal acts physically done by another because in the eye of the law they are regarded as the employer's acts. The delegation principle was operative in *Allen v. Whitehead*: "The acts of the manager and his mens rea (knowing that the women present were prostitutes) were both to be imputed to his employer, not simply because he was an employee, but because the management of the house had been delegated to him."[31] In *Sherras v. De Rutzen*, the *actus reus* of the bartender was attributed to the person holding the license to sell alcohol in the bar. Only the licensee can be the seller, and therefore even though the bartender poured the drinks and collected the money, it was the licensee who illegally sold the alcohol.[32]

---

a person is held liable for the act of another where the act of the other person amounts to an offense of strict liability (Leigh, *Strict and Vicarious Liability*, 1).

30 Indeed, the superior is entirely innocent, having neither an *actus reus* nor a *mens rea*, but is declared guilty by imputation.

31 Ormerod and Laird, *Smith, Hogan, and Ormerod's Criminal Law*, 270.

32 Similarly, in *Coppen v. Moore* (1898) an owner of several shops was convicted of fraudulent sales because one of the branch assistants sold hams as "Scotch hams," despite the owner's strict instructions to describe them only as "breakfast hams" and nothing more. Since only the person who initially owned the hams can be the seller, the assistant's wrongful acts were imputed to the owner. Under the delegation principle, the owner would not have been vicariously liable for the assistant's acts, since the control of the premises had not been delegated

In cases of vicarious liability we thus have clear instances, wholly apart from the use of legal fictions, for the imputation of criminal wrongdoing and guilt to a blameless third party. We thus have a decisive defeater of the objection that there is nothing in our experience involving the imputation of sin and guilt to an innocent person.

Emmanuel Mwale disputes the relevance of vicarious liability to Christ's vicarious atonement on the ground of various obvious disanalogies.[33] We shall examine Mwale's disanalogies in the sequel (chapter 11). For now it suffices to observe that Mwale conflates vicarious liability with what he calls "vicarious atonement" (= penal substitution).[34] That is a fundamental mistake, which vitiates his objection. Vicarious liability is offered as an analogy to the imputation of sins, not to penal substitution. (Later we shall consider whether the analogy can be extended to approximate penal substitution.) Disanalogies between vicarious liability and penal substitution do not undermine its analogy to imputation of sins.

Thus, the vicarious liability that exists in the law suffices to show that the imputation of our sins to Christ is not wholly without parallel in our experience. In the law's imputation of guilt to another person than the actor, we actually have a very close analogy to the doctrine of the imputation of our sins to Christ.[35]

---

to the assistant. But in virtue of the law governing the sale of certain products, the owner was the seller.

33 Mwale, "Jesus Christ's Substitutionary Death," 181.

34 See Mwale, "Jesus Christ's Substitutionary Death," 180, where he equates the "illegality of vicarious atonement" with the "illegality of vicarious liability." He compares apples and oranges when he asserts, "While the employer may be held *vicariously liable* for the criminal offence or tort of the employee, the employee is not always released from personal liability. . . . But *vicarious atonement* is different in that Christ's death releases the offender from all liability" (emphasis added).

35 Murphy might complain that our experiences of imputation involve only a legal and not a moral transaction. But it is characteristic of the Reformation doctrine of salvation that "justification" and "condemnation" are precisely forensic terms and that imputation is a legal transaction. See, e.g., Leon Morris, *The Atonement: Its Meaning and Significance* (Downers Grove, Ill.: InterVarsity, 1983), chap. 8: "Justification," esp. 187, 196; John Murray, *The Imputation of Adam's Sin* (Grand Rapids: Eerdmans, 1959), 84, who insists, "And neither are we to posit any such notion as the *transfer* from Adam to us of the moral character involved in his trespass" (cf. 86–87). Indeed, the forensic nature of justification is Pauline (see supra, chap. 4, n16, particularly the statement by Andrew Lincoln, p. 60, and infra,

Imputation of wrongdoing or guilt to a blameless party is thus a widely accepted feature of our justice system. Now sometimes the ascription of vicarious liability is denounced as unjust, though tolerated as a sort of necessary evil because of practical considerations arising from the human impossibility of administering a system of pure justice. That serves only to reinforce the point made above, that the *prima facie* demands of retributive justice can be outweighed by greater goods. But when would the imposition of vicarious liability be even *prima facie* unjust? Arguably, it could be only in cases in which it is nonvoluntary. Consider a case of voluntary corporate vicarious liability. Ormerod and Laird note that in cases of corporate vicarious liability it is unclear whether it is necessary for a conviction that an individual controlling mind be identifiable. This leads them to ask, "Can a company waive the need to establish that fact by pleading guilty on the basis that, although no controller was identifiable, the corporation is prepared to accept liability? There would seem no reason in principle why not."[36] Similarly, if an employer knows that the exaction of justice's demands from his employee would ruin him and out of compassion for his employee and his family wishes to act mercifully by voluntarily being held vicariously liable for his employee's wrongdoing, how is that unjust or immoral? In the same way, if Christ voluntarily invites our sins to be imputed to him for the sake of our salvation, what injustice is there in this? Who is to gainsay him?

Whether we think of imputation as God's adopting the legal fiction that Christ committed the sins for which we are condemned or as God's holding Christ vicariously liable for our wrongdoing, Christ is as a result of imputation legally guilty before God, that is, legally liable to punishment. In this light we can see how confused is Reformed theologian Oliver Crisp's characterization of penal substitution as a forensic fiction:

---

chap. 12, pp. 233–34). Michael Horton reports that there is now a "considerable" and "settled" "scholarly consensus," including advocates of the new perspective on Paul and Roman Catholic exegetes such as Joseph Fitzmeyer, Raymond Brown, and Karl Rahner, that "justification is a declarative, judicial verdict" (Michael S. Horton, "Traditional Reformed View," in Beilby and Eddy, *Justification*, 93); also Michael S. Horton, "Roman Catholic View: Traditional Reformed Response," in Beilby and Eddy, *Justification*, 293. Cf. the verdicts of James D. G. Dunn, "Traditional Reformed View: New Perspective Response," 118; Michael F. Bird, "Roman Catholic View: Progressive Reformed Response," in Beilby and Eddy, *Justification*, 296.

36 Ormerod and Laird, *Smith, Hogan, and Ormerod's Criminal Law*, 255.

> In the theological literature, the relation between Christ's penal substitution for the sinner and the sinner's sin and/or guilt is usually (though not always) interpreted according to what I shall call a *forensic fiction*. God treats Christ as if he is guilty of the sin of fallen human beings and "punishes" him accordingly, bringing about his death on the cross, which is a suitable act of atonement. God also treats the sinner as if she were sinless in view of Christ's work on the cross, provided the sinner appropriates that work for herself. How that is done is beyond the scope of this chapter. However, the important thing to see here is that on this forensic fiction account of penal substitution, the innocent Christ really is treated as if he were the guilty sinner, though he is not. And God really does punish the innocent in the place of the guilty.[37]

Crisp's first sentence misrepresents the majority tradition among penal substitution theorists, who do not take a fictionalist view of imputation, much less of penal substitution. On the view that Christ is vicariously liable for our sins, Christ's being declared legally guilty is no more fictitious than an employer's being held legally guilty by the court for wrongful acts done by his subordinate. Even if we take the view that the imputation of our sinful deeds to Christ is a legal fiction adopted by God, it does not follow that God treats Christ as if he were guilty of our sins. Rather, in virtue of the adoption of the legal fiction that Christ had done those deeds, Christ is legally guilty of those sins before God's bar, just as a ship is legally guilty of violating embargo laws in virtue of the court's adopting the fiction of ship personification. Similarly, *pace* Crisp, the redeemed sinner is not treated merely as if he were righteous; rather, in virtue of the imputation of Christ's obedience to him, he is legally righteous.

The view that Crisp describes in his last two sentences is, in fact, more akin to the Augustinian/Grotian non-imputative view of penal substitution than to the Reformers' view, which involves imputation of sin or righteousness. But even on the Augustinian/Grotian perspective, there is nothing fictitious about Christ's suffering the punishment we deserved or God's pardon of us on such grounds, and so the appellation "forensic fiction" is misleading.

Part of the difficulty here, I think, is that Crisp takes guilt to be the property of having committed a crime, a property that Christ did not exemplify, since he committed no crimes. While this understanding of

---

37 Oliver D. Crisp, *The Word Enfleshed: Exploring the Person and Work of Christ* (Grand Rapids: Baker Academic, 2016), 129.

guilt is in line with the opinions of many courts, it is problematic, as I shall argue in chapter 12, for on such an understanding our guilt could never be removed, in contradiction to Scripture (Ps 51:1, 9).

CONCLUDING REMARKS

In sum, the objection to penal substitution based on the justification of punishment is insufficiently nuanced. (1) It applies only to theories that affirm that Christ was punished for our sins. (2) It makes unwarranted assumptions about the ontological foundations of moral duty independent of God's commands. (3) It presupposes without warrant that God is by nature an unqualified negative retributivist. (4) It overlooks the possibility that the *prima facie* demands of negative retributive justice might be overridden in Christ's case. (5) And it takes it for granted that Christ was legally innocent, in opposition to the doctrine of imputation. Its failure in any one of these respects is sufficient for the argument's defeat. It thus fails to show any injustice in God's punishing Christ in our place.

Chapter 11

Satisfaction of Divine Justice

INTRODUCTION

In addition to penal substitution, any biblically adequate atonement theory must include the notion of propitiation, that is to say, the appeasement of God's just wrath against sin. The source of God's wrath is His retributive justice, and so appeasement of wrath is fundamentally a matter of the satisfaction of divine justice. How are the demands of divine justice satisfied? Biblically speaking, the satisfaction of God's justice primarily takes place, not as Anselm thought, through compensation, but through punishment.

We have seen that some penal substitution theorists deny that God punished Christ for our sins. Christ on such accounts stands in as our substitute and suffers the harsh treatment that we deserved and that would have been our punishment had it been inflicted on us, thereby freeing us from punishment.[1] An attractive feature of this kind of account is that

---

1 These features serve to distinguish such an account from satisfaction theories like Anselm's. On a penal substitutionary account, in contrast to satisfaction theories, the harsh treatment deserved by sinners is still administered or vicariously endured, even if it is not punishment. For discussion of what they characterize as penal substitution theories of various strengths, i.e., the degree to which they affirm that God punished Christ, see Daniel J. Hill and Joseph Jedwab, "Atonement and the Concept of Punishment," in *Locating Atonement:*

195

it enables the Christian theologian to avert so easily the standard objections against both the coherence and justice of penal substitution. For on
such accounts it is false that God punished an innocent person for our
sins, an assumption that lies at the root of the standard objections. Even
Socinus recognized that God might inflict nonpunitive harsh treatment
on an innocent person,[2] Job being the paradigmatic biblical example, and
the discussion of such treatment takes us out of the philosophy of law
and the theory of punishment and into the familiar concerns of theodicy.

Unfortunately, a penal substitutionary theory that does not affirm
that God punished Christ for our sins seems less promising when it
comes to satisfying the demands of God's justice. Penal substitutionary
theories hold that the satisfaction of divine justice, whether by a necessity of God's nature or by a free choice of God's will, is a precondition of God's pardon and salvation of sinners. Here the superiority of
a theory involving Christ's punishment emerges over penal substitutionary theories according to which God does not punish Christ. For it is
hard to see how divine justice could be satisfied by Christ's voluntarily
taking suffering upon himself if it were not a punishment meted out
for our sins. If the punishment for an offense were, say, deportation,
how could justice be satisfied by someone else's voluntarily going or even
being sent into exile unless it were intended to be a punishment for the
wrongdoing in question? If the suffering or harsh treatment is not punishment, then the demands of retributive justice seem to go unsatisfied.[3]

Explorations in Constructive Dogmatics, ed. Oliver D. Crisp and Fred Sanders
(Grand Rapids: Zondervan, 2015), 139–53.

2 Socinus, *De Jesu Christo Servatore* 3.10.

3 For more on the possibility of nonpunitive vicarious satisfaction, see Blaine
Swen, "The Logic of Divine-Human Reconciliation: A Critical Analysis of
Penal Substitution as an Explanatory Feature of Atonement" (Ph.D. dissertation, Loyola University, Chicago, 2012), 226–39. Swen's focus in this section is
not on whether vicarious punishment can be satisfactory but whether vicarious
satisfaction in any form is possible. Accordingly, his discussion will be relevant
to penal substitution theorists who claim that Christ was not punished for our
sins but nonetheless by his suffering discharged the debt of punishment we owe
to God. Swen argues that penal and pecuniary debts, *pace* Socinus, are similarly
compensatory and similarly flexible with regard to the dissolution of the debt.
As a non-necessitarian, Swen holds that God has the freedom simply to cancel our debt; accordingly, He has the freedom to stipulate whatever conditions
must be met in order for the debt to be dissolved. In other words, God sets the

THE ALLEGED UNSATISFACTORINESS
OF PENAL SUBSTITUTION

Socinus objected, however, that neither could punishing Christ in our place possibly meet the demands of divine retributive justice.[4] For punishing another person for my crimes would not serve to remove my liability to punishment. So how can penal substitution satisfy God's justice? We can formulate this objection as follows:

(1) Unless the person who committed a wrong is punished for that wrong, divine justice is not satisfied.

(2) If God practices penal substitution, then the person who committed a wrong is not punished for that wrong.

(3) Therefore, if God practices penal substitution, divine justice is not satisfied.

It follows that penal substitution is thus unsatisfactory.

RESPONSES TO THE ALLEGED
UNSATISFACTORINESS OF PENAL SUBSTITUTION

Metaethical Contextualization

To address the question of the satisfactoriness of penal substitution adequately, we must view it within the context of an overarching metaethical theory about the foundation of moral values and duties. Who or what determines what satisfies the demands of justice? The classic proponents of penal substitutionary theories all held to a view of God as at once the supreme Legislator, Judge, and Ruler of the moral order. Contrast once more the U.S. separation of powers, according to which Congress defines crimes and their punishments, the judiciary interprets and applies those laws and punishments, and the executive holds the power of pardon.[5] In God's case all these powers are vested in the same individual. So if He

---

conditions for the satisfaction of the debt, and when the conditions are to be met by a third party, the satisfaction is vicarious.

4 Socinus, *De Jesu Christo Servatore* 3.3. For contemporary statements of the objection, see, e.g., Philip L. Quinn, "Christian Atonement and Kantian Justification," *Faith and Philosophy* 3, no. 4 (1986): 440–62; and Eleonore Stump, *Aquinas* (New York: Routledge, 2003), 436.

5 Jeffrey Crouch, *The Presidential Pardon Power* (Lawrence: University Press of Kansas, 2009), 14.

determines that the demands of justice are met by Christ's punishment, who is to gainsay Him? He is the source of the moral law, its interpreter, and its executor. He Himself determines what meets justice's demands. So what is the problem?

The above response might seem to imply an unsettling account of satisfaction as so-called *acceptation*. John Duns Scotus suggested that God might have accepted any sacrifice He pleased as satisfactory for the demands of His retributive justice (*Distinctiones in quatuor libros Sententiarum* 3.19.1). Defenders of penal substitution have not been sympathetic to acceptation accounts.[6] For then God might have accepted as satisfactory the death of any ordinary human being or even an animal. But then it is not true, as Scripture affirms, that "it is impossible that the blood of bulls and goats should take away sins" (Heb 10:4). Retributive theories of justice require not merely that the guilty deserve punishment but also that the punishment be proportionate to the crime if justice is to be satisfied. The objector to substitutionary satisfaction would find a sympathetic ear among penal substitution theorists if he affirmed that retributive justice, as we know and understand it, is essential to God's nature and so could not be satisfied by mere animal sacrifices. But then the question persists: How does the punishment of Christ satisfy the demands of retributive justice?

Penal Substitution in Our Justice System

Perhaps some progress can be made toward answering this question by considering whether any analogies to penal substitution exist in our secular justice system. If something like penal substitution appears in our justice system, that would lend credibility to the claim that it can be satisfactory of divine justice's demands. After all, if we are talking about retributive justice as we know and understand it, then divine justice must be significantly analogous to enlightened human justice systems. Otherwise, the defender of penal substitution can just assert that

---

6   See Oliver Crisp, "Salvation and Atonement: On the Value and Necessity of the Work of Christ," in *The God of Salvation: Soteriology in Theological Perspective*, ed. Ivor J. Davidson and Murray A. Rae (Farnham, UK: Ashgate, 2011), 105–20. Contrast Swen, who speaks approvingly of Scotus' acceptation view (Swen, "Logic of Divine-Human Reconciliation," 251; cf. 134), despite acknowledging that on this view each of us could without Christ provide satisfaction for his own sin.

God's essential retributive justice is quite unlike our understanding of retributive justice—Problem solved!

The Anglo-American system of justice, in point of fact, does countenance and even endorse cases that are significantly analogous to substitutionary punishment. David Lewis claims that although we do not think that a criminal offender's friend can serve his prison sentence or death sentence, we do believe that a friend can pay a criminal's fine if both agree to the arrangement. "Yet this is just as much a case of penal substitution as the others."[7] Lewis rejects the view that these fines are not really punishments. Some of these fines, Lewis remarks, are just as burdensome as prison sentences and convey the same opprobrium. If we were single-mindedly against penal substitution, Lewis says, then we should conclude that fines are an *unsatisfactory* form of punishment, that such punishment, in other words, fails to satisfy justice's demands. But we do not.[8] Lewis draws the lesson that both secularists and Christians agree that "penal substitution sometimes makes sense after all, even if none can say how it makes sense. And if both sides agreed to that, that is some evidence that somehow they might both be right."[9]

We can press the analogy even further. For as we saw in chapter 10, in criminal law there are cases involving vicarious liability for criminal acts. One lesson to be learned from cases of vicarious liability is that what is required for the satisfaction of justice is that only persons who are *liable* for a wrong are punished for that wrong. Accordingly, (1) should be revised to:

> (1*) Unless a person who is liable for a wrong is punished for that wrong, divine justice is not satisfied.

---

7   David Lewis, "Do We Believe in Penal Substitution?" *Philosophical Papers* 26, no. 3 (1997): 207.

8   In response to Lewis, Quinn makes the interesting observation that courts have sometimes expressed diffidence about allowing companies to purchase insurance policies to cover possible penalties (Philip L. Quinn, *"Papers in Ethics and Social Philosophy* by David Lewis," *Noûs* 38, no. 4 [2004]: 722–30). For in such cases the insurance company, rather than the guilty party, pays the penalty demanded by the law. But such cases do not show that penal substitution is unsatisfactory; quite the contrary, in fact. Rather, such cases furnish a good example of the way in which *ultima facie* considerations can justify penal substitution, thereby meeting justice's demands in a specific action.

9   Lewis "Do We Believe in Penal Substitution?" 209.

That person might be the wrongdoer himself or someone vicariously liable for that wrong.

Now in affirming that justice is satisfied only if a person who is liable for a crime is punished for that crime, we have not yet arrived at an analogy to penal substitution. For in a case involving vicarious liability both parties, the subordinate who did the wrong and the blameless superior to whom the wrong is imputed may be found guilty and punished for the crime.

Intriguingly, however, it is sometimes the case that only the vicariously liable superior is prosecuted and punished. The state may forgo prosecution of the subordinate or forgo exacting a penalty at his hand in favor of the employer's satisfying justice's demands. Such cases are especially common when a corporation is held vicariously liable for crimes committed by employees. In cases in which the demands of justice are too heavy for individuals to bear, the corporation may be held solely responsible for satisfying justice's demands. Such a case seems to be as much an instance of penal substitution as Lewis' example of fines being paid by a third party. At the least, we can say that it appears that (1) is false in our Anglo-American justice system. Sometimes the demands of justice are met not by the wrongdoer himself but by someone held vicariously liable for that wrong.

I mentioned in the previous chapter that Emmanuel Mwale disputes the relevance of vicarious liability to Christ's vicarious atonement on the ground of various disanalogies. He claims that the relationship subsisting between employer and employee "is completely different from that between God and man."[10] For example, God is not some third party but the Creator of the human being who has offended Him. In civil cases involving vicarious liability three parties are involved: the employer, the employee, and the person who suffers damage as a result of the employee's act or omission, whereas in the case of the atonement only two parties are involved: God and man. Again, an innocent employer cannot choose, as Christ did, to die in place of an employee who has committed a capital offense. Again, while the employer may be held vicariously liable for the criminal offense or tort of the employee, the employee is not always released from personal liability. Vicarious

---

10 Emmanuel Mwale, "Jesus Christ's Substitutionary Death: An Attempt to Reconcile Two Divergent Seventh-Day Adventist Teachings" (Th.M. thesis, University of South Africa, 2015), 181.

atonement is different in that "Christ's death releases the offender from all liability."[11]

Disanalogies, however, are always to be expected when an analogy is drawn, so the question is whether they are so significant as to subvert the analogy that does exist between penal substitution and certain cases involving vicarious liability. I think not. The number of parties involved in a case is irrelevant to the fact that a blameless person may be found vicariously liable for another's wrong and punished instead of him (not mention the fact that in a criminal case only two parties are involved). The divine status of the superior party is again just not relevant to the analogy.[12] The fact that in our justice system an employer cannot choose to die in the place of his employee does not subvert Lewis' point that cases of penal substitution are to be found in our justice system. Finally, Mwale recognizes that there are cases involving vicarious liability in which only the employer is prosecuted and punished—and, moreover, that it is up to each jurisdiction to decide.[13]

Mwale seems to assume that in appealing to certain cases involving vicarious liability as analogous to penal substitution, one is trying to construct a doctrine of the atonement based on human justice systems. But one is not engaged in such a silly project. Theological construction of a doctrine of the atonement will be based on the teaching of Scripture. Rather, in appealing to the analogy of certain cases involving elements of vicarious liability, one is merely offering a defeater of the objection raised to penal substitution that it is unsatisfactory because our legal system

---

11 Mwale, "Jesus Christ's Substitutionary Death," 181.

12 Intriguingly, a necessary condition of a finding of vicarious liability is that the superior be so related to the subordinate as to have either the right, the power, or the duty to prevent the subordinate's wrongdoing. Christ, of course, stands in such a relationship to us, since he possesses both the power and the right to prevent our sinning, even if he has no duty to do so. Equally intriguing is the fact that a delegation of authority by the superior to the subordinate can be crucial. In *Vane v. Yiannopoullos* (1965), the licensed owner of a restaurant was initially found vicariously liable for a sale in breach of license by a waitress. The House of Lords reversed the decision on the grounds that the waitress had not been left in charge of the premises and all the effective management handed over to her. A striking feature of the Genesis creation story is that God gives to the man and woman authority over creation to act on His behalf and delegates to them the responsibility of managing creation (Gen 1:27-28). Thus, the analogy between God and the employer is unexpectedly close!

13 Mwale, "Jesus Christ's Substitutionary Death," 181.

allows only the wrongdoer to be punished for his wrong. In fact, we do sometimes penalize or punish in place of the wrongdoer blameless persons held vicariously liable for wrongs they did not commit.

Now the objector might reply at this point that in cases of vicarious liability in which only the superior is punished the demands of justice are not really satisfied but merely waived. When the state declines either to prosecute a subordinate for his wrongdoing or to exact the penalty from him that justice demands, it is not because his superior has met the demands of justice on his behalf. Rather, the demands of justice are just overlooked. Hence, (1) remains true.

It seems to me, however, that intuitions can reasonably differ here. It is the state that determines whether justice has been satisfied in a particular case. If the state is satisfied in such cases with the penalty exacted from the superior and requires nothing further from the subordinate, then the demands of justice are met. Even in cases in which both parties are convicted and sentenced, we can imagine scenarios in which only the superior discharges justice's demands. Criminal law theorist Antony Duff explains:

> If both are convicted, the question turns to sentencing: . . . If the punishment is a fine, for both the employer and the employee, it seems to be a demand of penal justice that the size of the fine be related to the defendant's means—a wealthy defendant's fine should be much larger than that imposed on a poor person (hence the attraction of "day fines" or "unit fines," which fine a person a specified proportion of his income). We could therefore expect that the employer's fine will be, in dollar terms, much greater than the employee's—which will serve the ends of penal justice.[14]

In Duff's view, even in the case in which the state prosecutes both parties, just desert is not absolute but relative to the defendants' means. If the employee for some reason had no means, then the demands of justice would be fully met by the employer alone.

We as condemned sinners are, as Anselm saw, utterly bereft of any means of satisfying divine justice apart from enduring the punishment

---

14 Antony Duff to William Lane Craig, March 13, 2019. The envisioned case concerns criminal liability for an oil spill. As for the civil liability of cleaning up the mess, Duff opines, "It doesn't look to me as if justice is frustrated if the employer/company has to pay a massive amount (assuming that it is just to hold them vicariously liable in the first place) and the employee whose misconduct directly caused the spill avoids any civil liability."

of hell. If God does not want to send His children to hell, then He must alone satisfy the demands of justice instead of us. It is God, as the analogue of the state, who determines whether the demands of divine justice have been met by Christ's substitutionary punishment. God may be satisfied with the infinite penalty exacted from Christ for my sins. He may therefore issue a pardon to us, freeing us from condemnation.

The objector's reply, then, is not decisive. We do seem to have some analogy in our justice system to penal substitution. In any case (1) seems to be defeated.

Substitution and Representation

Even more can be said. For now consider as well

> (2) If God practices penal substitution, then the person who committed a wrong is not punished for that wrong.

In cases of penal substitution, is it always the case that the person who did the wrong is not punished for that wrong?

Contemporary theologians have disputed the point by distinguishing between exclusionary place-taking (*exkludierende Stellvertretung*) and inclusionary place-taking (*inkludierende Stellvertretung*).[15] This important distinction requires a word of explanation about substitution and representation, respectively. In cases of simple substitution, someone takes the place of another person but does not represent that person. For example, a pinch hitter in baseball enters the lineup to bat in the place of another player. He is a substitute for that player but in no sense represents that other player. That is why the batting average of the player whom he replaces is not affected by the pinch hitter's performance. By contrast, a simple representative acts on behalf of another person and serves as his spokesman but is not a substitute for that person. For example, the

---

15 Alternatively, *ausschliessende* vs. *einschliessende Stellvertretung*. See, e.g., the influential work of Hartmut Gese, "The Atonement," in *Essays on Biblical Theology*, trans. Keith Crim (Minneapolis: Augsburg, 1981), 106; Otfried Hofius, "Sühne und Versöhnung: Zum paulinischen Verständnis des Kreuzestodes Jesu," in *Paulusstudien*, 2nd rev. ed., WUNT 1/51 (Tübingen: J. C. B. Mohr [Paul Siebeck], 1994), 41. The distinction is already to be found in Albrecht Ritschl, *The Christian Doctrine of Justification and Reconciliation: The Positive Development of the Doctrine*, ed. H. R. Mackintosh and Alexander Beith Macauley (Clifton, N.J.: Reference Book, 1966), 163–75.

baseball player has an agent who represents him in contract negotiations with the team. The representative does not replace the player but merely advocates for him.[16]

These roles can be combined, in which case we have neither simple substitution nor simple representation but rather substitutional representation (or representative substitution). A good illustration of this combination of substitution and representation is to be found in the role of a proxy at a shareholders' meeting. If we cannot attend the meeting ourselves, we may sign an agreement authorizing someone else to serve as our proxy at the meeting. He votes for us, and because he has been authorized to do so, his votes are our votes: we have voted via proxy at the meeting of shareholders. The proxy is a substitute in that he attends the meeting in our place, but he is also our representative in that he does not vote instead of us but on our behalf, so that we vote. This combination is an inclusionary place-taking.

Turretin believes that Christ, in bearing our punishment, was both our substitute and our representative before God. He states, "The curse and punishment of sin which he received upon himself in our stead secures to us blessing and righteousness with God in virtue of that most strict union between us and him by which, as our sins are imputed to him, so in turn his obedience and righteousness are imputed to us."[17] This relation is not one of simple substitution; there is an inclusive union here that is the basis of the imputation of our sins to Christ and of his righteousness to us. According to Turretin, so long as Christ is outside of us and we are out of Christ, we can receive no benefit from his righteousness. But God has united us with Christ by means of a twofold bond, one natural (namely, communion of nature by the incarnation), the other mystical (namely, the communion of grace by Christ's mediation), in virtue of which our sins might be imputed to Christ and his righteousness imputed to us. Christ was punished in our place and bore the suffering we deserved, but he also represented us before God, so that

---

16 Representation in this sense needs to be distinguished from representation in the sense of symbolization. A baseball scorecard is a representation of the playing field, and marks on it represent hits, outs, runs, etc. Christ's death as a representation in this sense would be akin to the popular misunderstanding of Grotius' governmental theory of the atonement as a representation to the world of what it would look like if Christ were punished for our sins.

17 Francis Turretin, *Institutes of Elenctic Theology*, 3 vols., trans. George Musgrave Giger, ed. James T. Dennison Jr. (Phillipsburg, N.J.: P&R, 1992), 16.3.

his punishment was our punishment. Christ was not merely punished instead of us; rather, we were punished by proxy.[18] For that reason, divine justice is satisfied.

How does it come to pass that we are so represented by Christ? As mentioned, Turretin proposes two ways in which we are in union with Christ, first, by way of his incarnation and, second, by way of our mystical union with him. Although theologians often appeal to this latter union of believers with Christ to explain the efficacy of his atonement,[19] such an account seems to be viciously circular.[20] Turretin emphasizes that it is our union with Christ that is the basis of the imputation of sins to Christ and of our justification.[21] But the problem is that the mystical union of believers with Christ is the privilege only of persons who are regenerate and justified. There is here a vicious explanatory circle: to be in mystical union with Christ, one must first be justified, but to be justified one must first be in mystical union with Christ. What is needed is

---

18 As mentioned earlier, atonement theorists have identified examples of such punishment by proxy even in human affairs, such as a team captain's being punished for his team's failings or a squad leader's being punished for his troops' failings (Steven L. Porter, "Swinburnian Atonement and the Doctrine of Penal Substitution," *Faith and Philosophy* 21, no. 2 [2004]: 236–37). Of course, Christ has been uniquely appointed by God to be our proxy, which may make his case sui generis.

19 See, e.g., Steve Jeffery, Michael Ovey, and Andrew Sach, *Pierced for Our Transgressions: Rediscovering the Glory of Penal Substitution* (Wheaton, Ill.: Crossway Books, 2007), 144–47, 242–43. While recognizing a problem of "timing" occasioned by the fact that neither we nor our sins existed at the time of Christ's death, the authors do not seem cognizant of the logical problem of vicious circularity.

20 As recognized by Reformed theologian Henri Blocher, "Justification of the Ungodly (*Sola Fide*): Theological Reflections," in *Justification and Variegated Nomism: A Fresh Appraisal of Paul and Second Temple Judaism*, 2 vols., ed. D. A. Carson, Peter T. O'Brien, and Mark A. Seifrid, vol. 2, *The Paradoxes of Paul*, WUNT 2/181 (Tübingen: Mohr Siebeck, 2004), 497–98. Cf. the discomfiture of Bruce L. McCormack, "What's at Stake in Current Debates over Justification? The Current Crisis of Protestantism in the West," in *Justification: What's at Stake in the Current Debates*, ed. Mark Husbands and Daniel J. Treier (Downers Grove, Ill.: InterVarsity), 101–2.

21 He calls our union with Christ the "cause and foundation" of our sharing in all his benefits, including justification (remission of sins and adoption as sons [Turretin, *Institutes of Elenctic Theology*, 16.6]).

a union with Christ that is explanatorily prior to (even if chronologically simultaneous with) imputation and justification.

Turretin's first proposal is therefore to be preferred.[22] In virtue of Christ's incarnation (and, I should say, his baptism, whereby Jesus identified himself with fallen humanity), Christ is appointed by God to serve as our proxy before Him. The Logos, the second person of the Trinity, has voluntarily consented to be appointed, by means of his incarnation and baptism, to serve as our proxy before God so that by his death he might satisfy the demands of divine justice on our behalf.

Herein we see the organic connection between Christ's incarnation, death, and resurrection. God's raising Jesus from the dead is not only a ratification to us of the efficacy of Christ's atoning death; it is a necessary consequence of it. For by his substitutionary death Christ fully satisfied divine justice. The penalty of death having been fully paid, Christ can no more remain dead than a criminal who has fully served his sentence can remain imprisoned. Punishment cannot justly continue; justice demands his release. Thus, Christ's resurrection is both a necessary consequence and a ratification of his satisfaction of divine justice.

In summary, while proponents of penal substitutionary theories that do not feature Christ's being punished for our sins may have difficulty rebutting the charge that on such theories Christ's suffering is unsatisfactory, the proponents of penal substitutionary theories that do feature Christ's being punished for our sins are not so clearly vulnerable to this charge. We need to keep in mind that God, as the supreme Legislator, Judge, and Ruler, Himself determines what satisfies the demands of His justice. If we insist that retributive justice, as we know and understand it, belongs essentially to God, the question will then become why

---

22 So-called realist accounts of the union, which appeal to mereological fusions like "fallen humanity" and "redeemed humanity" as a basis for original sin and Christ's redemption (Oliver D. Crisp, "Original Sin and Atonement," in *The Oxford Handbook of Philosophical Theology*, ed. Thomas P. Flint and Michael C. Rea [Oxford University Press, 2009], 437–46; cf. Oliver D. Crisp, *The Word Enfleshed: Exploring the Person and Work of Christ* [Grand Rapids: Baker Academic, 2016], 137–41), are implausible and unavailing, being dependent upon a principle of apparently unrestricted mereological composition and a tenseless theory of time and implying a view of human personhood incompatible with divine punishment and rewards (William Lane Craig, *Time and Eternity: Exploring God's Relationship to Time* [Wheaton, Ill.: Crossway, 2001], chap. 5; William Lane Craig, *God over All: Divine Aseity and the Challenge of Platonism* [Oxford: Oxford University Press, 2016], chap. 6).

substitutionary punishment cannot satisfy the demands of retributive justice so known and understood. We saw that in both civil law and criminal law we find cases of penal substitution that are regarded as satisfactory of justice's demands because guilt or liability is vicariously borne. We may think of Christ as being held vicariously liable for our sins and his punishment as satisfying for us, just as an employer might satisfy justice's demands on behalf of his employee.

Moreover, an inclusionary penal substitutionary theory does not preclude that we are punished for our sins in Christ's being punished for our sins. For Christ's being divinely and voluntarily appointed to act not merely as our substitute but as our representative enables him to serve as our proxy before God, so that when he is punished, we are punished by proxy, to the satisfaction of divine justice.

FURTHER OBJECTIONS TO THE SATISFACTORINESS OF CHRIST'S PENAL SUBSTITUTION

It will be recalled that Socinus pressed other objections against the satisfactoriness of Christ's substitutionary punishment. These have been rehearsed afresh by Eleonore Stump in her important study of the atonement.

Incompatibility of Remission and Satisfaction

Socinus argued that satisfaction of divine justice is actually logically incompatible with the remission of sins, for remission, by definition, entails that the creditor forgoes satisfaction of the debt and that the debtor is forgiven of his obligation. Stump similarly objects that penal substitutionary theories "do not in fact seem to present God as foregoing anything owed him by human beings or omitting any of the punishment deserved by human beings."[23] For "God . . . visits the whole punishment deserved" on Christ.[24] "There may be something specially benevolent in God's . . . bearing himself deserved human punishment, but it remains the case that no part of what is owed is left unpaid or unpunished."[25]

---

23 Eleonore Stump, *Atonement* (Oxford: Oxford University Press, 2018), 24.
24 Stump, *Atonement*, 24.
25 Stump, *Atonement*, 24.

So formulated, this is hardly an objection to penal substitutionary theories. Indeed, the genius of such a theory is that it enables the demands of divine retributive justice to be fully met, not simply swept under the rug, while giving full expression to God's love for condemned sinners. What God forgoes is punishing sinners in their proper persons; instead, out of His love for them He bears their punishment Himself. As Grotius rightly saw, the acceptance of a substitute for what is owed does require a special dispensation on the part of the creditor or judge.[26]

In a later iteration of this objection, Stump objects that penal substitution shows God to be unmerciful. "Mercy . . . is a matter of foregoing at least some of what is owed; and, contrary to what it intends, the penal substitution theory of the atonement does not, in fact, present God as foregoing what is owed him because of human sin."[27] This surprising claim depends on her loose characterization of mercy, which fails to take account of the fact that mercy is person-directed.[28] If Christ's freely giving his life so that justly condemned persons might live does not count as mercy toward such persons, that only goes to call into question Stump's characterization of mercy. Stump notes that the penal substitution theorist might say that "God's foregoing what is owed to God consists precisely in God's not requiring that human beings endure the punishment for their sins," but she responds that "it remains the case that on the penal substitution theory no part of the punishment due is omitted."[29] That is right on both counts, and it is one of the great strengths of the theory that it thus fully expresses God's justice as well as His mercy toward sinners.

Stump notes that the penal substitution theorist might say that God's justice requires that sin be punished, and so Christ's enduring our punishment for us constitutes mercy even though God does not forgo punishment for sin. Significantly, Stump's reply to this necessitarian

---

26 Recall that we have already faulted Stump's formulation because of her construal of God as a private party to a personal dispute. The necessity of a special dispensation is all the more evident in a criminal case.

27 Stump, *Atonement*, 77.

28 Cf. H. R. T. Roberts' rough working explication of acting mercifully: "In all justice I am entitled to A from *x*, but it is *mine* to exact and I choose not to" (H. R. T. Roberts, "Mercy," *Philosophy* 46, no. 178 [1971]: 353 [emphasis original]). Roberts' intention is clearly to give a characterization of my acting mercifully toward *x*. If out of benevolence for *x* I choose not to exact A from *x* but pay A myself, then I am acting mercifully toward *x*.

29 Stump, *Atonement*, 77.

perspective is faltering.[30] She does not deny that God is in such a case merciful; rather, she falls back onto the objection that penal substitution would be unjust. Her objection therefore ultimately collapses into the objection to the justice of penal substitution and so fails to stand as an independent objection. We have already addressed the justice of penal substitution at some length in chapter 10.

The Satisfactoriness of Christ's Suffering

Socinus argues that even if Christ's rendering satisfaction for our sins were possible, he did not in fact do so. For the penalty each of us faces is eternal death, but Christ did not literally endure this.[31] Similarly, Stump writes, "On orthodox theological doctrine, the penalty for sin is damnation, permanent absence of union with God. And yet it is not the case on any version of the Anselmian interpretation, even Calvin's, that Christ suffered permanent absence of union with God, so that this variation on the Anselmian interpretation has to construct some equivalence to human damnation that Christ does undergo."[32]

It seems to me that Reformed thinkers like Turretin adequately respond to Socinus on this score by doing exactly as Stump suggests.[33] According to Turretin, Christ was forsaken by God the Father by His withdrawing from him the beatific vision and by suspending the joy and comfort and sense and fruition of full felicity. While Christ's punishment was not infinite as to duration, still in its intensity it was equivalent to the eternal suffering of the damned in hell on account of the infinite dignity of the person suffering.[34] Interestingly, in the American criminal justice system, this sort of difference is recognized though not, to my

---

30 Stump, *Atonement*, 77.

31 Socinus, *De Jesu Christo Servatore* 3.4.

32 Stump, *Atonement*, 25; cf. 78.

33 Turretin, *Institutes of Elenctic Theology*, 14.11.

34 Stump objects, "No matter what sort of agony Christ experienced in his crucifixion, it certainly was not (and was not equivalent to) everlasting damnation, if for no other reason than that Christ's suffering came to an end" (Stump, *Atonement*, 78). This is an obvious non sequitur, since intensity can more than make up for limited duration. Indeed, since the future is merely potentially infinite, at no point will the damned ever have experienced more than finite suffering.

Stump also asserts that suffering cannot be both voluntary and punishment (*Atonement*, 78). This seems evidently false, since a person may volunteer—and doubtless many have volunteered, as in cases of civil disobedience—to be punished.

knowledge, countenanced. It is recognized that different prisoners may experience the same sentence in radically different ways. For a hardened criminal the punishment may be a mere annoyance, but for a person who is frail or sensitive, the same punishment may occasion terrible suffering. Our legal system will not allow these differences in persons to come into play in sentencing for obvious reasons: it could lead to outrageous exploitation of the system by certain persons. So the subjective suffering of persons is not allowed to play a role in the assigning of punishment. But God is obviously not susceptible to the sort of abuses that a human legal system is and so may take into account such subjective differences. In that case, Christ could be said to suffer subjectively the same pains as the damned. Turretin says that we cannot doubt the infinite value of Christ's satisfaction, for although his human nature was finite, the satisfaction is infinite, since it is relative to the person, who is the efficient cause and to whom the obedience and suffering are to be attributed.

Stump objects to the sort of view Turretin espouses by recurring to her objection to the justice of penal substitution: "Interpretations of the Anselmian kind emphasize both God's justice and Christ's perfect sinlessness. . . . But how could a sinless man be abandoned by a good and just God? What goodness or justice would there be in God's separating himself from a human person who is himself perfectly good and just?"[35] So this objection, like the first, also collapses into the objection to the justice of penal substitution. Moreover, we see again Stump's failure to understand the Reformers' doctrine of forensic imputation and justification.[36] As a result she interprets Calvin's view to imply that God deceived Christ into thinking that he had been forsaken when in fact he was not:

---

35 Stump, *Atonement*, 33; see further chap. 5.

36 In *Atonement*, 75, Stump has some very critical things to say with regard to a forensic understanding of justification. But a closer reading reveals that her complaint is not with theorists who hold that God has granted us a pardon through Christ but with those who say (sloppily, I think) that God has declared a verdict of acquittal over us. She is quite right in rejecting this latter understanding as a miscarriage of justice. God's judicial verdict of condemnation is not reversed by any verdict of acquittal; rather, we receive a legal pardon from God and are therefore no longer liable to punishment.

It must be said that Stump has no place for the Reformers' understanding of justification as a forensic declaration of righteousness. This is a significant deficit in her treatment, since Paul's doctrine of justification is forensic. See chap. 10, n30. One of the great advantages of penal substitution is that it meshes so well with a forensic understanding of justification.

"On Calvin's explanation, God brings it about that Christ experiences as real what is in fact not real. . . . On this view, then, God causes Christ to have an illusory experience; and to this degree God deceives Christ."[37] This is a misunderstanding; for Reformed thinkers like Calvin and Turretin, Christ is legally guilty before God and therefore justly punished by the Father's withdrawal of the blessings listed by Turretin.

Satisfaction and Universal Salvation

Unlike Socinus, who understood his interlocutors' views well, Stump objects that on penal substitutionary theories, Christ's atoning death ought to have been sufficient for universal salvation, which is inconsistent with the doctrine that some persons are not saved. "God's justice or goodness . . . are satisfied completely by Christ's atoning work. If so, however, then no human beings owe anything further to satisfy God. Why then does any human person have to do anything more? And why

---

Stump is right, of course, that neither pardon nor acquittal effects a moral transformation in the life of the wrongdoer, but that only underlines the necessity of sanctification in addition to forensic justification. She recognizes that "typically, the Anselmian kind of interpretation adds something to the basic account of atonement to explain how some human beings are in fact sanctified, so that some people are saved and others are not; and, often enough, there is a role for the Holy Spirit in this story of sanctification" (Stump, *Atonement*, 76). But she complains that

> on the Anselmian kind of interpretation, the work of Christ's atonement itself is just the obtaining of a pardon from God for human wrongdoers. The rest of the process resulting in the salvation of some human beings is not itself part of Christ's atonement. Consequently, on this view, Christ alone is not sufficient for salvation. But this conclusion is a *reductio* of this view, since, on traditional Christian teaching, there are indisputable biblical texts claiming or implying that in his person and work Christ is the sole savior of humankind. (76)

This attempted *reductio* is simplistic and unfair. Recall that Christ's exercise of his priestly office is but a part of his work. Christ's being the sole savior of mankind does not imply that his atonement does *everything* pertinent to salvation; for there are those for whom Christ died who remain unsaved (1 John 2:2), who are not sanctified (1 Cor 3:1-3), and who do not persevere (Heb 10:29). Indeed, on Stump's own theory of *at onement* Christ plays a relatively minor role, and the central figure in her account turns out to be the Holy Spirit.

37 Stump, *Atonement*, 157.

212 ATONEMENT AND THE DEATH OF CHRIST

are there any human beings who are not saved?"[38] Ironically, just this
consideration led Reformed thinkers like Turretin to embrace the doctrine of limited atonement, which holds that Christ died only on behalf
of the elect.[39] Thus, Stump's objection is not to penal substitution per se
but to the universal scope of Christ's atonement.[40]

So the objection fails to show any unsatisfactoriness of penal substitution as such. But why think that Christ's suffering the punishment for
all humanity's sins implies universal salvation? The assumption seems
to be that our actual redemption was achieved on Golgotha that fateful
day rather than our potential redemption. But, as Turretin sees, since we
did not even exist at that time, it is difficult to see how we could have
been actually redeemed at that moment. Christ suffered the punishment
due to all humanity's sins that God had previously passed over, thereby
meeting the demands of God's justice, a payment that is of infinite value
and therefore more than sufficient to pay for all humanity's sins yet to

---

38 Stump, *Atonement*, 25; cf. 78.
39 Advocacy of limited atonement is precisely the response to Stump's objection by
   Jeffery, Ovey, and Sach, *Pierced for Our Transgressions*, 270–78.
40 In a footnote, Stump acknowledges the doctrine of the limited atonement, to
   which she does not initially object. Instead, she mentions one particular argument sometimes offered for the doctrine of limited atonement; namely, that
   if Christ paid the penalty for the sins of the non-elect, then "God would be
   inflicting punishment for [the same] sins twice," once on Christ and once on
   the non-elect (Stump, *Atonement*, 421n67). She concludes, "This argument for
   limited atonement seems to me another reason for rejecting the penal substitution variant on the Anselmian kind of interpretation." This conclusion does not
   follow. Either this argument for limited atonement is a good one or not. If, as
   I am inclined to think, it is not a good argument, then it does not count in any
   way against penal substitution. But if it is a good argument, as Stump seems
   to think, then the atonement is only on behalf of the elect, and so there is no
   problem with the punishment of the non-elect.
   In chapter 3, Stump does object to the doctrine of limited atonement as such,
   saying that "this variant is inconsistent with God's justice in another way, since
   justice requires giving equal treatment to equal cases" (*Atonement*, 78). But limited atonement need not imply that God would not extend the atonement to
   cover the non-elect if He knew that they would freely respond to His saving
   grace, which is universally proffered to men. Such a non-Reformed, Molinist
   view of limited atonement holds that if the non-elect were to respond to God's
   extrinsically efficacious grace, then Christ would have died for them as well.
   Knowing that they would not freely so respond, God has limited the atonement
   to those persons He knew would respond.

be committed as well;[41] but that payment of our debt needs to be freely received by faith in order to achieve our actual redemption.

In fact, Reformed thinkers themselves recognize this truth in distinguishing between redemption as *accomplished* and as *applied*. They will say that our redemption was accomplished at the cross but that it is applied individually when persons are regenerated and place their faith in Christ.[42] This distinction is vital because otherwise the elect would be born redeemed. They would never be unregenerate sinners but would be justified and saved from the instant of their conception. But Scripture teaches that believers once were "children of wrath like the rest of mankind" (Eph 2:3). The distinction between redemption accomplished and applied makes sense only if we say that Christ's death wins our potential redemption and that that potential is actualized in individual lives through repentance and faith.

Stump is, however, puzzled by what she calls "the problem of application": "Even on the Anselmian kind of interpretation, a human being needs to do something to apply the benefits of the *at onement* to himself. He needs to have faith, or appropriate Christ's payment of the debt to himself in some other way. But why?"[43] It seems to me that the answer is that a pardon may be refused, as we shall see,[44] in which case it is inefficacious and the guilty party remains liable to punishment. Redemption is a historical process that takes place in individual lives as people are born, called and convicted by the Holy Spirit, and by faith actualize

---

41 Such an understanding would accord with the very widespread intuition that pre-punishment for a crime not yet committed is impossible or immoral. See, e.g., C. New, "Time and Punishment," *Analysis* 52, no. 1 (1992): 35–40; Bill Wringe, "Pre-punishment, Communicative Theories of Punishment, and Compatibilism," *Pacific Philosophical Quarterly* 93 (2012): 125–36.

42 See, e.g., Jeffery, Ovey, and Sach, *Pierced for Our Transgressions*, 243, 270–78. They would solve what they call the problem of timing by holding that God, timelessly foreknowing the sins of the elect, imputes them to Christ at the time of the crucifixion, but the benefits of Christ's death are applied to a person when he by faith becomes united with Christ. But even if God can impute foreknown sins to Christ, that does not suffice to explain how a person's redemption is actually accomplished at the cross, since the person at that time is not yet in union with Christ. It seems that the only persons whose redemption is actually, as opposed to potentially, accomplished at the cross are people who had actually existed by that time.

43 Stump, *Atonement*, 25.

44 See pp. 249–57.

the redemption potentially won for them by Christ.[45] As Stump herself emphasizes, faith is just the non-meritorious acquiescence to the prevenient grace of God. By freely refusing the grace of God, people can prevent their redemption's actualization. The situation is really no different from the situation on Stump's view that God has forgiven everyone's sins, and yet not all are saved because of their refusal of God's grace.

CONCLUDING REMARKS

Given the doctrine of the imputation of sin, to which parallels exist in our own justice system, the demands of divine justice may be satisfied by Christ's substitutionary punishment. Moreover, since Christ's substitutionary suffering is inclusionary, rather than exclusionary, we are punished in his being punished, to the fulfillment of divine justice.

God's graciously accepting a substitute for what we by justice owed is an expression of God's mercy toward us. We should not, in any case, think of our sinful condition primarily on the analogy of the debt owed by a debtor to a creditor nor of God's forgiveness in terms of remission of a debt; rather, our condition is like that of a condemned criminal before the court and divine forgiveness like a legal pardon, which is not at all incompatible with satisfaction of divine justice as a precondition of a full pardon. Penal substitution enables God to be both merciful and just. Because Christ is God Himself, the suffering of the Son in his human nature is ample to satisfy justice's demands for all humanity. Christ's atoning death on behalf of all mankind need not entail that all people will freely avail themselves of redemption. For while Christ's death has the potential to wipe away all men's sins, it does so only for those who avail themselves of it.

---

45 See Wolfhart Pannenberg, *Systematic Theology*, 3 vols. (Grand Rapids: Eerdmans, 1991), 2:412, 248.

Chapter 12

REDEMPTION
Divine Pardon and Its Effects

INTRODUCTION

Redemption through Christ's blood will be a third, vital facet of any biblical atonement theory. Christ's atoning death frees us from the bondage of sin, death, and hell and so liberates us from Satan's power. This emphasis is characteristic of classic *Christus Victor* theories. Contemporary *Christus Victor* theorists recognize that the ransom price of our redemption need not be thought of as paid to Satan to secure our release from bondage. Rather, the ransom price is paid to God to discharge the debt of punishment that we owe to divine justice. Just as we speak of a criminal's having "paid his debt to society" by suffering the punishment prescribed for his crime, so we may speak of Christ's having paid the debt of punishment we owe to God. Talk of ransom is thus a metaphor for penal substitution. Atonement theories emphasizing redemption should thus not be seen as stand-alone theories but rather serve to highlight one aspect of a multifaceted atonement theory that has penal substitution at its center.

DIVINE FORGIVENESS AS LEGAL PARDON

How, then, are condemned prisoners set free? If they are not to endure further punishment for their crimes, they must receive a full pardon. We have seen that it is more accurate to think of divine forgiveness on the analogy of a legal pardon by a ruler rather than on the analogy of the forgiveness extended by a private person. The philosophical literature typically treats forgiveness as a subjective change of attitude on the part of the person wronged, a determination to put away feelings of resentment, bitterness, or anger, a relinquishing of the desire for revenge or schadenfreude.[1] But God's forgiveness accomplishes much more than a change of attitude toward sinners on God's part.[2] God's forgiving sins removes our liability to punishment and thus obviates the demands of retributive justice upon us: the just desert of our sins is gone. Because

---

1   *Stanford Encyclopedia of Philosophy*, s.v. "Forgiveness," by Paul M. Hughes, §1, December 23, 2014, https://plato.stanford.edu/entries/forgiveness/. Hughes proceeds in §3.1 to differentiate legal pardon from forgiveness, concluding that "despite some similarities, pardon and forgiveness are significantly different notions." See also discussion in Kathleen Dean Moore, *Pardons: Justice, Mercy, and the Public Interest* (Oxford: Oxford University Press, 1989), chap. 16. For a helpful survey of the literature on the nature of divine forgiveness as either change of emotions or forbearance of punishment, see Brandon Warmke, "Divine Forgiveness I: Emotion and Punishment-Forbearance Theories," *Philosophy Compass* 12, no. 9 (2017): e12440, https://doi.org/10.1111/phc3.12440. Obviously, these alternatives are not mutually exclusive. Warmke's characterization of pardon as mere punishment-forbearance is inadequate, however, since an executive power could choose to forswear punishment without pardoning the lawbreaker. See n48 below. N.B. that if we take the nature of divine forgiveness to be pardon, then what Warmke calls the "standing question" and the "normativity question" simply evaporate, since God as chief executive has the standing to pardon crimes and the right to pardon third parties.

2   We encounter here the debate over whether the Levitical sacrifices and Christ's sacrificial death served to propitiate God, to change His attitude toward sinners from wrath to acceptance. It has become conventional wisdom among contemporary theologians that because the NT authors use *katalassō* (reconcile) and its cognates only with respect to human beings, not God, God does not need to be reconciled to humanity, but only humanity to a welcoming God. I leave aside whether such an argument from silence is cogent. But if God does not need to be reconciled to sinners, that fact shows all the more that divine forgiveness is not a change of attitude on God's part, in the way that forgiveness is usually understood by contemporary philosophers analyzing human relationships.

of the forgiveness that is to be found in Christ, one is no longer held accountable for one's sins. "There is therefore now no condemnation for those who are in Christ Jesus" (Rom 8:1).

It is evident, then, that divine forgiveness is much more akin to legal pardon than to forgiveness as typically understood.[3] Kathleen Moore has made the point forcefully by observing that when people ask God to forgive their sins, they are clearly hoping that God will not inflict the full measure of punishment they know they deserve. "These people would discover the seriousness of their conceptual confusion if God forgave their sins and punished them nevertheless—which is always an option for God."[4]

Samuel Morison, an attorney-advisor in the Office of Pardon Attorney, has therefore appropriately called the practice of executive clemency "the secular institutional expression of the traditional religious

---

3   The nature of divine forgiveness as legal pardon would be all the more obvious if some theorists were right in arguing that it is logically impossible for God to forgive sins, in the usual sense of the word (H. J. N. Horsbrugh, "Forgiveness," *Canadian Journal of Philosophy* 4, no. 2 [1974]: 269–82; Anne C. Minas, "God and Forgiveness," *Philosophical Quarterly* 25, no. 99 [1975]: 138–50; "Forgiveness," by Paul M. Hughes, §7; cf. the contrary view expressed by Meirlys Lewis, "On Forgiveness," *Philosophical Quarterly* 30, no. 120 [1980]: 236–45). For the proffered arguments against God's forgiving sins are admittedly inapplicable to His legally pardoning sins.

For better or worse, however, the arguments for the claim that it is logically impossible for God to forgive sins are scarcely plausible. God's attitude toward sinners could obviously go from wrath to acceptance, which is sufficient for forgiveness in the usual sense of the word. The fact that God, being omnipotent, cannot be harmed by sinners' wrongdoing does not entail that He be indifferent to their wrongdoing rather than incensed by it, as His holiness and love of the victims of sin demand. Moreover, if God is wronged, if not harmed, by sin, then His forgiveness is not a case of third-party forgiveness, which many theorists claim to be impossible. As St. Anselm understood, sinners' failure to give God His due in honor and obedience is a gross wrong committed against God. *Pace* Hughes, God's interests in establishing His Kingdom among mankind can be obviously set back, despite His omnipotence, through the free rebellion of creatures, as discussions of theodicy have made plain.

4   Moore, *Pardons*, 184. One may forgive without pardoning and pardon without forgiving. But recall that punishment and forgiveness are not incompatible with each other.

conception of reconciliation."⁵ Now, of course, there will be significant disanalogies between divine pardon and the pardoning power as it exists in Anglo-American systems of justice—for example, a president may issue pardons for personal political advantage⁶—but, still, given the similarities, we may expect to gain a good deal of insight into divine pardon by exploring the pardoning power vested in heads of government.

PARDON AND ITS EFFECTS

From ancient times, including the NT era,⁷ heads of state have exercised the power to pardon crimes.⁸ So the framers of the U.S. Constitution naturally included the pardoning power in the Constitution. Article 2, section 2 of the U.S. Constitution grants the president "Power to grant Reprieves and Pardons for Offences against the United States, except in Cases of Impeachment." Since this power is not defined in the

---

5   Morison, "Politics of Grace," 137. Recall that biblically speaking reconciliation is atonement in the broad sense. See also Mark W. Osler, "A Biblical Value in the Constitution: Mercy, Clemency, Faith and History," *University of St. Thomas Law Journal* 9, no. 3 (2012): 769–82.

6   Noah Messing lists seven motivations underlying presidential pardons: (1) justice: correcting excessive or improper punishments; (2) mercy: exercising compassion; (3) cronyism: extending favors to political loyalists and the wealthy; (4) military strategy: helping to win and end military conflicts; (5) legislative overreach: countering illegal or immoral legislation; (6) inter-administration consistency: lessening the punishments meted out during an overly harsh prior administration; (7) economic efficiency: offering relief from laws that harm economic growth (Noah A. Messing, "A New Power? Civil Offenses and Presidential Clemency," *Buffalo Law Review* 64 [2016]: 732–38). Most of these motivations are obviously inapplicable to divine pardon.

7   An executive pardon plays a pivotal role in the crucifixion of Jesus, according to Luke. The Roman prefect Pontius Pilate pardons the insurrectionist Barabbas instead of releasing Jesus, thereby condemning the Nazarene to the cross.

8   It is intriguing that much of the New Testament was written by a man who near the end of his life became embroiled in a legal dispute within the Roman justice system. When Paul appealed to the Roman emperor to try his case, he was not asking the emperor to pardon him, though that lay within Caesar's power. Nor was Paul appealing the verdict in his case, since Paul had never been tried and convicted. Rather, as a Roman citizen, Paul was exercising his right to be tried within the Roman system of justice rather than within the Jewish justice system and, moreover, asking for a change of venue for his case from Jerusalem to Rome, since Jewish pressures made it impossible for him to get a fair trial even before Roman officials resident in Palestine.

Constitution, U.S. courts have interpreted the presidential power to pardon on the model of the pardoning power of English monarchs, which the framers doubtless presupposed.[9] The power of English monarchs to pardon was, in turn, understood as a divine right, an act of grace reflecting God's ability to pardon sins.[10] William Blackstone characterizes the granting of "the king's most gracious pardon" as "the most amiable prerogative of the Crown."[11] So it is not surprising that the power of the executive to pardon strongly resembles divine pardon.

The U.S. Supreme Court has interpreted the pardon clause to comprise not only full pardons but by implication lesser acts of clemency,

---

9   Helpful surveys of the history of the pardon power may be found in Crouch, *Presidential Pardon Power*; W. H. Humbert, *The Pardoning Power of the President* (Washington, D.C.: American Council on Public Affairs, 1941); and Moore, *Pardons*.

10 In Moore's pithy conclusion, "Presidents used pardons as they chose, having been given a pardoning power patterned after that of the English Kings, which was patterned after God's" (*Pardons*, 51). She says that the pardoning power of English monarchs "was analogous in theory and practice to divine grace. Like grace . . . a royal pardon was thought of as a personal gift. Therefore, it required no justification and was not subject to criticism" (Kathleen Dean Moore, "Pardon for Good and Sufficient Reasons," *University of Richmond Law Review* 27, no. 2 [1993]: 282). So "pardon has historically been understood as an act of grace, a gift freely given from a God-like monarch to a subject" (Moore, *Pardons*, 9). Crouch suggests that in ancient cultures where the law was synonymous with justice, there would be no need to create exceptions to the law in order to further justice. The law was by definition just, so if an exception to the law was granted, it had to be for reasons unrelated to rectifying injustices. Ancient Judaism would seem to be a good example, for the Torah was God-given and therefore infallible. If an exception were granted, it could only be by an act of divine grace. While corrupt or incompetent judges might make the pardoning power of the king necessary in order to correct injustices, in God's case injustices are impossible, and so divine pardons could only be acts of mercy.

11 William Blackstone, *Commentaries on the Laws of England in Four Books*, 2nd ed. rev. (Chicago: Callaghan, 1879), 4:395. Interestingly, Blackstone opines that the power to pardon could never subsist in a republic, since then the power of judging and the power of pardoning would be vested in the same person, forcing him to undo his own pronouncements. The U.S. framers solved this problem by separating the judicial and executive branches of government and vesting the power to pardon solely in the latter. As observed above, in God's case the legislative, judicial, and executive functions of government are all rolled into one, but since God is both omniscient and morally perfect, injustice in His government of the world is logically impossible.

including commutations of sentence, reprieves, remissions of fines and penalties, and amnesties. Commutations are reductions of sentence for crimes of which the criminal is guilty. A reprieve is a temporary delay in the carrying out of a sentence. Remission of fines and penalties is the cancelation of such monetary obligations owed to the federal government for wrongdoing. Amnesties are similar to pardons but concern not individuals but classes of people.

What is a pardon? In a landmark decision, Chief Justice John Marshall describes a pardon as follows:

> A pardon is an act of grace, proceeding from the power entrusted with the execution of the laws, which exempts the individual, on whom it is bestowed, from the punishment the law inflicts for a crime he has committed.[12]

Marshall's description was later cited by the Supreme Court as a correct characterization of a pardon in *Burdick v. United States*, 236 U.S. 79, 89 (1915). According to this characterization, a pardon is an act of mercy, coming from the person(s) possessing the power of the executive, which removes a criminal's liability to punishment for a specific crime he has committed.

Marshall's description seems an apt characterization of a divine pardon as well. God is the power Who executes His divine *torah*, and His pardon is an act of grace by which He exempts elect sinners, who have violated His law, from the punishment they deserve. Every element of Marshall's definition finds a theological analogue. No wonder Daniel Kobil characterizes Marshall's vision of a pardon as "something akin to divine forgiveness"![13]

There are very few limitations on the U.S. presidential pardoning power: (1) the president may pardon only federal offenses ("Offences against the United States") and so is powerless to grant clemency in state criminal or civil cases, (2) the Constitution expressly prohibits the president from granting pardons "in Cases of Impeachment," (3) the president may not pardon a crime before it occurs, and (4) the president may not pardon someone held in contempt in a case between private parties.[14]

---

12 *United States v. Wilson*, 32 U.S. 150 (1833).
13 Daniel T. Kobil, "The Quality of Mercy Strained: Wresting the Pardoning Power from the King," *Texas Law Review* 69 (1991): 594.
14 Messing, "A New Power?" 668–69.

Only the third of these limitations is theologically interesting. Plausibly, God cannot pardon sins before they are committed, since at that time the person has not yet done anything wrong (and may not yet even exist!) and so cannot be guilty.[15] Hence, there is nothing to be pardoned. Pardon must take place after the sins have been committed.

One of the remarkable features of a presidential pardon is its absoluteness. It is not subject to either judicial review or to legislative restrictions. Even future presidents do not have the power to reverse a pardon. The president has the power to pardon whomever he wants for any reason he wants, and his pardon is irrevocable. The analogy to divine pardon is obvious. God as the supreme Ruler has absolute power to pardon sinners, and no one can gainsay His action. "Who will bring any charge against God's elect? It is God justifies. Who is to condemn?" (Rom 8:33-34).

What are the effects of a pardon? Marshall says that it exempts the individual from the punishment prescribed by the law for his crime. This much is uncontroversial.[16] But pardons do much more than merely exempt a convicted criminal from punishment for his crime. A pardon removes *all* the legal consequences of the criminal's conviction. A pardon thus restores to a person any civil rights which were restricted as a result of his conviction, such as the right to vote, to serve on a jury, or to obtain a business license. In *Knote v. United States*, the Supreme Court explained the effect of a pardon on its recipient:

> A pardon is an act of grace by which an offender is released from the consequences of his offence, so far as such release is practicable and within control of the pardoning power, or of officers under its direction. It releases the offender from all disabilities imposed by the offense, and restores to him all his civil rights. In contemplation of law, it so far blots out the

---

15 Thus, Turretin argues that prior to a person's birth his sins cannot be said to have been remitted because nonentities have no properties and, hence, no sin and guilt to be remitted (Francis Turretin, *Institutes of Elenctic Theology*, 3 vols., trans. George Musgrave Giger, ed. James T. Dennison Jr. [Phillipsburg, N.J.: P&R, 1992], 16.5). Such a person is not yet in union with Christ and so not yet justified. For Turretin, justification, though eternally decreed, takes place in this life in the moment of God's effectual calling, by which the sinner is transferred from a state of sin to a state of grace and is united to Christ, his head, by faith.

16 "Most jurists and scholars who have discussed this issue accept Chief Justice Marshall's dictum that '[a] pardon . . . exempts the individual, on whom it is bestowed, from the punishment the law inflicts for a *crime* he has committed'" (Messing, "A New Power?" 678).

offence, that afterwards it cannot be imputed to him to prevent the assertion of his legal rights. It gives him new credit and capacity, and rehabili-
tates him to that extent in his former position.[17]

We shall return to the effect of a pardon in restoring a person's civil
rights, a feature of pardons that is also uncontroversial, even if in some
cases difficult to adjudicate.

The controversial question concerning pardons is whether a pardon
serves to remove the criminal's guilt. Following the English model, the
U.S. courts were at first emphatic as to the effect of a pardon in expiating
guilt.[18] In *Ex parte Garland*[19] the Supreme Court famously declared:

> The inquiry arises as to the effect and operation of a pardon, and on this
> point all the authorities concur. A pardon reaches both the punishment
> prescribed for the offence and the guilt of the offender; and when the par-
> don is full, it releases the punishment and blots out of existence the guilt,
> so that in the eye of the law the offender is as innocent as if he had never
> committed the offence. If granted before conviction, it prevents any of
> the penalties and disabilities consequent upon conviction from attaching;
> if granted after conviction, it removes the penalties and disabilities, and
> restores him to all his civil rights; it makes him, as it were, a new man,
> and gives him a new credit and capacity.[20]

Like Marshall's description of a pardon, this characterization of the
effects of a full pardon is a marvelous description of a divine pardon. "If
anyone is in Christ, he is a new creation; the old has passed away, behold,
the new has come" (2 Cor 5:17). The pardoned sinner's guilt is expiated, so
that he is legally innocent before God.

---

17 *Knote v. United States*, 95 U.S. 149, 153 (1877).
18 See Samuel Williston, "Does a Pardon Blot Out Guilt?" *Harvard Law Review*
    28, no. 7 (1915): 648–52.
19 A. H. Garland, a former member of the Confederate Senate, received a full
    presidential pardon in July 1865 but was barred from practicing law because of an
    oath enacted by Congress as a prerequisite to appearing before a federal court.
    One had to swear that one had never supported, aided, or served in office in the
    Confederacy. Unable to take this oath, Garland sued to set aside this congres-
    sional prerequisite. The Supreme Court ruled that the oath was an improper
    legislative encroachment on the president's pardoning power.
20 *Ex parte Garland*, 71 U.S. 333, 380–81 (1866).

But as a description of the effects of human pardons, *Garland's* sweeping assertions have been eroded by subsequent court decisions.[21] In the *Harvard Law Review* of 1915 Samuel Williston published what has been called a "seminal" and "landmark" article, "Does a Pardon Blot Out Guilt?" in which he criticized *Garland* and its judicial progeny and which has been frequently cited by the courts.[22] Williston complained, "Everybody . . . knows that the vast majority of pardoned convicts were in fact guilty; and when it is said that in the eye of the law they are as innocent as if they have never committed an offense, the natural rejoinder is, then the eyesight of the law is very bad."[23] The truth, says Williston, is rather as Lord Coke wrote: *Poena mori potest, cupla perennis erit.*[24] A moment's reflection suggests that Williston must understand by "guilt" simply the property or fact of having committed the crime. On this understanding, to be guilty of a crime is just to have committed the crime.

That this is how Williston understands guilt is evident from the remainder of his article. He blames the verdict of the English Court in *Cuddington v. Wilkins* (80 Eng. Rep. 231 [K.B. 1615]) as laying the main foundation for the view that after a pardon the law could not see the criminal's guilt. Cuddington had brought an action against Wilkins for calling him a thief. Wilkins justified his appellation because Cuddington had once been convicted of theft. But Cuddington replied that he had been pardoned by the king for the alleged felony. The court decided for Cuddington, "for the whole court were of opinion that though he was a thief once, yet when the pardon came it took away, not only *poenam*, but *reatum.*"[25]

Williston disagrees:

> The true line of distinction seems to be this: The pardon removes all legal punishment for the offense. Therefore if the mere conviction involves certain disqualifications which would not follow from the commission of the crime without conviction, the pardon removes such disqualifications. On the other hand, if character is a necessary qualification and the commission of the crime would disqualify even though there had been no criminal

---

21 For a thorough review of the relevant judicial decisions see *In re Sang Man Shin*, 125 Nev. 100, 104–9 (2009); *Robertson v. Shinseki*, 26 Vet. App. 169, 176–79 (2013).
22 E.g., *Robertson v. Shinseki* at 177.
23 Williston, "Does a Pardon Blot Out Guilt?" 648.
24 "Punishment may expire, but guilt will last forever."
25 *Hob.* 67, 81, cited by Williston, "Does a Pardon Blot Out Guilt?" 651.

prosecution for the crime, the fact that the criminal has been convicted
and pardoned does not make him anymore eligible.[26]

The point is this: a pardon removes the legal disqualifications (abridgment of civil rights) resulting from the fact of conviction, but a pardon
does not affect any disqualifications resulting from the commission of
the crime.[27] The fact that a crime has been committed cannot be erased.
It is this fact that Williston identifies as guilt. Though pardoned, the
person still stole or lied or acted recklessly and so remains guilty of the
crime he committed. As such he may, despite his pardon, be disqualified
from certain activities, such as giving testimony or practicing law.

Thus, Williston blasts the New York Court of Appeals for the following "unpardonable reasoning" in a case involving disbarment of a pardonee:

> The pardon does reach the offence for which he was convicted, and does
> blot it out, so that he may not now be looked upon as guilty of it. But it
> cannot wipe out the act that he did, which was adjudged an offence. It was
> done, and will remain in effect for all time.[28]

Williston marvels, "How a man who 'may not now be looked upon as
guilty' of a crime, nevertheless did the act which was a crime and must
now be disbarred for it, it is difficult to imagine."[29] Henry Weihofen in
a later review, citing Williston's criticism of the court's opinion in this
case, complains of "the mischief that results when a court applies literally
the unfounded dictum of *Ex parte Garland* that a pardon 'blots out' guilt,
and makes the offender a 'new man,' etc."[30] The effect of a pardon (other
than on grounds of innocence) is "to absolve from further punishment
and restore civil rights, but *not to undo what is past or blot out of existence*

---

26 Williston, "Does a Pardon Blot Out Guilt?" 653.

27 Among the effects of a pardon Morison includes preventing deportation, easing
    foreign travel restrictions, restoring firearms rights, and facilitating the acqui-
    sition of a wide variety of valuable goods, such as naturalized citizenship, wel-
    fare, veterans and other government benefits, military enlistment, government
    contracts, various business and professional licenses, and employment in many
    regulated industries. But a pardon does not create the fiction that the offense
    never occurred or entitle the recipient to an expungement of his criminal record
    (Morison, "Politics of Grace," 32–34).

28 *In re an Attorney*, 86 N.Y. 563, 569 (1881).

29 Morison, "Politics of Grace," 656.

30 Henry Weihofen, "The Effect of a Pardon," *University of Pennsylvania Law
    Review* 88 (1939): 181; cf. 189–90.

a fact, namely, that *the person has committed a crime and been sentenced and punished* for it."[31]

An examination of various district, state, and appellate court cases walking back the assertions of *Garland* reveals that the courts in such cases tend to presuppose this same understanding of guilt as the property of having committed a crime. Consider the following examples:

> It is petitioner's contention that these pardons under Texas law wiped out the convictions as thoroughly as though they had never occurred, and that, therefore, giving full faith and credit to the law, no fact as to prior convictions existed. . . . It may be true (we do not so hold) that the Texas pardon law goes all the way and prohibits the Texas courts from giving any consideration to a pardoned offense. Yet such a law could not turn back the hand of time long enough to delete an actuality from its long course. It still remains true that petitioner was the subject of two prior final convictions when the law of California overtook him in the commission of another felony. Notwithstanding the Texas pardons, the stubborn fact remains that the *habit* of crime was upon him.[32]

> The offender's past conduct, including the commission of an offense against another sovereign, may be taken into account even though the offender has been pardoned by such other sovereign. The Constitution, which confers upon the President the power to pardon, does not confer upon him power to wipe out guilt.[33]

> If *Garland* ever had the broad impact on post-pardon proceedings which the sweep of its language implies, a century of judicial sculpturing has left more form than substance to the opinion. It can no longer be seriously contended, for example, that a pardon erases an offender's past, making it "as if he had never committed the offense." . . . While a pardon removes all legal punishments and disabilities attached to a conviction, we hold that it cannot erase the *fact* that the offender was convicted of an infamous crime and it is the fact of conviction alone, not its continuing viability, which renders the offender ineligible to hold public office. . . . As this Court said in *Grant*, 133 A. at 791: "[A pardon] . . . removes the disability, but does not change the common-law principle that the conviction of an infamous offense is evidence of bad character for truth."[34]

---

31 Weihofen, "Effect of a Pardon" (emphasis added).
32 *Groseclose v. Plummer,* 106 F.2d 311, 313 (9th Cir. 1939).
33 *People ex rel. Prisament v. Brophy,* 287 N.Y. 132, 137–38 (1941).
34 *State ex rel. Wier v. Peterson,* 369 A.2d 1076, 1080, 1081 (Del. 1976).

The undisputed legal effect of a pardon is to restore the civil rights to an ex-felon (suffrage, jury service, and the chance to seek public office). However, the Governor cannot overrule the judgment of a court of law. He has no "appellate" jurisdiction. There can be no doubt but that a final judgment was entered against the ex-felon. Regardless of the post-judgment procedural maneuvering, a final conviction does not disappear. A pardon implies guilt. Texas Courts may forgive, but they do not forget. The fact is not obliterated and there is no "wash." Moreover, the granting of a pardon does not in any way indicate a defect in the process. It may remove some disabilities, but does not change the common-law principle that a conviction of an infamous offense is evidence of bad character.[35]

[A]lthough the presidential pardon set aside Abrams' convictions, as well as the consequences which the law attaches to those convictions, it could not and did not require the court to close its eyes to the fact that Abrams did what he did. . . . According to Abrams, the quoted language requires this court, in effect, to pretend that his pardoned wrongdoing never happened. . . . The implications of Abrams' position are troubling to say the least. Let us consider an apt analogy. Suppose that an alcoholic surgeon performs an operation while intoxicated. He botches the surgery. The patient dies. The surgeon is convicted of manslaughter and is sentenced to imprisonment. The President grants him a full and unconditional pardon. According to Abrams, the surgeon now has the right, as a result of the pardon, to continue to operate on other patients, without any interference from the medical licensing authorities. . . . The presidential pardon would undoubtedly have precluded a sanction based on Abrams' conviction. . . . Instead, the proceeding was brought to discipline Abrams for engaging in *conduct* which, according to Bar Counsel, violated the Code of Professional Responsibility.[36]

Pursuant to the current expunction statute, a person will only qualify for a certificate of eligibility if he "[h]as not been adjudicated guilty of, or adjudicated delinquent for committing, any of the acts stemming from the arrest or alleged criminal activity to which the petition to expunge pertains." § 943.0585(2)(e), Fla. Stat. (2002). . . . While a pardon removes the legal consequences of a crime, it does not remove the historical fact that the conviction occurred; a pardon does not mean that the conviction is gone. If a pardon had the effect of allowing an individual to declare that he had not been adjudicated guilty of a crime, the end result would be that all pardoned individuals would be eligible for expungement of their

---

35 *Dixon v. McMullen*, 527 F. Supp. 711, 717–18 (N.D. Tex. 1981).
36 *In re Abrams*, 689 A.2d 6, 7, 10–11 (D.C. 1997).

criminal history records. Today, we hold that a pardon does not have the effect of erasing guilt so that a conviction is treated as though it had never occurred.[37]

To summarize: the legal effect of a presidential pardon is to preclude further punishment for the crime, but not to wipe out the fact of conviction. The CFTC did not violate the pardon clause by considering the conduct underlying Hirschberg's conviction in determining whether he was qualified to do business as a floor trader, because its decision was grounded in protection of the public rather than in punishing Hirschberg as a convicted felon. . . . The effect of a pardon is not to prohibit all *consequences* of a pardoned conviction, but rather to preclude future *punishment* for the conviction. . . . In cases where governmental action has been held to violate the pardon clause, . . . the pardoned individual is stripped of his rights based not on the conduct underlying the conviction, but on the fact of conviction alone. . . . evidence of the CFTC's non-punitive purpose in denying Hirschberg's application is the fact that the conduct underlying Hirschberg's mail fraud conviction would be cause for denial even if he had not been criminally convicted for it.[38]

A pardon does not prevent any and all consequences of the pardoned offense: collateral consequences of the offense may still follow. For example, an attorney who has been pardoned for the offense of forgery may not be punished for that crime, but may be disbarred as a result of that offense. Our predecessor court also recognized that a gubernatorial pardon does not restore the character of the witness/pardonee, so that he or she could still be impeached as a felon. Thus, while a pardon will foreclose punishment of the offense itself, it does not erase the fact that the offense occurred, and that fact may later be used to the pardonee's detriment.[39]

The authorities cited are in accord: expunction is not a civil right. Based upon these well-reasoned authorities, we hereby retreat from our prior decisions . . . to the extent that they imply that a pardon blots out guilt and erases the historical fact of the underlying conviction. . . . Because we conclude that the effect of the pardon does not erase the historical fact of the conviction, we hold that there is nothing in the Nevada Constitution

---

37 *R. J. L. v. State*, 887 So.2d 1268, 1280–81 (Fla. 2004).
38 *Hirschberg v. Commodity Futures Trading Commission*, 414 F.3d 679, 682, 683 (7th Cir. 2005).
39 *Fletcher v. Graham*, 192 S.W.3d 350, 362–63 (Ky. 2006).

that creates a civil right to an expunction of the record of a criminal conviction.[40]

The Court is bound by the Supreme Court's eventual adoption of Professor's Williston's view of the effect of a Presidential pardon—namely, that a Presidential pardon relieves the pardonee of the legal disabilities incident to a conviction of an offense (in this case, the legal punishment of a general court-martial conviction), but does not eliminate the consideration of the conduct (being AWOL for 313 days) that led to that conviction. . . . Therefore, Mr. Robertson's argument, that his Presidential pardon "blots out" the conduct that led to his discharge and prohibits VA from considering that conduct as a bar to benefits, must fail.[41]

These cases have typically to do with whether a pardon serves to expunge one's criminal record or to remove a particular disqualification (such as disbarment, banishment from the trading floor, or denial of veteran's benefits) suffered by the pardonee as a consequence of his being convicted of the crime for which he received a pardon. In holding that *Garland* overstepped in asserting that a pardon blots out guilt because a pardon does not blot out the past conduct leading to the conviction, these courts equate guilt with having carried out the conduct that led to the conviction.[42]

---

40 *In re Sang Man Shin*, 125 Nev. at 110.

41 *Robertson v. Shinseki* at 179.

42 So also Ashley M. Steiner, "Remission of Guilt or Removal of Punishment? The Effects of a Presidential Pardon," *Emory Law Journal* 46 (1997): 996–97, who, without ever defining "guilt," claims that it is "illogical to assert that the pardon 'blots out of existence the guilt' of the offender," since "the acts leading to the conviction, whether or not they are punished, remain." She observes that after Williston's article, courts generally adopted one of three views regarding the effects of a presidential pardon: (1) a pardon obliterates both the conviction and the guilt; (2) a pardon obliterates the conviction but not the guilt (which she inexplicably identifies as Williston's view); or (3) a pardon obliterates neither the conviction nor the guilt (Williston's actual view). She takes no cognizance of a fourth alternative staring us in the face; namely, (4) a pardon obliterates the guilt but not the conviction. Alternative (2) is incoherent, since in the absence of a conviction, *legal* (as opposed to moral) guilt cannot exist. Moreover, given a retributive theory of justice, both (2) and (3) are incoherent, as explained below, since—a criminal being forever after guilty—a pardon could not obviate punishment. Although some courts have affirmed (1) in stating that not simply the guilt of the offender but the offense itself is blotted out, *Garland* does not

While such an understanding of the word "guilt" may accord with much of ordinary language, a little reflection reveals that, given standard retributive theories of justice, such a conception of guilt has bizarre consequences. For on this view a person's guilt could never be expunged, whether by pardon or punishment. Even if a person has served his full sentence and so satisfied the demands of justice, he remains guilty, since it will be ineradicably and forever the case that once upon a time he did commit the crime. But then on standard theories of retributive justice, he still deserves punishment! For it is an axiom of retributive justice that the guilty deserve punishment. Such an understanding of guilt would thus, in effect, sentence everyone to hell, even for the most minor of crimes, since guilt could never be eradicated and, hence, the demands of justice satisfied. Indeed, even a divine pardon would not serve to remove guilt and save us from punishment, since even God cannot change the past. But such a conclusion is incoherent, since it is the function of pardon to cancel one's liability to punishment. Therefore, this understanding of guilt is incompatible with standard theories of retributive justice.

The *Garland* court and its progeny should not be thought to consider a pardon to be a sort of judicial time machine, capable of erasing the past. It is logically incoherent to bring it about that an event which has occurred has not occurred, and it would be ungracious to attribute to our courts the absurd opinion that a pardon can erase from the past a person's wrongdoing or conviction for a crime. Rather what the *Garland* court was doing, and what its detractors have failed to do, is what contemporary philosophers of time call "taking tense seriously."[43] When the Supreme Court declared that a pardon "blots out of existence the guilt, so that in the eye of the law the offender is as innocent as if he had never committed the offence," it takes seriously the tenses of the verbs involved. It recognizes that the offender *was* guilty, but as a result of his

---

affirm that a pardon blots out the offense. Accordingly, *Garland* and its progeny are best interpreted as affirming (4).

43 The phrase was apparently inspired by the great Oxford tense logician A. N. Prior, who, in reaction to W. V. O. Quine's extolling the tenselessness of modern logic, praised medieval logic because it "took tenses far more seriously than our own common logic does" (Prior, "The Syntax of Time Distinctions," *Franciscan Studies* 18, no. 2 [1958]: 117). I am grateful to Prior scholar David Jakobsen for alerting me to this article, which was originally Prior's presidential address to the New Zealand Congress of Philosophy in 1954.

pardon he *is now* innocent in the law's eyes. It is precisely for that reason that in the court's opinion Congress' attempt to prescribe further punishment for Mr. Garland was illegitimate: as a result of the pardon he is no longer guilty.[44] Moreover, the counterfactual conditional signaled by "as if . . ." reveals that the law is not blind to his offense. The law can see his offense, but as a result of the pardon the offender is now as innocent as he would have been if he had never committed the offense.

From the beginning, courts that held that a pardon expunges a person's guilt recognized the importance of tense. In *Cuddington v. Wilkins*, for example, the court opines that while Cuddington was once rightly called a thief, as a result of the king's pardon he should no longer be called a thief. In Hobart's report on the case, we read, "It was said, that he could no more call him thief, in the present tense, than to say a man hath the pox, or is a villain after he be cured or manumised, but that he had been a thief or villain he might say."[45] The court's decision turns upon taking tense seriously. Similarly, the reasoning of the New York Court of Appeals, which Williston found unpardonable, emphasizes that though the pardonee was once guilty of the offense, "he may not now be looked upon as guilty of it." The opinion is admittedly sloppy in saying that it is the offense rather than the guilt that is blotted out by a pardon, but in view of the court's insistence that the criminal act cannot be "wipe[d] out," its intention to agree with *Garland* is evident. Moreover, contrary to the opinions of several lower courts,[46] *Garland* is wholly consistent with the Supreme Court's opinion in *Burdick v. United States* that the pardon of an accused person, if accepted, actually implies his guilt (otherwise there would be nothing to be pardoned), for *Garland*

---

44 See discussion by Samuel E. Schoenburg, "Clemency, War Powers, and Guantánamo," *New York University Law Review* 91, no. 4 (2016): 930–31.

45 *Hob.* 81, 82 (1615), cited in Williston, "Does a Pardon Blot Out Guilt?" 652. Williston notes that "the principal case was followed in *Leyman v. Latimer*, 3 Ex. D. 15 (1877), on very similar facts, and the court upheld the validity of the distinction taken in *Cuddington v. Wilkins*, between the legality of using the present and the past tense," and yet fails himself to appreciate the importance of this distinction.

46 For example, the opinion of the Supreme Court of Nevada, which states, "In *Burdick*, the Court implicitly acknowledged that the mere act of accepting a preconviction pardon carried an unremovable social stigma, an acknowledgement that is inconsistent with a position that a pardon blots out all existence of guilt" (*In re Sang Man Shin* at 105). A pardon can take away the guilt that it implies, and enduring social stigma is definitely not guilt.

has no interest in denying that the offender was guilty, so that the pardon, in taking away his guilt, implies that he was guilty. A pardon does not have an "appellate" function, as the courts have recognized, in that it does not imply a miscarriage of justice; the correctness of the guilty verdict rendered is not undermined.[47] But now the person is pardoned, and so the effect of that verdict is canceled: though once guilty, the pardonee no longer is.[48]

The opinion in *Garland* was properly explicated in *In re Spenser* (1878) as follows:

> This is probably as strong and unqualified a statement of the scope and efficacy of a pardon as can be found in the books. And yet I do not suppose the opinion is to be understood as going the length of holding that while the party is to be deemed innocent of the crime by reason of the pardon from and after the taking effect thereof, that it is also to be deemed that he never did commit the crime or was convicted of it. The effect of the pardon is prospective and not retrospective. It removes the guilt and restores the party to a state of innocence. But it does not change the past and cannot annihilate the established fact that he was guilty of the offence.[49]

The opinion in *Garland* is thus fully in accord with the prevailing view that a pardon has no effect upon the criminal conduct and conviction of the person pardoned.

---

47 The Supreme Court of Indiana was in accord with *Garland* when it wrote, "An innocent man suffering from an illegal sentence, procured by fraud or extorted by violence, may desire a trial and an acquittal which shall remove from his character the stain of guilt, and this the exercise of the pardoning power cannot do" (*Sanders v. State*, 85 Ind. 318, 322 [1882]). A pardon cannot remove the stain of past guilt, even if it renders the pardonee no longer guilty.

48 A number of scholars have noted that pardons differ from other forms of executive clemency in that the latter, unlike pardons, do not negate the criminal's conviction but leave intact the judgment of guilt. For example, President Carter, in proclaiming an amnesty for Vietnam War draft dodgers, said poignantly that their crimes have been forgotten, not forgiven. Similarly, recipients of commutations and reprieves remain guilty (Kobil, "Quality of Mercy Strained," 577; Stacy Caplow, "Governors! Seize the Law: A Call to Expand the Use of Pardons to Provide Relief from Deportation," *Boston University Public Interest Law Journal* 22 [2013]: 299; Messing, "A New Power?" 672; Schoenburg, "Clemency, War Powers, and Guantánamo," 924). This distinction seems to make sense only if a pardon annuls the guilt of the offender.

49 *In re Spenser*, 22 F. Cas. 921, 922 (Cir. Ct. D. Or. 1878).

Not only so, the opinion in *Garland* is also consistent with the view that some things (for example, having one's criminal records sealed) may be prohibited to a pardonee because there is no civil right that may be restored in such cases; in other cases a pardon has no effect upon the susceptibility of the pardonee to certain actions because the actions involve private lawsuits. *Garland* is thus in accord with the prevailing opinion that a pardon serves to release a person from all the legal consequences of his conviction, including punishment, taken in abstraction from the wrongdoing itself.

It is obvious that the *Garland* court has a very different conception of guilt than lower courts that see themselves as departing from *Garland*. Rather than assume the incoherent understanding that equates guilt with the facticity of a past event, *Garland* assumes that guilt is a property that can be temporarily exemplified and then lost though pardon or appropriate punishment. So what is this property? In criminal law guilt is typically determined by establishing that someone has committed a wrongful act (*actus reus*) while possessing a blameworthy mental state (*mens rea*).[50] Perhaps guilt is the property of being a culpable wrongdoer, a property that can be temporarily exemplified but lost through sufficient punishment or pardon. But wrongdoing and culpability are merely sufficient, not necessary, conditions for guilt. Guilty verdicts in cases of strict liability (in which there may be neither wrongdoing nor culpability) show that guilt cannot be equated merely with being a culpable wrongdoer.[51]

So what is guilt? It may be convenient to think of guilt just as *liability to punishment*. A verdict of "guilty" is plausibly a declaration that the person is liable to punishment. To be guilty of a crime is to be liable to punishment for that crime. Such an understanding of guilt makes it perspicuous why punishment or pardon serves to expiate guilt. A person who has served his sentence has "paid his debt to society" and so is now no longer guilty, that is to say, no longer liable to punishment. Similarly, a person who has been pardoned is by all accounts no longer liable to punishment for the crime he committed. In any case, however we define

---

50 These just are the conditions Michael Moore identifies as just desert (*Placing Blame: A Theory of Criminal Law* [Oxford: Oxford University Press, 1997], 33, 91, 168, 403–4).

51 On strict liability see L. H. Leigh, *Strict and Vicarious Liability: A Study in Administrative Criminal Law*, Modern Legal Studies (London: Sweet and Maxwell, 1982); David Ormerod and Karl Laird, *Smith, Hogan, and Ormerod's Criminal Law*, 15th ed. (Oxford: Oxford University Press, 2018), chap. 5.

guilt, if at all, given a retributive theory of justice, guilt entails liability to punishment. It follows logically that if a pardon removes one's liability to punishment, then it also blots out guilt. It is impossible that a person be pardoned and yet remain guilty.

To return, then, to the concerns of theology, it seems to me that *Garland*'s statement of the effects of a pardon is a marvelous description of the effects of a divine pardon of a person's sins. By taking tense seriously, we understand how a person who was once guilty may, in virtue of a pardon, be no longer guilty, despite the ineradicable fact that he did commit the sin for which he was condemned. The decisions of certain lower U.S. courts do not compromise *Garland*, for they are assuming a different understanding of guilt, which equates guilt with the facticity of the past offense, which *Garland* would not think to deny. Like punishment, pardon expiates a person's guilt, so that he is no longer condemned and liable to punishment.

These debates over the effects of a pardon provide insight into the nature of divine justification. In contrast to Catholic theologians, who saw justification as involving only infused righteousness, the Protestant Reformers recaptured the Pauline doctrine of imputed righteousness. Alister McGrath highlights three distinctive features of the Protestant doctrine of justification:

(1) Justification involves a *forensic declaration* of righteousness that effects a change in *legal status before God*, as opposed to a process that actually makes one righteous.

(2) There is a clear conceptual difference between justification ("the act by which God declares the sinner to be righteous") and either regeneration or sanctification (the actual "internal process of renewal by the Holy Spirit").

(3) Justifying righteousness is understood as an external, "alien" righteousness graciously *imputed* to the Christian through the act of faith.[52]

Not that the Reformers denied that God infuses righteousness into us, that is to say, makes us righteous by a moral transformation of our character! They affirmed such an infused righteousness but saw it as belonging properly to sanctification, that gradual transformation of character into conformity with Christ's image by the power of the indwelling Holy

---

52 Alister McGrath, "Forerunners of the Reformation? A Critical Examination of the Evidence for Precursors of the Reformation Doctrines of Justification," *Harvard Theological Review* 75, no. 2 (1982): 223.

Spirit (2 Cor 3:18).[53] Justification in Paul's view is a forensic notion, God's legal declaration that we are righteous. While justification may involve more than divine pardon of our sins, at the heart of forensic justification lies divine pardon. By God's pardon we are freed of our liability to punishment, so that legally we are innocent before the bar of His justice.

Our legal pardon by God no more transforms our character and makes us virtuous people than does a human pardon a convicted criminal. Again and again, the courts have insisted that a person may suffer various disabilities, despite his pardon, because of the flawed character that led to his conviction. The conviction alone, now pardoned, may not serve as grounds of disability, but it may serve as evidence of a corrupt character and conduct that are disabling. So, for example, in the case *In re Abrams*, Elliott Abrams was deemed unfit to practice law despite his pardon because a pardon did nothing to restore the moral character necessary for him to continue to practice law. Although the District of Columbia Court of Appeals agreed with Abrams that his pardon set aside his convictions and the legal consequences thereof, still his pardon "could not and did not require the court to close its eyes to the fact that Abrams did what he did."[54] Similarly, in *Hirschberg v. Commodity Futures Trading Commission*, the Seventh Circuit U.S. Court of Appeals found that "the conduct underlying Hirschberg's mail fraud conviction would be cause for denial even if he had not been criminally convicted for it. . . . The CFTC appropriately considered the conviction as evidence of Hirschberg's inability to work as an ethical floor broker."[55] These cases nicely illustrate Williston's point that "while pardon dispenses with punishment, it cannot change character, and where character is a qualification for an office, a pardoned offence as much as an unpardoned offence is evidence of a lack of the necessary qualification."[56]

---

53 For example, Turretin emphasizes that imputation is a purely forensic notion and does not involve an infusion of Christ's righteousness into us (Turretin, *Institutes of Elenctic Theology*, 14.16). While agreeing that by the grace of Christ righteousness is infused into us, Turretin insists that it plays no role in justification: "For the righteousness of Christ alone imputed to us is the foundation and meritorious cause upon which our absolutary sentence rests, so that for no other reason does God bestow the pardon of sin and the right to life than on account of the most perfect righteousness of Christ imputed to us and apprehended by faith" (16.1).
54 *In re Abrams* at 7.
55 *Hirschberg v. Commodity Futures Trading Commission*, 414 F.3d at 683, 684.
56 Williston, "Does a Pardon Blot Out Guilt?" 657.

Similarly, while a divine pardon makes us legally innocent before God, free of liability to punishment, it is powerless of itself to effect moral transformation of character. To that end we need regeneration through the Holy Spirit and His sanctifying influence to make us over time into the men and women that God wants us to be.[57] Sanctification in this sense is not a forensic transaction but a moral transformation of character and is not therefore wrought by divine pardon alone.

CONCLUDING REMARKS

In summary, at the heart of redemption lies divine pardon. Our liberation from sin and death and hell and our victory over Satan, so emphasized by the *Christus Victor* theory, is achieved via a divine pardon procured as a result of Christ's atoning death, which satisfied the demands of divine justice, so that we might go free. A pardon annuls our liability to punishment, and so blots out our guilt, and constitutes us new persons, now as innocent in God's sight as if we had never committed sin. The effect of a divine pardon may be supplemented, if we like, by affirming a positive imputation of righteousness to us, so that we are much more than merely innocent but have the new legal standing of being positively righteous in God's eyes.[58]

---

57 Emphasis upon the work of the Holy Spirit in achieving what she calls "*at one-ment*" with God is the principal merit of Eleonore Stump's recent study of the atonement. Unfortunately, she knows nothing of imputed righteousness but only infused righteousness and has no place in her theory for satisfaction of divine justice.

58 Whether that righteousness is procured by Christ's complete obedience to the law or is immediately from God is an in-house debate that need not be finally resolved.

Chapter 13

REDEMPTION
Justification and Appropriation of a Divine Pardon

INTRODUCTION

We have seen that redemption is a function of divine pardon. As a result of Christ's atoning death, a divine pardon is procured that blots out our guilt, sets us free, and gives us a new start. In this chapter we want to explore the justification and appropriation of such a pardon. Once again, it can prove insightful to examine first how executive pardons are justified and appropriated in our justice system.

THE JUSTIFICATION OF A PARDON

Like the question of whether a pardon blots out the guilt of the pardoned offender, a question that has seemingly divided our courts is whether pardons are acts of mercy, and if so, what justifies such an act of clemency. H. R. T. Roberts provides a rough working explication of acting mercifully: "In all justice I am entitled to A from *x*, but it is *mine* to exact and I choose not to."[1] Alwynne Smart would add that the choice is made "solely through benevolence" and not, for example, out of constraint,

---

1   H. R. T. Roberts, "Mercy," *Philosophy* 46, no. 178 (1971): 353.

self-interest, or ulterior motives.[2] Morison makes the application to exec-utive pardons:

> The institutional expression of mercy through executive clemency means . . . the partial or complete mitigation of justly imposed punish-ment (including the removal of the collateral consequences attendant upon a felony conviction) by the chief executive on *non-retributive* grounds, that is to say, for reasons which do not necessarily have anything to do with what a criminal justly deserves as punishment for the commission of a particular offense.[3]

The central question to be answered in this connection is, in Moore's words, the following: given a retributivist theory of justice and of the role of the state, under what conditions is a pardon justified and under what conditions is it not justified?[4] I hope to show that this question has profound theological significance.

As we have seen, early Supreme Court opinions, following English precedent, considered pardons to be acts of mercy on the part of the executive power. The landmark decision in this respect was *United States v. Wilson* (1833), in which Chief Justice Marshall wrote:

> The constitution gives to the president, in general terms, "the power to grant reprieves and pardons for offences against the United States." As this power had been exercised, from time immemorial, by the executive of that nation whose language is our language, and to whose judicial institutions ours bear a close resemblance; we adopt their principles respecting the operation and effect of a pardon, and look into their books for the rules prescribing the manner in which it is to be used by the person who would avail himself of it.
>
> A pardon is an act of grace, proceeding from the power intrusted with the execution of the laws, which exempts the individual, on whom it is bestowed, from the punishment the law inflicts for a crime he has committed. It is the private, though official, act of the executive magis-trate, delivered to the individual for whose benefit it is intended, and not communicated officially to the court.[5]

2   Alwynne Smart, "Mercy," *Philosophy* 43, no. 166 (1968): 359.
3   Samuel T. Morison, "The Politics of Grace: On the Moral Justification of Exec-utive Clemency," *Buffalo Criminal Law Review* 9, no. 1 (2005): 18–19.
4   Kathleen Dean Moore, *Pardons: Justice, Mercy, and the Public Interest* (Oxford: Oxford University Press, 1989), 9.
5   *United States v. Wilson*, 32 U.S. 150, 160–61 (1833).

In this opinion we see clearly the reliance on English precedent, the subsequent characterization of a pardon as an act of grace, and the interesting characterization of a pardon as a private, though official, transaction between the executive and the criminal. We shall have more to say of this last element in the sequel; for now we focus on the description of a pardon as an act of grace.

According to Humbert, "In virtue of the stress which Marshall placed upon the grace and upon the private character of the presidential act, mercy or grace became, in strict legal theory, the reason for a pardon."[6] In 1927 a case came before the Supreme Court involving President Taft's commutation of a criminal's death sentence to life imprisonment, a commutation that the criminal, in a complex legal maneuver, claimed was invalid because he had not accepted it. Chief Justice Oliver Wendell Holmes wrote curtly:

> We will not go into history, but we will say a word about the principles of pardons in the law of the United States. A pardon in our days is not a private act of grace from an individual happening to possess power. It is a part of the Constitutional scheme. When granted it is the determination of the ultimate authority that the public welfare will be better served by inflicting less than what the judgment fixed.[7]

In this opinion, Holmes brushes aside English precedent and appears to repudiate in no uncertain terms Marshall's characterization of a pardon as an act of grace, and his opinion has been so interpreted.[8] In fact, however, appearances are misleading: what the *Biddle* court rejects is not that a pardon is an act of grace but that it is a private transaction between the person in office and the criminal. It is the privacy of the act of grace to which Holmes objects.

Holmes' opinion was carefully explicated by the Oregon Supreme Court in 2013 in a case involving a criminal's rejection of the governor's reprieve of his death sentence:

---

6 W. H. Humbert, *The Pardoning Power of the President* (Washington, D.C.: American Council on Public Affairs, 1941), 22.

7 *Biddle v. Perovich*, 274 U.S. 480, 486 (1927).

8 For example, Humbert asserts that in *Biddle v. Perovich* the Supreme Court "rejected the elements of grace and of the private character of the act of pardon" (Humbert, *Pardoning Power of the President*, 22). In fact, only the second element was rejected.

> To the extent that this court's cases indicate that acts of clemency are ineffective if rejected, the cases suggest that the recipient has that right of rejection because grants of clemency are acts of grace. A grant of clemency may be an act of grace in some cases, but, as the Court stated in *Biddle*, under our constitutional scheme, a grant of clemency is not a *"private* act of grace from an individual *happening* to possess power."[9]

The Oregon court emphasizes that while pardons may be acts of grace, they are not, according to *Biddle*, private acts of grace. The court goes on to recognize that "historically, governors and presidents have granted clemency for a wide range of reasons, including reasons that may be political, personal, or 'private.' . . . Nonetheless, . . . the Governor's clemency power is far from private: It is an important part of the constitutional scheme envisioned by the framers."[10]

On the basis of the Supreme Court decisions mentioned above, Jeffery Crouch concludes that the presidential clemency power has two equally valid rationales: "the idea that a pardon is an act of grace shown by the president to the offender and the diametrically opposed view that clemency should be granted as part of the constitutional scheme—that is, for the good of the public rather than for the benefit of the individual offender."[11] Crouch errs in seeing these rationales as opposed rather than complementary. Pardons can be granted for either reason—perhaps even for both. Two unanimous Supreme Court decisions have established these rationales, and *Wilson* was never overruled. Noting that the former U.S. pardon attorney Roger Adams has referred to pardon decision making as "all a matter of grace," Crouch concludes that both rationales remain valid law today.[12]

---

9 *Haugen v. Kitzhaber*, 353 Or. 715, 736 (2013) (emphases added).

10 *Haugen v. Kitzhaber*, 742.

11 Crouch, *Presidential Pardon Power*, 28–29.

12 Crouch, *Presidential Pardon Power*, 28–29. The president's pardoning power is administered by the Office of Pardon attorney. Samuel Morison, who works in that office, observes, "The court itself evidently does not see any inconsistency between Holmes's dictum and the traditional view of clemency as an act of mercy, because cases decided after *Biddle* continue to describe clemency in precisely those terms." Citing a number of examples, Morison concludes, "Consequently, there is no authority for the proposition that the Supreme Court has formally rejected the conception of clemency as an act of mercy" ("Politics of Grace," 113).

Pure retributivists like Kathleen Moore have, however, sharply challenged the validity of pardons issued solely on grounds of mercy.[13] These theorists argue that pardons given for any other reason than furthering justice are of necessity unjust and therefore immoral, even if legal. In particular, pardons given out of mercy violate the principles of (positive) retributive justice because in such cases the guilty do not receive their just desert. On retributive theories of justice it is axiomatic that the guilty deserve punishment. To pardon someone out of mercy is therefore to subvert justice and so to act unjustly. Moreover, if pardons are acts of mercy, they may be given out arbitrarily, subverting the principle of equal treatment under the law.

Moore argues that the major shift from consequentialism to retributivism that has occurred among legal philosophers with respect to the justification of punishment needs to be accompanied by a similar shift with respect to the justification of pardon. In Moore's view retributivism *requires* pardons when there is no legal liability to punishment, and it *permits* pardons when there is liability without moral culpability. With respect to a pardon two questions control: (1) Is the offender legally liable to punishment (a lawbreaker)? If not, then he should be pardoned if convicted. (2) Is the offender morally deserving of punishment (without excuse or justification for his lawbreaking)? If he is, then punishment is obligatory; if not, the offender may be pardoned.[14] So pardons are

---

13 Morison, "Politics of Grace," provides this useful bibliography: Dan Markel, "Against Mercy," *Minnesota Law Review* 88 (2004): 1421; Emilios A. Christodoulis, "The Irrationality of Merciful Legal Judgment," *Law & Philosophy* 18 (1999): 215; Daniel Statman, "Doing without Mercy," *Southern Journal of Philosophy* 32 (1994): 331; Ross Harrison, "The Equality of Mercy," in *Jurisprudence: Cambridge Essays*, ed. Hyman Gross and Ross Harrison (Oxford: Clarendon, 1992), 107–25; Daniel T. Kobil, "The Quality of Mercy Strained: Wresting the Pardon Power from the King," *Texas Law Review* 69 (1991): 569; Kathleen Dean Moore, *Pardons: Justice, Mercy, and the Public Interest* (Oxford: Oxford University Press, 1989); Jeffrie G. Murphy, "Mercy and Legal Justice," in *Forgiveness and Mercy*, ed. Jean Hampton and Jeffrie Murphy (Cambridge: Cambridge University Press, 1988), 162–86; H. R. T. Roberts, "Mercy," *Philosophy* 46 (1971): 352–53.

14 Moore, *Pardons*, 125. She also permits adjustment to sentences to prevent undeserved suffering (e.g., legal disabilities and shame, which are not properly punishments) or to prevent an unwarranted, cruel punishment. Moore's conception of legal liability seems excessively narrow, for if a person has justification or excuse for his lawbreaking, then he is counted not guilty in our justice system and so not legally liable to punishment. In that case, pardons are required just in

appropriate on retributive grounds only in cases of innocence, excusable crime, justified crime, and prevention of undeserved suffering.

The claim of the pure retributivists has enormous theological implications for divine pardon.[15] For God is portrayed in the Bible as acting mercifully toward us and His pardoning our sins as an act of grace. "For by grace you have been saved through faith, and this is not your own doing; it is the gift of God—not the result of works, so that no one may boast" (Eph 2:8-9). "So it depends not upon man's will or exertion, but upon God's mercy" (Rom 9:16). Although we deserve condemnation and death, having neither excuse nor justification for our breaking of His law (Rom 1:32; 2:1-3; 3:20), God out of His great mercy has pardoned our sins and graciously reckoned us righteous. Thus, a divine pardon is, indeed, in Marshall's words, "an act of grace."

At the same time, the Bible portrays God as a positive retributivist with respect to justice (Exod 34:7). As we have seen, God's judgment is described in the Bible as ultimately eschatological. God, in effect, carries out what Kant deemed to be necessary for a just society about to dissolve: to execute any prisoners condemned to death.[16] In any case,

---

case a person has been mistakenly found by some court to be legally liable, that is to say, they are required to rectify injustices.

15 See Morison's poignant observation:

> The theoretical controversy surrounding the exercise of executive clemency really only arises when . . . the president acts for reasons unrelated to the offender's just deserts. The interesting philosophical question is whether *this* sort of leniency constitutes a serious injustice of some kind. Understood in this way, the practice of executive clemency for reasons unrelated to the offender's just deserts does seem to give rise to a real dilemma, because it apparently permits a departure from the demands of justice, which, according to some theorists, renders the dispensation of mercy in a legal context inherently immoral. But this result is at least puzzling, since mercy has occupied a central place in the philosophical tradition, not merely as chief among the human virtues, but indeed as an attribute of divine perfection. ("Politics of Grace," 27 [emphasis original])

For a theological version of the argument of the pure retributivists, see David Londey, "Can God Forgive Us Our Trespasses?" *Sophia* 25, no. 1 (1986): 4–10; along with responses by Andrew Brien, "Can God Forgive Us Our Trespasses?" *Sophia* 28, no. 2 (1989): 35–42; Dean Geuras, "In Defense of Divine Forgiveness: A Response to David Londey," *Sophia* 31, no. 1–2 (1992): 65–77.

16 Immanuel Kant, *Metaphysical Elements of Justice*, 2nd ed., trans. John Ladd (Indianapolis: Hackett, 1999), 140.

the biblical view is that the wicked deserve punishment—"those who do such things deserve to die" (Rom 1:32; cf. Heb 10:29)—so that retributive justice belongs to God's character.

Indeed, it is plausible, I think, that retributive justice belongs essentially to God. Brian Leftow observes that "the more central and prominent an attribute is in the Biblical picture of God, the stronger the case for taking it to be necessary to being God, *ceteris paribus*: this is the only reason philosophers usually treat being omniscient or omnipotent as thus necessary."[17] It is hard to think of an attribute more central and prominent in the biblical picture of God than His righteousness or justice.[18] "Shall not the Judge of all the earth do right?" (Gen 18:25). "Is there injustice (*adikia*) on God's part? By no means!" (Rom 9:14). It would have been inconceivable to the biblical authors that God might act unjustly.

But then God faces "the dilemma of the merciful judge":[19] when a judge tries to treat an offender mercifully, either the offender *is* given the penalty he deserves (in which case he is being shown justice, not mercy) or the offender is *not* given the penalty he deserves (in which case the judge acts unjustly). Thus, a judge in his official capacity cannot exercise either pseudo-mercy or real mercy; his choice is between being just or unjust. God in His capacity of Judge acts in conformity with the strict demands of justice, so that we sinners find ourselves condemned before His bar (Rom 3:19-20).

The official remission of punishment can be justified only through pardon by the executive. Since God is both Ruler and Judge, He is as Ruler in the rather odd situation described by Blackstone of undoing His own verdict as Judge. Not that He second-guesses the Judge's determination of guilt, for He as Judge is infallible in His determination of justice. Justification should not, contrary to careless statements by some NT scholars, be thought to be a verdict of acquittal. The guilty verdict stands. But as Ruler God pardons us, so that whereas we were once guilty, we are now innocent before Him. God as Ruler thus does not contradict what He as Judge has determined.

But now God as Ruler faces a similar dilemma to the one described above: if the pardon is given by the executive to rectify some injustice,

17 Brian Leftow, *God and Necessity* (Oxford: Oxford University Press, 2012), 412.
18 See John Owen, *A Dissertation on Divine Justice; Or, The Claims of Vindicatory Justice Asserted* (Latin version 1653) (London: L. J. Higham, n.d.).
19 Moore, *Pardons*, 192; cf. Murphy, "Mercy and Legal Justice," 167–69; Roberts, "Mercy," 352–53; Smart, "Mercy," 349–53.

then the pardon is not an act of grace given out of mercy but is an expression of justice; but if it is given out of mercy, then the executive violates the principles of retributive justice and so is unjust. Clearly, God cannot give pardons to rectify some injustice, since His judicial condemnation of sinners is perfectly just. If He pardons, it must be out of mercy. But then He would seem to be acting unjustly. But given that retributive justice belongs to God's character, it is impossible that He so act. He must give people what they deserve, on pain of acting contrary to His own nature.

Critics of the pure retributivists have argued that the demands of retributive justice can be overridden by other considerations, so that the executive who pardons out of sheer mercy is not immoral. In a recent, lengthy review of the question Samuel Morison argues that sometimes leniency is morally justified when satisfying the *prima facie* demands of retributive justice is immoral or practically impossible. He criticizes Moore's "moral rigorism," commenting:

> The implications are, to put it mildly, fairly drastic. For if Moore is correct, it would seem to invalidate not only the merciful exercise of the clemency power, but also the relevant portions of the Bill of Rights, which presuppose precisely the opposite moral principle, namely that it is more important to protect the rights and liberties of innocent citizens than it is to punish even those who are likely to be guilty, and that some level of unrequited justice is thus the price worth paying for the promotion of these other, equally important social values.[20]

What is striking about Morison's concerns is that they are inapplicable in God's case, since God's administration of eschatological justice will in no way infringe upon the rights and liberties of innocent citizens, so that divine justice is never unrequited, even if deferred (Matt 13:24-30; cf. Gen 18:22-33). Morison raises other concerns to show that the *prima facie* duty to punish retributively may not be an *ultima facie* duty. It is evident, however, that none of these concerns, such as protecting people against self-incrimination, unreasonable searches and seizures, and so on, is remotely relevant to the case of God's administration of justice.

---

20 Morison, "Politics of Grace," 77–78. Cf. Leo Zaibert's denunciation of Michael Moore's "legal moralism," which would require the state to punish every moral wrong, an impossible task that would drive one crazy (Leo Zaibert, *Punishment and Retribution* [Aldershot, U.K.: Ashgate, 2006], 183–85). Of course, such a task is only humanly impossible.

An omniscient deity need not rely on self-incrimination or searches and seizures to convict the guilty. Morison actually admits that "such protections are merely a concession to the contingent imperfections of human nature" but thinks that "this is not an adequate reply to the foregoing objection, because it implicitly concedes that giving the guilty what they deserve is not, after all, of greater moral worth than avoiding the punishment of the innocent."[21] The theist, however, is not forced to play off the demands of positive and negative retributive justice against each other in this way; God can be equally committed to both insofar as human beings are concerned, delaying the full satisfaction of positive retributive justice while satisfying the demands of negative retributive justice in the meantime. He can give the guilty what they deserve while protecting the rights of the innocent.

Morison also complains that

> Moore's extravagant claim about the imposition of deserved punishment also betrays a certain air of unreality, which fails to adequately grasp the actual complexity of events encountered by practitioners in the criminal justice system. For in the practical world of "retail" justice, a conscientious prosecutor is routinely confronted by a dizzying array of conflicting and not wholly commensurable moral demands, depending upon the nature of the particular case under consideration and the context in which it arises.[22]

Again, since God does not inhabit the world of retail justice, such worries are irrelevant to His administration of justice.

Noting that it is a ubiquitous feature of the criminal justice system that for both pragmatic and ethical reasons the large majority of persons accused of a crime do *not* receive the full measure of punishment that they arguably deserve based on retributive considerations alone, Morison warns that

> the myopic insistence that it is a mandatory obligation to give each offender the full measure of deserved punishment would render the practice of resolving criminal charges by mutual agreement morally intolerable in most cases, except in the relatively rare instance in which a defendant pleads guilty without any expectation of receiving a reduced sentence.[23]

---

21 Morison, "Politics of Grace," 78.
22 Morison, "Politics of Grace," 80.
23 Morison, "Politics of Grace," 82.

Since God neither needs nor offers plea bargains, this limitation of divine retributive justice also falls to the wayside.

Turning from practical considerations to normative political theory, Morison contends that "it is also difficult to conceive any rational warrant for believing that it is the proper business of a liberal state to pursue the sort of moral objectives Moore envisions through the practice of punishment."[24] Obviously, this concern is irrelevant to divine justice. In fact, it is telling when Morison quotes approvingly Jeffrie Murphy's declamation, "The liberal tradition would thus view it as silly (and perhaps impious) to make God's ultimate justice the model for the state's legal justice; and thus any attempt to identify *criminal* with *sinner* is to be avoided."[25] In fact, Morison states plainly, "The pursuit of the legitimate interest in securing social peace via state-sponsored legal punishment (as distinguished from divine retribution) does not entail any prima facie obligation to exact the full measure of morally justified punitive suffering merely because the offender deserves it."[26] Morison thus recognizes God's obligation to exact the full measure of morally justified punitive suffering.

Perhaps I have belabored the point unnecessarily; but Morison's defense of pardons on grounds of mercy is the fullest I have encountered in the literature, and yet it is stunningly irrelevant, as he recognizes, to the case of divine pardon.[27] In the end Morison rejects "the implicit

---

24 Morison, "Politics of Grace," 83.

25 Jeffrie G. Murphy, "Retributivism, Moral Education, and the Liberal State," *Criminal Justice Ethics* 4, no. 1 (1985): 6, cited by Morison, "Politics of Grace," 84. Morison adds, "Murphy is surely correct that we are never in a position to play God."

26 Morison, "Politics of Grace," 86.

27 Cf. Daniel Kobil's reservations about the view of the pure retributivists:

> Retributive concerns alone, however, do not sufficiently describe the goals of punishment. The . . . problem with the strict approach to clemency that Moore and other Kantian philosophers advocate is its presumption that retributive principles are the only justification for punishment and must be the sole guideposts in clemency decisions. The better view . . . is that deserts provide only a starting point, with utilitarian and other societal concerns establishing secondary limits on the remission of punishment generally, and in individual cases. Once a determination as to deserts has been made, other considerations such as general or specific deterrence of crime may limit both the imposition and remission of punishment. ("Quality of Mercy Strained," 581–82)

conflation of morality and justice, which assumes that the legitimate exercise of mercy always must be consistent with the demands of justice."[28] He cites George Rainbolt: "The fact that mercy counsels unjust acts on occasion does not imply that it is a vice. It only reflects the unfortunate fact that mercy and justice can conflict."[29] But that is precisely the problem for the Christian theist: God's justice and mercy are both essential to Him and so neither can be sacrificed. We can agree with Morison "that the moral basis for the merciful extension of clemency is thus whatever 'is right and good as judged against *all* moral considerations, rather than only those of justice. *Any* pertinent moral consideration may be taken into account."[30] One should not, indeed, simply identify morality with justice. But none of the considerations that Morison has adduced for tempering justice with mercy in the case of the state applies to God. So how can God legitimately exercise mercy if doing so is inconsistent with the demands of His justice? Morison admits that that "there is no tidy conceptual solution to the problem of reconciling justice and mercy in the abstract."[31] He concludes that "the practice of punishment is informed by a plurality of values that may not be ultimately commensurable."[32]

If none of the reasons that go to justify pardons based on mercy rather than on justice applies in the case of divine pardon, then it is difficult to see how God can mercifully pardon sins; indeed, it is difficult to see how divine pardon is possible at all, since neither can it be justified on grounds of justice. What seems to be needed is a way of reconciling divine mercy and justice that justifies a pardon without sacrificing the demands of either virtue.

In fact, we seem to have backed into a persuasive argument for the conviction of Anselm and the Reformers that the satisfaction of divine justice is a necessary condition of salvation. Theologians have long debated the question of whether God could have simply pardoned

---

Such concerns arise only on a human level, so that they do not serve to qualify the *prima facie* demands of divine retributive justice.

28 Morison, "Politics of Grace," 100.
29 George W. Rainbolt, "Mercy: An Independent, Imperfect Virtue," *American Philosophical Quarterly* 27, no. 2 (1990): 192, cited by Morison, "Politics of Grace," 101.
30 Morison, "Politics of Grace," 104, citing Andrew Brien, "Mercy within Legal Justice," *Social Theory & Practice* 24 (1998): 91 (emphasis added).
31 Morison, "Politics of Grace," 102.
32 Morison, "Politics of Grace," 102.

our sin without Christ's atoning death or, more broadly, the satisfaction of divine justice. Thomas Aquinas followed most of the early Church Fathers in thinking that this is possible, although less suitable for God's purposes. Following the rise of Socinianism, most Protestant theologians, with the notable exception of Hugo Grotius, followed Anselm's lead in holding that divine justice had to be satisfied if salvation from sin were to be possible. Our inquiry suggests the following argument in support of the necessitarian perspective:

(1) Necessarily (Retributive justice is essential to God.)
(2) Necessarily (If retributive justice is essential to God, then God justly punishes every sin.)
(3) Necessarily (If God justly punishes every sin, then divine justice is satisfied.)

Therefore,

(4) Necessarily (Divine justice is satisfied.)

Therefore,

(5) Necessarily (If some human beings are saved, divine justice satisfied.)

Let me say a word about each of the premises.

In support of (1) we have seen that the centrality and prominence of divine retributive justice in the biblical scheme supports its being essential to God. Moreover, to mention an ad hominem consideration, neo-Socinian opponents of penal substitution need (1) if they are to argue successfully for the injustice of penal substitution, for otherwise God may determine that it is not unjust to punish a substitute in our place. Given that there is no higher law to which God must conform, He will be bound only by His own nature in determining what is just or unjust.

The support for (2) lies in the absence of any apparent justification for pardons of sheer mercy on God's part. It is difficult to see what would justify waiving the demands of retributive justice essential to God's nature. We say "justly punishes" to ensure the truth of (3), since only proportionate punishment of sins committed will satisfy the demands of retributive justice.

From the three premises, (4) follows. Divine justice is satisfied so long as no sin goes unpunished. This will be the case whether there are no human beings and, hence, no sin, or whether there are in fact sinners.

(5) in turn follows, since any proposition implies a necessary truth. It also follows that if divine justice is not satisfied, then no human beings are saved; indeed, that it is impossible that any human beings are saved.

If this is right, then God's pardoning us for our sins demands the satisfaction of God's justice. This is exactly what the atonement theories of Anselm and the Reformers offer. On the Reformers' view Christ as our substitute and representative bears the punishment due for every sin, so that the demands of divine retributive justice are fully met. The demands of divine justice thus satisfied, God can in turn pardon us of our sins. God's pardon is thus predicated on Christ's satisfying for us the demands of divine retributive justice. Indeed, in a sense, such a divine pardon meets the requirements of even the pure retributivists, for given Christ's satisfaction of divine retributive justice on our behalf, nothing more is due from us. God's pardon of us is therefore required by justice. Nonetheless, God's provision of Christ as our penal substitute is an active expression of God's mercy and grace, giving us what we did not deserve. The whole scheme is motivated by and justified by God's grace: "For by grace you have been saved through faith, and this is not your own doing; it is the gift of God—not the result of works, so that no one may boast" (Eph 2:8-9). In this passage the word "this," being masculine in the Greek, does not take "faith," which is feminine, as its antecedent; rather the antecedent is the whole salvific arrangement of salvation by grace through faith. This atoning arrangement is a gift of God to us, not based on human merit. In this sense God's pardon of us, while consistent with divine justice, is a pardon grounded ultimately in mercy.

THE APPROPRIATION OF A PARDON

A final question of theological significance that remains to be addressed is whether a pardon, to be effective, must be accepted by the criminal who is the intended beneficiary. Courts and legal theorists have tended to answer this question based on whether a pardon is considered a private communication of the executive to the criminal or a public proclamation of the executive that is known to the court. Again, *United States v. Wilson* is the seminal case here.[33] Drawing upon English precedent, Chief Justice Marshall held that a presidential pardon

---

33 Background: Having been convicted of robbing the mail and endangering the carrier's life, George Wilson was pardoned by President Jackson. Facing further charges, Wilson was asked by the court whether he wished to avail himself of

is the private, though official, act of the executive magistrate, delivered to the individual for whose benefit it is intended, and not communicated officially to the court. It is a constituent part of the judicial system, that the judge sees only with judicial eyes, and knows nothing respecting any particular case, of which he is not informed judicially. A private deed, not communicated to him, whatever may be its character, whether a pardon or release, is totally unknown, and cannot be acted on.[34]

The idea here is that something that is not brought officially before the court must be treated as though it were nonexistent. A pardon is just such an item, since it is not communicated by the executive to the court but to the accused and so remains, in effect, unknown until the accused introduces it into court. By contrast, "The reason why a court must *ex officio* take notice of pardon by act of parliament, is that it is considered as a public law; having the same effect on the case, as if the general law punishing the offence had been repealed or annulled."[35] So in the case of *United States v. Wilson*, "This court is of opinion, that the pardon in the proceedings mentioned, not having been brought judicially before the court, by plea, motion or otherwise, cannot be noticed by the judges."[36]

But Marshall goes further than this. Wilson had already accepted the pardon; otherwise, he would have been executed. He was simply declining to bring the existence of the pardon to the attention of the court in another trial.[37] But Marshall held not merely that a pardon may be rendered judicially invisible by the pardonee's refusing to plead it; he held that a pardon may be rendered ineffectual by one's refusing to accept it. "A pardon is a deed, to the validity of which, delivery is essential, and delivery is not complete without acceptance. It may then be rejected by the person to whom it is tendered; and if it be rejected, we have discovered no power in a court to force it on him."[38] Marshall cites English precedent for this opinion:

---

the pardon to avoid sentencing in the particular case. Wilson answered that he did not wish to avail himself of the pardon referred to.

34 *United States v. Wilson*, 32 U.S. at 161.

35 *United States v. Wilson* at 163.

36 *United States v. Wilson* at 163.

37 See Mark Strasser, "The Limits of the Clemency Power on Pardons, Retributivists, and the United States Constitution," *Brandeis Law Journal* 41 (2002): 110–11.

38 *United States v. Wilson* at 161. When is a pardon delivered? Humbert relates that in *In re DePuy*, Fed. Case No. 3,814, 7 Fed. Cas. 506 (1869), the president

Hawkins says, § 64, "it will be error to allow a man the benefit of such a pardon, unless it be pleaded." In § 65, he says, "he who pleads such a pardon must produce it *sub pede sigilli*, though it be a plea in bar, because it is presumed to be in his custody, and the property of it belongs to him." Comyn, in his Digest, tit. Pardon, H, says, "if a man has a charter of pardon from the king, he ought to plead it, in bar of the indictment; and if he pleads not guilty, he waives his pardon." The same law is laid down in Bacon's Abridgment, title Pardon; and is confirmed by the cases these authors quote.[39]

On this view, then, failure to bring one's pardon to the attention of the court is to waive it; it becomes ineffectual.

Marshall's opinion was ratified in *Burdick v. United States* 236 U.S. 79 (1915).[40] In answer to the question "Is the acceptance of a pardon necessary?" the court followed *United States v. Wilson* to a tee, since "all of the principles upon which its solution depends were there considered."[41] Citing Marshall's words, the court declared:

> That a pardon by its mere issue has automatic effect resistless by him to whom it is tendered, forcing upon him by mere executive power whatever consequences it may have or however he may regard it . . . was rejected by the court with particularity and emphasis. The decision is unmistakable.

granted a pardon to one Moses DePuy but then rescinded it before the marshal could deliver it to the prison warden. Depuy obtained a writ of habeas corpus and demanded release. But the federal court held that the prisoner should not be discharged because the pardon had not been delivered. In order to be considered delivered, the pardon had to be placed in the hands of the warden (Humbert, *Pardoning Power of the President,* 67–68; cf. p. 72).

39 *United States v. Wilson* at 162.

40 Background: In 1913 George Burdick, the city editor of the *New York Tribune,* refused to testify before a grand jury concerning his sources of information for certain stories in the *Tribune* on alleged custom frauds, on the grounds that his answers might tend to incriminate him. To secure Burdick's testimony, President Wilson issued "a full and unconditional pardon for all offenses against the United States" that Burdick may have committed in the matter, "thereby absolving him from the consequences of every such criminal act" (*Burdick v. United States,* 236 U.S. 79, 86 [1915]). Burdick remained adamant and refused to accept the pardon, so that a New York district court found him to be in contempt. When Burdick's case was brought before the Supreme Court the following year, the solicitor general argued that acceptance of a pardon is not a necessary condition of its efficacy.

41 *Burdick v. United States* at 88.

A pardon was denominated as the "private" act, the "private deed," of the executive magistrate, and the denomination was advisedly selected to mark the incompleteness of the act or deed without its acceptance.[42]

Here a pardon is called private to signal "its functional deficiency if not accepted by him to whom it is tendered."[43]

Like the *Wilson* opinion, the *Burdick* opinion considers a pardon to be an act of grace. But the court takes a realistic view:

The grace of a pardon, though good its intention, may be only in pretense or seeming; in pretense, as having purpose not moving from the individual to whom it is offered; in seeming, as involving consequences of even greater disgrace than those from which it purports to relieve. Circumstances may be made to bring innocence under the penalties of the law. If so brought, escape by confession of guilt implied in the acceptance of a pardon may be rejected,—preferring to be the victim of the law rather than its acknowledged transgressor—preferring death even to such certain infamy.[44]

The pardon in Burdick's case was really intended to wrest testimony from him, not to benefit him personally, and so might be thought of as a pretense; and in accepting the pardon Burdick would be implicitly admitting his guilt, so that his pardon, in bringing this shame upon him, might only *seem* to relieve his predicament. As the court notes, an innocent man might well reject the pardon and suffer the consequences rather than implicitly confess to being guilty of a crime he did not commit. All this goes to undergird the right of the accused to refuse a pardon proffered him.

In 1927, the Supreme Court considered the case of a convicted criminal who, to claim wrongful imprisonment, disputed the commutation of his death sentence to life imprisonment. As we have seen, Chief Justice Holmes curtly declared, "A pardon in our days is not a private act of grace from an individual happening to possess power. It is a part of the Constitutional scheme. When granted it is the determination of the ultimate authority that the public welfare will be better served by inflicting less than what the judgment fixed."[45] Marshall would, of course, have

---

42 *Burdick v. United States* at 90.
43 *Burdick v. United States* at 90.
44 *Burdick v. United States* at 90–91.
45 *Biddle*, 274 U.S. at 486.

agreed with Holmes that a pardon is part of our constitutional scheme. So wherein lies their disagreement?

Holmes seems to think that pardons are granted solely out of consideration for the public welfare. He repeatedly returns to this theme in the opinion:

> Just as the original punishment would be imposed without regard to the prisoner's consent and in the teeth of his will, whether he liked it or not, the public welfare, not his consent determines what shall be done.
>
> The opposite answer . . . would deprive him [the president] of the power in the most important cases and require him to permit an execution which he had decided ought not to take place unless the change is agreed to by one who on no sound principle ought to have any voice in what the law should do for the welfare of the whole.[46]

The idea that pardons are granted always for the public welfare is, however, patently false. While some pardons are granted for the sake of the public welfare, such as President Ford's pardon of Richard Nixon, other pardons have notoriously been granted for considerations wholly apart from the public good.[47] Moreover, as a number of legal theorists have remarked, the fact that a pardon has been granted for the public welfare is irrelevant to whether it requires acceptance in order to be efficacious.[48]

---

46 *Biddle* at 486, 487.

47 Crouch draws attention to President Clinton's notorious pardons of members of the Puerto Rican nationalist group FALN to curry favor with Puerto Rican voters in New York City for his wife's Senate campaign and of Marc Rich, whose ex-wife had donated a half million dollars to Clinton's presidential library (Crouch, *Presidential Pardon Power*, 3–4). Crouch says that since Watergate presidents have been more willing to use their pardoning power not merely as an act of grace or for the public welfare, as the framers of the Constitution intended, but also as a political weapon to close investigations of their allies or to reward political contributors. See also Kobil, "Quality of Mercy Strained," 610, for many other examples.

48 See, e.g., Strasser, "Limits of the Clemency Power," 110, who comments on the *Wilson* opinion:

> Although the Court's analysis of when a pardon becomes effective was offered in a context in which the pardon was viewed as an act of grace, the same analysis might have been offered had the Court instead suggested that pardons are to promote the public good—the Court might still have maintained that the pardonee would have to bring the pardon to the attention of the court in order for it to be effective.

Holmes does give some additional argument for why a commutation of sentence ought not to be refusable by the convicted criminal:

> No one doubts that a reduction of the term of an imprisonment or the amount of a fine would limit the sentence effectively on the one side and on the other would leave the reduced term or fine valid and to be enforced, and that the convict's cansent [sic] is not required.
>
> When we come to the commutation of death to imprisonment for life it is hard to see how consent has any more to do with it than it has in the cases first put.[49]

The claim here is that if the original sentence was justified and enforced without the criminal's consent, then the reduced sentence is automatically implicit in it and therefore requires no consent from the criminal. This argument, however persuasive it might be for commutations and reprieves, does not apply *pari passu* to pardons. From the fact that a man deserves imprisonment of, say, thirty years, it does not follow that he deserves no imprisonment.[50] On the contrary, from the fact that he deserves an imprisonment of thirty years, it follows that he deserves some imprisonment. Therefore, pardons are not implicit in sentences issued. Moreover, pardons may be issued prior to conviction and sentencing (not to mention after sentence has been served) and in such cases are independent of criminal sentences.[51] It is noteworthy that the court in *Biddle* did not overturn *Burdick* but concluded merely that the reasoning of *Burdick* "is not to be extended to the present case."[52]

By the same token, even if a pardon is an act of grace, "there is nothing inherent in the concept of private grace which suggests that the individual benefited must voluntarily accept that grace in order for it to be effective."

49 *Biddle* at 486–87.

50 To illustrate: From the fact that there are seven apples on the table, it follows that there are three apples on the table. But it does not follow that there are no apples on the table; quite the opposite, in fact. Since a pardon involves no punishment, it cannot be implied in any punishment to be meted out.

51 Caplow comments on the *Burdick* opinion, "Noting that a retrospective pardon might eradicate guilt, the Court recognized that a pardon accepted without any adjudication may effectively constitute a confession of guilt and thus no one could be forced to accept one" (Caplow, "Governors! Seize the Law," 303n40).

52 *Biddle* at 488. Humbert comments, "The decision . . . does not overrule the decision in the Burdick case to the effect that a full pardon must be accepted, but the later decision limits the doctrine of the earlier case by holding that commutations do not require acceptance" (*Pardoning Power of the President*, 69).

The key phrase in Holmes' opinion seems to be "the determination of the ultimate authority." Holmes sees a pardon as a unilateral determination of the sovereign authority that cannot be gainsaid. Similarly, the Oregon Supreme Court said,

> We recognize that, historically, governors and presidents have granted clemency for a wide range of reasons, including reasons that may be political, personal, or "private," and that many such decisions—such as Governor Kitzhaber's decision here—may be animated by both public and private concerns. Nonetheless, the executive power to grant clemency flows from the constitution and is one of the Governor's only checks on another branch of government. As part of the system of checks and balances, the Governor's clemency power is far from private: It is an important part of the constitutional scheme envisioned by the framers.[53]

Here the concern with public welfare recedes; rather, the concern is with the executive's power in checking the courts. This concern is again not always relevant to pardons, however, since pardons may be and have been issued prior to conviction and sentencing. Moreover, in this scenario the person on whom a pardon is bestowed tends to get run over by the government. The worries raised in *Burdick* are just ignored. A potential pardonee who believes himself innocent may want his day in court, rather than to be summarily pardoned, whether or not accepting a pardon is thought to imply guilt.[54]

In any case, the courts remain unclear on whether a pardon requires acceptance in order to be efficacious.[55] Fortunately, or perhaps unfortunately, this question is unlikely to come before the Supreme Court today,

---

Similarly, in *Haugen v. Kitzhaber* the Oregon Supreme Court limited its opinion to reprieves, stating, "We need not—and do not—decide whether a *pardon* must be accepted to be valid. We note only that none of the definitions of 'reprieve' contains a similar notion of acceptance" (*Haugen v. Kitzhaber*, 353 Or. at 724 [emphasis original]).

53 *Haugen v. Kitzhaber* at 742.

54 It is interesting that prior to his pardon of Richard Nixon, President Ford, cognizant of *Burdick*'s ruling, sent a secret emissary to Nixon to ensure that he was willing to accept both the pardon and the guilt implied by it. Nixon said that he was so willing.

55 The situation remains the same as when Humbert concluded that the president "cannot under existing law make a full pardon effective without the consent of the prisoner. The latter must be willing to receive and accept a full pardon before it can be put into effect" (*Pardoning Power of the President*, 135).

since pardons are virtually always given in response to applicants to the Office of Pardon Attorney asking for a pardon and not bestowed upon unwitting criminals. People who receive pardons are those who want them.

The theological analogue to this question is whether a divine pardon must be accepted in order to be efficacious. Taking divine pardons to be acts of grace does not serve to resolve this question, since theologians have differed on whether grace is intrinsically efficacious and so irresistible by him upon whom it is bestowed or whether grace is extrinsically efficacious and so requires the free consent of the creaturely will in order to produce its effect. The concern with checks and balances is hardly appropriate to the divine government, since God is both Supreme Judge and Executive. Divine pardons are never bestowed to rectify judicial injustices but must be acts of grace motivated by mercy and love. Given God's love for those whom He pardons, God's pardons are intensely personal and in this sense private. Though official acts, they are motivated out of concern for the individual and not just for the general welfare. Whether a divine pardon requires acceptance by the person to whom it is granted is going to depend more on theological considerations such as freedom of the will and the nature of divine grace than upon the nature of a pardon.

In any case, what we have not mentioned thus far is that pardons may be conditional, in which case they undisputedly depend for their effect upon the pardonee's agreeing to the conditions of the proffered pardon.[56] While the president may not demand just any condition for a pardon—for example, that the pardonee vote forever after only for the president's political party—nevertheless the conditions that the president may lay down for a pardon are endless. In fact, no federal court has ever held any condition invalid.[57] A divine pardon, then, can be granted on the conditions of repentance and faith.[58] If God desires people to come

---

56 *Ex parte Wells*, 59 U.S. 307, 314 (1855). See comment by Humbert, *Pardoning Power of the President*, 72: "Before conditional pardons or conditional commutations go into effect, physical delivery takes place and actual acceptance has been and is required by providing for the signature of the prisoner and by obtaining it on a form of acceptance which is embodied in the warrant of clemency." Cf. 23–24.

57 Schoenburg, "Clemency, War Powers, and Guantánamo," 928.

58 Humbert, *Pardoning Power of the President*, 74–75, explains that in a conditional pardon the conditions can be either precedent or subsequent. If the conditions

freely into His Kingdom, then He may offer His pardon to everyone who will freely accept it. Anyone who refuses a divine pardon therefore remains guilty before God's bar and so liable to punishment.

CONCLUDING REMARKS

We have seen that redemption is accomplished legally via a divine pardon, which frees us from the prison house of sin. The Church Fathers' instincts were thus correct when they insisted that we ought to think of redemption as accomplished in accord with justice rather than by raw power alone. Moreover, contra Socinus, given God's roles in the government of the world as Judge and Ruler, divine forgiveness is much more akin to a legal pardon of a condemned criminal than to the remission of a debt or the forgiveness of an offense.

But can God pardon us of our sins if Christ has satisfied divine justice by being vicariously punished for those sins? Absolutely; it is precisely on the basis of Christ's vicariously meeting the demands of divine justice that a perfectly just God can in His mercy pardon us. Pardons granted on grounds of innocence and wrongful conviction already show that a pardon is wholly compatible with justice's demands' being satisfied.[59] Pardons to achieve remedial justice do not imply the guilt of the person involved or his failure to satisfy the demands of justice. Indeed, quite the opposite is the case. Moreover, the vast majority of pardons are granted *after* the criminal's sentence has been fully served. The U.S. Office of Pardon Attorney will not even permit applications for a presidential pardon until at least five years have elapsed since the sentence of the criminal has been fully satisfied. A pardon in such a case does not imply that the pardonee has failed to satisfy justice's demands. Even though the convicted person is no longer liable to punishment, a pardon serves to restore to him all his civil rights voided by his conviction. Similarly, a divine pardon serves to bestow upon us the full rights and privileges of a child of God, such as adoption into God's family (Eph 1:5), an inheritance in heaven (1 Pet 1:4),

---

are precedent, the pardon becomes operative when the recipient has fulfilled the conditions, but not until then. If the conditions are subsequent, the pardon takes effect upon delivery and acceptance but becomes void upon the violation of the specified conditions. Both precedent and subsequent conditions have theological analogues with respect to justification and perseverance.

59 See discussion by Weihofen, "Effect of a Pardon," 178–79.

citizenship in God's Kingdom (Phil 3:20), access to the Father (Rom 5:2), and so on (all, interestingly, legal notions).

Because Christ has borne the punishment for our sins, God can be both just and the justifier of him who has faith in Jesus (Rom 3:26). Because God's justice has been fully satisfied, God can pardon us on the basis of Christ's sacrifice without prejudice to His justice. Paul says, "When you were dead in trespasses . . . , God made you alive together with him, when he forgave us all our trespasses, erasing the record that stood against us with its legal demands. He set this aside, nailing it to the cross" (Col 2:13-14). Forgiveness in this legal sense is based on the fact that the penalty has been fully paid and therefore we may be pardoned.

A divine pardon is rooted in God's grace, for it is by His mercy that God determines to supply a satisfaction of His justice that we might in turn be pardoned. Because it is Christ and not we who has discharged the sentence for our sins, our redemption is not accomplished unless and until we receive God's pardon. In contrast to the criminal who has fulfilled his sentence, we remain in our state of judicial condemnation until we accept the pardon offered us by God. If anyone refuses the pardon offered by God, then Christ's sacrifice avails him nothing, for he has rejected the satisfaction of God's justice wrought by Christ. The necessity of accepting God's pardon is especially evident if it is conditional on repentance and faith, for apart from fulfillment of its conditions, the pardon is ineffectual. Thus, "those who receive the abundance of grace and the free gift of righteousness will reign in life through the one man Jesus Christ" (Rom 5:17).

Chapter 14

THE MORAL INFLUENCE
OF CHRIST'S PASSION

INTRODUCTION

A multifaceted atonement theory should also include the moral influence of Christ's death upon humanity, which helps to draw people to faith in Christ and to persevere in faith through trials and even martyrdom.

MORAL INFLUENCE IN ABSTRACTION
FROM PENAL SUBSTITUTION

Taken in isolation, the moral influence theory is hopeless as an atonement theory. Not only is it biblically inadequate, but, *pace* Abelard, it is powerless to explain how redemption is accomplished for all those believers who lived prior to the time of Christ and who had no expectation of his coming, upon whom his death had therefore no influence whatsoever. Moreover, taken in abstraction from penal substitution, the moral influence theory becomes bizarre. In his classic work *The Death of Christ*, James Denney contrasts the case of someone who drowns to save me from drowning with the case of someone who throws himself into the water and drowns to show his love for me.[1] The first case prompts

---

1 James Denney, *The Death of Christ: Its Place and Interpretation in the New Testament* (London: Hodder & Stoughton, 1907), 177; cf. R. W. Dale, *The Atonement*,

259

me to say, "Greater love hath no man than this," but the second case is unintelligible. Penal substitution thus lies at the heart of the moral influence of the death of Christ.

PENAL SUBSTITUTION AND MORAL INFLUENCE

Although moral influence will properly play a role in any penal substitutionary theory, non-necessitarian penal substitution theorists like Hugo Grotius have especially stressed the moral influence of Christ's substitutionary death, which motivated God's contingent choice of satisfying His justice through penal substitution. Blaine Swen, taking his cue from Thomas Aquinas, finds in God's choice of penal substitution the provision of both disincentives for human beings to continue in their sinful state of alienation from God and positive incentives for them to embrace God's offer of reconciliation.[2] These are critically important in bringing people freely to a state of reconciliation with God.

Disincentives to Continued Alienation from God

Swen claims that God's making satisfaction through penal substitution discourages persistence in a state of alienation from God in two ways: First, penal substitution, by showing God's wrath upon sin, alerts sinners to the danger of their remaining in a state of alienation from God. Swen is concerned that even if God were to waive His active wrath in punishing sin, there would still remain His passive wrath, which is the personally destructive consequences of sin. Given human freedom, God's passive wrath cannot be waived. By expressing His active wrath in punishing Christ, God warns sinners of the dangers to them of persisting in a state of alienation from God. Swen's point is doubly true if, as Grotius held, God's essential retributive justice prevents His waiving His active wrath upon the sins of the unrepentant. His punishing Christ displays the punishment that awaits the unrepentant as well as the natural consequences of sin.

9th ed. (London: Hodder & Stoughton, 1884), liv.

2 Blaine Swen, "The Logic of Divine-Human Reconciliation: A Critical Analysis of Penal Substitution as An Explanatory Feature of Atonement" (Ph.D. dissertation, Loyola University, Chicago, 2012), 165–75.

Second, God, by insisting on exacting so high a price of salvation at Christ's hand, demonstrates the high value of His offer of salvation. Given the deity of Christ, the price of our salvation is nothing less than divine, penal Self-substitution. As Turretin maintains, the divinity of Christ's person makes his sacrifice of infinite value. Consideration of the cost that was paid as a condition of our salvation could discourage the sinner from ignoring the value of the offer of salvation and persisting in an alienated state.

Incentives to Embracing Reconciliation

On the positive side, Swen argues that Christ's making satisfaction through penal substitution encourages sinners to embrace God's offer of forgiveness in three ways. First, penal substitution demonstrates God's objectively expunging a person's guilt, thereby helping him to overcome his sense of shame. One obstacle to personal reconciliation is an offender's sense of shame for his wrongdoing. By removing a person's guilt through penal substitution, God can allay a person's fear that he is too guilty to be forgiven. Swen's point underlines the importance of God's pardon's blotting out our guilt on the basis of Christ's satisfaction.

Second, penal substitution demonstrates God's justice, thereby encouraging victims of injustice to be open to a loving relationship with God. The demonstration of divine justice in punishing Christ can help to quell fears of the victims of injustice that God is not just. While God could waive the debt of punishment we owe, so doing would not be an act of justice that is visible to human victims of sin. It would be, as we have seen, an act of mercy rather than retributive justice. By choosing instead to exercise active wrath through penal substitution God visibly displays His justice and demonstrates His seriousness about sin. Knowing that God is just can help victims of injustice to be open to reconciliation with God.

Third, penal substitution demonstrates God's love of sinners, as He substitutes Himself for them in bearing their just desert, thereby encouraging in turn a loving response to Him. Since Christ is himself God, we can see in the cross the extent to which God will go to win sinners back to Him. While God could simply pardon sinners without satisfaction, penal substitution affords God the opportunity, through Self-substitution, to convincingly display the depth of His desire for reconciliation with fallen humanity. Through penal Self-substitution God offers "a shocking display of God's deep love for sinners," a display "so shocking that it can combat our ability to ignore or doubt it."[3]

CONCLUDING REMARKS

Although for Grotians like Swen such incentives and disincentives play a more crucial role in motivating God's choice of penal substitution than they do in necessitarian theories, still it is evident that such disincentives to persistence in alienation from God and incentives to freely embracing God's offer of forgiveness will attend necessitarian theories as well. And, of course, even on necessitarian theories, God's choosing the particular means of Christ's substitutionary punishment remains contingent, in which case Christ's passion may be motivated by its production of such benefits.

Swen might be accused of exaggerating the thoughtfulness of unbelievers concerning Christ's atoning death. But there can be no doubt, I think, about the impact of the graphic display of God's wrath and mercy in Christ's passion. The moral influence of Christ's self-sacrificial death upon mankind has truly been inestimable. Repeatedly represented figuratively in literature and graphically in art, the death of Christ has, even more than his teaching, more than his character, made Jesus of Nazareth an arresting and captivating person for hundreds of millions, if not billions, of people and has inspired countless people to bear with courage and faith terrible pain and even death. As mentioned earlier, it is not at all implausible that only in a world that includes such an atoning death would the optimal number of people come freely to love and know God and so to find eternal life. As Gregory of Nyssa saw, God's wisdom, as well as His love and holiness, are thus manifest in the atoning death of Christ.

> When I survey the wondrous cross
> On which the Prince of glory died,
> My richest gain I count but loss,
> And pour contempt on all my pride.
>
> See from His head, His hands, His feet,
> Sorrow and love flow mingled down!
> Did e'er such love and sorrow meet,
> Or thorns compose so rich a crown?

---

3   Swen, "The Logic of Divine-Human Reconciliation," 176.

Were the whole realm of nature mine,
That were a present far too small;
Love so amazing, so divine,
Demands my soul, my life, my all.

—Isaac Watts

Chapter 15

Conclusion

INTRODUCTION

Our exploration of atonement and the death of Christ has yielded rich rewards. Simply acquiring a clearer understanding of the meaning of the English word "atonement" represents a major advance, which enables us to see the inadequacy of many contemporary theories of the atonement offered by Christian philosophers. For while their theories may offer an account of the atonement in the broad, etymological sense of the word, they have little to say, if anything, about atonement in the narrow, biblical sense of the word. But biblically speaking, atonement in the narrow sense (*kippēr, hilaskesthai*) is the means to atonement in the broad sense (*katallagē*). To borrow the terminology of our German colleagues, a theory of *Versöhnung* that does not have at its heart *die Sühne* is empty.

Since we have no conciliar guidance concerning the atonement, our theories of the atonement must be guided and assessed by biblical exegesis and philosophical analysis. Although we have distinguished between the doctrine of the atonement and a theory of the atonement, we should not be misled into thinking that the biblical doctrine of the atonement is the simple affirmation that "Christ died for our sins," so that theory construction can proceed with little regard to biblical teaching. Rather, we have seen that the biblical doctrine of the atonement is a multifaceted doctrine replete with various motifs and metaphors and therefore capable of guiding us in finding acceptable theories of the atonement. Even the formulaic affirmation "Christ died for our sins" (1 Cor 15:3) is in all probability, as we have seen, a reference to the righteous Servant of the LORD of Isaiah 53, whose vicarious, punitive suffering makes many to be accounted righteous.

On the other hand, we want a theory of the atonement that is philosophically coherent and can therefore withstand the attacks of its critics. Contemporary theologians exhibit a disturbing tendency to shun accounts of the mechanism of atonement and to content themselves with mystery or metaphor. Such an approach to the atonement not only precludes our gaining insight into this important doctrine but leaves Christianity vulnerable to the attacks of its critics. We must therefore seek an account of the atonement that is both biblically adequate and philosophically coherent.

BIBLICAL DATA CONCERNING THE ATONEMENT

We have seen that the biblical doctrine of the atonement is like a multifaceted jewel with sacrifice as its table. Moreover, a study of sacrifice in OT Judaism reveals that the Levitical animal sacrifices, to which NT authors compare the death of Christ, were not, like the bloodless grain offerings, offered as gifts to God but rather served the twin functions of expiation of sins/impurity and propitiation of God. A death was prescribed, and through the hand-laying ritual, which accompanies every animal sacrifice, it is plausible that the offerer identifies himself symbolically with the animal, so that the animal dies in his place, suffering the fate that the worshipper deserved as the punishment for his sin. In the eyes of the NT authors, these sacrifices were an arrangement graciously given by God that were merely provisional in nature, an understanding of the sacrifices already intimated in the OT, until Christ should come and by his self-sacrificial death offer once for all a truly efficacious sacrifice for sin. Moreover, Christ's death propitiated God's wrath, which hung over mankind as the result of its condemnation before the bar of God's justice.

The substitutionary, punitive nature of Christ's death, already limned in the Levitical sacrifices, comes to the fore in the NT authors' identification of Christ with Isaiah's Servant of the LORD, who "bore our sins in his body on the tree" (1 Pet 2:24). The common Hebrew idiom of bearing sin/iniquity means *to be liable to punishment* or *to endure punishment*. This Christ did in our place and on our behalf.

By bearing the punishment of our sins, Christ satisfied the demands of divine justice. We have seen how replete the NT is with justice terminology and metaphors of the courtroom. Because Christ has borne the punishment for our sins, we can be declared righteous by God and our legal status changed from condemnation to exoneration. Divine forgiveness of sin is thus seen to be much more than a change of attitude toward us on God's part but is analogous to a legal pardon. More than that, however, God's justification of us is much more than a bare declaration of "not guilty." Rather, God's righteousness is imputed to us, as we are reckoned to be righteous by God. Though less clearly attested than the imputation of God's righteousness to us, our sins were similarly apparently imputed to Christ, for he became accursed instead of us (Gal 3:13) and so is said to have "become sin" for our sake (2 Cor 5:21). Christ's atoning death is thus closely connected to a forensic view of justification.

We have seen that Christ's atoning death is taken by Paul to be not simply substitutionary but representational as well. Christ somehow represents every human being before God, such that his death can be said to be our death. But to become beneficiaries of his death, we must be united with Christ in a yet more intimate way through faith culminating in baptism, whereby we identify with his death and resurrection. It is only in so far as we are "in Christ" that his sacrifice on our behalf becomes efficacious.

Finally, the death of Christ on our behalf is the means of our redemption, as we are set free from sin and death. Christ's life is the ransom paid for our redemption. Thereby Christ through the cross achieves a triumphant victory over the principalities and powers that had bound us.

It is evident, then, that a biblical doctrine of the atonement is so much more than a simple affirmation that Christ died for our sins but is a rich, variegated doctrine that places significant constraints on any Christian theory of the atonement.

DOGMATIC HISTORY OF THE
DOCTRINE OF THE ATONEMENT

In part 2 of this work we surveyed some of the highlights of the premodern dogmatic history of the atonement. Perhaps the most important result of our survey is the realization of the way in which these traditional atonement theories are so often misrepresented and even caricatured by some modern writers. In particular, we have seen that the Church Fathers were by no means committed to a single-faceted atonement theory of *Christus Victor*, much less to a ransom model of the same. Rather, the diversity of NT motifs and metaphors concerning the atonement is well represented in the Fathers.

Similarly, Anselm's satisfaction theory should not be caricatured as portraying God as a feudal lord too vain to forgive an insult. Rather, Anselm's great advance over the Church Fathers lies in his emphasis on divine justice and its satisfaction as a prerequisite of human salvation. Abelard, though emphasizing the moral influence of Christ's passion, was also not an advocate of a single-faceted theory but seemed to recognize Christ's payment of the penalty for our sins as well. Finally, Hugo Grotius has been hugely misrepresented and maligned, I think, in the secondary literature as an advocate of a so-called governmental theory of the atonement, when, in fact, he offered a brilliant defense of a non-necessitarian penal substitutionary theory of the atonement.

It is a curiosity of contemporary discussions of the atonement in English that Faustus Socinus is so consistently overlooked. Doubtless this is due to the surprising fact that no English translation of his hugely influential critique of satisfaction and penal substitutionary atonement theories has been published. Contemporary neo-Socinian objections, though widespread, are typically perfunctory and pale in comparison to Socinus' own incisive criticisms. Also overlooked in contemporary discussions is the work of Francis Turretin, who, reflecting the work of Grotius, offers a powerful defense of penal substitution. Contemporary discussions of the atonement are the more impoverished for ignoring the contributions of these thinkers, who can serve as a rich source of insight.

PHILOSOPHICAL REFLECTIONS ON THE DOCTRINE OF THE ATONEMENT

Drawing upon the insights gained from the dogmatic history of the doctrine of the atonement, I have tried in part 3 to articulate the parameters of an atonement theory that is philosophically coherent while remaining faithful to the biblical doctrine. I have argued that at the heart of such a theory must be penal substitution. Because of the punitive nature of Christ's vicarious suffering, the philosophy of law and particularly discussions of the theory of punishment provide a rich resource for the contemporary penal substitution theorist. One important insight, in line with biblical teaching but rarely appreciated in contemporary discussions, is that God should not be construed as merely a private person in a personal dispute but as Judge and Ruler of the world.

I have rejected the attempt to show that the doctrine of penal substitution is incoherent. The claim that harsh treatment inflicted on a substitute cannot be punishment is flawed on multiple grounds. Not every advocate of penal substitution holds that Christ was punished for our sins, though that is my predilection. Christian philosophers need not adopt, in any case, an expressivist definition of punishment, which is said to be the source of the incoherence. If we do accept an expressivist theory of punishment, the typical articulations of expressivist theories are perfectly compatible with penal substitution. Finally, even if we adopt a definition of punishment that is so narrowly construed as to rule out normal cases of penal substitution, that does not subvert the Reformers' doctrine of penal substitution, since it is predicated on the doctrine of the imputation of our sin to Christ, which removes any incoherence arising from the definition of punishment.

The attempt to show that the doctrine of penal substitution is theologically incoherent is even less impressive. At least this objection recognizes, in contrast to many contemporary caricatures of penal substitution, that the theory is predicated on God's love for people, which motivates His provision of a substitute! But the objection is a fundamental failure because it misconstrues God as a sort of private person setting conditions for personal love and forgiveness rather than as supreme Judge and Ruler, whose legal pardon has preconditions, which God Himself graciously supplies precisely because He is loving and forgiving.

The more important neo-Socinian objection to the justice of penal substitution, though formidable, is not unanswerable. Again, the objection applies only to theories that affirm that Christ was punished for our sins. More importantly, given a Divine Command Theory of ethics or something similar, God Himself by His commands determines what is just or unjust. Since He presumably does not issue commands to Himself, God has no moral prohibitions to abide by. He can do whatever He wants, so long as it is consistent with His nature. This fact makes it difficult for the objection even to get off the ground, since there is no one to prohibit God from punishing a substitute. The only way to rescue the objection, it seems, is to maintain, against Socinus, that retributive justice as we know and understand it is part of God's nature, so that God cannot act contrary to the principles of retributive justice. This development in the dialectic is interesting because neo-Socinians seem so often opposed to divine retributive justice. In fact, they need retributive justice to be essential to God, lest God choose to punish the innocent.

But now the reformulated objection lacks nuance. It presupposes without warrant that God is by nature an unqualified negative retributivist. God could be a positive retributivist and even a negative retributivist with respect to human persons yet reserve for Himself the right to punish an innocent divine person in an act of divine Self-sacrifice. Furthermore, the objection overlooks the possibility that the *prima facie* demands of negative retributive justice might be overridden by weightier moral considerations in Christ's case. Finally, the objection takes for granted that Christ was legally innocent, in opposition to the Reformers' doctrine of imputation. The rejection of that doctrine on the grounds that there is nothing analogous to imputation in human experience betrays an ignorance of the law. Through the long established, widespread, and indispensable device of legal fictions, wrongful acts can be attributed to an individual other than the actor, so that the other individual is held legally guilty for the acts. Moreover, in both civil law and criminal law, persons can be held vicariously liable for wrongful acts, even though they did not commit such acts or any other wrongful acts related to such behavior. The point is not—God forbid!—that we should build our theology on the pattern of our justice system. Rather, the point is that the all-too-often repeated assertion that there is nothing in our experience analogous to the imputation of wrongdoing or guilt to an innocent person is simply mistaken. Imputation is, on the contrary, a familiar and relatively uncontroversial feature of our legal system.

If the coherence and justice of Christ's penal substitution is thus defensible, the question then arises as to whether penal substitution satisfies divine justice. Again, the doctrine of imputation plays a key role in answering this question. For the lesson of vicarious liability is that punishment of only persons who are liable for wrongdoing satisfies justice's demands. In some such cases, punishment of the vicariously liable superior alone satisfies the demands of justice. Given the doctrine of imputation of our sin to Christ, Christ was in God's eyes legally liable for our sins. His punishment on our behalf can therefore meet the conditions for the satisfaction of divine justice. Moreover, Christ's vicarious suffering was not merely substitutionary; it was representational. He was voluntarily our divinely appointed proxy before God, so that when he was punished we were punished, to the satisfaction of divine justice.

Neo-Socinian objections to the satisfactoriness of Christ's penal substitution are not very compelling. Although Socinus thought that remission of sins and satisfaction for those sins is logically incompatible, Grotius' claim seems plausible that the acceptance of a substitute for what is legally required does require a special dispensation on the part of the creditor or judge. In forgoing punishing us in our proper persons, God does act mercifully toward us. Socinus' complaint that Christ did not suffer eternally for our sins is met by the affirmation of the deity of his person, for the intensity of what Christ suffered can more than offset the finitude of its duration. Indeed, since the future is potentially infinite only, the damned never suffer more than a finite amount of punishment.

The objection that Christ's suffering the punishment due for all men's sins would imply universal salvation need not be met by affirming the doctrine of limited atonement. For Christ's atoning death may be taken to have potentially accomplished the redemption of all men, but this redemption is actualized progressively throughout history, only as people come to be united with Christ through repentance and faith. Like a pardon that has been issued and yet refused, Christ's redeeming work remains inefficacious in the lives of those who refuse him.

The NT doctrine that we are redeemed from sin and death by Christ's atoning death is illuminated by the way in which pardon functions in our legal system. A full pardon, granted, as in our case, after conviction for a capital crime, removes the convict's liability to punishment and restores to him his civil rights. God's forgiveness of our sins is like a legal pardon, since it is issued by executive authority to remove our liability to punishment. While a pardon does not erase the fact that criminal conduct has been committed, a pardon does expunge guilt, lest we be forced to say that a person who has been pardoned is still guilty and therefore deserving of further punishment, which is incoherent. Similarly, God's pardon blots out our guilt, so that we are no longer liable to punishment.

Moreover, just as a pardon restores a pardonee's civil rights, so a divine pardon bestows on us such benefits as adoption as sons, citizenship in the Kingdom of God, and inheritance of eternal life. A pardon is a legal action that does nothing to reform the criminal's character. Similarly, a divine pardon is a forensic act that does not transform us into virtuous people. It simply changes our legal status. Moral transformation requires the sanctifying work of the Holy Spirit to shape us gradually into the people that God wants us to be.

Pardons are traditionally taken to be acts of grace, issued on grounds of mercy. Certainly God's pardon of us is presented in the NT as an act of grace toward us undeserving sinners. Yet this occasions a tension with God's essential justice. Socinus thought that God's acting mercifully would be impossible were retributive justice essential to God. But penal substitution provides a wonderful resolution of this tension. God's essential justice and mercy are both exhibited in the cross of Christ, for Christ by his death satisfies the demands of divine justice, enabling God in turn to pardon our sins. The whole arrangement is an expression of God's mercy. Thus, while a necessitarian view of the atonement may not be theologically required, it does, I think, make the best sense of the way in which Christ's atonement displays both the mercy and justice of God.

We have noted that pardons can be refused, in which case they are rendered inefficacious, and can be conditional, in which case failure to meet the conditions nullifies the pardon. Similarly, refusal to accept a divine pardon renders Christ's work on one's behalf inefficacious in one's life, and if one fails to meet the conditions of repentance and faith, a divine pardon avails one nothing.

Finally, we have noted various ways in which the death of Christ exerts a tremendous moral influence upon mankind, especially in the moving demonstration of God's love in His Self-substitution for us in bearing awful suffering and in the fearsome demonstration of God's righteous wrath in what it cost Christ to win our redemption.

CONCLUSION

As a result of our investigation, we have thus arrived at a rich, multifaceted atonement theory featuring penal substitution, satisfaction of divine justice, imputation of sin and divine righteousness, pardon, and moral influence. These aspects of the theory do justice to the biblical motifs of sacrifice, including expiation of sin and propitiation of God, Isaiah's Servant of the LORD, whose vicarious, punitive suffering serves to make many accounted righteous, divine justice and forensic justification, redemption from sin and death, and Christ's representation of us before God. Not only does such an account do justice to the biblical data, but it is arguably philosophically tenable as well.

Bibliography

Adams, Robert Merrihew. *Finite and Infinite Goods: A Framework for Ethics.* Oxford: Oxford University Press, 1999.

Alston, William P. "What Euthyphro Should Have Said." In *Philosophy of Religion: A Reader and Guide*, edited by William Lane Craig, 283–98. Edinburgh: Edinburgh University Press, 2002.

Anderson, Gary A. "Sacrifice and Sacrificial Offerings: Old Testament." In *The Anchor Bible Dictionary, O–Sh*, edited by David Noel Freedman, 870–86. New York: Doubleday, 1992.

Aulén, Gustaf. *Christus Victor: An Historical Study of the Three Main Types of the Idea of Atonement.* Translated by A. G. Herbert. New York: Macmillan, 1969.

Averbeck, Richard E. "Christian Interpretations of Isaiah 53." In *The Gospel According to Isaiah 53: Encountering the Suffering Servant in Jewish and Christian Theology*, edited by Darrell L. Bock and Mitch Glaser, 33–60. Grand Rapids: Kregel, 2012.

Averbeck, Richard E. "kpr [4105/4106]." In *New International Dictionary of Old Testament Theology and Exegesis*, edited by Willem A. VanGemeren, 689–710. Grand Rapids: Zondervan, 1997.

Averbeck, Richard E. "Sacrifices and Offerings." In *Dictionary of the Old Testament: Pentateuch*, edited by T. Desmond Alexander and David W. Baker, 706–33. Downers Grove, Ill.: IVP Academic, 2003.

Bailey, Daniel P. "Atonement in the Hebrew Bible, Early Judaism, and the New Testament: An Overview." *Biblical Research* 60 (2015): 5–6.

Bailey, Daniel P. "Biblical and Greco-Roman Uses of *Hilastērion* in Romans 3:25 and 4 Maccabees 17:22 (Codex S)." In *Biblical Theology of the New Testament*, by Peter Stuhlmacher, translated and edited by Daniel P. Bailey with the collaboration of Jostein Ådna, 824–68. Grand Rapids: Eerdmans, 2018.

Bailey, Daniel P. "Concepts of *Stellvertretung* in the Interpretation of Isaiah 53." In *Jesus and the Suffering Servant: Isaiah 53 and Christian Origins*, edited by William H. Bellinger Jr. and William R. Farmer, 223–50. Harrisburg, Penn.: Trinity Press International, 1998.

Bailey, Daniel P. "Jesus as the Mercy Seat: The Semantics and Theology of Paul's Use of *Hilasterion* in Romans 3:25." Ph.D. diss., University of Cambridge, 1999. https://doi.org/10.17863/CAM.17213.

Bailey, Daniel P. "Jesus as the Mercy Seat: The Semantics and Theology of Paul's Use of *Hilasterion* in Romans 3:25." *Tyndale Bulletin* 51, no. 1 (2000): 155–58.

Bell, Richard H. "Sacrifice and Christology in Paul." *Journal of Theological Studies* 53, no. 1 (2002): 1–27.

Benz, Ernst, and Erich Klostermann, eds. *Origenes Werke: Die Griechischen Christlichen Schriftsteller der ersten drei Jahrhunderte*. Vol. 10, *Origenes Matthäuserklärung*. Leipzig: J. C. Heinrich'sche Buchhandlung, 1935.

Benz, Ernst, and Erich Klostermann, eds. *Origenes Werke: Die Griechischen Christlichen Schriftsteller der ersten drei Jahrhunderte*. Vol. 11, *Origenes Matthäuserklärung*. Leipzig: J. C. Heinrich'sche Buchhandlung, 1933.

Bird, Michael F. "Progressive Reformed View." In *Justification: Five Views*, edited by James Beilby and Paul Rhodes Eddy, 131–57. Downers Grove, Ill.: IVP Academic, 2011.

Bird, Michael F. "Roman Catholic View: Progressive Reformed Response." In *Justification: Five Views*, edited by James Beilby and Paul Rhodes Eddy, 296–300. Downers Grove, Ill.: IVP Academic, 2011.

Blackstone, William. *Commentaries on the Laws of England in Four Books*. 2nd ed. rev. Chicago: Callaghan, 1879.

Blocher, Henri. "Justification of the Ungodly (*Sola Fide*): Theological Reflections." In *Justification and Variegated Nomism: A Fresh Appraisal of Paul and Second Temple Judaism*, edited by D. A. Carson, Peter T. O'Brien, and Mark A. Seifrid, 465–500. Vol. 2, *The Paradoxes of Paul*. WUNT 2/181. Tübingen: Mohr Siebeck, 2004.

Borg, Marcus J., and John Dominic Crossan. *The First Paul: Reclaiming the Radical Visionary Behind the Church's Conservative Icon*. San Francisco: HarperOne, 2009.

Botha, M. M., and D. Millard. *The Past, Present and Future of Vicarious Liability in South Africa*. Pretoria: Pretoria University Press, 2014.

Botha, Monray Marsellus, and Daleen Millard. "The Past, Present and Future of Vicarious Liability in South Africa." *De Jure Law Journal* 45, no. 2 (2012): 225–53.

Breiner, Nikolaus. "Penal Substitution but Not Substitutionary Punishment: Aquinas on the Atonement." Paper presented at the Eastern Regional Meeting of the Society of Christian Philosophers, Wilmore, Ky., September 2017.

Breiner, Nikolaus. "Punishment and Satisfaction in Aquinas's Account of the Atonement: A Reply to Stump." *Faith and Philosophy* 35, no. 2 (2018): 237–56.

Brien, Andrew. "Can God Forgive Us Our Trespasses?" *Sophia* 28, no. 2 (1989): 35–42.

Brien, Andrew. "Mercy within Legal Justice." *Social Theory & Practice* 24 (1998): 83–110.

Brunner, Emil. *The Mediator: A Study of the Central Doctrine of the Christian Faith*. 2nd ed. Translated by Olive Wyon. Lutterworth Library 3. London: Lutterworth Press, 1934.

Calvin, John. *Institutes of the Christian Religion*. 2 vols. Translated by Henry Beveridge. Grand Rapids: Eerdmans, 1972.

Caplow, Stacy. "Governors! Seize the Law: A Call to Expand the Use of Pardons to Provide Relief from Deportation." *Boston University Public Interest Law Journal* 22 (2013): 299–339.

Carson, D. A. "Atonement in Romans 3:21–26." In *The Glory of the Atonement: Biblical, Historical, and Practical Perspectives*, edited by Charles E. Hill and Frank A. James III, 119–39. Downers Grove, Ill.: InterVarsity, 2004.

Carson, D. A. "The Vindication of Imputation: On Fields of Discourse and Semantic Fields." In *Justification: What's at Stake in the Current Debates*, edited by Mark Husbands and Daniel J. Treier, 46–79. Downers Grove, Ill.: InterVarsity, 2004.

Cassuto, Umberto. *A Commentary on the Book of Genesis*. Part 1, *From Adam to Noah: Genesis I–VI. 8* (1944). Translated by Israel Abrahams. Skokie, Ill.: Varda Books, 2005.

Childs, Brevard S. *Introduction to the Old Testament as Scripture*. Philadelphia: Fortress Press, 1979.

Clines, David J. A. *The Theme of the Pentateuch*. 2nd ed. Journal for the Study of the Old Testament Supplement Series 10. Sheffield, England: Sheffield Academic Press, 1987.

Craig, William Lane. *The Atonement*. Cambridge: Cambridge University Press, 2018.

Craig, William Lane. *God over All: Divine Aseity and the Challenge of Platonism*. Oxford: Oxford University Press, 2016.

Craig, William Lane. *Time and Eternity: Exploring God's Relationship to Time*. Wheaton, Ill.: Crossway, 2001.

Crisp, Oliver D. "Original Sin and Atonement." In *The Oxford Handbook of Philosophical Theology*, edited by Thomas P. Flint and Michael Rea, 430–51. Oxford: Oxford University Press, 2009.

Crisp, Oliver D. "Salvation and Atonement: On the Value and Necessity of the Work of Jesus Christ." In *The God of Salvation: Soteriology in Theological Perspective*, edited by Ivor J. Davidson and Murray A. Rae, 105–20. Farnham, UK: Ashgate, 2011.

Crisp, Oliver D. *The Word Enfleshed: Exploring the Person and Work of Christ*. Grand Rapids: Baker Academic, 2016.

Crouch, Jeffrey P. *The Presidential Pardon Power*. Lawrence: University Press of Kansas, 2009.

Dale, R. W. *The Atonement*. 9th ed. London: Hodder & Stoughton, 1884.

Denney, James. *The Death of Christ: Its Place and Interpretation in the New Testament*. London: Hodder & Stoughton, 1907.

DeSilva, David. *4 Maccabees: Introduction and Commentary on the Greek Text in Codex Sinaiticus*. Leiden: Brill, 2006.

Dodd, C. H. "Ἱλασκεσθαι, Its Cognates, Derivatives, and Synonyms, in the Septuagint." *Journal of Theological Studies* 32, no. 128 (1931): 352–60.

Donnellan, Keith. "Reference and Definite Descriptions." *Philosophical Review* 75, no. 3 (1966): 281–304.

Dunn, James D. G. "New Perspective View." In *Justification: Five Views*, edited by James Beilby and Paul Rhodes Eddy, 176–201. Downers Grove, Ill.: IVP Academic, 2011.

Dunn, James D. G. "The New Perspective: Whence, What and Whither?" In *The New Perspective on Paul*, rev. ed., 1–97. Grand Rapids: Eerdmans, 2008.

Dunn, James D. G. "Traditional Reformed View: New Perspective Response." In *Justification: Five Views*, edited by James Beilby and Paul Rhodes Eddy, 117–21. Downers Grove, Ill.: IVP Academic, 2011.

Edwards, Jonathan. *The Works of Jonathan Edwards*. Vol. I, *The Great Christian Doctrine of Original Sin Defended* (1834). Peabody, Mass.: Hendrickson, 1998.

Farmer, William R. "Reflections on Isaiah 53 and Christian Origins." In *Jesus and the Suffering Servant: Isaiah 53 and Christian Origins*, edited by William H. Bellinger Jr. and William R. Farmer, 260–80. Harrisburg, Penn.: Trinity Press International, 1998.

Feinberg, Joel. *Doing and Deserving: Essays in the Theory of Responsibility*. Princeton, N.J.: Princeton University Press, 1970.

Feinberg, Joel, and Hyman Gross, eds. *Philosophy of Law*. 2nd ed. Belmont, Calif.: Wadsworth, 1980.

Finlan, Stephen. *Options on Atonement in Christian Thought*. Collegeville, Minn.: Liturgical Press, 2007.

Forsyth, Peter Taylor. *The Work of Christ*. 2nd ed. London: Independent Press, 1938.

Franks, Robert S. *A History of the Doctrine of the Work of Christ in Its Ecclesiastical Development*. 2 vols. London: Hodder & Stoughton, 1918.

Fuller, L. L. "Legal Fictions." Pts. 1, 2, and 3. *Illinois Law Review* 25, no. 4 (1930): 363–99; no. 5 (1931): 513–46; no. 8 (1931): 877–910.

Gathercole, Simon. *Defending Substitution: An Essay on Atonement in Paul*. Grand Rapids: Baker Academic, 2015.

Gerrish, B. A. *A Prince of the Church: Schleiermacher and the Beginnings of Modern Theology*. Philadelphia: Fortress Press, 1984.

Gese, Hartmut. *Essays on Biblical Theology*. Translated by Keith Crim. Minneapolis: Augsburg, 1981.

Gestrich, Christoph. "Sühne V: Kirchengeschichtlich und dogmatisch." In *Theologische Realenzyklopädie*, edited by Gerhard Müller. Vol. 32, *Spurgeon-Taylor*, 348–55. Berlin: Walter de Gruyter, 2001.

Geuras, Dean. "In Defense of Divine Forgiveness: A Response to David Londey." *Sophia* 31, nos. 1–2 (1992): 65–77.

Godbey, John Charles. "A Study of Faustus Socinus' *De Jesu Christo Servatore*." Ph.D. diss., University of Chicago Divinity School, 1968.

Gomes, Alan W. "Faustus Socinus' *De Jesu Christo Servatore*, Part III: Historical Introduction, Translation, and Critical Notes." Ph.D. diss., Fuller Theological Seminary, 1990.

Green, Joel B. "Kaleidoscopic View." In *The Nature of the Atonement: Four Views*, edited by James Beilby and Paul R. Eddy. Spectrum Multiview Books, 157–85. Downers Grove, Ill.: IVP Academic, 2006.

Greenberg, Jim. "An Assessment of Jacob Milgrom's View of the *ḥaṭṭā't*
Offering Using a Text-Immanent Approach to Reading the Priestly
Texts." Paper presented at the annual meeting of the Society of
Biblical Literature, Boston, November 18–21, 2017.

Grensted, L. W. *A Short History of the Doctrine of the Atonement.* Theological Series 4. Manchester: Manchester University Press, 1920.

Greshake, Gisbert. *Gnade als konkrete Freiheit.* Mainz: Matthias-
Grünewald-Verlag, 1972.

Grotius, Hugo. *A Defence of the Catholic Faith concerning the Satisfaction
of Christ, against Faustus Socinus.* Translated by Frank Hugh Foster.
Andover, Mass.: Warren F. Draper, 1889.

Groves, J. Alan. "Atonement in Isaiah 53." In *The Glory of the Atonement:
Biblical, Historical, and Practical Perspectives,* edited by Charles E.
Hill and Frank A. James III, 61–89. Downers Grove, Ill.: Inter-
Varsity, 2004.

Gundry, Robert H. "The Nonimputation of Christ's Righteousness." In
Justification: What's at Stake in the Current Debates, edited by Mark
Husbands and Daniel J. Treier, 17–45. Downers Grove, Ill.: Inter-
Varsity, 2004.

Hall, Jerome. "Biblical Atonement and Modern Criminal Law."
Washington University Law Quarterly 65, no. 4 (1987): 694–710.

Hamilton, Victor P. *The Book of Genesis: Chapters 1–17.* The New International Commentary on the Old Testament. Grand Rapids:
Eerdmans, 1990.

Harnack, Adolf. *Lehrbuch der Dogmengeschichte.* 4th ed. Vol. 3, *Die Entstehung des kirchlichen Dogmas II, III.* Tübingen: J. C. B. Mohr, 1909.

Hart, H. L. A. *Punishment and Responsibility.* Oxford: Oxford University Press, 1968.

Hiecke, Thomas. "Participation and Abstraction in the Yom Kippur Rit-
ual according to Leviticus 16." Paper presented to the "Ritual in the
Biblical World" section of the Society of Biblical Literature, San
Antonio, Tex., November 21, 2016.

Hermisson, Hans-Jürgen. "The Fourth Servant Song in the Context
of Second Isaiah." In *The Suffering Servant: Isaiah 53 in Jewish and
Christian Sources,* edited by Bernd Janowski and Peter Stuhlmacher
(1996), translated by Daniel P. Bailey, 16–47. Grand Rapids: Eerdmans, 2004.

Hilborn, David. "Atonement, Evangelicalism and the Evangelical Alliance: The Present Debate in Context." In *The Atonement Debate:
Papers from the London Symposium on the Theology of Atonement,*

edited by Derek Tidball, David Hilborn, and Justin Thacker, 15–33. Grand Rapids: Zondervan, 2008.

Hill, Charles E., and Frank A. James III, eds. *The Glory of the Atonement: Biblical, Historical, and Practical Perspectives*. Downers Grove, Ill.: InterVarsity, 2004.

Hill, Daniel J., and Joseph Jedwab. "Atonement and the Concept of Punishment." In *Locating Atonement: Explorations in Constructive Dogmatics*, edited by Oliver D. Crisp and Fred Sanders, 139–53. Grand Rapids: Zondervan, 2015.

Hoffman, Karen D. "Forgiveness without Apology: Defending Unconditional Forgiveness." *Proceedings of the American Catholic Philosophical Association* 82 (2008): 135–51.

Hofius, Otfried. "Erwägungen zur Gestalt und Herkunft des paulinischen Versöhnungsgedankens." *Zeitschrift für Theologie und Kirche* 77, no. 2 (1980): 186–99.

Hofius, Otfried. "The Fourth Servant Song in the New Testament Letters." In *The Suffering Servant: Isaiah 53 in Jewish and Christian Sources*, edited by Bernd Janowski and Peter Stuhlmacher (1996), translated by Daniel P. Bailey, 163–88. Grand Rapids: Eerdmans, 2004.

Hofius, Otfried. "Sühne IV: Neues Testament." In *Theologische Realenzyklopädie*, edited by Gerhard Müller, 342–47. Vol. 32, *Spurgeon-Taylor*. Berlin: Walter de Gruyter, 2001.

Hofius, Otfried. "Sühne und Versöhnung: Zum paulinischen Verständnis des Kreuzestodes Jesu." In *Paulusstudien*, 2nd rev. ed, edited by Otfried Hofius, 33–49. WUNT 1/51. Tübingen: J. C. B. Mohr (Paul Siebeck), 1994.

Hofius, Otfried. "Sühne und Versöhnung: Zum paulinischen Verständnis des Kreuzestodes Jesu." In *Versuche, das Leiden und Sterben Jesu zu verstehen*, edited by Wilhelm Maas, 25–46. Schriftenreihe der Katholischen Akademie der Erzdiözese Freiburg. Munich: Verlag Schnell & Steiner, 1983.

Hofius, Otfried. "Versöhnung: Neues Testament." In *Theologische Realenzyklopädie*, edited by Gerhard Müller. Vol. 35, *Vernunft III–Wiederbringung aller*, 18–22. Berlin: Walter de Gruyter, 2003.

Hooker, M. D. "Interchange in Christ." *Journal of Theological Studies* 22, no. 2 (1971): 349–61.

Horsbrugh, H. J. N. "Forgiveness." *Canadian Journal of Philosophy* 4, no. 2 (1974): 269–82.

Horton, Michael S. "Roman Catholic View: Traditional Reformed Response." In *Justification: Five Views*, edited by James Beilby and Paul Rhodes Eddy, 291–95. Downers Grove, Ill.: IVP Academic, 2011.

Horton, Michael S. "Traditional Reformed View." In *Justification: Five Views*, edited by James Beilby and Paul Rhodes Eddy, 83–111. Downers Grove, Ill.: IVP Academic, 2011.

Hughes, Paul M. "Forgiveness." In *The Stanford Encyclopedia of Philosophy*, edited by Edward N. Zalta. Spring 2015 ed. https://plato.stanford.edu/entries/forgiveness.

Hultgren, Stephen. "*Hilastērion* (Rom. 3:25) and the Union of Divine Justice and Mercy. Part I: The Convergence of Temple and Martyrdom Theologies." *Journal of Theological Studies* 70, no. 1 (April 2019): 69–109.

Hultgren, Stephen. "*Hilastērion* (Rom. 3:25) and the Union of Divine Justice and Mercy. Part II: Atonement in the Old Testament and in Romans 1–5." *Journal of Theological Studies* (forthcoming).

Humbert, W. H. *The Pardoning Power of the President*. Washington D.C.: American Council on Public Affairs, 1941.

Husak, Douglas. "*Malum Prohibitum* and Retributivism." In *Defining Crimes: Essays on the Special Part of the Criminal Law*, edited by R. A. Duff and Stuart P. Green, 65–90. Oxford Monographs on Criminal Law and Justice. Oxford: Oxford University Press, 2005.

Irons, Charles Lee. *The Righteousness of God: A Lexical Examination of the Covenant-Faithfulness Interpretation*. WUNT 2/386. Tübingen: Mohr Siebeck, 2015.

James, Frank A., III. General introduction to *The Glory of the Atonement: Biblical, Theological, and Practical Perspectives*, edited by Charles E. Hill and Frank A. James III, 15–20. Downers Grove, Ill.: InterVarsity, 2004.

Janowski, Bernd. "He Bore Our Sins: Isaiah 53 and the Drama of Taking Another's Place." In *The Suffering Servant: Isaiah 53 in Jewish and Christian Sources*, edited by Bernd Janowski and Peter Stuhlmacher (1996), translated by Daniel P. Bailey, 48–74. Grand Rapids: Eerdmans, 2004.

Janowski, Bernd. *Stellvertretung: Alttestamentliche Studien zu einem theologischen Grundbegriff*. Stuttgarter Bibelstudien 165. Stuttgart: Verlag Katholisches Bibelwerk, 1997.

Janowski, Bernd. *Sühne als Heilsgeschehen: Studien zur Sühnetheologie der Priesterschrift und zur Wurzel KPR im Alten Orient und im Alten*

Testament. WMANT 55. Neukirchen-Vluyn, Germany: Neukirchener (Vandenhoeck & Ruprecht Verlage), 1982.

Jeffery, Steve, Michael Ovey, and Andrew Sach. *Pierced for Our Transgressions: Rediscovering the Glory of Penal Substitution.* Wheaton, Ill.: Crossway Books, 2007.

Jensen, Paul. "Forgiveness and Atonement." *Scottish Journal of Theology* 46, no. 2 (1993): 141–60.

Jeremias, Joachim. *The Eucharistic Words of Jesus.* Translated by Norman Perrin. New York: Charles Scribner's Sons, 1966.

Kant, Immanuel. *Metaphysical Elements of Justice.* 2nd ed. Translated by John Ladd. Indianapolis: Hackett, 1999.

Kessler, Hans. *Die theologische Bedeutung des Todes Jesu: Eine traditionsgeschichtliche Untersuchung.* Düsseldorf: Patmos-Verlag, 1970.

Kinzig, Wolfram, and Thomas Brüggemann, eds. *Kyrill von Alexandrien: Werke.* Vol. 1, *Gegen Julian.* Part 2, *Buch 6–10 und Fragmente.* Die Griechischen Christlichen Schriftsteller der ersten Jahrhunderte, Neue Folge 21. Berlin: Walter de Gruyter, 2017.

Kobil, Daniel T. "The Quality of Mercy Strained: Wresting the Pardoning Power from the King." *Texas Law Review* 69 (1991): 569–641.

Korsch, Dietrich. "Versöhnung: Theologiegeschichtlich und dogmatisch." In *Theologische Realenzyklopädie*, edited by Gerhard Müller. Vol. 35, *Vernunft III–Wiederbringung aller*, 22–40. Berlin: Walter de Gruyter, 2003.

Leftow, Brian. *God and Necessity.* Oxford: Oxford University Press, 2012.

Leigh, L. H. *Strict and Vicarious Liability: A Study in Administrative Criminal Law.* Modern Legal Studies. London: Sweet and Maxwell, 1982.

Levine, Baruch A. *In the Presence of the Lord: A Study of Cult and Some Cultic Terms in Ancient Israel.* Studies in Judaism in Late Antiquity. Leiden: Brill, 1974.

Lewis, David. "Do We Believe in Penal Substitution?" *Philosophical Papers* 26, no. 3 (1997): 203–9.

Lewis, Meirlys. "On Forgiveness." *Philosophical Quarterly* 30, no. 120 (1980): 236–45.

Lincoln, Andrew T. "From Wrath to Justification: Tradition, Gospel, and Audience in the Theology of Romans 1:18–4:25." In *Pauline Theology*, vol. 3, *Romans*, edited by David M. Hay and E. Elizabeth Johnson, 130–59. Minneapolis: Fortress, 1995.

Lind, Douglas. "The Pragmatic Value of Legal Fictions." In *Legal Fictions in Theory and Practice*, edited by Maksymilian Del Mar and

William Twining, 83–109. Law and Philosophy Library 110. Cham, Switzerland: Springer Verlag, 2015.

Londey, David. "Can God Forgive Us Our Trespasses?" *Sophia* 25, no. 2 (1986): 4–10.

Longenecker, Richard N. *The Epistle to the Romans*. The New International Greek Testament Commentary. Grand Rapids: Eerdmans, 2016.

Luther, Martin. *A Commentary on St. Paul's Epistle to the Galatians*. Translated by Theodore Graebner. Grand Rapids: Zondervan, 1939.

Marshall, I. Howard. *Aspects of the Atonement: Cross and Resurrection in the Reconciling of God and Humanity*. London: Paternoster, 2007.

Marshall, I. Howard. "The Theology of the Atonement." In *The Atonement Debate*, edited by Derek Tidball, David Hilborn, and Justin Thacker, 49–68. Grand Rapids: Zondervan, 2008.

Matthews, Kenneth A. *Genesis 1–11:26*. The New American Commentary 1A. Nashville: B&H, 1996.

McCormack, Bruce L. "What's at Stake in Current Debates over Justification? The Crisis of Protestantism in the West." In *Justification: What's at Stake in the Current Debates*, edited by Mark Husbands and Daniel J. Treier, 81–117. Downers Grove, Ill.: InterVarsity, 2004.

McGrath, Alister. "Forerunners of the Reformation? A Critical Examination of the Evidence for Precursors of the Reformation Doctrines of Justification." *Harvard Theological Review* 75, no. 2 (1982): 219–42.

McGrath, Alister E. *Iustitia Dei: A History of the Christian Doctrine of Justification*. 3rd ed. Cambridge: Cambridge University Press, 2005.

Messing, Noah A. "A New Power? Civil Offenses and Presidential Clemency." *Buffalo Law Review* 64, no. 4 (2016): 661–743.

Migne, J.-P., ed. *Patrologia Græca*. Vol. 69. Paris: 1864.

Migne, J.-P., ed. *Patrologia Græca*. Vol. 76. Paris: 1859.

Milgrom, Jacob. *Leviticus 1–16*. The Anchor Bible 3. New York: Doubleday, 1991.

Milgrom, Jacob. *Leviticus 17–22*. Anchor Yale Bible 3A. New Haven, Conn.: Yale University Press, 2000.

Minas, Anne C. "God and Forgiveness." *Philosophical Quarterly* 25, no. 99 (1975): 138–50.

Mitros, Joseph F. "Patristic Views of Christ's Salvific Work." *Thought* 42, no. 3 (1967): 415–47.

Moberly, Walter. *The Ethics of Punishment*. Hamden, Conn.: Archon Books, 1968.

Moffitt, David M. *Atonement and the Logic of Resurrection in the Epistle to the Hebrews.* Supplements to Novum Testamentum 141. Leiden: Brill, 2013.

Moo, Douglas J. *Encountering the Book of Romans.* Grand Rapids: Baker Academic, 2002.

Moo, Douglas J. *The Epistle to the Romans.* New International Commentary on the New Testament. Grand Rapids: Eerdmans, 1996.

Moo, Douglas J. *Romans.* NIV Application Commentary. Grand Rapids: Zondervan, 2000.

Moore, Kathleen Dean. "Pardon for Good and Sufficient Reasons." *University of Richmond Law Review* 27, no. 2 (1993): 281–88.

Moore, Kathleen Dean. *Pardons: Justice, Mercy, and the Public Interest.* Oxford: Oxford University Press, 1989.

Moore, Michael. *Placing Blame: A Theory of Criminal Law.* Oxford: Oxford University Press, 1997.

Moreland, J. P., and William Lane Craig. *Philosophical Foundations for a Christian Worldview.* 2nd ed. Downers Grove, Ill.: InterVarsity, 2017.

Morison, Samuel T. "The Politics of Grace: On the Moral Justification of Executive Clemency." *Buffalo Criminal Law Review* 9, no. 1 (2005): 1–138.

Morris, Leon. *The Atonement: Its Meaning and Significance.* Downers Grove, Ill.: InterVarsity, 1983.

Morris, Leon. "The Meaning of ἱλαστήριον in Romans III.25." *New Testament Studies* 2, no. 1 (1955): 33–43.

Murphy, Jeffrie. "Mercy and Legal Justice." In *Forgiveness and Mercy*, edited by Jeffrie G. Murphy and Jean Hampton, 162–86. Cambridge: Cambridge University Press, 1988.

Murphy, Jeffrie G. "Retributivism, Moral Education, and the Liberal State." *Criminal Justice Ethics* 4, no. 1 (1985): 3–11.

Murphy, Mark C. "Not Penal Substitution but Vicarious Punishment." *Faith and Philosophy* 26, no. 3 (2009): 253–73.

Murray, John. *The Imputation of Adam's Sin.* Grand Rapids: Eerdmans, 1959.

Murray, Michael, and Michael Rea. "Philosophy and Christian Theology." In *The Stanford Encyclopedia of Philosophy*, edited by Edward N. Zalta. Summer 2012 ed. https://plato.stanford.edu/entries/christian theology-philosophy/.

Mwale, Emmanuel. "Jesus Christ's Substitutionary Death: An Attempt to Reconcile Two Divergent Seventh-Day Adventist Teachings." Th.M. thesis, University of South Africa, 2015.

New, Christopher. "Time and Punishment." *Analysis* 52, no. 1 (1992): 35–40.

Nicole, Roger. "C. H. Dodd and the Doctrine of Propitiation." *Westminster Theological Journal* 17, no. 2 (1955): 117–57.

Nicole, Roger. "Postscript on Penal Substitution." In *The Glory of the Atonement: Biblical, Theological, and Practical Perspectives*, edited by Charles E. Hill and Frank A. James III, 445–52. Downers Grove, Ill.: InterVarsity, 2004.

O'Collins, Gerald. "Traditional Reformed View: Roman Catholic Response." In *Justification: Five Views*, edited by James K. Beilby and Paul Rhodes Eddy, 127–30. Downers Grove, Ill.: IVP Academic, 2011.

Onesti, K. L., and M. T. Brauch. "Righteousness, Righteousness of God." In *Dictionary of Paul and His Letters*, edited by Gerald F. Hawthorne, Ralph P. Martin, and D. G. Reid, 827–37. Downers Grove, Ill.: InterVarsity, 1993.

Origen. *The Commentary of Origen on the Gospel of St. Matthew*. Translated by Ronald E. Heine. 2 vols. Oxford Early Christian Texts. Oxford: Oxford University Press, 2018.

Ormerod, David, and Karl Laird. *Smith, Hogan, and Ormerod's Criminal Law*. 15th ed. Oxford: Oxford University Press, 2018.

Osler, Mark W. "A Biblical Value in the Constitution: Mercy, Clemency, Faith and History." *University of St. Thomas Law Journal* 9, no. 3 (2012): 769–82.

Oswalt, J. N. "Theology of the Pentateuch." In *Dictionary of the Old Testament: Pentateuch*, edited by T. Desmond Alexander and David W. Baker, 845–59. Downers Grove, Ill.: InterVarsity, 2003.

Owen, John. *A Dissertation on Divine Justice; Or, The Claims of Vindicatory Justice Asserted* (Latin version 1653). London: L. J. Higham, n.d.

Pannenberg, Wolfhart. *Systematic Theology*. 3 vols. Grand Rapids: Eerdmans, 1991.

Peterson, David. "Atonement in the Old Testament." In *Where Wrath and Mercy Meet: Proclaiming the Atonement Today*, edited by David Peterson, 1–25. Oak Hill School of Theology Series. Carlisle, Cumbria, U.K.: Paternoster, 2001.

Pitre, Brant. *Jesus and the Last Supper*. Grand Rapids: William B. Eerdmans, 2015.

Plantinga, Alvin. "Comments on 'Satanic Verses: Moral Chaos in Holy Writ.'" In *Divine Evil? The Moral Character of the God of Abraham*, edited by Michael Bergmann, Michael J. Murray, and Michael C. Rea, 109–14. Oxford: Oxford University Press, 2011.

Plantinga, Alvin. "Self-Profile." In *Alvin Plantinga*, edited by James E. Tomberlin and Peter van Inwagen, 3–97. Profiles 5. Dordrecht: D. Reidel, 1985.

Plasger, Georg. *Die Notwendigkeit der Gerechtigkeit: Eine Interpretation zu* "Cur Deus homo" *v. Anselm v. Canterbury.* Beiträge zur Geschichte und Philosophie des Mittelalters. Neue Folge 38. Münster: Aschendorff, 1993.

Porter, Steven J. "Swinburnian Atonement and the Doctrine of Penal Substitution." *Faith and Philosophy* 21, no. 2 (2004): 228–41.

Preuschen, Erwin, ed. *Origenes Werke*. Vol. 2, *Der Johanneskommentar*. Leipzig: J. C. Heinrich'sche Buchhandlung, 1903.

Prior, A. N. "The Syntax of Time Distinctions." *Franciscan Studies* 18, no. 2 (1958): 105–20.

Purtill, Richard. "Justice, Mercy, Supererogation, and Atonement." In *Christian Philosophy*, edited by Thomas P. Flint, 37–50. Notre Dame, Ind.: University of Notre Dame Press, 1990.

Quinn, Philip L. "Christian Atonement and Kantian Justification." *Faith and Philosophy* 3, no. 4 (1986): 440–62.

Quinn, Philip L. *Divine Commands and Moral Requirements*. Oxford: Clarendon Press, 1978.

Quinn, Philip L. *"Papers in Ethics and Social Philosophy* by David Lewis," *Noûs* 38, no. 4 (2004): 711–30.

Quinton, A. M. "On Punishment." *Analysis* 14, no. 6 (1954): 133–42.

Rainbolt, George W. "Mercy: An Independent, Imperfect Virtue." *American Philosophical Quarterly* 27, no. 2 (1990): 169–73.

Ripstein, Arthur. "Philosophy of Tort Law." In *The Oxford Handbook of Jurisprudence and Philosophy of Law*, edited by Jules Coleman and Scott Shapiro, 656–86. Oxford: Oxford University Press, 2002.

Ritschl, Albrecht. *The Christian Doctrine of Justification and Reconciliation: The Positive Development of the Doctrine*, edited by H. R. Mackintosh and Alexander Beith Macauley. Clifton, N.J.: Reference Book, 1966.

Ritschl, Albrecht. *A Critical History of the Christian Doctrine of Justification and Reconciliation* (1870). Translated by John S. Black. Edinburgh: Edmonston and Douglas, 1872.

Rivière, Jean. *The Doctrine of the Atonement: A Historical Essay*. 2 vols. Translated by Luigi Cappadelta. London: Kegan Paul, Trench, Trübner, 1909.

Roberts, H. R. T. "Mercy." *Philosophy* 46, no. 178 (1971): 352–53.

Ruane, Nicole. "Constructing Contagion on Yom Kippur: Reflections on the Scapegoat as Hatta't." Paper presented to the "Ritual in the Biblical World" section of the Society of Biblical Literature, San Antonio, Tex., November 21, 2016.

Schauer, Frederick. "Legal Fictions Revisited." In *Legal Fictions in Theory and Practice*, edited by Maksymilian Del Mar and William Twining, 113–30. Law and Philosophy Library 110. Cham, Switzerland: Springer Verlag, 2015.

Schenker, Adrian. "Sühne II: Altes Testament." In *Theologische Realenzyklopädie*, edited by Gerhard Müller, 335–38. Vol. 32, *Spurgeon-Taylor*. Berlin: Walter de Gruyter, 2001.

Schoenburg, Samuel E. "Clemency, War Powers, and Guantánamo." *New York University Law Review* 91, no. 4 (2016): 917–53.

Schreiber, Stefan. "Weitergedacht: Das versöhnende Weihegeschenk Gottes in Röm 3,25." *Zeitschrift für die Neutestamentliche Wissenschaft* 106, no. 2 (2015): 201–15.

Schwartz, Baruch J. "The Bearing of Sin in the Priestly Literature." In *Pomegranates and Golden Bells: Studies in Biblical, Jewish, and Near Eastern Ritual, Law, and Literature in Honor of Jacob Milgrom*, edited by David P. Wright, David Noel Freedman, and Avi Hurvitz, 3–22. Winona Lake, Ind.: Eisenbrauns, 1995.

Seifrid, Mark A. "Paul's Use of Righteousness Language against Its Hellenistic Background." In *Justification and Variegated Nomism: A Fresh Appraisal of Paul and Second Temple Judaism*, edited by D. A. Carson, Peter T. O'Brien, and Mark A. Seifrid, 39–74. Vol. 2, *The Paradoxes of Paul*. WUNT 2/181. Tübingen: Mohr Siebeck, 2004.

Seifrid, Mark A. "Righteousness Language in the Hebrew Scriptures and Early Judaism." In *Justification and Variegated Nomism: A Fresh Appraisal of Paul and Second Temple Judaism*, edited by D. A. Carson, Peter T. O'Brien, and Mark A. Seifrid, 415–42. Vol. 1, *The Complexities of Second Temple Judaism*. WUNT 2/140. Tübingen: Mohr Siebeck, 2001.

Sklar, Jay. "Pentateuch." In *Companion to the Doctrine of Sin*, edited by Keith L. Johnson and David Lauber, 3–26. London: T&T Clark, 2016.

Sklar, Jay. *Sin, Impurity, Sacrifice, Atonement: The Priestly Conceptions*. Hebrew Bible Monographs 2. Sheffield: Sheffield Phoenix Press, 2005.

Sklar, Jay. "Sin and Atonement: Lessons from the Pentateuch." *Bulletin for Biblical Research* 22, no. 4 (2012): 467–91.

Sklar, Jay. "Sin and Impurity: Atoned or Purified? Yes!" In *Perspectives on Purity and Purification in the Bible*, edited by Baruch J. Schwartz, David P. Wright, Jeffrey Stackert, and Naphtali S. Meshel, 18–31. Library of Hebrew Bible / Old Testament Studies 474. London: T&T Clark, 2008.

Smart, Alwynne. "Mercy." *Philosophy* 43, no. 166 (1968): 345–59.

Smeaton, George. *The Doctrine of the Atonement, as Taught by the Apostles.* Edinburgh: T&T Clark, 1870. Reprint: *The Apostles' Doctrine of the Atonement.* Grand Rapids: Zondervan, 1957.

Socinus, Faustus. *De Jesu Christo Servatore* [*On Jesus Christ Our Savior*]. In Wissowatius, Andreas, ed. *Bibliotheca Fratrum Polonorum quos Unitarios vocant.* Irenopoli (Amsterdam), 1668.

Spieckermann, Hermann. "The Conception and Prehistory of the Idea of Vicarious Suffering in the Old Testament." In *The Suffering Servant: Isaiah 53 in Jewish and Christian Sources*, edited by Bernd Janowski and Peter Stuhlmacher (1996), translated by Daniel P. Bailey, 1–15. Grand Rapids: Eerdmans, 2004.

Steindl, Helmut. *Genugtuung: Bibliische Versöhnungsdenken—eine Quelle für Anselms Satisfaktionstheorie?* Studia Friburgensia NS 71. Freiburg, Switzerland: Universitätsverlag,

Steiner, Ashley M. "Remission of Guilt or Removal of Punishment? The Effects of a Presidential Pardon." *Emory Law Journal* 46 (1997): 959–1003.

Stephan, Hayden C. "Is the God of Anselm Unloving? A Response to Eleonore Stump." *Religious Studies*, August 23, 2019, 1–16. doi:10.1017/S0034412519000416.

Stott, John. *The Cross of Christ.* Leicester, UK: InterVarsity, 1986.

Strasser, Mark. "The Limits of the Clemency Power: On Pardons, Retributivists, and the United States Constitution." *Brandeis Law Journal* 41 (2002): 85–154.

Stuhlmacher, Peter. *Reconciliation, Law, and Righteousness: Essays in Biblical Theology.* Translated by Everett R. Kalin. Philadelphia: Fortress Press, 1986.

Stump, Eleonore. *Aquinas.* New York: Routledge, 2003.

Stump, Eleonore. *Atonement.* Oxford: Oxford University Press, 2018.

Swen, Blaine. "The Logic of Divine-Human Reconciliation: A Critical Analysis of Penal Substitution as an Explanatory Feature of Atonement." Ph.D. diss., Loyola University, Chicago, 2012.

Tonry, Michael, ed. *Retributivism Has a Past: Has It a Future?* Studies in Penal Theory and Philosophy. Oxford: Oxford University Press, 2011.

Turretin, Francis. *Institutes of Elenctic Theology.* 3 vols. Translated by George Musgrave Giger, edited by James T. Dennison Jr. Phillipsburg, N.J.: P&R, 1992.

Vaihinger, Hans. *The Philosophy of "As If"* (1911). Translated by C. K. Ogden. 2nd ed. International Library of Psychology, Philosophy, and Scientific Method. London: Kegan Paul, Trench, Trübner, 1935.

Vidu, Adonis. *Atonement, Law, and Justice: The Cross in Historical and Cultural Contexts.* Grand Rapids: Baker, 2014.

Walen, Alec. "Retributive Justice." In *The Stanford Encyclopedia of Philosophy*, edited by Edward N. Zalta. Summer 2014 ed. http://plato.stanford.edu/entries/justice-retributive/.

Warmke, Brandon. "Divine Forgiveness I: Emotion and Punishment-Forbearance Theories." *Philosophy Compass* 12, no. 9 (2017): e12440. https://doi.org/10.1111/phc3.12440.

Warmke, Brandon. "Divine Forgiveness II: Reconciliation and Debt-Cancellation Theories." *Philosophy Compass* 12, no. 9 (2017): e12439. https://doi.org/10.1111/phc3.12439.

Watts, Rikki E. "Jesus' Death, Isaiah 53, and Mark 10:45: A Crux Revisited." In *Jesus and the Suffering Servant: Isaiah 53 and Christian Origins*, edited by William H. Bellinger Jr. and William R. Farmer, 125–51. Harrisburg, Penn.: Trinity Press International, 1998.

Weihofen, Henry. "The Effect of a Pardon." *University of Pennsylvania Law Review* 88, no. 2 (December 1939): 177–93.

Weiss, Alexander. "Christus Jesus als Weihegeschenk oder Sühnemal? Anmerkungen zu einer neueren Deutung von hilasterion (Röm 3,25) samt einer Liste der epigraphischen Belege." *Zeitschrift für die Neutestamentliche Wissenschaft* 105, no. 2 (2014): 294–302.

Wellum, Steve. "Penal Substitution as the Ground for Forensic Justification and Imputation." Paper presented at the annual meeting of the Evangelical Theological Society, Providence, R.I., November 15–17, 2017.

Wenham, Gordon J. "The Theology of Old Testament Sacrifice." In *Sacrifice in the Bible*, edited by Roger T. Beckwith and Martin J. Selman, 75–87. Grand Rapids: Baker Book House, 1995.

Wenz, Gunther. *Geschichte der Versöhnungslehre in der evangelischen Theologie der Neuzeit.* 2 vols. Munich: Chr. Kaiser, 1984.

White, Mark D., ed. *Retributivism: Essays on Theory and Policy*. Oxford: Oxford University Press, 2011.

Whybray, R. N. *Thanksgiving for a Liberated Prophet: An Interpretation of Isaiah Chapter 53*. Journal for the Study of the Old Testament Supplement Series 4. Sheffield: JSOT, 1978.

Williston, Samuel. "Does a Pardon Blot Out Guilt?" *Harvard Law Review* 28, no. 7 (May 1915): 647–63.

Wright, N. T. *The Day the Revolution Began: Reconsidering the Meaning of Jesus's Crucifixion*. San Francisco: HarperOne, 2016.

Wringe, Bill. "Pre-punishment, Communicative Theories of Punishment, and Compatibilism." *Pacific Philosophical Quarterly* 93, no. 2 (2012): 125–36.

Zaibert, Leo. *Punishment and Retribution*. Aldershot, UK: Ashgate, 2006.

ANCIENT AND MEDIEVAL SOURCES

Abelard, *Commentary on the Epistle to the Romans*

Anselm, *Cur Deus homo*

Aquinas, *Compendium theologiae*

Aquinas, *Summa contra gentiles*

Aquinas, *Summa theologiae*

Augustine, *Against Faustus*

Augustine, *Confessions*

Augustine, *Enchiridion*

Augustine, *The Merits and Forgiveness of Sins*

Augustine, *On the Christian Struggle*

Augustine, *On the Trinity*

Augustine, *Sermons*

Basil, *Homily on Psalm xlviii*

Bernard of Clairvaux, *Letter to Pope Innocent, Against Certain Heads of Abaelard's Heresies*

Cyril of Alexandria, *Ad reginas de recta fide, Oratio altera*

Cyril of Alexandria, *Contra Julianum*

Cyril of Alexandria, *Glaphyrorum in Exodum*

Cyril of Jerusalem, *Catechesis*

Dio Chrysostom, *Orations*

Eusebius, *Demonstration of the Gospel*

Gregory Nazianzus, *Against Apollinarius*

Gregory Nazianzus, *Orations*

Gregory of Nyssa, *Catechetical Oration*
Irenaeus, *Against Heresies*
John Chrysostom, *Homilies on I Timothy*
John Chrysostom, *Homilies on II Corinthians*
John Duns Scotus, *Distinctiones in quatuor libros Sententiarum*
Josephus, *Antiquities of the Jews*
The Lindos Chronicle
Origen, *Commentary on the Epistle to the Romans*
Origen, *Commentary on the Gospel of John*
Origen, *Commentary on the Gospel of Matthew*
Origen, *Homilies on Leviticus*
Origen, *Homilies on Numbers*
Philo, *On the Life of Moses*
Sibylline Oracles

COURT OPINIONS

U.S. Supreme Court
Flemming v. Nestor, 363 U.S. 603 (1960)
Biddle v. Perovich, 274 U.S. 480 (1927)
Burdick v. United States, 236 U.S. 79 (1915)
The John G. Stevens, 170 U.S. 113 (1898)
Knote v. United States, 95 U.S. 149 (1877)
Ex parte Garland, 71 U.S. 333 (1866)
Ex parte Wells, 59 U.S. 307 (1855)
United States v. Wilson, 32 U.S. 150 (1833)

U.S. Appeals Court
Hirschberg v. Commodity Futures Trading Commission, 414 F.3d 679 (7th Cir. 2005)
Groseclose v. Plummer, 106 F.2d 311 (9th Cir. 1939)
Robertson v. Shinseki, 26 Vet. App. 169 (2013)

Delaware
State *ex rel.* Wier v. Peterson, 369 A.2d 1076 (Del. 1976)

District of Columbia
In re Abrams, 689 A.2d 6 (D.C. 1997)

Florida
R.J.L. v. State, 887 So.2d 1268 (Fla. 2004)

Indiana

Sanders v. State, 85 Ind. 318 (1882)

Kentucky

Fletcher v. Graham, 192 S.W.3d 350 (Ky. 2006)

Nevada

Sang Man Shin v. State (*In re* Sang Man Shin), 125 Nev. 100 (2009)

New York

People *ex rel.* Prisament v. Brophy, 38 N.E.2d 468 (1941)
In re an Attorney, 86 N.Y. 563 (1881)
In re DePuy, 7 F. Cas. 506 (S.D.N.Y. 1869)

Oregon

Haugen v. Kitzhaber, 306 P.3d 592 (2013)
In re Spenser, 22 F. Cas. 921 (1878)

Texas

Dixon v. McMullen, 527 F. Supp. 711 (N.D. Tex. 1981)

United Kingdom

Pharmaceutical Society of Great Britain v. Storkwain Ltd., [1986] 2 All
    ER 635 (H.L.)
Allen v. Whitehead, [1930] 1 K.B. 211
Sherras v. De Rutzen, [1895] 1 Q.B. 918
Mostyn v. Fabrigas, (1774) 1 Cowp. 161
Cuddington v. Wilkins, (1615) 80 Eng. Rep. 231 (K.B.)

INDEX OF AUTHORS AND SUBJECTS

Abelard, Peter, 121–24, 181, 268
Abraham, 46, 73, 74n50, 177
acceptation, 198
acquittal: divine, 44, 56n6, 60n16, 127, 210n36, 243; legal, 231n47
act: from duty *vs.* in accordance with duty, 177; quality of *vs.* effect of, 179–80
actus reus, 156, 158, 180, 189, 232
Adam, 80, 100, 103, 187, 190n35
Adams, Robert, 177
Alcestis, 159n29
Alston, William, 177
altar, 21, 23, 25, 26, 27n33, 30, 31; *see also* expiation; forgiveness
amnesty, 220, 231n48
animal sacrifice: of birds, 24n25, 25, 30; and blood: *see* blood; and burnt offering, 20–22, 31; descriptions of rituals, 20–22, 24–26, 27n33, 30–31; foreignness to modern mind, 18; functions of, 18–19, 20, 22; and guilt offerings, 20, 21,

43–45; and hand-laying ritual, 24, 27n33, 28n34, 28n35, 43, 79, 93; identification of offerer with animal, 24–25, 27n33, 28, 43, 79–80, 93; Levitical system of, 20, 22–23, 43–45, 63, 72, 79–80, 93, 94, 216n2; Levitical system of (prior to), 20n12, 25n28; pagan systems of, 24n24, 27n33; and peace offerings, 20, 21, 27n32, 28n34; as "preliminary event," 29–30; and scapegoat ritual: *see* scapegoat; and sin offerings, 15, 17, 21, 23, 25n27, 30, 33, 69, 98, 177; symbolic nature of, 18, 24–25, 27, 42, 43, 79–80; and transferral of sin, 27n33; and Yom Kippur, 30–31, 42, 66, 69, 80; *see also* expiation; grain offering; guilt, offering; propitiation; representation; sacrifice; substitution
annihilation, 175
Anselm, 92, 111, 113–18, 119n4, 120,

121, 122, 124, 169, 195, 217n3,
247–48, 268; *see also* satisfaction;
satisfaction theory; theories of the
atonement
anti-supernaturalism, 111n19
apologetics, 14n2
apostasy, 23–24, 30
Aquinas, Thomas, 118–21, 129, 182,
248; *see also* satisfaction; satisfaction
theory
Aristotle, 180
ark of the covenant, 2, 66
'āšām, 20, 43–44; *see also* guilt, offering
associations, unincorporated: 187n27;
see also corporations
atonement: concept in Isaiah 53,
44, 45; confusion about term,
3–5, 265; as covering of sin in
God's sight, 3n3, 62; Day of: *see*
animal sacrifice, and Yom Kippur;
distinctions in types of, 31; doctrine
of: *see* doctrine of the atonement;
English *vs.* German treatments
of, vii–viii, 3; and human sacrifice,
45–46; limited, 165n40, 212, 271;
meanings of 'atonement,' 1–5;
Pentateuchal narratives on, 28; as
ransom: *see* ransom; theories of: *see*
theories of the atonement; *see also*
death of Christ; doctrine of the
atonement; *hilas*; imputation; *kpr,
kippēr*; reconciliation; substitution;
suffering; theories of the atonement
"at-onement" or "at onement," 1–2,
4–5, 211n36, 213, 235n57; *see also*
atonement; Christ, union with;
God, union with
attribution principle, 189
Augustine, 103–7, 109–10; affirmation
of penal substitution, 105–6
Averbeck, Richard, 26n31, 32, 44n17,
45n18, 68n38
Ayer, A.J., 8–9
Azazel: *see* scapegoat

Bailey, Daniel, 2n2, 35n48, 63n27,
67n38, 68
baptism, 83, 206, 267
beatific vision, 134, 148n4, 209
Beckwith, Francis, 150n6, 186n25
Bernard of Clairvaux, 123
Blackstone, William, 219, 243
blame, blamelessness,
blameworthiness, 55, 156, 158,
180, 188–91, 200–202, 232; *see also*
innocence
Blocher, Henri, 55n4, 62n23
blood: of Christ: *see* Christ, blood of;
of the covenant, 16; rite of animal
sacrifice, 22n18, 26–27, 29–31, 66,
69, 85
Borg, Marcus, 184n20
Breiner, Nikolaus, 119n5
Brunner, Emil, 9n13

Calvin, John, 126–27, 209, 210–11
canonical criticism, 14n1
Caplow, Stacy, 254n51
Carson, D. A., 53, 55n4, 56n6, 62, 64,
66, 180
Cassuto, Umberto, 25n28
censure: *see* condemnation
Childs, Brevard, 14n1
Christ: as advocate before divine judge,
33; baptism of, 206; as bearer of
sins, 7n7, 47–49, 75, 94, 96–97, 104,
258; blood of, 15, 63, 69–70, 86,
104, 122, 126; corporate solidarity
with, 80–83; death of: *see* death of
Christ; deity of, 95, 97, 128, 261,
271; as deliverer from wrath: *see*
death of Christ, as propitiatory;
faith in, 52, 54, 62, 71, 73, 75, 77,
85, 88, 96, 99, 118, 119n4, 126,
128, 129, 138, 181, 213–14, 259; as
high priest, 4, 32, 80n1, 99, 211n36;
incarnation of: *see* incarnation; as
mediator: *see* mediator/mediation;
as mercy seat, 63n27, 65–66; as

Messiah, 16, 39n3, 61n20, 70n45; passion of: *see* death of Christ; personal virtue of, 182; punishment of: *see* punishment, of Christ; as representative, 79–85, 204–5; resurrection of, 5–6, 39n3, 81n1, 83–85, 100, 101, 103, 128, 206, 267; as sacrifice for sin, 4, 32, 80–82, 94–95, 98–99, 103, 104, 177–78; self-understanding of, 49; as Servant of the Lord, 17, 47–49, 81n2; sin imputed to: *see* imputation; as sin offering, 33, 76–77; threefold role of, 134; two natures of, 118; union with, 83–84, 127, 136–37, 204–6, 213n42, 221n15; as victim, 102, 106; work of: *see* atonement; *see also* God, union with; Servant of the Lord

Christian philosophers: *see* philosophers/philosophy

Christus Victor theory, 101, 102, 103, 107, 110, 111, 113, 215, 235, 267–68

Chrysostom, John, 98

Church Fathers, 91–92, 98, 110, 111, 141, 181, 257; Latin Fathers, 102, 111; *see also* Augustine; Chrysostom, John; doctrine of the atonement; Eusebius; Gregory Nazianzus; Gregory of Nyssa; Irenaeus; Origen

civil law, 114n1, 141, 149, 176, 188, 207, 217, 270; and God as private party, 167–72, 208n26, 214; *see also* creditor; criminal law

cleansing, 3, 22n18, 23, 27n33, 30–31, 45, 63, 85, 94–95

clemency, 72, 142, 217, 238, 240, 242, 244, 246n27, 247, 255, 256n56; forms of, 219–20, 231n48; *see also* mercy; pardon

Clines, David J. A., 14n1

commutation, 29n37, 169, 231n48,

239, 252–54, 256n56; definition of, 220

companies: *see* corporations

compensation, 114n1, 116–18, 119n4, 120, 121, 122, 157, 169, 186, 195, 196n3; *see also* satisfaction; satisfaction theory

compensation theory: *see* satisfaction theory

condemnation, 6, 34, 53, 60, 72, 149n5, 151–52, 153–55, 156–59, 203, 210, 217, 242, 266; and expressivism, 160–61; as forensic, 190n35; legal, 161, 171, 244, 258, 267; *see also* expressivism

Constitution, U.S., 159, 218–19, 225, 238, 244, 255

corporations, 187n27, 191, 199n8, 200, 202; *see also* associations, unincorporated; employer/ee

councils, ecumenical: *see* doctrine of the atonement, conciliar guidance on

counterfactuals, 155, 182, 230

covenant: ark of the, 2, 66; blood of the, 16; concept of, 52; -faithfulness interpretation: *see* divine justice; Paul, new perspective on; new, 16–17, 18, 71, 86–87; old, 16–17, 24, 57, 86–87

creditor, 114n1, 129–30, 133, 136, 141–42, 207–8, 214, 271; contrasted with judge, 168; contrasted with ruler, 139; *see also* civil law

Cremer, Hermann, 54–55

crime: *see* punishment, of crimes; sin, as crime

criminal law, 114n1, 149, 156–58, 168, 188–89, 191, 198–203, 207, 209, 214, 232, 237, 245, 270; *see also* civil law; God, as judge or ruler; judge

criminal liability, 187n27, 189, 202n14, 223; *see also* strict liability; vicarious liability

Crisp, Oliver, 170, 171, 191–92
cross, the, 2, 6, 47, 83–85, 94, 95, 101, 102n8, 121–22, 126, 128, 148–49, 171, 192, 213, 218, 261, 267; as metaphor of Gospel message, 5
Crossan, John Dominic, 184n20
Crouch, Jeffery, 219n10, 240, 253n47
Cur Deus homo, 92, 113, 115, 116, 118, 122, 124
Cyril of Alexandria, 107n15

damnation: *see* hell
Day of Atonement: *see* animal sacrifice, and Yom Kippur
death: *see* animal sacrifice; death of Christ; punishment; sin, consequences or penalty of
death of Christ, 1, 3, 5, 52, 98–99, 180, 181, 218n7, 259, 267, vi; as compensatory: *see* compensation; as expiatory, 32–34, 63n27, 69–72, 95, 119n4, 121, 126–27, 128, 184; infinite value of, 95, 118, 119, 131, 134–35, 209–10, 212, 261; interpretation of, 15–16, 32–35, 37; Jesus' attitude toward, 15–18; NT motifs for, 32, 35, 37–38; OT background of, 18, 37; as propitiatory, 33–34, 53, 63–67, 96, 99, 119n4, 121, 125–27, 171, 184, 196–98, 200; as ransom payment, 98–99, 100, 101, 102n8, 108, 111, 122, 267; as sacrifice, 4, 32–34, 69, 70, 92–93, 94–95, 98–99, 104, 113–14, 171, 177, 259–62; substitutionary nature of, 16, 80, 83, 97–98, 104, 118, 125–27, 134, 140–41, 148, 174, 177; universal scope of, 62, 80, 82n2, 84–85, 88, 95, 212; *see also* punishment, of Christ; representation; substitution; theories of the atonement
debt: pecuniary, 116, 130, 133, 136, 139, 168, 185, 196n3, 207, 220;

penal, 114n1, 117–20, 121, 129–31, 133, 134, 140–42, 171, 196n3, 213, 214, 215; *see also* creditor
delegation principle, 189, 201n12
Denney, James, 259–60
desert, just, 87, 96, 104, 175, 178, 202, 216, 241, 242n15, 246n27, 261; conditions for, 232n50
DeSilva, David, 65n30, 65n31
deterrence: *see* punishment, consequentialist view of
devil, the: *see* Satan
dik-: *dikaiōma*, 52, 74; *dikaioō*, 52, 59–60; *dikaios*, 52; *dikaiōs*, 52; *dikaiōsynē*, 52, 53–62, 74
"dilemma of the merciful judge," 242n15, 243–44
distributive, 58, 132
Divine Command Theory, 116, 133, 177, 178n3, 269
divine justice: as conqueror of Satan, 103–5; as eschatological, 34n47, 72, 72n47, 175, 242, 244; as essential property of God, 54, 77, 115, 116, 129, 132–33, 135, 178–80, 182, 198–99, 206, 243, 247; not an activity of God, 56n6; NT motifs for, 52, 53–61, 62, 63–68, 69, 70, 71–77; OT motifs for, 51–52; as retributive, 57, 178–79; satisfaction of: *see* satisfaction; Septuagintal language for, 58, 59–60, 63, 64, 66; Turretin on, 132–37; *see also* justice; retributive justice
divine righteousness: *see* divine justice
doctrine of the atonement: Anselm's advance over Church Fathers, 268; central NT question of, 6; Church Fathers' motifs for, 92, 93, 94, 96, 98, 102n8, 103–6, 110–11, 267–68; conciliar guidance on, 6, 91–92, 265; methodology of formulating, 7–9, 13–15, 202; as morally contemptible, 8–9; as

multifaceted, 13, 15, 34n48, 35, 94, 112, 215, 266–68; nineteenth-century literature on, viii, 9n13; NT motifs for, 15, 32, 74n50, 92, 266–67; in Origen, 94–102; Reformers' view of, 5, 132, 137, 161; summary of biblical data on, 266–67; summary of dogmatic history on, 267–68; thematic *vs.* authorial study of, 14–15; *vs.* theory of, 6–9; in Turretin, 133–37; and use of legal fictions, 185; *see also* divine justice; reconciliation; redemption; representation; sacrifice; satisfaction; theories of the atonement

Dodd, C. H., 63–64, 64n28

Duff, Anthony, 202

Dunn, J. D. G., 61, 62n23, 85n4

eisegesis, 7n7, 8

employer/ee, 188–89, 190n34, 191, 192, 200–202, 207; *see also* corporations

Eusebius, 92–94

Euthyphro Dilemma, 116

exegesis, 7n7, 8

exiles, Jewish, 16n5, 40, 41, 45n18

expiation: in Christ: *see* death of Christ, as expiatory; definition of, 18; legal theory of, 94; in Levitical sacrifices, 20–30, 32, 93, 94; as necessary for forgiveness, 23, 82n2, 96, 107, 129, 163; in Passover sacrifice, 33n45; *see also* propitiation

expiatory sacrifices, 20–30; *see also* animal sacrifice; death of Christ, as expiatory; propitiation; satisfaction

expressivism, 151, 155–56, 158–59, 162, 269; without condemnation of Christ, 160–61

expungement, 31n41, 33, 224n27, 226, 227, 228, 229, 230, 271

faith: *see* Christ, faith in

Farmer, William, 39

Feinberg, Joel, 151, 152n11, 153–54, 156, 159, 160, 179

forgiveness: in philosophical literature, 216; as result of sacrifice, 22–23, 30, 32, 42n10, 70, 92, 171; third-party, 217n3; *see also* God, forgiveness of; pardon; sin, forgiveness of

Forsyth, P. T., 3n3, 9, 143n11

Gathercole, Simon, 159n29

Gentiles, 17, 49, 57, 61n20, 68, 70n45, 76

Gese, Hartmut, 28n35, 81n2, 82n2

Gestrich, Christoph, viii

God: as analogous to an employer, 201n12; emotion in, 72n47, 107n14, 217n3; fellowship with, 17; as feudal lord, 114, 268; forgiveness of, 23n21, 42n10, 62, 70, 71, 85, 97, 114, 128, 129, 166, 269; forgiveness of—as legal pardon, 72, 171, 214, 216–18, 220–22, 233–35, 242, 246–49, 256–58, 270–72; forgiveness of—as unconditional, 163–65; free choice of, 116, 120–21, 129, 132, 133, 137, 138, 165, 196; hatred of sin: *see* sin, hatred of; hatred of sinners: *see* sinner/s, hatred of; holiness of, 19, 59, 133, 142, 182, 217n3, 262; honor owed to, 69n44, 114–16, 217n3, 268; as judge or ruler, 51–52, 56–57, 114n1, 129, 137, 139, 142, 167–72, 183, 186, 197–98, 206, 219n11, 243–44; judgment of, 16, 17, 19, 33, 58n13, 87, 126, 175, 242; justice of: *see* divine justice; love of: *see* love of God; as monarch, 114, 170, 219n10; omniscience of: *see* omniscience; pardon of: *see* pardon, divine; power of, 103, 109–10, 217n3, 243, 257; as private party,

167–72, 208n26, 214; righteousness of: *see* divine justice; threefold role of, 133–34; union with, 3–5, 82n2, 166–67, 169, 171, 209; *see also* Christ, union with; wrath of: *see* wrath of God

Godbey, John Charles, 128n6

Gomes, Alan, 128n6

governmental theory, 137–42, 204n16, 268; *see also* theories of the atonement

grace: infused, 5; prevenient, 214

grain offering, 20, 22n15, 24n25, 25, 32, 266; *see also* sacrifice

Green, Joel, 15

Greenberg, Jim, 22n18

Gregory Nazianzus, 102n8

Gregory of Nyssa, 101, 107–9, 262

Grotius, Hugo, 137–42, 159, 167–68, 171, 177, 181, 208, 248, 260, 268, 270

Groves, J. Alan, 43n14, 45

guilt, 22, 98, 105, 180, 182, 192–93, 222, 223–25, 229; confession of, 252, 254n51; definition of, 232–33; expungement of: *see* expungement; offering, 43–45; replication of, 187; transfer of, 98, 127, 161, 182–83, 186–87; *see also* animal sacrifice; imputation

Gundry, Robert, 73n49

Hall, Jerome, 150n6, 176n2

Hamilton, Victor, 25n28

hand-laying ritual: *see* animal sacrifice, and hand-laying ritual

Hart, H. L. A., 154, 155–56

hatred: *see* sin, hatred of; sinner/s, hatred of; wrath of God

Heine, Ronald, 97n4, 99n6

hell, 101, 105n13, 111–12, 117, 126, 175, 203, 209, 229, 235; *see also* punishment, infinite (duration or intensity)

Hermisson, H.-J., 40–41

Hezekiah, 33n45

high priest: *see* Christ, as high priest; priest, Levitical

hilas-, 3, 32, 62, 64n28; *hilaskesthai*, 2, 32, 35n48, 63, 64n28, 265; *hilaskomai*, 2n2, 66; *hilasmos*, 2n2, 32; *hilastērion*, 2n2, 32, 34, 35n48, 63–68, 64n29, 69–70

Hilborn, David, 148n2

historical criticism, 14n2

Hofius, Otfried, 40, 41, 43, 47n23, 69n44, 72n47, 81n2, 84n3

Holmes, Oliver Wendell, 239, 252–55

Holy of Holies, 2n2, 19, 65, 80, 81n1

Holy Spirit, 3–5, 211n26, 213, 271; indwelling of the, 5, 233–35

Horton, Michael, 191n35

Hultgren, Stephen, 34n48

Humbert, W. H., 239, 250n38, 254n52, 255n55, 256n58

identification doctrine, 187n27; *see also* corporations

impurity: *see* sin

imputation: analysis of, 73–74, 131, 184n20; as forensic, 126, 135–36, 188, 190n35, 210, 234n53; of guilt to innocent person, 189–90, 270; of righteousness to sinners, 54, 55, 71, 73–75, 77, 87, 126, 135–37, 140, 184n10, 204–5, 213n42, 233, 242, 270; of sin to Christ, 76–77, 87, 93–94, 97, 98, 102n8, 105, 125–27, 135–37, 140, 161, 182–83, 184, 186–87, 191, 204–5, 213n42; *see also* guilt; penal substitution; vicarious liability

incarnation, viii, 6, 92, 95–96, 101, 107, 108n15, 114, 118, 123, 136, 204–6

infinity: potential, 209n34, 271; *see also*

punishment, infinite (duration or intensity)
innocence, 130, 134, 138, 140, 153n12, 154–55, 173–74, 190, 231, 235, 270; *see also* blame, blamelessness, blameworthiness; Servant of the Lord, innocence of
Institutes of Elenctic Theology, 132
Irenaeus, 100, 111
Irons, Charles, 58–61
Isaac, 46, 177

Janowski, Bernd, 24n24, 40n6, 44n17, 81n2
Jeffery, Steve, 148, 205n19, 212n39, 213n42
Jesus of Nazareth: *see* Christ
John Chrysostom: *see* Chrysostom, John
judge (role), 168; *see also* creditor; criminal law; God, as judge or ruler
justice: consequentialist theory of, 174–76; corrective, 157; desert *vs.* virtue, 132; distributive, 58–59, 132; divine: *see* divine justice; human *vs.* divine systems of, 149–50; NT motifs for, 52, 53–77; OT motifs for, 51–52, 56–59, 61; punitive, 57, 61, 70, 116, 129–30, 132, 150, 157, 160, 169, 202; retributive theories of: *see* retributive justice; system: *see* law; and wrath of God: *see* wrath of God; *see also* divine justice; righteousness
justification, 33–34, 57, 60n16, 71–75, 136, 140, 205, 233; doctrine of, 32, 51, 210, 233–34; as forensic, 51, 127, 169n49, 184n20, 186, 190n35, 210, 233–34, 267, 272; *see also* divine justice; righteousness

Kant, Immanuel, 242; *see also* philosophers/philosophy, Kantian

katalassō, 216n2; see also *hilas-*; *kpr*, *kippēr*
katallagē, 1, 2, 265; *see also* atonement; reconciliation
Kobil, Daniel, 220, 246n27
Korsch, Dietrich, 115n1
kpr, *kippēr*, 2–3, 22–23, 26, 28, 31n41, 44, 63, 64n28, 85, 265; *kapporēt*, 2n2, 27n33, 66; *kippurim*, 2n2; *kōper*, 2n2, 28; *see also* atonement; mercy seat; ransom

Last Supper, the, 39, 86
law: civil: *see* civil law; criminal: *see* criminal law; Germanic, 116; natural, 133; OT, 53; philosophy of: *see* philosophers/philosophy, of law; positive, 139, 140; relaxation of, 133, 134, 139, 140, 142; Roman, 116–17, 218n8; rule of, 168; tort, 156–57; *see also* legal fictions; penal substitution theories, law and forgiveness on
Leftow, Brian, 243
legal fictions, 74n50, 183–86, 191–92; *see also* imputation; penal substitution
legal moralism, 178–79, 181, 244n20
Lewis, David, 155, 199–201
liability: *see* criminal liability; punishment, liability to; strict liability; vicarious liability
Lind, Douglas, 186
Longenecker, R. N., 68
love of God: expressed by or quality of God, 110, 122, 126n3, 163, 166, 182, 208, 269; expressed to God, 122–23; as unconditional, 163, 164n40, 166; *see also* God, forgiveness of
Luther, Martin, 126
lytrōsis, 85–86; *see also* ransom

mala in se, 157n23
mala prohibita, 157
Marshall, I. H., 2, 72n47
Marshall, John, 220–22, 238–39, 242, 249–51, 252–53
Matthews, Kenneth, 25n28
McGrath, Alister, 233
meaning, linguistic, 41n10, 148n3; and literal *vs.* figurative meaning, 67; *vs.* reference, 66–67; *see also* metaphorical language
mediator/mediation, 24, 86, 96, 106n14, 132, 134, 136, 137, 204
mens rea, 156, 158, 180, 188n29, 189, 232
mercy, 67–68, 116, 179, 191, 208, 220, 239–42, 242n15, 246–47; consistency with retributive justice, 168; as essential property of God, 129, 247; explication of, 208n28; *see also* clemency; pardon, as act of grace or mercy
mercy seat, 2n2, 63n27, 65, 99–100; *see also* Christ, as mercy seat; *hilas-*, *hilastērion*; place-taking; righteousness
mereological fusions, 206n22
Messiah, 16, 39n3, 48; *see also* Christ, as Messiah
Messing, Noah, 218n6
metaphorical language, 34, 42, 63n27, 65, 67–69, 215, 265–67; *see also* meaning, linguistic
Milgrom, Jacob, 20n13, 23, 24, 28n34, 30n39, 43
Mitros, Joseph, 111
Moberly, Walter, 25n29
modern synthesis, the, 7n8
Moffitt, David, 29n38, 81n1
Moo, Douglas, 56n6, 59n14, 59n16, 66–67
Moore, Kathleen Dean, 176n2, 217, 219n10, 238, 241, 244, 245, 246

Moore, Michael, 181, 232n50
moral influence theory, 121–24, 128, 137, 138, 181–82; in abstraction from penal substitution, 259–60; disincentives to alienation, 260–61; incentives to reconciliation, 261–62
moral transformation: *see* sanctification
Moreland, J.P., 112n20
Morison, Samuel, 217–18, 224n27, 238, 240n12, 242n15, 244–47
Morris, Leon, 29n37, 51, 52, 63n25, 63n27, 64n28, 86, 190n35
Moses, 16, 28, 45–46, 93, 104, 177
Murphy, Jeffrie, 168, 246
Murphy, Mark, 151–55, 156–58, 160–62, 182–83, 186, 190n35
Mwale, Emmanuel, 186n25, 187n26, 190, 200–201

Nazianzus, Gregory, 102n8
negligence, 156, 158, 188
new perspective on Paul: *see* Paul, new perspective on
Nicole, Roger, 63n27, 64n28

O'Collins, Gerald, 184n20
omnipotence: *see* God, power of
omniscience, 219n11, 243, 245
On Jesus Christ Our Savior, 128
Origen, 94–102, 106, 107
Oswalt, J.N., 19n10
Ovey, Michael, 148, 205n19, 212n39, 213n42

pardon, 20n13, 23n21, 24, 60n16, 169–71, 179n10, 211n36, 213; as act of grace or mercy, 219–21, 238–42, 244, 246, 249, 252, 253n48, 271; appropriation of, 249–57; conditionality of, 256–57; definition of, 220; divine, 77, 216–18, 219, 220–22, 233–35, 242, 246–49, 256–58, 271–72; effects

of, 218, 221–35; and English legal
precedence, 219, 222, 238–39,
249–51; as executive prerogative,
60n16, 62n24, 72, 172, 183n18,
197, 217, 218–20, 231n48, 238–39,
242n15, 243–44, 249–52, 255, 271;
as expression of justice, 241–42,
244; justification of, 237–49;
limitations on, 220–21; as political
weapon, 253n47; private *vs.* public
construals of, 238–40, 249–50,
252–53, 254n48, 255, 256; without
satisfaction, 182; *see also* clemency;
forgiveness; mercy
passion of Christ: *see* death of Christ
Passover, the: as explanatory setting,
16, 86
Passover elements: symbolic nature of,
16
Paul, 1, 3, 5, 6, 32, 33, 34, 51, 77, 83,
84–85, 159n29, 184n20, 190n35,
218n8, 267; new perspective on,
16n5, 54–62, 70–71, 191n35; and
use of righteousness language,
53–62, 233; *see also* pre-Pauline
formula
peace offering: *see* animal sacrifice
penal substitution: analogs in justice
system, 198–203; analogs in
other human affairs, 205n18;
consistency with expressivism,
160–61, 269; definition, nature of,
conditions for, 82n2, 134, 147–49;
and "definitional stop" to debate,
154; justification of, 176, 177, 178,
179–82; legal fictions and, 184–86;
metaethical context of, 116, 177,
197–98; objections to—moral,
130–31, 134, 136, 140, 152, 173–76,
182, 196, 209, 269; objections
to—philosophical coherence or
possibility, 128, 130, 149, 150–52,
153, 155, 159, 160–62, 172, 190,

196, 217n3, 269; objections to—
theological coherence, 162–64,
171, 172, 269; and the Servant of
the Lord, 40–43, 46n20; theories:
see penal substitution theories;
as unsatisfactory, 197; without
expressivism, 155–60; without
punishment, 153–55, 176, 195–96;
see also imputation; place-taking;
punishment; Socinus, Faustus;
substitution; vicarious liability
penal substitution theories, 125–37,
163n39, 169, 170, 173, 192, 195n1,
196, 206; inclusionary, 207, 214;
law and forgiveness on, 166–67;
objections to: *see* penal substitution,
objections to; of the Reformers,
125–27, 132–37; *see also* penal
substitution; place-taking
penalty: *see* punishment, *vs.* penalties;
sin, consequences or penalty of
penance, sacrament of, 117, 119n4
Pentateuch: categories of sin in: *see*
sin; centrality of death in, 28;
consequences for sin in, 25n28,
43; *see also* sin; *see also* atonement,
Pentateuchal narratives on
personhood, 206n22
philosophers/philosophy: analytic,
vii–viii, 8; Christian, vii, viiin2,
7–8, 149, 169, 265, 269; Kantian,
177, 246n27; of law, 149–50, 162,
196, 268; Molinist, 167, 212n40; of
time, 229
place-taking, 40n6, 82n2, 203–4; *see*
also mercy seat; representation;
substitution
Plantinga, Alvin, 111n19, 177n6
pre-Pauline formula, the, 6; *see also*
Christ, resurrection of
priest, Levitical, 20, 21, 22, 25–26,
28n4, 30, 32, 42, 44, 71–72, 80; *see*
also animal sacrifice; expiation

Prior, A. N., 229n43

propitiation: in Christ: *see* death of Christ, as propitiatory; definition of, 18, 195; in dogmatic history, 96, 99, 119n4; in Levitical sacrifices, 19–20, 63; in NT thought, 33, 34, 63–69, 77; in Passover sacrifice, 19; place of, 34, 67n38; *see also* expiation

propitiatory sacrifices, 19–20; *see also* animal sacrifice; death of Christ, as propitiatory; expiation; satisfaction

proxyhood, 204–7

punishment, 25, 27n33, 29, 58n13, 96, 98, 104, 130, 139; of Christ, 97, 104, 117, 126–27, 134–35, 138, 141, 148–49, 151–52, 171, 174, 176, 177, 182, 196, 204, 209–10, 212, 261, 267; consequentialist theory of, 138, 139, 174, 241; of crimes, 116, 131, 133, 154, 156–57, 227, 229, 232, 238, 245, 271; debt of: *see* debt, penal; "defective," 151–53; definition, nature of, conditions for, 140, 150–51, 152, 154, 156, 159, 160, 178, 269; and expressivism: *see* expressivism; and harsh treatment, 120, 149n5, 150–55, 156, 158, 161, 168, 195–96, 218n6, 269; infinite (duration or intensity), 134–35, 203, 209; of the innocent, 153n12, 154–55, 174, 176; justification of, 134, 150, 159, 179–82; liability to, 41–42, 76, 127, 140, 171, 189, 191, 210n36, 213, 220, 232–34, 241, 257, 266; *vs.* penalties, 153–60, 176, 199; practice of, 159, 162, 179, 244, 246, 247; of Servant of the Lord: *see* Servant of the Lord; substitutionary: *see* penal substitution; terminology for, 132; *see also* animal sacrifice; death of Christ; guilt; hell; justice, punitive; penal substitution; sin

Quine, W. V. O., 229n43
Quinn, Philip, 177, 199n8
Quinton, Anthony, 154–55

Rainbolt, George, 247

ransom, 26, 28–29, 63, 86, 93, 95n3, 98–99, 108; as metaphor for penal substitution, 215; paid to God, 215; theory, 108, 122, 267–68; *see also* death of Christ; *kpr*, *kippēr*; substitution; theories of the atonement

reconciliation: between God and Israel, 17, 18, 28, 30–31, 46; between God and man, 1–2, 23, 29, 65n32, 84, 111, 117, 121, 122–23, 126, 163n39, 216n2; in human relationships, 8; ministry of, 1, 2, 84; *see also hilaskesthai*; *katallagē*; *kpr*, *Versöhnung*

redemption, 62–63, 85–87, 98, 103, 105, 123, 141; accomplished *vs.* applied, 213; actual *vs.* potential, 213n42; role of divine power in, 107–8, 110; *see also* ransom

regeneration, 5

relationship with God, 19n10, 23n21, 44–45, 51, 57n8, 60n16, 114n1, 167, 169, 200, 201n12, 261; *see also* restoration

relaxation (of law): *see* law, relaxation of

remission, 72, 104–6, 116, 119n4, 120n6, 128, 129–30, 132–33, 137, 138, 139, 141–42, 152, 205n21, 243, 246n27, 257; compatibility with satisfaction, 207–9; definition of, 220

repentance, 23, 24, 129, 166, 256, 272

representation: by Christ: *see* Christ, as representative; and Levitical sacrifices, 79–80; personal, 79–85; and representative substitution, 203–4, 267; simple, 203–4; *vs.* symbolization, 80, 204n16; *see also*

animal sacrifice, Levitical system of;
Christ, corporate solidarity with;
Christ, union with; substitution
reprieve, 70, 218, 231n48, 238, 239,
254–55; definition of, 220
respondeat superior, 188
restoration: of civil rights, 224, 232,
257; of Israel's fortunes, 16–17, 41,
45n18; of moral character, 227, 234;
of relationship, 23n21, 29, 120n6;
see also God, forgiveness of
retributive justice, 129, 133, 138, 140,
167, 168–69, 171, 174, 175, 196,
198–203, 229, 245; compatibility
with satisfaction, 207–9; definition
of, 178; as essential property of
God, 107, 178–79, 182, 243–44,
247–48, 269; negative, 178, 179–81,
182, 193, 245, 270; positive,
178–79, 181, 241, 242, 245,
270; prima facie *vs.* ultima facie
demands of, 179–82, 191, 244,
247n27, 270; pure, 179n10, 241–42,
244, 246n27, 249; renaissance
in theories of, 175–76, 241; *see
also* divine justice; justice; penal
substitution; punishment
retributivism: *see* retributive justice
righteousness: alien, 73n49, 233;
of Christ, 104, 135; as covenant
faithfulness: *see* Paul, new
perspective on; Dead Sea Scrolls'
language for, 58n13; divine: *see*
divine justice; extrabiblical Greek
language for, 59, 66; imputed: *see*
imputation; infused, 5, 74, 135,
169n49, 233, 234n53, 235n57; as
moral property, 56; as normative
concept, 54–56, 59; reckoned
to sinners: *see* imputation; and
"righteousness of God" (expression),
53–54, 56n6; *see also* divine justice;
imputation; justice
Ripstein, Arthur, 156–57

Ritschl, Albrecht, 3n3, 114n1, 123,
203n15
ritual: *see* animal sacrifice
Rivière, Jean, 95n3
Roberts, H. R. T., 168n47, 208n28,
237

Sach, Andrew, 148, 205n19, 212n39,
213n42
sacrifice: animal: *see* animal sacrifice;
expiatory: *see* expiatory sacrifices;
human: *see* atonement, and
human sacrifice; NT motifs for,
32–35; OT background of, 18–31;
Passover, 15, 16n8, 18, 33n45,
86; propitiatory: *see* propitiatory
sacrifices; as "table" of atonement
doctrine, 15, 35, 266; Yom Kippur:
see animal sacrifice, and Yom
Kippur; *see also* death of Christ, as
sacrifice; punishment; satisfaction;
substitution
sacrificial offering: *see* animal sacrifice;
death of Christ; expiation;
propitiation
sālaḥ: *see* God, forgiveness of
salvation, 96, 247; universal, 83–84,
182, 211–14, 271
sanctification, 33, 127, 211n36,
233–35, 271
Satan, 95n3, 98, 99n6, 100–102,
103–6, 107n15, 108, 113–14, 121,
126, 215; existence of, 111n19; as
having rights over man, 102, 103,
110, 111, 122
satisfaction, 69–70, 87, 95n3, 96, 106,
107, 114, 119n4, 141–42, 163–64,
165, 170, 205; Anselm's view of,
116–18, 119n4, 129, 169, 195, 247;
Aquinas' view of, 118–20, 129;
compatibility with remission, 207–9;
as independent of punishment,
117, 195–96; legal concepts in,
114n1; misrepresentations of

Anselm's theory, 114–15, 268; as necessary for salvation: *see* theories of the atonement, necessitarian; Reformers' view of, 117, 125–27, 247; Socinus' view of, 129–30, 141–42, 197, 207, 209; theory: *see* satisfaction theory; *see also* compensation; divine justice; pardon, without satisfaction; penal substitution; Stump, Eleonore

satisfaction theory: of Anselm, 110, 113–18, 119n4, 121, 123, 268; taken up by Aquinas, 119–21, 119n4, 124

scapegoat, 30–31, 32, 42; not a representative of the people, 80; *see also* animal sacrifice; representation; substitution

Schleiermacher, Friedrich, 143–44

Schreiber, Stefan, 65n32

Schwartz, Baruch, 41n10

sedek, 51, 55, 58: *see* divine justice; justice

Seifrid, Mark, 56n8, 57, 59n14, 59n16

Servant of the Lord, 34n47, 37–51, 75, 81–82, 96, 147, 180, 266, 272; as bearer of sins, 17–18, 41–42, 43–45, 46, 75, 96; eschatological context of, 18, 37; as guilt offering, 43–45; innocence of, 46n21; in NT: *see* Christ, as Servant of the Lord; punishment of, 40–43, 46n20, 47n23, 180; suffering of, 7n7, 39n3, 41–42, 46–47, 96

ship personification: 185–86, 192; *see also* legal fictions

sin: consequences or penalty of, 53, 87, 94, 96, 98, 101, 103–4, 117–19; as crime, 75, 133, 142, 216n1, 271; debt of: *see* debt; as dishonor, 115; as enmity with God, 106, 127n3, 133; forgiveness of, 41n10, 60n16, 70–72, 96, 212–13, 216–18; hatred of, 107, 141, 142, 181; high-handed, 23–24, 30; as impurity, 19, 22,

24n21, 71; infused, 182; offering: *see* animal sacrifice, and sin offerings; original, 9, 103n9, 106n14, 187, 206n22; Pentateuchal categories of, 23–24; remission of: *see* remission; sins as object of forgiveness, 72; universality of, 53

sin-bearing, 27n33, 41, 42, 43n11, 48; *see also* Christ, as bearer of sins; Servant of the Lord; substitution

sinner/s, 2, 41, 42n10, 60, 69, 70, 72, 72n47, 81n2, 102, 120n5, 123, 129, 130, 134, 140, 163n39, 165, 169, 171, 192, 202, 208, 213, 216n2, 217n3, 221n15, 246, 260, 261; hatred of, 107, 163n39, 166

Sklar, Jay, 25n28, 29

Smart, Alwynne, 168n47, 237

Smeaton, George, 63n26, 110

Socinus, Faustus, 9, 127–37, 138–43, 149, 151, 168, 171, 196n3, 197, 207, 209, 268, 270

Spieckermann, Hermann, 43n11, 46, 47

Steiner, Ashley M., 228n42

Stellvertretung, 40n6, 81, 203; *see also* place-taking; representation; substitution

Stephan, Hayden, 163n39

Stott, John, 148

Strasser, Mark, 253n48

strict liability, 157–58, 180, 187, 189, 232, 241; *see also* criminal liability; vicarious liability

Stump, Eleonore, 3–5, 119n3, 173, 235n57; and atonement theory assessment criteria, 7n7; objections to penal substitution, 162–65, 166–67, 168–72, 207–8, 209–10, 211–14; and "problem of application," 213; *see also* God, as judge or ruler; penal substitution; theories of the atonement, "Anselmian" substitution: -al representation, 203–4; -ary death, 27n33, 28n34, 29, 81n2, 93, 123, 125, 141, 159; -ary punishment: *see* penal substitution; -ary suffering, 7n7, 40, 42, 43, 46, 47–48, 81–82, 87, 93, 137, 148–49, 154, 168, 182, 214, 268, 270; exclusionary *vs.* inclusionary, 81–82, 204, 214; penal: *see* penal substitution; principle of, 26n31; simple, 136, 203–4; *see also* animal sacrifice; death of Christ; penal substitution; theories of the atonement

suffering: infinite, 209n34; punitive, 40, 42, 48, 246, 266, 268; representational, 81–82, 267, 270; unjust, 41; vicarious: *see* substitution, -ary suffering

suffering Servant, the: *see* Servant of the Lord

Sühne, 3, 4, 5, 265; *see also* expiation

superabundance: *see* death of Christ, infinite value of

superior/subordinate: *see* employer/ee

Supreme Court, U.S., 159, 219–20, 229, 238, 239, 240, 252, 255; *see also* List of Court Opinions in this volume

Swen, Blaine, 196n3, 198n6, 260, 261, 262

symbolization, 16, 24–25, 27n33, 29–31, 42–43, 93; *vs.* representation, 80, 204n16

tense/tenselessness, 206n22, 229–30, 233; *see also* time and timelessness

theodicy, 4, 196, 217n3

theologians/theology: analytic, vii–viii; Arminian, 167; Catholic, 233; contemporary, 111, 123, 149, 169, 176n2, 183n16, 184n20, 203, 216n2, 266; German, vii–viii, 3, 7n8, 54; liberal, vii–viii, 3n3,

7, 9n13, 114n1, 123; Lutheran, 54, 167; Molinist, 167, 212n40; Protestant, 4, 248; Reformed, 73n49, 132, 161, 167, 191, 209–10, 211–13, 233; systematic, vii, 8

theories of the atonement: Anselmian, 61n20, 113; "Anselmian," 163–64, 170, 173–74, 209–10, 211n36; canonical approach toward, 13–14, 266–67; *Christus Victor*: see *Christus Victor* theory; criteria of adequacy for, 7–9, 13, 35, 87, 195, 215; *vs.* doctrine of, 6–9; eisegetical treatments of, 7n7, 8; governmental: *see* governmental theory; medieval theories of, 113, 121; moral influence: *see* moral influence theory; necessitarian, 109–10, 121, 143n11, 163n39, 165, 171, 174n1, 196, 208–9, 247–48, 262, 272; non-necessitarian, 121, 137, 165, 171, 181n15, 196n3, 260, 268; paganized, 143n11; penal substitution: *see* penal substitution theories; punishment-forbearance, 8n9, 216n1; ransom: *see* ransom; Reformers', 5, 61n20, 117, 125–27, 137, 161; and relationship to biblical doctrine, 13; satisfaction: *see* satisfaction theory; Socinian, 127–28, 136; summary of philosophical reflections on, 268–72

time and timelessness, 213n42; *see also* tense/tenselessness

Torah, 51, 219n10

torts, 156, 190, 200; *see also* law

Turretin, Francis, 131, 132–37, 204–5, 209, 210, 221n15, 234n53, 268

universalism: *see* salvation, universal

vengeance, 55n4, 129, 151

Versöhnung, 3, 4, 265; *see also* reconciliation

vicarious liability, 180, 186–93, 199,
    200–202, 207, 270; *see also* criminal
    liability; imputation; strict liability
vicarious suffering: *see* substitution,
    -ary suffering
vicious circularity, 205
Vidu, Adonis, 150n6
vigilantism, 151
von Harnack, Adolf, 114n1

Walen, Alex, 151, 160
Warmke, Brandon, 216n1
Weiss, Alexander, 65n32
Wenham, Gordon, 20n11, 26n31
Whybray, R. N., 40
Williston, Samuel, 223–24, 228n42,
    230n45, 234
wrath of God, 28n34, 34, 53, 63–66,
    72, 77, 87, 107, 126, 129, 175,
    195, 217n3, 260, 261, 266, 272;
    Augustine's account of, 106–7; and

moral influence theory, 123; and
    Reformation theories, 127; *see also*
    sin, hatred of; sinner/s, hatred of
Wright, N. T., 16, 27n33, 29–30,
    34n47, 61n20, 70n45, 143n11; *see
    also* Paul, new perspective on

Yahweh, 40, 46, 47n23, 57
Yom Kippur: *see* animal sacrifice, and
    Yom Kippur

Zaibert, Leo, 154n17, 159, 178–79,
    244n20

INDEX OF ANCIENT SOURCES

ABELARD

Commentary on the Epistle to the Romans

2	122–24

ANSELM

Cur Deus homo

1.8	122
1.11	115
1.12	114n1, 116
1.13	116
1.19	116
1.23	113
1.24	116
2.7	118
2.11	118
2.11.18b	124
2.18b	118
2.19	118
2.20	118
12.19	113

AQUINAS

Compendium theologiae

200	120n6
227	119n5
231	119n5

Summa contra gentiles

4.54.9	120n6
4.55.22	119n5

Summa theologiae

3.1.2	121
3.46.2 *ad* 3	120
3.46.3	121
3.47.3	119n4
3.48.2	119
3.48.4	119n4
3.48.6 *ad* 3	119
3.49.3	119

AUGUSTINE

Against Faustus

14.4	104

14.6–7 — 104
14.7 — 105

Confessions
10 — 106

Enchiridion
10.33 — 106n14
14.48 — 103n9
14.51 — 105n13

The Merits and Forgiveness of Sins
1.61 — 105n11

On the Christian Struggle
100.11 — 109–10

On the Trinity
4.12.15 — 104, 105
4.13.16 — 103, 105n12
13.10.13 — 104, 109, 110
13.11.15 — 106
13.12.16 — 103n9, 105
13.13.17 — 103
13.14.18 — 103–4, 106, 110
13.15.19 — 106
13.16.20 — 105, 106–7, 109

Sermons
171.3 — 105

BASIL

Homily on Psalm xlviii
3 — 95n3

BERNARD OF CLAIRVAUX

Letter to Pope Innocent, Against Certain Heads of Abaelard's Heresies — 123

CYRIL OF ALEXANDRIA

Ad reginas de recta fide, Oratio altera
31 — 108n15

Contra Julianum
8.36–37 — 107n15

Glaphyrorum in Exodum
2.2 — 108n15

CYRIL OF JERUSALEM

Catechesis
13.33 — 95n3

DIO CHRYSOSTOM

Orations — 64n29

EUSEBIUS

Demonstration of the Gospel
1.10 — 93
10.1 — 92

GREGORY NAZIANZUS

Against Apollinarius
69–72 — 102n8

Orations
30.5 — 102n8
45.22 — 101n8

GREGORY OF NYSSA

Catechetical Oration
17 — 108
22 — 101, 108–9
23 — 109
24 — 101
26 — 109n16
32 — 109n16

IRENAEUS

Against Heresies
3.23 — 100

JOHN CHRYSOSTOM

Homilies on I Timothy
homily 7.3 — 98

Homilies on II Corinthians
    homily 1   98
    homily 11   98

JOHN DUNS SCOTUS

*Distinctiones in quatuor libros
Sententiarum*
    3.19.1   198

JOSEPHUS

Antiquities of the Jews
    2.312   33n45

ORIGEN

*Commentary on the Epistle to the
Romans*
    2.8.1   99
    2.8.11   99–100
    2.13.29   99n6
    3.7.14   98
    3.8.1   96

Commentary on the Gospel of John
    2.21   97
    6.37   101
    28.18.19   95

Commentary on the Gospel of Matthew
Series 113   96
    XVI.8   98–99

Homilies on Leviticus
    14.4.2   94

Homilies on Numbers
    24.1.6   96
    24.1.6–8   94–95

PHILO

On the Life of Moses
    2.95   68

Sibylline Oracles
    1.167   64n28
    3.625   64n28
    3.628   64n28
    7.138   64n28
    8.333   64n28

The Lindos Chronicle
    B49   64n29

Index of Scripture

**APOCRYPHA AND
PSEUDEPIGRAPHA**

JUBILEES

49:19-21   33n45

2 MACCABEES

7:38   65

4 MACCABEES

17:22   65

WISDOM

12:12   34

OLD TESTAMENT

GENESIS

1:27-28   201n12
8:21   19n10, 20, 20n12
15:6   60

18:22-33   244
18:25   51, 178, 243
22:1-19   46, 177

EXODUS

6:6   86
9:27   57
12:1-27   19
12:13   19
19:6   86
23:7   62n23
24:8   16
30:11-16   2n2
30:12   2n2, 26
30:15   2n2
30:16   2n2, 26
30:30-34   28
32:11-14   24
32:30-34   45, 177
32:34   46
33:3   19
33:5   19
34:6-7   41n10

34:7, 30	178, 242
52:13	46

LEVITICUS

1-9	19n10
1:4	24, 43
1:5	21
1:9	19, 21
1:10	21
1:11	21
1:13	19, 21
1:14	21
1:15	21
1:17	19, 21
2:2	19
3:1	21
3:2	21
3:3-4	21
3:5	19
3:6	21
3:8	21
3:9-10	21
3:12	21
3:14-15	21
4-5	26
4:3	21
4:6-7	21
4:17-18	21
4:8-10	21
4:11-12	21
4:13-14	21
4:15	25n27
4:21	21
4:22-23	21
4:25	21
4:27-28	21
4:30	21
4:31	19
4:32	21
4:35	21, 22, 33, 72
5:1	41

5:6	33
5:7-13	20n13
5:15	21
6:10	33
6:21	30
6:25-26	21
6:29	21
7:2	21
7:3-4	21
7:6	21
7:8	21
7:15-21	21
7:18	41
7:31-34	21
8:21	19
9:7	22n15
10:1-2	19
10:1-7	19n10
10:8-15:33	19n10
10:17	42
14:2-7	31
14:20	22n15
16	30
16:1	19
16:2	2n2
16:16-17	31
16:17	77, 80
16:24	22n15, 31
16:30	31
16:33	31
17:11	20n13, 26–28, 31, 44, 63, 66, 85, 93
19:8	41
24:15	41

NUMBERS

5:31	41
9:13	41
11:2	24
14:13-20	24
14:34	41

16:22	24
17:6-15	24
25:7-13	28
25:8	24
31:50	26
35:33	29n36

DEUTERONOMY

16:5-7	33n45
21:1-8	28
24:16	178
25:1	62n23

JUDGES

20:26	22n15

1 SAMUEL

13:12	22n15

2 SAMUEL

24:21-25	22n15

2 CHRONICLES

12:1-6	57
30:17	33n45

NEHEMIAH

1:10	86
9:33	57

JOB

1:5	20n12, 22n15
42:8	20n12, 22n15

PSALMS

7:10	57
7:12	57
11:5-7	57
19:14	10
50:6	57

51:1	193
51:9	193
143:2	53

PROVERBS

17:15	62n23

ISAIAH

1:27	57
3:13	52
5:15-16	57
5:23	62n23
6:1	46
10:22	57
28:17	57
33:10	46
41:21	52
42:6	17
43:3-4	86
49:6	17
52:13-53:12	37
52:14-53:1	40
53	92
53:4	41, 42, 119
53:4a	48
53:4-6	40
53:5	42, 48
53:6	42, 48
53:7	44, 47
53:8	42
53:8a	48
53:9	48
53:9b	47
53:10	17, 33, 40, 43
53:11	41, 48, 49
53:11-12	42
53:11c	48
53:11d	48
53:12	17, 39, 47n22, 48, 75
53:12b	48
53:12c	48

53:12	127
57:15	46

JEREMIAH

31:31-34	16–17

LAMENTATIONS

1:18	57

EZEKIEL

4:4-6	42–43
18:20	43n11
43:14	66
43:17	66
43:20	66
45:15	22n15
45:17	22n15

DANIEL

7:14	17
9:7	57
9:14	57
9:16	57

AMOS

9:1	66

MICAH

6:1-2	52

HABAKKUK

2:4	60

ZECHARIAH

7:2	64n28
8:22	64n28
9:9-12	16

MALACHI

1:9	64n28

NEW TESTAMENT

MATTHEW

13:24-30	244

MARK

10:33-34	16
10:45	17, 48, 86
11:1-10	16
11:13-18	16
14:22-24	16
15:6-15	72

LUKE

18:13	2n2
22:20	16n7
22:37	17
24:25-27	39n3

JOHN

1:29	33
3:16	5, 143n11

ACTS

3:13	39n3
3:18	39n3
8:30-35	39
17:30	70

ROMANS

1-3	34, 65
1:17	54
1:18	53, 56, 57
1:18-3:20	52
1:29-31	56
1:32	175, 242, 243
2:1-3	242
2:2	56
2:4	70
2:5	175
2:13	60n16

2:15	53
3:5	54
3:19-20	53, 243
3:20	60n16, 242
3:21	56n5
3:21-26	34, 52–77
3:22	53, 54, 62, 73n50
3:24	62
3:24-26	121–22
3:25	2n2, 32, 34, 63, 65n32, 69, 73n50
3:25-26	54
3:25b-26	70
3:26	54, 71, 258
3:27	62
3:27-31	71
3:28	73n50
3:30	74n50
4:1	71
4:3	52
4:4-5	62
4:5	62n23, 74n50
4:6-8	71
4:9	74n50
4:22	74n50
4:23-24	52
4:23-25	72
4:24	52
4:25	6, 48, 124
4:26	52
5:1	74n50
5:2	258
5:7-8	159n29
5:9	33, 34
5:10	2
5:17	74n50, 83, 258
5:18-19	33, 80
6:3	83
6:3-11	83
8:1	72, 83, 217
8:3	33
8:4	74
8:33	60n16

8:33-34	221
9:14	243
9:16	242
9:30-32	74n50
10:3	54, 55n5
11:9	175
11:27	72
12:19	175
16:1-2	68

1 CORINTHIANS

1:18	5
2:2	5
3:1-3	211n36
6:20	63, 86
7:23	63, 86
11:25	16n7
15:3	48, 266
15:3-5	6
15:11	6

2 CORINTHIANS

2:8	111
3:18	234
5:11-21	84
5:14	80
5:17	222
5:17-20	1–2
5:18	2
5:19	77
5:20	2
5:21	48, 54, 94, 267
5:21a	76
5:21b	75
6:14	56

GALATIANS

1:8-9	76
3:10-14	76
3:13	63n26, 92, 94, 104, 267
6:14	5

EPHESIANS

1:5	257
1:7	63n26, 72, 86
2:3	213
2:8-9	242, 249

PHILIPPIANS

3:6-9	53, 55
3:8-9	75
3:9	54, 55n5
3:20	258

COLOSSIANS

1:14	72
1:19-22	2
2:12	83
2:13-14	171, 258
2:15	111
2:20	83

2 THESSALONIANS

1:5-9	55n4

2 TIMOTHY

2:26	111

HEBREWS

2:9	80n1
2:17	2n2, 32
9:5	66
9:9-10	20n13
9:12	86
9:15	86
9:22	33
9:26	33
9:26b-28	48
9:28	33, 39
10:4	198
10:6, 8	33
10:10	33
10:11	33
10:14	24, 32
10:29	175, 211n36, 243

1 PETER

1:4	257
1:18-19	86
1:19	63n26
2:21-24	47
2:22-25	39
2:24	266

1 JOHN

1:5	97
2:1-2	33
2:2	2n2, 32, 211n36
4:10	2n2, 32, 33
5:19	111

REVELATION

5:9	63n26
5:9-10	86

Index of Court Opinions

U.S. SUPREME COURT

Flemming v. Nestor, 363 U.S. 603 (1960) — 160
Biddle v. Perovich, 274 U.S. 480 (1927) — 238–39, 252–54
Burdick v. United States, 236 U.S. 79 (1915) — 220, 230n46, 251, 252, 254–55
The John G. Stevens, 170 U.S. 113 (1898) — 186n23
Knote v. United States, 95 U.S. 149 (1877) — 221–22
Ex parte Garland, 71 U.S. 333 (1866) — 222–25, 228–33
Ex parte Wells, 59 U.S. 307 (1855) — 256
United States v. Wilson, 32 U.S. 150 (1833) — 220, 238, 250–52, 253n48

U.S. APPEALS COURT

Hirschberg v. Commodity Futures Trading Commission,
    414 F.3d 679 (7th Cir. 2005) — 227, 234
Groseclose v. Plummer, 106 F.2d 311 (9th Cir. 1939) — 225
Robertson v. Shinseki, 26 Vet. App. 169 (2013) — 223n21, 228

DELAWARE

State *ex rel.* Wier v. Peterson, 369 A.2d 1076 (Del. 1976) — 225

DISTRICT OF COLUMBIA

In re Abrams, 689 A.2d 6 (D.C. 1997) — 226, 234

FLORIDA

R.J.L. v. State, 887 So.2d 1268 (Fla. 2004)   227

INDIANA

Sanders v. State, 85 Ind. 318 (1882)   231n47

KENTUCKY

Fletcher v. Graham, 192 S.W.3d 350 (Ky. 2006)   227

NEVADA

Sang Man Shin v. State (*In re* Sang Man Shin),
     125 Nev. 100 (2009)   223n21, 228, 230n46

NEW YORK

People *ex rel.* Prisament v. Brophy, 38 N.E.2d 468 (1941)   225
In re an Attorney, 86 N.Y. 563 (1881)   224
In re DePuy, 7 F. Cas. 506 (S.D.N.Y. 1869)   250n38

OREGON

Haugen v. Kitzhaber, 306 P.3d 592 (2013)   239, 255
In re Spenser, 22 F. Cas. 921 (1878)   231

TEXAS

Dixon v. McMullen, 527 F. Supp. 711 (N.D. Tex. 1981)   226

UNITED KINGDOM

Pharmaceutical Society of Great Britain v. Storkwain
     Ltd., [1986] 2 All ER 635 (H.L.)   158
Allen v. Whitehead, [1930] 1 K.B. 211   188–89
Sherras v. De Rutzen, [1895] 1 Q.B. 918   189
Mostyn v. Fabrigas, (1774) 1 Cowp.   74n50, 161, 185
Cuddington v. Wilkins, (1615) 80 Eng. Rep. 231 (K.B.)   223, 230